Ivory
Coast

A World Bank Country Economic Report

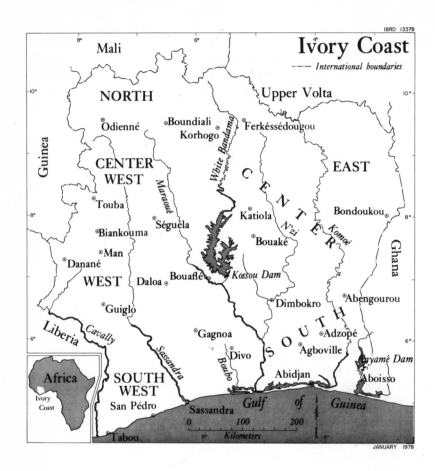

Mali

Ivory Coast

----- *International boundaries*

NORTH

Upper Volta

Odienné

Boundiali
Korhogo

Ferkéssédougou

Guinea

CENTER
WEST

EAST

Touba

White Bandama

Katiola

Bondoukou

Maraoué

Séguéla

Bouaké

N'zi

Komoé

Ghana

Biankouma

Man

Danané

Bouaflé

Kossou Dam

WEST   Daloa

Dimbokro

Abengourou

Guiglo

Cavally

SOUTH

Liberia

Gagnoa

Adzopé

Sassandra

Divo

Bandama

Agboville

yamé Dam

Africa

SOUTH
WEST

Abidjan

Aboisso

Ivory
Coast

San Pédro

Sassandra

Gulf   of   Guinea

0   100   200

Tabou

Kilometers

Ivory Coast
The Challenge of Success

Report of a mission sent
to the Ivory Coast
by the World Bank

Bastiaan A. den Tuinder
Chief of Mission and Coordinating Author

Published for the World Bank
The Johns Hopkins University Press
Baltimore and London

The views and interpretations in this book are the author's and should not be attributed to the World Bank, to its affiliated organizations, or to any individual acting in their behalf. The map serving as frontispiece has been prepared by the staff of the World Bank exclusively for the convenience of readers of this book. The denominations used and the boundaries shown do not imply, on the part of the World Bank and its affiliates, any judgment on the legal status of any territory or any endorsement or acceptance of such boundaries.

Library of Congress Cataloging in Publication Data

Tuinder, Bastiaan A. den, 1936–
    Ivory Coast, the challenge of success.

    Includes index.
    1. Ivory Coast—Economic conditions.   2. Ivory
Coast—Economic policy.   I. International Bank for
Reconstruction and Development.   II. Title.
HC547.I8T84   338.9666'8   76-47395
ISBN 0-8018-1939-3
ISBN 0-8018-2099-5 pbk.

Foreword

THIS IS THE FIFTEENTH IN THE CURRENT SERIES of World Bank country economic reports, all of which are listed on the following page. They are published, in response to a desire expressed by scholars and practitioners in the field of economic and social development, to aid and encourage research and the interchange of knowledge.

Economic reports on borrowing countries are prepared regularly by the Bank in support of its own operations. These surveys provide a basis for discussions with the governments and for decisions on Bank policy and operations. Many of these reports are also used by the governments themselves as an aid to their economic planning and by consortia and consultative groups of governments and institutions providing assistance in development. All Bank country reports are subject to the agreement of—and several have been published by—the governments concerned.

The present study results from the work of a mission to the Ivory Coast in 1975 under the leadership of Bastiaan A. den Tuinder and was reviewed with Ivorian authorities in 1976. It accordingly does not take account of developments in the economy since then, such as the exceptionally high prices for coffee and cocoa, the major expansion in public investments in the 1976–77 period, and recent government decisions to review and modify the public investment program. These developments show both the sensitivity of the Ivorian economy to external factors and the growing social pressures for improved education and public services, regional development, and diversified economic opportunities; they also confirm the determination of the country's economic management to adapt economic policies to changing circumstances, to maintain growth and social progress while preserving the country's internal and external financial equilibrium.

HOLLIS CHENERY
Vice President for Development Policy
The World Bank

Washington, D.C.
June 1978

WORLD BANK COUNTRY ECONOMIC REPORTS

Published for the Bank by The Johns Hopkins University Press

Ivory Coast: The Challenge of Success
Korea: Problems and Issues in a Rapidly Growing Economy
Kenya: Into the Second Decade
Yugoslavia: Development with Decentralization
Nigeria: Options for Long-Term Development
Economic Growth of Colombia

Published by the World Bank

Papua New Guinea: Its Economic Situation and Prospects for Development
The Philippines: Priorities and Prospects for Development
Lesotho: A Development Challenge
Turkey: Prospects and Problems of an Expanding Economy
Senegal: Tradition, Diversification, and Economic Development
   (also published in French)
Chad: Development Potential and Constraints (also published in French as
   Le Développement du Tchad: Possibilités et Limites)
Current Economic Position and Prospects of Peru
Current Economic Position and Prospects of Ecuador
Employment in Trinidad and Tobago

Contents

Tables

Acronyms

AfDB	African Development Bank
AOF	Afrique Occidentale Française (Federation of French West Africa)
ARSO	Autorité pour l'Aménagement de la Région du Sud-Ouest (Development Authority for the Southwest Region)
AVB	Autorité pour l'Aménagement de la Vallée du Bandama (Bandama Valley Authority)
BCEAO	Banque Centrale des Etats de l'Afrique de l'Ouest (Central Bank)
BDI	Bureau de Développement Industriel (Industrial Development Bureau)
BICICI	Banque Internationale pour le Commerce et l'Industrie de la Côte d'Ivoire (International Bank for Commerce and Industry of the Ivory Coast)
BNDA	Banque Nationale pour le Développement Agricole (National Agricultural Development Bank)
BNEC	Banque Nationale d'Epargne et de Crédit (National Savings and Credit Bank)
BNETD	Bureaux nationaux d'Etudes Techniques et de Développement (National Offices for Technical and Development Studies)
BOAD	Banque Ouest Africaine de Développement (West African Development Bank)

BSIE	Budget Spécial d'Investissement et d'Equipement (Investment Budget)
CAA	Caisse Autonome d'Amortissement (Debt Amortization Fund)
CCCE	Caisse Centrale de Coopération Economique (Central Fund for Economic Cooperation)
CCI	Crédit de la Côte d'Ivoire (Credit Bank of the Ivory Coast)
CEAO	Communauté Economique de l'Afrique de l'Ouest (West African Economic Community)
CEDA	Arabusta trial centers
CEDEAO	Communauté des Etats de l'Afrique de l'Ouest (Community of West African States)
CENAPEC	Centre National de la Promotion des Entreprises Coopératives (National Center for the Promotion of Cooperatives)
CFDT	Compagnie Française pour le Développement des Fibres Textiles (French Company for the Development of Textile Fibers)
CIC	Conseil Ivoirien des Chargeurs (National Council of Shippers)
CICE	Centre Ivoirien du Commerce Extérieur (Ivorian Foreign Trade Center)
CIDA	Canadian International Development Agency
CIDT	Compagnie Ivoirienne pour le Développement des Textiles (Ivorian Textile Development Company)
CIMAO	Ciments de l'Afrique de l'Ouest (West African Cement Company)
COMARAN	Compagnie Maritime de l'Afrique Noire (Black African Maritime Company)
CSSPPA	Caisse de Stabilisation et de Soutien des Prix de Produits Agricoles (Stabilization Fund)
CTFT	Centre Technique Forestier Tropical (Technical Center for Tropical Forestry)
CTR	Centre Technique Régional (regional technical center)
CTU	Centre Technique Urbain (urban technical center)

DATAR   Direction de l'Aménagement du Territoire et de l'Action Régionale (French Regional Development Agency)

DDI   Direction du Développement Industriel (Industrial Development Directorate)

DGDA   Direction Générale du Développement de l'Agriculture (Directorate General of Agricultural Development)

DPW   Department of Public Works

DRC   Domestic resource cost

EC   European Communities

ECOWAS   Economic Community of West African States

EIB   European Investment Bank

EPC   Effective protection coefficient

FAC   Fonds d'Aide et de Coopération (French Aid and Cooperation Fund)

FED   Fonds Européen de Développement (European Development Fund)

FNI   Fonds National d'Investissement (National Investment Fund)

FRAR   Fonds Régionaux d'Aménagement Rural (Regional Rural Development Funds)

IDA   International Development Association (World Bank Group)

IFCC   Institut Français pour le Café et le Cacao (French Institute for Coffee and Cocoa)

IRAT   Institut de Recherches Agronomiques Tropicales et des Cultures Vivrières (Institute for Research in Tropical Agriculture and Foodcrops)

IRCT   Institut de Recherches du Coton et des Fibres Exotiques (Institute for Research on Cotton and Exotic Fibers)

IRHO   Institut de Recherches des Huiles et Oléagineux (Institute for Research on Edible Oils and Oleaginous Products)

MOTORAGRI   Société pour le Développement de la Motorisation de l'Agriculture (Company for the Development of Agricultural Motorization)

NORAD   Norwegian Aid Agency

OCAM   Organisation Commune Africaine et Mauricienne
               (Common Organization of African and Mauritian
               States)

ONFP   Office National de Formation Professionnelle (Office
               of Professional Training)

ONPR   Office National de Promotion Rurale (National
               Office for Rural Development)

OPEI   Office National de Promotion de l'Entreprise
               Ivoiriene (National Office for the Development of
               Ivorian Enterprises)

ORSTOM   Office de la Recherche Scientifique et Technique
               d'Outre-Mer (Office of Overseas Scientific and
               Technical Research)

OSHE   Office pour le Soutien de l'Habitat Economique
               (Office for Promotion of Low-income Housing)

RAN   Régie du Chemin de Fer Abidjan-Niger (Abidjan-
               Niger Railroad)

SATMACI   Société d'Assistance Technique pour le
               Modernisation Agricole de la Côte d'Ivoire
               (Technical Assistance Company for the
               Agricultural Modernization of the Ivory Coast)

SITRAM   Société Ivoirienne des Transports Maritimes (Ivorian
               Maritime Transport Company)

SOCATCI   Société des Caoutchoucs de Côte d'Ivoire (Ivory
               Coast Rubber Company)

SODE   Société de Développement (Development Company)

SODEFEL   Société pour le Développement des Fruits et
               Légumes (Fruit and Vegetable Development
               Company)

SODEFOR   Société pour le Développement des Plantations
               Forestières (Forestry Development Company)

SODEMI   Société pour le Développement Minier en Côte
               d'Ivoire (Ivory Coast Mining Development
               Company)

SODEPALM   Société pour le Développement et l'Exploitation du
               Palmier à l'Huile (Oil Palm Development
               Company)

SODEPRA	Société pour le Développement des Productions Animales (Livestock Production Development Company)
SODERIZ	Société pour le Développement de la Riziculture (Rice Development Company)
SODESUCRE	Société pour le Développement des Plantations de Cannes à Sucre, l'Industrialisation et Commercialisation du Sucre (Sugar Development Company)
SOGEFIHA	Société de Gestion Financière de l'Habitat (Company for the Financial Management of Housing)
SONAFI	Société Nationale de Financement (National Finance Company)
SSE	Small-scale enterprise
UDAO	Union Douanière entre les Etats de l'Afrique Occidentale (former West African Customs Union)
UDEAO	Union Douanière des Etats de l'Afrique de l'Ouest (West African Customs Union)
UMOA	Union Monétaire Ouest-Africaine (West African Monetary Union)
UNDP	United Nations Development Programme
Unesco	United Nations Educational, Scientific, and Cultural Organization
UNIDO	United Nations Industrial Development Organization
USAID	United States Agency for International Development

Currency Equivalents

The currency unit of the Ivory Coast is the CFA Franc [CFAF]. A fixed parity exists between the CFA franc and the French franc: FF1 = CFAF50. The CFA franc floats against the dollar; between February 12, 1973, and the end of 1976, the rate fluctuated as follows: US$1 = CFAF205–255. Throughout this book the following rates have been used for the conversion of CFA francs into US dollars and vice versa:

1968 and earlier years: US$1 = CFAF247
1969: US$1 = CFAF256
1970: US$1 = CFAF278
1971: US$1 = CFAF278
1972: US$1 = CFAF252
1973: US$1 = CFAF223
1974: US$1 = CFAF241
1975: US$1 = CFAF214
1976 and beyond: US$1 = CFAF230

Acknowledgements

THIS WORLD BANK COUNTRY ECONOMIC REPORT is based on the findings of an economic mission that was headed by Bastiaan A. den Tuinder and included Chuong Ngoc Phung (economist and balance-of-payments specialist); John D. Shilling (macroeconomist for the long-run model); Wolfgang F. Stolper (consultant and economist on employment and income distribution); Bernard Verdier (economist on the private sector); Luc H. De Wulf (International Monetary Fund fiscal economist); Marto Ballesteros (agricultural economist); Christopher Redfern (consultant and agricultural economist); Bernard Decaux (consultant and industrial economist); Peter Koenig (tourism specialist); Roy Knighton (consultant and transport economist); Robin W. Bates (public utilities economist); Michael A. Cohen (urban development specialist); and David Davies (education economist). The book also draws on the findings of several restricted-circulation documents of the World Bank—a special report on employment and a sector study on industry—as well as on a World Bank research project studying comparative advantage and effective protection.

Principal among those whose contributions deserve acknowledgement are three staff members of the World Bank's Western Africa Regional Office: Luis de Azcarate, chief economist, and Michael Payson, senior economist, who guided the report through the internal review and redrafting process, and Richard Westebbe, senior economist, who undertook this task for the latter part of the process leading to publication. The administrative and secretarial work in preparing various drafts of the report was the responsibility of Suzanne M.

Lorang. Jane H. Carroll coordinated the editorial effort in preparing the book for publication; Pamela K. Brennan, John W. Sifton, and Frances R. Glennon edited successive drafts of the text; and Rachel C. Anderson edited the tables and supervised production of the book. Florence Robinson prepared the index.

The report does not necessarily reflect the views of the government of the Ivory Coast, and its scope and overall conclusions remain the responsibility of the chief of mission and coordinating author.

Ivory Coast

CHAPTER ONE

Introduction

FEW COUNTRIES, DEVELOPED OR DEVELOPING, can match the economic growth record of the Ivory Coast. Its annual growth rate in real terms of over 7 percent during the past twenty-five years is unique on the African continent. With no mining activity to speak of, cocoa, coffee, and timber have been and still are the pillars of the economy; 1975 exports of these commodities were respectively four, five, and thirty times the 1950 exports in volume. In 1950, with a per capita income of around $70,[1] the Ivory Coast ranked among the poorest nations. At independence in 1960, income had risen to $145, and in 1974 had reached $450.[2]

Circumstances and Achievements

Identification and analysis of the factors responsible for the Ivory Coast's outstanding performance is an unusual exercise in that it seeks to find out what went right instead of what went wrong. Luck is frequently given as the main factor to explain the "Ivorian miracle," but closer scrutiny of the country's economic performance reveals that the miracle is man-made and capable of being analyzed. In addition to being directly responsible for many favorable developments, the government has capitalized on events of an exogenous nature.

1. Gross national income (GNY) in current prices. All dollar equivalents are in U.S. dollars for the relevant years.
2. In 1950 prices the income per capita in 1974 amounted to about $190.

Rapid economic growth has ranked high in Ivorian development strategy since the country first achieved independence. The government has consistently argued that, at the country's low level of income, rapid growth itself is the key to overcoming economic and social problems. The authorities were well aware of possible tradeoff between growth and distribution of income, but their decision to emphasize the former, without neglecting the latter, in their early development strategy seems justified by the circumstances. Many developing countries must regularly fight off disasters that threaten the lives of their citizens—droughts, floods, crop failures, and the most visible effect of these evils, starvation. When a country faces this type of problem, short-term relief and medium-term crash programs usually consume part of the funds originally allocated for what might be longer-term solutions. Sometimes solutions are hard to define, thus making any movement toward improvement extremely difficult. The Ivory Coast is not in this unfortunate group. With a population of 6.7 million in mid-1975, the average density was still only 21 inhabitants a square kilometer, and although densities are higher where the population clusters around existing infrastructure, fertile land is still available and is being made accessible through public investment. The north receives less rain than the south, but no part of the country extends into the drought-prone Sahel zone. Although the accumulation of wealth requires considerable effort, as it does everywhere, ecological circumstances in the Ivory Coast are relatively benign.

In this book the economic objectives chosen by the government are discussed as well as the instruments used to arrive at these goals. The country's performance will be evaluated primarily in terms of how well it has succeeded in accomplishing the objectives it chose for itself. In this respect, the government's policy decision to pursue growth and to orient development outward rather than inward has been successful. The orientation has been outward in the sense that it was recognized that the export sector would be the key to economic growth and that foreign production factors (capital, labor, and know-how) would be essential in developing the country's economic potential.

At independence, the government was quick to realize that the country's vast economic potential could be developed at a satisfactory rate only by a combination of local and foreign factors of production. Before 1960 managerial and skilled labor, mainly from France, and unskilled plantation and construction workers from neighboring countries had come to the Ivory Coast. They were encouraged to stay. The government's liberal and pragmatic economic policies, and its emphasis on political stability and the creation of an image of a modern growth-oriented economy, were instrumental in attracting even more capital and labor from abroad. Moreover, the government continued to encourage its export-oriented agricultural sector. At first this encouragement was mainly through public investment in infrastructure, but later it was broadened to a host of direct incentives to production, particularly relatively high and stable producer prices for the main agricultural products. Recognizing the economic vulnerability of too much dependence on three export commodities (unprocessed cocoa, coffee, and timber), the government diversified agriculture by introducing or expanding the cultivation of oil palm, coconut, pineapple, rice, rubber, cotton, and later sugarcane, and more emphasis was also placed on other sectors. An investment code was instituted in 1959 to help establish an industrial sector, which at that time constituted only 4 percent of gross domestic product (GDP).

The major credit for the Ivory Coast's impressive economic performance must go to the government, which has created an attractive atmosphere for investment. Foreign private investors were impressed by the political stability and the continuity in policy the government was able to provide. The public sector itself was able to finance a major share of its investment program that equalled about 60 percent of total investment in the early 1970s. The country's savings performance has been good and the amount of domestic savings generated was about 22 percent of GDP around 1970. It should be realized, however, that because of the large foreign community the level of national savings has been systematically about 6 percentage points lower. This savings record and the outstanding export performance are the major reasons that the foreign debt service has been kept within manageable limits. Given the magnitude of investment, this has surprised many observers. Balance of payments equilibrium has been maintained and reserves have been sufficiently large to cope with unexpected developments. The country has generally avoided large military expenditures and costly prestige projects, although the foreign impact on the economy has resulted in high standards in several sectors, standards that are not always the best ones for Ivorian circumstances.

Upcoming Constraints

As the government realizes, growth has not eliminated all problems. In fact the very success of its emphasis on growth has created new kinds of problems. For instance, since the Ivory Coast now ranks third among world cocoa and coffee producers, it has greater responsibility for maintaining world prices by keeping future production within forecast demand. The third major export product, timber, has reached levels of production that may be maintained for some years to come but can hardly be expected to increase further owing to supply limitations. Moreover, the government's diversification policy, although economically justified, has resulted in the development of crops and areas where there is less comparative advantage than there was earlier for coffee, cocoa, and, in the southern part of the country, timber. In industry, import substitution is running out of the more obvious opportunities. In general, a policy of growth leads to declining returns in any economy and this is already occurring in the Ivory Coast. The overall capital-output ratio, which was low (averaging 2.7 for the 1966–70 period), is rising.

Another constraint is the existence of differences in incomes between rural and urban areas, between the major rural zones, and between occupational and educational groups. Such gaps are the inevitable result of the fact that the Ivory Coast derives an increasing share of its national income from export-oriented commercial crops and from modern industrial activities in locations where optimal use can be made of natural resources. The response to these income and opportunity differences has been a shift of the Ivorian population to the more richly endowed south and to the cities, particularly Abidjan. These migration flows were originally beneficial to further growth. Unemployment, though not yet a major problem, is increasing, as is the cost of urban infrastructure in Abidjan. Urbanization is a rather recent phenomenon in the Ivory Coast: The portion of the population living in urban areas rose from 13 percent in 1955 to 31 percent in 1973.[3] Pressure is now being felt, particularly in Abidjan, which had about one million inhabitants in 1975 or some 50 percent of the urban population. Moreover, the voluntary movement toward the city has not solved the problems of those remaining in rural areas. These residents are becoming increasingly aware of a rural-urban gap in opportunities and services.

A third upcoming constraint arises from the heavy reliance on foreign factors. Although detailed results of the country's first population census in 1975 are not yet available, it is officially estimated that out of a total of 6.7 million residents, about 2 million were originally from other African countries. This situation occasionally creates tensions,

---

3. Population is considered urban if in centers of at least 4,000 inhabitants.

and Ivorians are asking whether such a ratio is acceptable. In recent years the foreign community seems to have grown more rapidly than the local one, while the demand from Ivorians for certain types of jobs is exceeding the supply. Furthermore, the Ivorian education system is starting to turn out sizable numbers of graduates who feel qualified to occupy jobs held by a community of some 50,000 expatriates, mainly French. There are also about 100,000 Syrians and Lebanese. Rapid economic growth has generally been accompanied by a widening gap between the expectations of an Ivorian labor force that is becoming better educated and the opportunities for what they regard as acceptable employment. Ivorianization is therefore becoming a more pressing issue.

In recent years dependence on foreign capital has resulted in a more rapid increase in debt and debt service than in exports or national income. Public foreign debt outstanding in 1975 amounted to about $200 per capita; public foreign debt payments reached a level of about 10 percent of exports of goods and nonfactor services, to which should be added an estimated 4 to 6 percent for foreign debt (including net direct investment income) in the private sector. The government, eager to maintain growth, and at the same time determined to correct the imbalances described above, has maintained a sizable investment program, with the public sector's proportion of total investments rising from 40 to 60 percent between the early 1960s and 1970s. With national savings falling behind investment and concessionary capital from abroad increasing too slowly, the public sector has contracted growing amounts of foreign capital on progressively harder terms. There is no doubt that the Ivory Coast will continue to need foreign production factors to support its future development, but the amounts cannot continue to grow disproportionately.

The Need for Policy Change

There is still impressive economic potential in the Ivory Coast, but it will be a major challenge in the next decade or two to develop it while reducing the existing gaps in income levels and opportunities. Without jeopardizing continued assistance from abroad in terms of manpower and money, the government needs to find a better way to mobilize more of its own resources and to integrate these resources more fully into the national economy. While ownership in agriculture is already mainly in local hands, foreign interests still dominate forestry, industry, and some services.

An important feature of past policies has been the subsidization of industrial development by agriculture. This system can be described briefly in this way: Good producer prices and a host of other incentives (which are discussed in Chapter 3) made it attractive for Ivorian farmers to expand production of export crops. Government-controlled wages in agriculture were kept relatively low, but sufficiently high to attract both Ivorian labor (mainly from the north) and large numbers of unskilled labor from neighboring countries, especially Upper Volta. The tax revenue from these operations enabled the government not only to encourage diversification of agriculture itself, but also to diversify the economy in a broader sense by subsidizing industrial development. Because the country had hardly any industrial experience, it was deemed necessary to rely heavily on foreign factors; a favorable climate for foreign investment was created and efforts were concentrated on import-substitution activities. The industry established under this policy was predominantly foreign-owned, applying production techniques, standards, and combinations of production factors that were basically foreign.

An integral component of this policy was Ivorianization; that is, Ivorians were to be gradually prepared by education and training to take over positions initially held by foreigners. It was also understood that ultimate ownership of capital was to be in the hands of the Ivorians as well. Some kind of job upgrading has resulted. Profits made in agriculture have been used to create jobs for skilled Ivorians, mainly by buying modern plants and technology abroad at relatively high cost. Experience now shows that replacement of foreign factors by Ivorian ones is not easy. It is a slow process if efficiency is not to be lost because the educational system does not always turn out the skills required. Often the skills are paper skills rather than real ones. Ivorianization of foreign capital has also taken time because of the difficulty of directing local savings to the industrial sector.

With increasing direct and indirect costs in agriculture and with the import-substitution industry running out of the more obvious opportunities, the policy to expand industrial production was not likely to solve the employment problem. The government has therefore set out to improve living conditions in rural areas and create an alternative to migrating to Abidjan, where most of the industry is located. It has embarked on an ambitious program to offer rural areas not only a production base that will provide a decent income, but also a rather complete package of services. In addition, by shifting emphasis from import-substitution to export-oriented processing of local raw materials, more industry will be established in the production areas in the interior of the country. These policy decisions seem promising because they will create employment where it is needed and probably at a lower cost than in Abidjan.

An area with considerable potential for job creation is the informal sector, which includes traditional artisan activities and small-scale industry and services. In the past, the form of modern industrialization emphasized has frequently worked to the detriment of what could have been complementary, that is, the development of industrial and service activities based predominantly on local factors. On several occasions government policies have discriminated against these types of activities, but they would seem to provide important potential for future economic growth. In fact, the informal sector is one of the more promising options the country has in combating unemployment. With greater purchasing power in the local market, such a change in emphasis seems not only feasible but highly desirable. The government should accelerate its efforts to create a better environment for the development of this type of activity through incentives and other forms of assistance. Such action would also help in mobilizing local savings and would strengthen the local private initiative needed to establish a viable private sector. The Ivorian population has shown itself to be very responsive to price and other incentives on numerous occasions in the past. The government could do much more in these areas than it has so far. Also, importing sophisticated plants and technology before the skills of its people are sufficiently developed can lead only to high costs. In general, therefore, schemes must be developed to mobilize Ivorian private initiative. In most cases this should be in addition to, not instead of, continuing activities by foreigners.

The Ivory Coast has made good use of its favorable endowments. These are: first, a strategic geographical location serving several landlocked countries (Mali, Upper Volta, Niger); second, an abundance of fertile land and forestry resources; and third, a climate favorable to agriculture, especially in the south. In addition, the government has been able to provide political stability and continuity, which have created confidence abroad, a prerequisite for obtaining know-how, capital, and technical and managerial skills to alleviate local constraints. A consistent part of this development strategy was the decision to remain a member of the franc area (which guaranteed the convertibility of its currency) and to participate in the West African Monetary Union. These memberships also created an outlet for Ivorian manufactured goods and gave the country continued access to the surplus of unskilled labor in neighboring countries without which the rapid economic development experienced during the past twenty-five years would not have been possible. There are, however, indications from the supply as well as from the demand side that limits of acceptability and absorptive capacity are being approached. To an increasing extent, future development will depend on how successfully the economy can be Ivorianized in the true sense of the word. While this does not mean elimination of foreign factors, the blend of local and foreign goods, services, and production factors should in the future contain a relatively larger local component. The success of this transformation will be closely correlated with future progress of the Ivorian economy.

Statistical data on past development will be found in the Statistical Appendix to this publication. More detailed information on achievements in the past can be found in Ivorian documents, such as the outstanding series of national accounts statistics dating from 1960 and the consecutive national plans as well as in earlier unpublished World Bank reports. The past will be used in this report to define trends that may have relevance for future developments and from which, it is hoped, lessons can be learned. The main questions addressed are whether it is possible and desirable to extend the development policies followed in the Ivory Coast thus far, or whether modifications will be required. If the latter, what kind of modifications are required and to what extent should they be made? Much, of course, depends on the social and economic objectives the government considers desirable to realize within a given period of time. As shown by its recent investment and other policy decisions, the government is fully aware that too much emphasis on growth for too long may trigger undesirable socioeconomic effects, which may in turn jeopardize future growth. When members of the World Bank visited the country in mid-1975, the authorities were preparing the next five-year development plan (1976–80), and were discussing and testing many ideas aimed at the correction of economic imbalances. These ideas were not sufficiently far advanced at the time to allow a final evaluation, but they had most of the features discussed above. It seemed clear, however, that the time span envisaged by the government for the implementation of its ambitious program was optimistically short. Structural change, and that is what is involved, requires time and this the Ivorian planners feel they have little of.

CHAPTER TWO

The Development of the Ivorian Economy

THIS BOOK ANALYZES TRENDS IN THE IVORY COAST since 1960, the year of independence and the first year of a consistent series of national accounts statistics. Some events prior to 1960 are vital to an understanding not only of achievements since then but also of future objectives and the choice of instruments of economic policy. These events are therefore discussed briefly.

Historical Perspective

The history of the country as a political unit dates from 1893 when it became a colony of the French Empire. Without the consent of the people most closely involved and for administrative convenience only, more than fifty ethnic groups, with as many different languages, were brought together in a political entity called the Ivory Coast. Agreements determining the eastern and western boundaries of the colony were signed with Liberia and Great Britain at about that time, while the northern boundary was not established until 1947.

In 1900 France initiated a policy of economic self-sufficiency for its colonies. Each colony was made responsible for raising the funds for its own administration and defense, while France was to offer assistance only when needed. The Ivory Coast, with a flourishing trade, had little difficulty in complying; for other countries, especially the landlocked ones, the new procedure posed difficult problems. In 1904 this situation resulted in the formation of the federation of French West Africa (Afrique Occidentale Française or AOF), which encompassed the territories known today as Mauritania, Senegal, Mali, the Ivory Coast, Upper Volta, Niger, Guinea, and Benin. The economic purpose of the federation was to pool the resources of all French West African colonies and make the richer ones help support the poorer. The Ivory Coast, however, objected to the fact that it had no direct control over the distribution of AOF funds. Other economic grievances developed over time. In the period between the two World Wars the expansion of coffee and cocoa production gave rise in the Ivory Coast to an African planter class that competed with the European planters. Colonial policy, however, favored the latter. During World War II, with production quotas and intensified recruitment of forced labor, resentment grew. This prompted Felix Houphouet-Boigny, a wealthy planter himself, to organize a movement to express the country's dissatisfaction. The movement, which affected the entire region, eventually produced the Ivory Coast's only political party.

French colonial policy, in principle, applied a theory of assimilation, which was based on the assumption that all men are equal and thus should be treated alike. It condemned slavery and colonial exploitation. The assimilation policy meant extension into the colonies of the French language, institutions, laws, and customs. The French trained a native elite in their administrative practices, and this corps in turn formed an intermediary group between the French and the Africans. This policy of assimilation, together with the lack of unity among the individual ethnic groups, is probably largely responsible for the absence of major outbursts of violent nationalism. It is also probably the reason opposition to colonial status centered mainly on economic grievances. By the late 1950s the local political leaders realized that assimilation could in fact never be achieved and that real equality could be obtained only through independence. In August 1960, of its own choice, the Ivory Coast withdrew from the French Community.[1] This was done quietly and without economic disruption.

The way in which the Ivory Coast gained independence very much carries the imprint of Houphouet-Boigny, the outstanding national political figure and president since independence. His policy of conciliation and dialogue has given the country political and economic stability. To mold a nation out of more than fifty groups with different identities and interests is a major achievement. Continuity in policy

---

1. The French Community, established in 1958, was a free association of autonomous republics of France and its former colonies. Other West and Central African French colonies also withdrew in 1960.

has probably been as important as the kind of policy followed. A recent poll among foreign industrialists in the Ivory Coast indicates that political stability ranks highest in the list of factors governing choice of location abroad. In the elections of November 1975 the president, at the age of 70, was given a mandate for another five years.

At the turn of the century, when plans were devised to make the colonies self-supporting or profitable, it was recognized that the Ivory Coast was potentially one of the richest colonies (probably second only to Guinea) because of its vast agricultural and forestry resources. From an agricultural standpoint, the Ivory Coast can be divided into two main regions: the south, where the natural vegetation is tropical forest, and the north, which consists of savannah grasslands. In the south, conditions are particularly favorable for perennial tree crops such as coffee, cocoa, oil palm, rubber, and coconuts. Annual food crops, including yams, plantains, cassava, and upland rice also do very well in this zone. Except under special conditions, perennial crops cannot be grown in the north, but considerable potential exists there for annual food crops, such as millet, sorghum, maize, and rice.

Around 1900 the Ivory Coast had the infrastructure to export to France and other foreign markets the products that could be grown in the south. Consequently, coffee and cocoa were introduced and experiment and research stations were established to improve varieties. Exports of cocoa started in 1905 with 2 tons; in the same year 29 tons of coffee were exported and 9,600 tons of logs. With ups and downs— a result of disease, weather conditions, and fluctuating world market prices—the production of timber, cocoa, and coffee has increased steadily. Logging was and still is largely foreign controlled, but coffee and cocoa, originally grown by Africans and Europeans, became an almost exclusively African enterprise after 1950 with hundreds of thousands of families involved. By maintaining attractive producer prices, the government not only induced farmers to expand production, but also brought purchasing power to substantial numbers of Ivorians.

The north, by contrast, had no market either abroad or locally for its foodstuffs. France was a food surplus market itself, and the Ivory Coast's neighbors were largely inaccessible, had little purchasing power, and in general produced the same foodstuffs on a subsistence level. Moreover, in the early days urbanization was limited. In 1955 Abidjan, which was by far the biggest city, had only 125,000 inhabitants. The south could easily produce the food needed by the urban population. For these reasons there was very little incentive for surplus production in the north. There was no place for the north in the early development strategy. The only valuable production factor the north had was labor, and its workers were encouraged to take on jobs in the south.

Two other important points should be made in explaining the pattern of growth in the past. First, there was a clear-cut division of tasks between the Ivory Coast and France. On the one hand, the Ivory Coast produced raw materials that were processed mainly in France. (In 1960 about 50 percent of each of the Ivory Coast's three main export products went to France; the other half, exported outside the franc area, was a precious source of hard currency for the franc area.) On the other hand, the Ivory Coast was a market for French manufactured goods; in 1960 about 70 percent of Ivorian imports originated in France. Second, as part of the changing relationship between France and its colonies after World War II, a vast investment program was started in the Ivory Coast with French technical and financial assistance. To stimulate the production of timber, cocoa, and coffee and to aid other developments, the transport infrastructure in the south was improved considerably. Most important, the Vridi Canal, opened in 1950, gave Abidjan an excellent deep-water port and marked the beginning of that city's rapid growth. Before the construction of the canal the Ivory Coast was relatively inaccessible from the sea. This had long hindered the country's economic development, and removal of this obstacle was consistent with the country's outward-oriented development. Furthermore, as the four north-south flowing rivers are not navigable, heavy investments had to be made in land transport. The Abidjan-Niger railway, begun in Abidjan in 1904, reached Ouagadougou, the capital of Upper Volta, in 1954. A rather complete network of reasonably good roads already existed in 1960 in the forest zone centered around Abidjan. Forestry activities in turn opened up new areas to agricultural activities.

Few statistics are available for the first half of the 1900s, but because exports have always been dominant, export data probably give quite reliable insight into Ivorian economic development in those days. Table 2.1 shows the following:

a. Export volume growth rates are high, with an acceleration after 1945. This was the result of earlier research in cocoa and coffee production and a new form of cooperation with France. Also, with an increase in income in Europe, the market for tropical hardwood expanded rapidly.

b. With the high proportion of cocoa, coffee, and timber in total exports and the high proportion of commodity exports in GDP,

TABLE 2.1. HISTORICAL DEVELOPMENT OF THE MAJOR EXPORT
             PRODUCTS

Year	Export (tons) Logs	Cocoa	Coffee	Export value of unprocessed logs, cocoa, coffee[a] (CFAF billion)	Value of total commodity exports (CFAF billion)	Commodity exports as a proportion of GDP (percent)
1900	13,420	n.a.	24	n.a.	0.01	n.a.
1920	46,000	1,036	17	0.02	0.06	n.a.
1940	23,220	45,360	15,610	n.a.	0.30	n.a.
1945	10,070	26,940	37,870	n.a.	0.82	n.a.
1950	106,000	61,690	54,190	12.00	13.80	n.a.
1955	169,400	75,200	84,800	24.20	25.60	n.a.
1959	444,200	63,260	104,700	30.60	33.80	n.a.
1960	640,000	62,870	147,500	33.30	40.20	28.6
1961	760,000	88,470	153,800	37.70	47.50	29.8
1965	1,500,000	126,400	185,700	51.80	70.50	29.8

n.a. Not available.

Source: J. Dirck Stryker, *Exports and Growth in the Ivory Coast: Timber, Cocoa and Coffee,* Yale University Economic Growth Center Discussion Paper no. 147 (New Haven: June 1972), Appendix Tables.

a. Exports of the three products in processed form had a value of CFAF0.7 billion in 1960 and CFAF4.6 billion in 1965.

high growth rates for these three products are equivalent to a high growth rate of GDP.

c. The drop in the proportion of the three main export revenues—from 91 percent in the 1950s to 78 percent in the 1960s—indicates that other export products grew rapidly as well.

d. The data for 1959–61 indicate that gaining independence did not disrupt production as it did in several other countries.

Continuation of an Outward Orientation

Given the positive results of the economic policies pursued earlier, it is not surprising that the government decided to continue along the same lines after becoming independent. At this time the economy was booming and prospects for further growth were very good. As early as 1960, ten-year projections of the economy were made outlining alternative scenarios of what the situation might be at the end of the decade. These forecasts were not directly integrated into a coherent and comprehensive investment program, but they provided the basis for a number of investment projects undertaken by the government. As part of the exercise, the decision was made to continue to promote outward-oriented development. With the low level of income and a population of only 3.7 million, the local market had a purchasing power that was low and would remain so for some time. Therefore, an inward-oriented development strategy was considered to have much less potential than one looking outward.

The government was fully aware that further economic success was dependent on more foreign capital and labor. Political and economic stability and growth, together with a liberal policy toward foreign investors, were considered essential in creating the confidence abroad needed to acquire these production factors. This was one of the reasons the government decided to stay in the franc area. This decision meant that the currency was tied to the French franc at the rate of CFAF50 to one French franc, the same rate as today, with guaranteed full and unlimited convertibility into French francs by France. The Ivory Coast's exchange and trade system is similar to that of other franc area countries. It maintains an operations account with the French treasury and is virtually free of restrictions on current international transactions. At the time of independence, the French government committed itself to substantial financial and technical aid to the Ivory Coast.

Given the outward-oriented policy chosen by the Ivory Coast, it was important to preserve and to cultivate close economic and political relations with France and with francophone neighbors. The country needed the former for capital, expertise, skilled labor, and markets, and the latter for both unskilled labor and markets. In an effort to regroup the former members of the French West African Community and salvage the advantages of the Community that existed before 1960, three organizations were established between 1959 and 1962: the Conseil de l'Entente in 1959, the Union Douanière des Etats de l'Afrique de l'Ouest (UDEAO) in 1959,[2] and the Union Monétaire Ouest-Africaine (UMOA) in 1962. Because the Ivory Coast was the most prosperous member, it was in a unique position to exert a dominant influence in these groups and lead the movement for unity of francophone West Africa. With the growth of nationalist sentiment and the affirmation of African identity, it soon became evident that the original concept of the community, whether between France and West Africa or among the African states, would have to be considerably relaxed. A series of reforms have transformed these three organizations to bring them into

2. The UDEAO emerged in 1966 from the Union Douanière entre les Etats de l'Afrique Occidentale (UDAO), which had been established in 1959.

better conformity with the aspirations of their members. A discussion of this is given in Chapter 5.

Diversification of Production and Markets

For greater economic and political stability, and in fact for real independence, it was recognized that the production base had to be broadened and that economic as well as political relations with non-francophone countries had to be established and intensified. This element in economic policy gained momentum around 1960.

Low world prices for cocoa and coffee in the early 1960s stimulated the expansion or introduction of other crops such as bananas,[3] pineapple, rubber, coconut, and palm oil. Only under the ecological conditions existing in the south, where ample land was still available, could these products be cultivated. This led to continued concentration of attention on the south. As for the savannah areas in the north, cotton cultivation was made feasible by the development of selected cotton varieties and crucial insecticides in the early 1960s. The north is well suited for this crop and it is increasingly grown in rotation with food-crops. The system of production has also been improved by the introduction of ox-drawn cultivation. This program is now gradually becoming a major element in transforming the north, integrating this region into the rest of the economy, and helping close the income gap with the south.

Industry, which had been neglected under colonial policies, was another desirable area for diversification. Manufacturing activities under the AOF were concentrated in the capital, Dakar, which at the time had the largest market and the best port facilities. In the Ivory Coast in 1960 manufacturing was limited mainly to the timber, textile, and food industries, and served only the local market. Rapid industrialization was hampered by the lack of an indigenous skilled labor force and the lack of management with industrial experience. This made it necessary to import Europeans—at two or three times their cost in Europe. Furthermore, African wages in industry were relatively high by the standards of countries at similar levels of development. To some extent this situation was a reflection of the shortage of skilled labor, but it was also a consequence of minimum wage and labor regulations the Ivory Coast inherited from the colonial era. For these reasons, the

3. In the early 1960s many European banana planters came to the Ivory Coast from Guinea as a result of that country's leaving the franc area.

Ivory Coast was at a disadvantage with respect to making manufacturing for export to Europe attractive. Moreover, the protection provided by the existing tariff structure did not seem sufficient to attract many import-substitution industries. To deal with this situation the government opted for a policy of providing substantial incentives to import-replacement industries. Under the 1959 investment code, priority firms were exempted from duties on imported raw materials and other intermediate inputs, while in a few cases quantitative import restrictions were also introduced.

In 1960 the government recognized that to create a solid, long-term industrial base, it was necessary first to develop sufficient domestic sources of raw materials, human resources, and domestic demand. In the short to medium term, while the basis for industrial development was being laid, growth would have to rest primarily on expansion and diversification in the sectors in which the Ivory Coast had the greatest immediate comparative advantage, agriculture, particularly export agriculture, and forestry. The implicit strategy was to rely on the short-run comparative advantage in these sectors to lay the foundation for the structural shift into development based on industrial expansion. This strategy would not only give the Ivory Coast a strong basis in the form of income and wealth in agriculture, but would also provide the infrastructure, training, capital, demand, and foreign exchange required for further development.

The Ivory Coast's outward orientation in the early days of independence was still predominantly francophone, but a diversification of markets and sources of capital was starting to emerge. In 1960 about 70 percent of total imports originated in France, whereas the proportion of exports going to other countries was already 55 percent. Through its association with the European Economic Community (EEC) these percentages, especially with regard to exports, changed quite rapidly and helped the country in its search for foreign investment capital. The Ivory Coast's performance has indeed led to confidence abroad, and in 1968 it was the first black African country to obtain a Eurodollar loan.

A New Type of Problem

The government's policy decisions at independence were logical in the sense that successful policies were retained and, to avoid ruptures, modifications were made only gradually. This strategy has led to impressive economic results, but it has not been able to prevent the emergence of structural and other complex problems.

Education is a case in point. At independence the government declared French the official national language. This seems a sensible decision in a country where over fifty different languages are spoken (close to a hundred if the languages of immigrants are included). The choice of a local language as national language would certainly have created problems and might have cost the country its vital political stability. In 1960 only 33 percent of the primary school age group was enrolled in school and it is not known what proportion of the population could understand or express themselves in the national language. It is therefore understandable that the government gave high priority to education. By 1975 about 55 percent of the primary school age group was enrolled and, as a result of the nationwide introduction of televised education, universal primary education may be achieved by 1985. To gain time, however, it was the French educational system that was introduced. The French curriculum was taught primarily by French teachers, maintaining French standards. In Appendix D on Education it is noted that the Ivory Coast spends a larger proportion of its current budget on education than any other country in the world. An impressive number of graduates is being turned out, but these graduates in many cases will not be able to find jobs matching their expectations. These unfulfilled expectations are turning what should have been a substantial benefit to the economy into a lesser one and in some cases even into an extra cost. The decision to transplant the French education system virtually in its entirety to the Ivory Coast may have been the most rapid way to help to make a nation out of so many different groups; however, problems have developed as a result of this decision and they will continue into the late 1970s.

This is just one example of how an initial and seemingly logical decision can have such adverse effects over time that only a drastic change in policy can bring the required relief. It is also an example of how the outward-oriented policy of the government has indirectly imposed standards that are not necessarily too high, but rather inadequate, inappropriate, and out of line with local conditions. The results of policy decisions tend to become entrenched, making adjustments all the more difficult. This report contains other examples of unbalanced standards that have affected policy choices and forced the government into situations that have become increasingly hard to correct. Further success in exploiting the still considerable potential for economic development will depend to a large extent on the government's decisiveness, ingenuity, and timing in correcting this type of problem.

CHAPTER THREE

Resource Allocation

THE IVORIAN ECONOMY HAS DEVELOPED in an atmosphere of controlled liberalism. It has been characterized by entrepreneurial freedom, with few physical controls and a favorable disposition toward foreign capital, labor, and expertise. The government has at the same time intervened in significant ways. It has regulated many agricultural prices for the producer as well as the consumer, established minimum wages, maintained a host of incentives in many sectors of the economy, carried out substantial public investment—lately at a pace of 60 percent of total investment, or some 13 percent of GDP—and set overall targets through development planning.

Objectives and Overall Performance

The general objectives of the government have changed little over time. In the broad context of responding as much as possible to the aspirations of the individual Ivorian, these goals have been and still are:

- to pursue the highest possible economic growth within the limits of budgetary and balance of payments equilibrium. A foreign-oriented growth model has been applied, because it was felt to be the only one permitting rapid growth, without which no development was considered possible.
- to improve distribution of the fruits of growth and to stimulate individual effort, especially with a view to strengthening national unity.

· to increase gradually the control of Ivorian citizens over economic development.

Indicators of growth

The Ivory Coast does not publish national accounts in constant terms. Using the data on volume in the government's statistics and the regularly published price indexes on the cost of living for different groups of consumers and on construction materials, the World Bank has calculated price deflators that probably adequately reflect price movements. For reasons of consistency, some of the national accounts estimates have been brought in line with balance of payments statistics (see appendix to Chapter 5). Growth of population and production and income growth[1] in constant 1973 prices, all in percentage by year, have been:

Item	1960–65	1966–70	1971–75	1960–70	1960–75
Gross domestic product (GDP)	9.2	7.4	5.6	8.3	7.4
Gross national product (GNP)	9.0	7.4	5.6	8.2	7.4
Gross national income (GNY)	8.2	10.2	3.7	9.2	7.4
Growth of resident population	2.8	4.0	4.5	3.4	3.8

Annual growth in GDP, GNP, and GNY averaged a remarkable 7.4 percent over the fifteen-year period between 1960 and 1975. GNP, which has been consistently some 6 to 7 percent lower than GDP, grew at about the same pace as GDP, while movements in the terms of trade as expressed in GNY[2] created greater irregularity in the pattern of growth. It is remarkable, however, that for the period as a whole the GNY and GNP growth rates were the same. Data on population growth is tentative, because only preliminary results of the first population census in 1975 are available. But even with this new information, the calculated population growth rate would still depend on the accuracy of earlier sample data. There is no doubt, however, that a marked acceleration in population growth has taken place and that increased immigration is mainly responsible. Despite such a population rise, real income per capita increased by 3.6 percent a year, although the growth of GNY per capita over the period 1971–75 was low.

1. Expressed as average annual rates of growth in CFAF.
2. GNY equals GNP at constant prices, corrected for the income effect of changes in the terms of trade.

Although data for 1974 and 1975 are only provisional, the trend over five-year periods since 1960 indicates a declining rate of growth. Growth in real terms in the 1960s was high but sometimes irregular, and the average rates conceal highs of 16.9 and 17.9 percent in 1963 and 1964 respectively, and lows of minus 2.2 and plus 1.4 percent in 1965 and 1967. These fluctuations reflect the performance of exports in general and agricultural exports in particular, to which the overall growth of the economy is directly related. To broaden the agricultural base, the government embarked on a diversification policy in this sector and put more emphasis on the other sectors as well. The policy has been successful. First, the proportion of unprocessed cocoa, coffee, and timber in total exports dropped from 90 percent of total exports in the 1950s to some 60 percent in the first half of the 1970s. Second, the contribution of manufacturing to GDP, which was 4 percent in 1960, had tripled in constant prices by 1975.

Table 3.1 summarizes the development of some selected macroeconomic indicators between the periods 1960–64 and 1970–74. Investment, including stocks, went up from 15.6 percent to 21.8 percent, a rather high level; in the process, the incremental capital-output ratio (ICOR) values went up. These increases were due not only to higher investments in social sectors, but also to the development of sectors in which the comparative advantage was lower than in previous activities, as will be discussed later in this chapter. Consumption as a proportion of GDP decreased. But the monetized part of private consumption remained at about the same level (60 percent of GDP), since the decline occurred almost entirely in the subsistence sector, which dropped to less than 10 percent of GDP. The foreign trade sector continued to be very important, with a level of close to 40 percent for both exports and imports (including nonfactor services).

Savings have increased considerably, but investments have gone up even more rapidly. Because of the large foreign population in the Ivory Coast, not all domestic savings are available to finance local investments. Part of the remuneration of factor services, capital, and labor is transferred as interest, profits, and workers' remittances. In 1960–64 this amounted to an average of about CFAF11 billion a year, but in 1970–74 went up to some CFAF40 billion a year. This means that in 1970–74 considerably more had to be borrowed from abroad a year than in the 1960–64 period. With limited availability of concessionary capital, the terms of foreign capital have hardened and the debt service, although still manageable, has increased considerably. The development of foreign borrowing will be discussed in Chapter 4.

The private sector has borrowed abroad surprisingly little, and most

TABLE 3.1. SELECTED MACROECONOMIC
INDICATORS
(Percent)

Indicator	1960–64	1970–74
Gross domestic product	100.0	100.0
Consumption		
Private	78.2	70.8
Subsistence	18.2	9.6
Public	4.1	6.7
Subtotal	82.3	77.5
Gross fixed investment	15.0	20.6
Stock changes	0.6	1.2
Exports (including nonfactor services)	37.6	39.5
Imports (including nonfactor services)	−35.5	−38.8
Gross domestic savings	17.7	22.5
Gross national savings[a]	12.0	16.4

Source: Statistical Appendix Table 7.
a. Corrected for retained earnings.

foreign borrowing was done by the public sector. In fact, as is evident from Table 3.2, the resource surplus of the private sector has been considerable. It will be noted that the outflow of private savings has gone up substantially. Reasons for this are the increasing earnings from earlier foreign investment, some reluctance lately on the part of foreigners to reinvest or engage in new ventures, and a continuous inflow of foreign labor, primarily African, who transfer part of their earnings abroad. By contrast, there has been a substantial deficit in the public sector, as the government has explored new opportunities and at the same time has continued to invest in social and supportive sectors.

TABLE 3.2. PUBLIC AND PRIVATE SECTOR SAVINGS
AND INVESTMENTS
(Annual average in CFAF billion)

Item	1960–65	1965–67	1971–74
Gross domestic public investment	14.9	26.2	69.9
Gross domestic public savings	11.3	19.1	47.4
Public sector savings deficit	3.6	7.1	22.5
Resource balance	3.8	3.6	5.7
Private sector savings surplus[a]	7.4	10.7	28.2

Sources: National accounts statistics; balance of payments; Loi Programme; Loi Plan.
a. Public sector savings deficit plus resource balance.

While the private sector has continued to transfer resources abroad, the public sector has been forced to borrow increasingly abroad to fill the gap between investments and savings. Thus it appears that with respect to investments and contribution to growth the private sector is declining in relative importance. Public investment as a proportion of total investment increased from an average of 40 percent in the early 1960s to slightly over 60 percent in 1971–74. The public debt service ratio[3] has recently gone up rapidly—from about 6 percent in 1969 to 8 percent in 1973, and to about 11 percent in 1975.

The terms of trade

In the financing of investments, the development of the terms of trade is an important factor. Deteriorating terms of trade indicate that the average price of a country's basket of exports did not keep pace with the average price of its imports. A way to compensate is to increase exports in volume, but this may be difficult in the case of the Ivory Coast since it is one of the world's largest producers of each of its main export products, and exporting much more could affect world prices negatively. Because terms of trade can only be seen to improve or worsen relative to a base year, in Table 3.3, 1973 has been arbitrarily chosen as the base year. It is clear from the table that defining 1970 as a normal year would make any other year look poor, while the reverse would be true if 1962 were declared normal. The table also shows that with 1973 as the base year, the terms of trade in 1974 were about back where they started in 1960. The annual value of the terms of trade over the period 1960–75 (with 1973 as 100) averages 96.7. As also shown by Figure 1, there has been no systematic deterioration of the terms of trade, but the fluctuations have been quite substantial. The deterioration between 1964 and 1965 cost the Ivory Coast CFAF14 billion, and in 1971 CFAF26 billion less was earned than trade would have generated under the price conditions of the year before. Forecasting the sometimes sharp price fluctuations for cocoa and coffee has proved hazardous. This has made economic planning difficult, especially the preparation of the next year's budget. Fluctuating revenues have a tendency to give the economy a stop-and-go character, which the Ivory Coast has been able to counter to some extent in the short run by establishing a price stabilization fund for agricultural products,

3. Debt service as a percentage of exports, plus nonfactor service earnings, minus workers' remittances abroad.

TABLE 3.3 TERMS OF TRADE FOR GOODS AND
NONFACTOR SERVICES, 1960–75
(1973 = 100)

Year	Terms of trade	Year	Terms of trade	Year	Terms of trade
1960	95.8	1965	83.9	1970	113.2
1961	90.5	1966	95.6	1971	98.6
1962	86.5	1967	97.6	1972	93.2
1963	97.3	1968	102.2	1973	100.0
1964	101.8	1969	109.4	1974	95.8
				1975	91.8[a]

Note: Based on historical series in CFAF.
Source: Statistical Appendix Table 10.
a. Preliminary.

FIGURE 1. DEVELOPMENT OF THE TERMS OF TRADE
(1973 = 100)

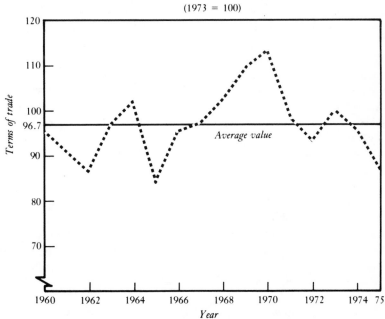

by drawing on reserves, and by borrowing from abroad. In the long run the fluctuations have been countered by a diversification policy.

Planning

A primary method of government regulation of the economy is the planning of the public investment program. This program now amounts to about 60 percent of total investment. The country has a distinguished record of planning. In 1960 a series of ten-year projections of the economy through 1970 was prepared, which called for a continuation of the policies followed during the final stage of the colonial era. After this came a four-year plan for 1967–70 and a five-year plan for 1971–75; the latest plan covers the 1976–80 period.

The plan

In the context of the liberal economy of the Ivory Coast the plan is very much a part of the French tradition of indicative planning and therefore allows a certain amount of flexibility. Since the publication of the 1967–70 four-year plan in 1966, the planning process has undergone continual improvement and refinement, and the 1971–75 plan has become a keystone of the development process in the Ivory Coast. Drawing up the plan required a large technical staff, which was and still is predominantly expatriate.

In contrast to development plans in many countries, the plan document for the Ivory Coast has been very detailed. Overall economic objectives are quantified as much as possible, sectoral and regional breakdowns of future investments are provided, and a financial plan is included. The Ministry of Planning has started to make a distinction between planning and programming, both of which are coordinated by the ministry. The planning process formulates the overall objectives, puts them in a general framework, assures consistency between objectives, and sets priorities. The development of an overall macroeconomic framework is part of this exercise. The programming process takes the projects as its units of account. The projects are the vehicles for meeting government objectives, and all changes each year in direction, emphasis, cost, progress of implementation, and other elements are taken into account in a three-year rolling program called the "Loi Programme."

This two-part procedure of going from the overall five-year targets of the plan (Loi Plan) to the annual project details in the three-year Loi Programme adds a great deal of flexibility to the whole planning process. This is an important asset in the light of the increasing worldwide uncertainty about future economic developments and the unpredictable changes that can actually take place in the economic order. Each year's Loi Programme contains the public investment program detailed down to the individual project and is aggregated thereafter to subprogram, major program, and region and to the specific sources of financing for the expenditures planned for the next three years. The first year of each Loi Programme is, in effect, the investment budget of the government proper for that year (Budget Spécial d'Investissement et d'Equipement or BSIE), plus the investment program of the public enterprises. By providing the link between the Loi Plan and its project-by-project execution, the Loi Programme provides a means of following the execution of the plan, of scheduling and coordinating the implementation of its projects, and of shifting resources as bottlenecks become apparent or circumstances change. The more general the Loi Plan becomes, the more crucial the role of the Loi Programme. Implementation of the Loi Programme has to be checked continuously against the objectives set in the Loi Plan. Debt service, budget, and balance of payments equilibria are important criteria in this respect.

The BSIE does not include public enterprises. Investments of these enterprises have, however, increased rapidly from 45 percent of public investment in 1965–69 to about 60 percent in 1975; in the proposals for 1976 this percentage went as high as 70 percent. It is not entirely clear how public enterprises received authorization for their investment spending. In theory, they have to submit their long-term investment plans to the Ministries of Finance and Planning and to the technical ministry involved. This is done in a sense when the Loi Programme is established, but the authorization for spending seems to have been given very much on a case-by-case basis. With the proliferation of public enterprises and their sometimes autonomous behavior, such an approach could jeopardize national economic objectives, physically and financially. To deal with this troublesome issue an interministerial committee was formed (see discussion in Chapter 4).

The Ministry of Planning does not, of course, design or select all the investment projects presented in the plan document. Rather it plays the important role of arbitrator between the technical ministries and the public enterprises on the one hand and the Ministry of Finance and the government (in its role as formulator of objectives) on the other. The Ministry of Planning translates the objectives of the government into a set of consistent projections covering the next five to ten years. These projections produce overall output and investment targets and the aggregate investment package. Then within the guidelines of the investment package and sectoral and other priorities, the Ministry of Planning, together with the technical ministries, selects from all the potentially worthwhile projects those which contribute most to achieving the targets of the plan and which can be achieved within the means estimated to be available. This process of *arbitrage* (arbitration) is a long and often difficult exercise in reconciling the programs of different ministries with the demands of different priorities. The process enables airing of different views within the government. In effect, the Ministry of Planning is responsible for the long-run coordination of the development projects, the Ministry of Finance for the annual investment financing, and the technical ministries for project preparation and execution.

The Ivory Coast has experimented for some years with this concept and, although its implementation is still far from perfect, the 1976–80 plan reflects much more than earlier plans the idea of planning by objective, thus showing much less project detail. The new concept will probably profoundly change the character of the next plan document because it is likely to be directed mainly to broad objectives. Because the Ivory Coast is in the fortunate position of having many opportunities for further development and also has imaginative planners, the new methodology has led to a cascade of investment proposals. Any arbitration to reduce the total amount of planned investments has proved to be difficult. It can be done effectively only if there is a clear understanding of what the priorities are. The president has always greatly influenced decisions such as these.

In making its final decisions, the government should realize that balanced development must recognize existing constraints. The means being finite, a railway in the southwest may have to compete with a water supply system in the north, and an accelerated program for sugar production may jeopardize objectives set for education. A decision that road users should be charged total costs, but that the railway and the port should be subsidized, is a question of the priorities set by the government. The same is true for a decision to provide free education and to charge the consumer the full cost of water and electricity. The country is autonomous in choosing its objectives and in determining priorities among them. For proper planning, however, these priorities cannot be left undefined. If too many things are left undecided, a maximum of flexibility may be obtained, but implementation of projects may become dependent on the skill and power of a particular ministry or the desire of bilateral sources to sell certain equipment. These dangers are visibly present in the Ivory Coast. It is true that a slavish adherence to a project-oriented five-year plan may not give the best results, and in this respect planning by objective is indeed an improvement. But planning by project injects a certain discipline into the system, which, for balanced development, is as essential as flexibility. Financial discipline would enter the system in the programming and budgeting stage, which to become more effective should be considerably improved.

Another facet of the problem is that planning concentrates on investment, while recurrent expenditure receives much less attention. The discussion of public finance in Chapter 4 takes note of the fact that current expenditure by the central government has grown more rapidly than revenue. The operating costs of the public enterprises are only partially known, but the conditions there do not seem any better. With recurrent expenditure increasing at a faster pace than revenue, savings available for investment are declining and more and more money has to be borrowed to finance a given investment program. It is therefore essential that the recurrent costs resulting from investment decisions be taken into account and that much more attention be given to this aspect of planning. The Loi Programme concept offers an opportunity to do this, but so far its implementation has been poor.

Record of plan implementation

Table 3.4 shows the allocation of public investment over the various major programs, the percentage forecast, and the percentage implemented. In 1960–66, the emphasis was clearly on economic infrastructure. Considerable assistance was received from France to improve roads and ports, and in this period the second small hydroelectric system was installed. The next largest investment category was government infrastructure. In 1967 in an analysis of 1960–66 performance, the government found a satisfactory real income growth of some 5 percent per capita a year, but at the same time expressed its concern about the imbalance in growth among the regions. Little progress had been made in changing the per capita income differences of 1960. These imbalances are discussed in Chapter 6. The government also observed that private initiative in the country's basic sector, agriculture, was lagging behind expectations and consequently public sector investment for agriculture was doubled for the 1967–70 period as com-

TABLE 3.4. FORECAST AND ACTUAL ALLOCATION OF PUBLIC INVESTMENT BY FIVE-YEAR PLANS BETWEEN 1960 AND 1980

Public investment	1960–66 Actual	1967–70 Forecast	1967–70 Actual	1971–75 Forecast	1971–75 Actual	1976–80 Forecast
Percentage						
Economic development[a]	19	36	33	37	32	36
Economic infrastructure[b]	46	39	35	32	37	36
Social development[c]	2	6	14	17	16	15
Cultural development[d]	9	7	7	9	8	6
Government infrastructure[e]	24	12	11	5	7	7
Total	100	100	100	100	100	100
Total (constant CFAF billion)	93.2	116[f]		277[g]		1,350
Total (current CFAF billion)			139.9		425.0	
Annual average (1975 CFAF billion)	31.1		61.9		109.5	270[h]

Source: Ministry of Planning, plan documents.
a. Almost entirely primary sector until 1971; about 6 percentage points for the secondary sector in 1971–75, and around 10 percentage points planned for 1976–80.
  b. Communications and energy.
  c. Urban development, health, and welfare.
  d. Education and culture.
  e. Research, defense, and general administration.
  f. 1967 prices.
  g. 1970 prices.
  h. 1975 prices; preliminary.

pared with 1960–66, while that for government infrastructure was cut in half. Implementation was remarkably close to plan forecasts.

Since 1970 the investment most directly related to production has continued to claim over 30 percent of public investment, although implementation has consistently fallen a few points short of what was projected. Expenditure for economic infrastructure continued at about 35 percent, reflecting the government's policy of providing sufficient high-quality capacity consistent with the foreign and efficiency-oriented economy. This trend also reflects the fact that two major projects were started during 1967–70. One of these was the Kossou Dam, a hydroelectric system on the Bandama River on the northern fringe of the forest zone south of Bouaké. The dam, with an installed capacity of 174 megawatts represented an investment cost of about CFAF25 billion in current prices. The second project was the port of San Pédro, which involved three general cargo berths, a timber park and accompanying road infrastructure in the port's hinterland. This project opened up the southwest's untapped forestry and land resources. Both projects were completed in 1972. They will continue to have an important impact on development in the next decade and to influence future policy decisions. Urbanization has progressed rapidly and urban infrastructure investment has greatly exceeded the amount forecast in 1967–70. The proportion of investment in education stayed at about the same level, but the emphasis here has been on current expenditure as already indicated.

The last line of Table 3.4 expresses amounts in 1975 prices. This series shows that in terms of implementation public investment increased by 13.4 percent a year between 1960–66 and 1967–70, and by 13.6 percent between 1967–70 and 1971–75. This is about 1.8 times as rapidly as real growth of income during the same period, reflecting the increase in investment from 15 percent to over 20 percent of GDP, and an increase in public investment as a proportion of total investment from 40 to 60 percent.

Investment in real terms has consistently been higher than anticipated, and, as net local savings have gone up at a slower pace than investment, borrowing from abroad has also consistently exceeded the limits set earlier. The public investment figure for 1976–80 refers to a very preliminary investment program drawn up by the Ministry of Planning before much arbitration had taken place. The size of the preliminary program suggests that a fair amount of scaling down will have to be done. Assuming for 1976–80 an annual real growth in GDP of 7 percent and a continuation of the trend of investment (that is, increasing to 25 percent of GDP, with public investment growing to 65 percent of total investment), annual public investment over the 1976–80 period would average about CFAF160 billion (in 1975 prices). But even this high level of public investment will be possible only if the local savings performance can be improved. A feasible development strategy for the next ten-year period is discussed in Chapters 7 and 8, with emphasis on the orientation and size of the public investment program.

Implementation of the 1971–75 plan

The 1971–75 plan was a much improved and more detailed one than its predecessor, although it followed the same general lines. The aggregate economic analysis was better developed and the system of rolling budgets was improved. The plan continued to put more emphasis on industrial development, while continuing the diversification and expansion of agriculture. It began the study of some very large-scale industrial projects, such as the iron ore mine and the pulp and paper project in the southwest. The plan also reflected an increased role for the government in the productive sectors of the economy, both directly and through the state enterprises.

External events have not been too favorable for this well-conceived plan. The oil crisis, the sharp inflation of 1974, and the worldwide recession of 1975 have made full implementation of the 1971–75 plan all but impossible. The combination of high export earnings in 1973–74 and increased concern about better regional distribution have led to sharp increases in government investment expenditure. As a result, as noted earlier, investments have exceeded plan targets in constant as well as current terms. On balance, the Ivory Coast was not seriously hurt in 1974 by external inflation since its exports also enjoyed high prices, but the world recession of late 1974 and 1975 and the high prices of imports slowed domestic production and exports in some areas, such as timber. This led to growth rates of GDP in constant terms below plan targets, although under the circumstances a real growth in GDP of 5.6 percent a year during 1971–75 can be considered a very good performance.

No comprehensive information is available as yet on the degree to which plan targets have been achieved in physical terms, but the World Bank has made estimates for two important sectors, agriculture and transportation. As for agricultural production, plan targets for commercial crops grown in the forest zone were more or less reached or exceeded in 1975. Coffee, cocoa, copra, rubber, and oil palm reached

90 percent of their targets; bananas, 85 percent; and pineapples, 125 percent. For other crops such as cotton, sugar, rice, and groundnuts, the targets have proved overoptimistic. Estimated production of traditional food crops appears to have kept pace with plan forecasts; at any rate, recovery of food production since the droughts of 1972 and 1973 (from which the Ivory Coast suffered only marginally) has been sufficient to avoid shortages on local markets. Taking the years 1970 and 1975 as points of comparison, it is estimated that the volume of commercial crop production (plus timber) has grown by about 28 percent over the plan period, or 5 percent a year, as against a plan forecast of 21 percent increase (3.9 percent a year). In effect, an increased rate of exploitation of timber resources has more than compensated for shortfalls in the realization of certain overoptimistic crop targets and the slow pace of diversification into new industrial crops such as kenaf,[4] tobacco, cashew nuts, avocados, and groundnuts.

During the plan period delays have occurred in the physical realization of certain expansion or replanting programs for perennial crops that are very important for future production. In addition, and measured in constant prices, there have been serious cost overruns in several cases. A tabulation of planned and actual figures for plantings and cost per hectare indicates the extent of these problems (see Table 3.5). The table compares cost in constant prices. For coffee, expenditure per hectare in constant terms was more than four times the original estimate; at these costs only 54 percent of the program was implemented. On the average, the cost in constant prices of the entire program was more than twice as high as forecast, and at these costs only 61 percent of the program was implemented. The cost of establishment of coffee, rubber, and, to a lesser extent, oil palm and sugar turned out to be higher than estimated.

Among a variety of possible reasons for the high cost overruns may be singled out the following: (a) underestimation of the extent to which public investment in buildings, roads, and social infrastructure would be necessary in order to reach project targets; (b) insufficient control over the size of overhead and spending programs of state companies; (c) the choice of what may be an overly sophisticated production technology, at least in the case of sugar; (d) delays in project execution; and (e) insufficient project preparation. The government is concerned about the cost overruns and is aware of the seriousness of the problems; in

---

4. This project was abandoned in 1974, the area developed will be used for rice and other crops.

TABLE 3.5. AREA AND COST OF
ESTABLISHMENT OF
PLANTATION CROPS, 1971–75
(Percent)

Crop	Area actually planted as a percentage of planned area	Actual cost per hectare as a percentage of planned cost per hectare[a]
Coffee	54	427
Cocoa	68	127
Rubber	51	313
Oil palm	54	200
Coconut	57	140
Sugar	100	150
Total	61	220

Source: Ministry of Planning (mainly the 1971–75 Plan and Loi Programmes) and World Bank estimates.
  a. The cost comparisons have been made in constant prices. Inflation over the 1971–75 period was low in the beginning but much higher later on; the average is estimated at about 50 percent.

some cases, such as control over state companies, corrective action has begun.

In the transport sector, it is estimated that implementation of the sector plan will have exceeded the initial financial targets, expressed in constant prices, by 22 percent (see Table 3.6). The table shows that the proportions invested in each subsector were largely according to plan, although during the plan period some projects were added and others deleted. A detailed analysis of the road sector program shows

TABLE 3.6. INVESTMENTS IN TRANSPORT SECTOR
UNDER THE 1971–75 PLAN
(Percent)

Subsector	Planned	Actual	Actual cost as a percentage of planned cost
Roads	48.9	49.0	123
Railways	21.0	22.3	130
Ports	19.5	19.5	123
Maritime transport and aviation	10.6	9.2	104
Total	100.0	100.0	—
Total (CFAF billion; 1968 prices)	43.0	52.6	122

Source: Ministry of Planning (mainly the 1971–75 Plan and Loi Programmes) and World Bank estimates.

that only about 50 percent of the original proposals will have been implemented; but taking into account the additions, about 75 percent of the road length originally foreseen will have been upgraded. For the road subsector, therefore, a physical realization of 75 percent ultimately cost 123 percent (in constant prices) of the amount originally estimated to pay for the entire program. For the railway subsector, the physical shortfall is estimated to be on the order of 40 percent. Implementation of only part of the transportation program at considerably higher cost than envisaged for the entire program suggests a serious underestimation of costs during plan preparation.

It is not known whether and how the high costs have affected the profitability of investments. Inasmuch as the cost comparisons were made in constant terms, it seems unlikely that the benefits in constant terms have been underestimated to the same degree. The data seem to support the earlier observation that the costs of development are increasing, that is, that the incremental capital-output ratios are going up. More evidence of this phenomenon will be found later in this chapter in the discussion of the comparative advantage of productive activities in, and outside of, agriculture.

Structural changes

The economy has changed substantially during the last fifteen-year period, as shown in Table 3.7. The share of agriculture in total production declined continuously between 1960 and 1974, but this decline should not be misinterpreted. In the table, agricultural production is

TABLE 3.7. PRODUCTION OF GDP AT MARKET
PRICES BY SECTOR
(Percent)

Sector	1960	1965	1970	1974
Agriculture	40.2	30.6	22.6 ⎫	
Forestry	2.6	4.5	4.0 ⎬	26.4
Fisheries	0.9	0.8	0.6 ⎭	
Mining	0.8	0.7	0.2	0.2
Manufacturing	4.0	6.9	10.8	12.3
Crafts	4.0	3.2	2.7	1.9
Public utilities	0.6	0.9	1.1	1.1
Construction	4.8	5.4	6.7	5.4
Tertiary sector	42.1	47.0	51.3	52.7
Total	100.0	100.0	100.0	100.0

Source: National accounts.

valued only at producer prices. Taxes, trade margins, and transportation are all attributed to other sectors. Furthermore, manufacturing makes over 50 percent of its value added by processing agricultural raw materials. Therefore the agricultural sector is much more important to the economy than the table suggests; in fact, it is the foundation of the economy and the mainspring of its growth, providing directly or indirectly a livelihood for 75 percent of the population and a similar percentage of export earnings, facts well recognized by the government. Forestry has expanded substantially as a result of increased European demand for tropical hardwood. Industry has also grown rapidly from its very low base in 1960, while mining activity remains virtually nonexistent.

The World Bank has been studying incentive systems and comparative advantages in selected West African countries, including the Ivory Coast. According to preliminary results,[5] the incentive system was found to have subsidized industry to a large extent with earnings in agriculture. Using effective subsidy[6] as a yardstick, a value of unity being neutral, coffee and cocoa have values between 0.5 and 0.6; palm, oil and copra between 0.8 and 0.9; cotton and maize, provided an appropriate production technique is used, around 1.0; and rice slightly above 1.0. The median for industry is 1.45. The analysis also demonstrates that in the case of agriculture all the incentives and stimulative measures given to the crops scoring a value below 1.0 are more than compensated for by taxes on those crops. In fact, there is a surplus benefit that can and has been used to stimulate other activities. Thus the government is providing a host of incentives and many services to agriculture, but in the end the agricultural sector pays for them. The products for which the comparative advantage is largest are taxed most, while new products in particular are taxed at a lower level. The agricultural price and taxation policies seem sound in general and appear to be based on the proper principles and considerations. These include a desire to diversify and to stabilize the economy, to avoid price-destructive overproduction, to redistribute the income from the best endowed areas, and to invest in longer term necessities such as industry.

5. Based on the 1972 situation but still generally considered valid.

6. The effective subsidy coefficient reflects the protection an activity receives in the form of tariffs and from tax and interest rates lower than what should be considered normal. Activities with a value exceeding 1.0 are those that receive a subsidy; those with a value below 1.0 are those that yield tax revenue.

Policies and Results in Agriculture

The emphasis the government correctly put on agricultural development in the south after independence has already been noted. It was also logical to continue efforts toward diversification. The soundness of these policies is confirmed by the findings of the World Bank study of incentive systems and comparative advantages mentioned earlier. The study indicates that the Ivory Coast has a clear advantage in the production of coffee, cocoa, oil palm products, copra, pineapple, and bananas—all products of the forest zone. An advantage also exists, but to a lesser extent, in the production of cotton, groundnuts, rice, and maize—all products of the savannah. Using the domestic resources cost (DRC) criterion, cocoa and coffee score 0.60–0.70 and cotton scores 0.70–0.80.[7] Rice scores around 1.05 if cultivated using simple techniques; grown in rotation with cotton its DRC drops to around 0.80. Thus, the comparative advantage appears particularly high for the major export crops originating in the south. It should be added that only after the appropriate insecticides and hybrids for cotton had become available in the early 1960s did the growing of cotton in the north become a real possibility.

The study also shows that cotton cultivation in the north becomes comparable in its national economic effects with the rich tree crops of the south if it is grown in rotation with other crops such as rice, maize, groundnuts, and the like. In the early days there was hardly a market for these foodstuffs, but the situation has changed. Urban centers have been growing rapidly as has their demand for food. Until 1973 cereals could be and were imported at subsidized prices from surplus stocks elsewhere in the world, but this is changing as well and it is conceivable that the future world food situation will be characterized by shortages rather than by surpluses.

---

7. DRC values represent the value of domestic resources spent in saving or earning a unit of foreign exchange expressed as a proportion of the actual exchange rate. Accordingly, a DRC greater than 1.0 shows that the implicit exchange rate representing the amount of domestic resources spent to earn a unit of foreign exchange is higher than the actual rate of exchange. Consequently, if the actual exchange rate appropriately represents the scarcity value of foreign exchange to the economy, it will be desirable to expand activities with DRCs lower than 1.0 and reduce those with DRCs exceeding 1.0.

The study reaches another interesting conclusion: Nonmotorized mechanization is possible for the types of crops grown in the northern savannah. At present factor costs, the study demonstrates that in the savannah zone ox-drawn cultivation is the most advantageous technique in all cases, while motorization imparts a comparative disadvantage. This is an important conclusion, which, together with the increased demand for food, indicates that the cultivation of cotton in rotation with other crops and with ox traction is able to earn the farmer in the north an adequate income. Introduction of these new techniques will not be easy, but if it is successful, the basis will have been laid for the introduction later of more advanced forms of mechanization (including motorization) and the higher incomes that accompany it. Considering the upward trend of wages and the possibility of labor shortages in agriculture, the opportunities for mechanization seem better in the north than in the south where tree crops are less suited to it. Although structural changes must take place, the north seems in the longer run to have very real economic potential, which is based primarily on agriculture integrated with livestock and on industrial possibilities as well, especially the processing of agricultural raw materials.

Thus it can be said that, although government policies seem to have given priority to growth, long-run policies have laid a foundation for improved equity. In 1960 it would have been possible to transfer more income from the south to the north, but it would mainly have been a transfer of consumption.[8] Instead, the government preferred to invest in longer-term solutions, for instance, efforts of research institutes to develop an income basis for the north where few real investment opportunities then existed. Moreover, not only people from neighboring countries but also those from the north of the Ivory Coast drifted south to fill the many jobs in industry, construction, and agriculture. The government did not want to stop this flow at the time because it was essential for successful implementation of an outward-oriented policy.

Incentives in agriculture

The system of government incentives affecting agricultural products operates at two levels. First, there are trade and other taxes, officially regulated producer and consumer prices, credit policies, general ex-

---

8. For regional differences in income see Chapter 6, "Employment, Income Distribution, and Ivorianization."

tension services, and publicly financed infrastructure—all of which are the result of decisions implemented by the central government. Second, specialized public institutions operating in the agricultural sector frequently intervene between the central government and the farmer to influence output and input prices, grant credit on favorable terms, provide subsidies in kind or cash, and otherwise affect the environment within which the farmer operates. The main policies have been to pay reasonable and stable producer prices, keep wages in agriculture relatively low, create an efficient and effective organizational structure, and allow the influx of unskilled and skilled labor from abroad.

Producer price policy.   The responsiveness of farmers to price changes is impressive. Most recently an increase in the producer price for rice not only induced farmers to step up production considerably but also led them to abandon crops that under the new system of prices had become less profitable. Such responsiveness can facilitate policymaking, but it is a double-edged sword since mistakes can be costly. For instance, again in the case of rice, the government was not able to buy all the paddy at the announced producer price in 1975 and most farmers had to sell their production on the parallel market, reportedly at about 60 percent of the announced price.

In 1960, with falling world prices for cocoa and coffee, one of the first things the government had to do was to lower producer prices (see Table 3.8). Probably partly as a reaction of the farmers to this reduction, there was a serious delay in the implementation of the government's agricultural development program in the mid-1960s. The government decided to step up its direct involvement and to spend 30 percent of its 1967–70 total public investment in agriculture, compared with 12 percent during 1960–66. Aware of demand constraints in coffee and cocoa and also of the impact of adverse weather conditions and lower world prices on two products on which the country relied heavily, it chose to reemphasize diversification.

The impact of the producer price policy should not be underestimated. Apart from some banana and pineapple plantations, virtually all interests in agriculture are Ivorian. Hundreds of thousands of families are involved in cocoa and coffee cultivation. These two products alone paid the farmers in 1975 about CFAF90 billion, or US$200 million after taxes. Over the last ten years producers have been paid an average of about 50 percent of the f.o.b. price for coffee and cocoa. This and the other incentives seem to have worked even better than anticipated. Early estimates of the area under cocoa and coffee culti-

TABLE 3.8. PRODUCER PRICES
OF COCOA AND COFFEE
(CFAF per kilogram)

Year [a]	Cocoa	Coffee
1958	90	115
1959	95	105
1960	70	95
1961, 1962	70	80
1963, 1964	70	90
1965	55	75
1966, 1967, 1968	70	90
1969	80	95
1970, 1971, 1972	85	105
1973	110	120
1974, 1975, 1976	175	150

Source: Stabilization Fund.
a. Year refers to crop year; thus 1958 stands for crop year 1958–59.

vation were 600,000 and 700,000 hectares respectively; by 1973–74 the agricultural census of the south registered 225,000 plots growing 920,000 hectares of cocoa and 350,000 plots growing 1,235,000 hectares of coffee.

Wages. Minimum wages are established by the government and have increased faster for nonagricultural workers than for agricultural. Between 1970 and 1974 agricultural minimum wages rose by 20 percent to CFAF25 an hour and nonagricultural minimum wages rose by 58 percent to CFAF92 an hour. Wages and income distribution are further discussed in Chapter 6. There it is shown that generally in agriculture the income from wages is supplemented by income from sharecropping and subsistence cultivation. Still, income in nonagricultural occupations in general is higher, which encourages urban migration. Most hired workers in agriculture are non-Ivorian Africans, and until recently the level of remuneration in cash and kind was generally able to attract the required labor. Lately, however, labor shortages have been reported in several rural areas and the government may have to reconsider agricultural wage levels.

The organization of agriculture. Between 1963 and 1966, a single ministry was responsible for agriculture, forestry, and livestock; now there are four. Project implementation and, so far, most project design is carried out by autonomous agencies (SODE),[9] placed under the supervision of the technical ministries. SODE are in most cases closely connected with specialized agricultural research institutes. The SODE are organized by product. The principal ones are SATMACI (coffee and cocoa), SODEPALM (oil and coconut palm), SOCATCI (rubber), SODESUCRE (sugar), SODEFEL (fruit and vegetables), SODERIZ (rice), CIDT (cotton), MOTORAGRI (agricultural motorization), and SODEPRA (livestock). In addition, agricultural programs are initiated by two regional organizations: One is the Autorité pour l'Aménagement de la Vallée du Bandama (AVB), established in 1969 with the primary objective of resettling the villagers who were to be displaced by the Kossou Dam hydroelectric scheme. The other is the Autorité pour l'Aménagement de la Région du Sud-Ouest (ARSO), whose principal activities so far have consisted of establishing facilities for new settlers in the southwest. Both are directly responsible to the presidency.

Supporting services also exist in the fields of research, credit, cooperative development, regional development, and price stabilization. Research on individual crops is carried out by specialized institutes under overall government supervision. The institutes dealing with coffee and cocoa (IFCC), oil crops (IRHO), and cotton (IRCT) have achieved excellent results, in close coordination with the corresponding SODE. Unfortunately little progress has been made so far in food crop research (IRAT).

Institutional agricultural credit is provided by BNDA (Banque Nationale pour le Développement Agricole), a mixed enterprise created in 1968 under the supervision of the Ministry of Agriculture. The volume of loans has grown rapidly, with an amount outstanding in 1975 of over CFAF15 billion, two-thirds of which is in the form of short-term loans. Interest rates to final borrowers vary between 7.5 percent and 10 percent, and credit recovery is good. BNDA operates mainly through the SODE, although it is enlarging its field staff considerably as a basis for expanding individual credit activities. It also assists in the development of cooperatives, working in close association with the Centre National de la Promotion des Entreprises Coopératives (CENAPEC), an autonomous agency under the supervision of the Ministry of Agriculture, which was established in 1968 with the assistance of ILO.

The role of CENAPEC is to foster the organization and development of farmers' cooperatives. The creation of cooperatives in a country

9. Sociétés de Développement.

where there is no tradition for this type of institution is a difficult task under the best of circumstances; the task is made even more difficult when, as in the Ivory Coast, there is a lack of trained manpower among the prospective membership. The recent growth in numbers of cooperatives has, however, been impressive: from 100 in 1970 to 300 in 1971, to 1,000 in 1972, and to 1,600 in 1973.

The Office National de Promotion Rurale (ONPR) was created in 1973 under the joint supervision of the Ministries of Planning and Agriculture. Its objective is to design programs aimed at training and motivating rural inhabitants, especially the youth, and to help peasant communities organize themselves so that they can eventually take charge of their own development. The Fonds Régionaux d'Aménagement Rural (FRAR) have a somewhat similar orientation, but with a broader scope of action and a distinctly regional character. The FRAR organizations are also of recent creation and are under interministerial supervision; their functions and responsibilities will probably be more clearly defined in the near future. The creation of both organizations reflects the increased preoccupation of the government with conditions in rural areas.

The Stabilization Fund (Caisse de Stabilisation et de Soutien des Prix des Produits Agricoles, CSSPPA) stabilizes producer prices of coffee, cocoa, vegetable oils, cotton, bananas, copra, tobacco, kenaf, and cashew nuts. In addition to price stabilization, CSSPPA is charged with the organization and supervision of domestic marketing and export handling of its products, the financing of investments designed to increase productivity and to promote domestic processing, and the conclusion and execution of international agreements. (See Chapter 4 for its financial role in price stabilization.) The prices for rice and some other basic foodstuffs are stabilized by the Caisse de Péréquation; in 1975 this organization was placed under the supervision of the Ministry of Commerce.

The proliferation and dispersion of decision centers is creating problems. There are conflicts between regional and product organizations, and, when product organizations compete for the same land, national economic interest does not always prevail. The government is confronted with these problems every day and has been working on solutions. Its strategy is to make the central ministry an effective agency for policymaking, program design and coordination, and supervision of the project-executing agencies (SODE); and to broaden the scope of the SODE from single-crop promotion to integrated regional agricultural development. The assignment of regional responsibilities to the different SODE is currently being discussed, and will primarily concern SAT-MACI, SODEPALM, SODERIZ, and CIDT. To a large extent, in fact, the activities of the last two agencies already go beyond their usual responsibilities of traditional single-crop promotion. CIDT, established in 1974 as a mixed company to carry on cotton development initiated by the Compagnie Française pour le Développement des Textiles (CFDT), has been given statutory responsibility for the integrated development of the cotton areas, which cover roughly one-third of the country's surface and engage one-fourth of its population. In a similar way, SODERIZ, although primarily responsible for rice development, is expected to assist in the development of other crops, such as maize and soybeans.

Foreign labor.   Another factor that has been crucial in achieving the remarkable record of growth in agriculture has been heavy immigration of hardworking manpower from neighboring countries. Immigrants have added a new stimulus to development and contributed to its acceleration. They provided the bulk of the labor force involved in the substantial increases in the production of cocoa and coffee from smallholder plots. Immigrants also provided the bulk of the workers needed for the establishment of large-scale plantations, particularly oil and coconut palm plantations. Moreover, the development of livestock in the north, limited as it is, has been assisted by non-Ivorian herders. This has opened up a limited avenue for possible livestock development, one that the Ivorian government has recently shown an interest in pursuing and supporting.

Another positive factor has been that the organization of agriculture has lent itself well to the employment of highly trained and motivated supervisory personnel (expatriates initially, but increasingly Ivorian) who have not only designed bold and far-reaching programs, but have had the skill and tenacity to carry them out. SODEPALM is perhaps the outstanding example. Finally, the generally favorable world market conditions for the country's main export crops provided the required conditions for the success of the sector. The Stabilization Fund has been skillful in its market operations and in general has chosen the proper moment for its activities.

Results in agriculture

The most remarkable achievement of Ivorian agriculture has been the satisfactory growth in production of both industrial crops and food crops (see Appendix A for details). The main industrial crops grew by 5 percent a year between 1965 and 1975, while diversification continued at a satisfactory rate. In 1975 crops other than coffee and cocoa accounted for 25 percent of total production, compared with 16 percent in 1970 and 11 percent in 1965. Oil palm, cotton, and pineapple have been the three key diversification crops.

The annual average growth rate of food crop production accelerated from about 3 percent a year in 1965–70 to 4 percent in 1970–75. Growth has been fairly uniform in cereals and root crops. Among cereals, sorghum and millet have shown little progress, while rice has increased at a rapid rate. The remarkable results of Ivorian farmers in food production during the past decade have surpassed the most optimistic forecasts of government planners and policymakers. From 1965 to 1975 the rural population increased 27 percent but produced 42 percent more food; imports of foodstuff for each urban inhabitant declined from 200 kilograms to 115 kilograms during the same period. The inference here is clear: In spite of the considerable increase in urban population and per capita incomes, the Ivory Coast has become less rather than more dependent on food imports. Since the increase in food production was largely a spontaneous response of farmers and traders to market forces, it must be concluded that a reasonably efficient private marketing network exists and that farmers respond readily to price signals and incentives transmitted by this network. This and the remarkable performance of Ivorian farmers in food production during the past decade should be taken into account by government planners and policymakers. A better appreciation of the responsiveness of farmers to prices would help to avoid problems such as those created by government intervention in the rice sector. The private sector is alive and reacting readily to incentives.

Livestock production has continued to lag far behind crop production; growth, if any, has been minimal.

Policies and Results in Forestry

After reaching a peak of some 150,000 cubic meters in the early 1920s, log exports declined. The transport infrastructure was not in place to allow deeper penetration into the forest zone. Around 1950 export volume was back to about 150,000 cubic meters and it continued to rise. Between 1960 and 1973 production of logs increased more than fivefold from 1 million to 5.2 million cubic meters. This dramatic growth was made possible by increasing demand and rising prices, together with considerable improvements in the transport infrastructure that made forests accessible and lowered transportation costs. The construction of the port of San Pédro in the southwest opened up the forest resources of that area, and in its second year, 1973, the port handled about 1 million cubic meters of logs, contributing substantially to the record exports of that year. Production in 1974 and 1975 fell back to 4–4.5 million cubic meters as a result of a slowdown in the European construction industry.

Tropical forests cover somewhat less than half of the country, that is, 15 million hectares. Areas of dense forest, which are the only ones that can be exploited economically, decreased from 9.8 million hectares in 1956 to 5.5 million hectares in 1973, or by 44 percent in seventeen years. However, this destruction of the forestry resources is not so much a matter of timber industry activities as it is encroachment by agricultural activities, especially in the regions opened by forestry sector roads. It is not known precisely how much forest is left; more inventories would have to be carried out to determine this. Until recently about thirty out of 1,000 identified species had been exploited. Four or five of these thirty species could be exhausted within a few years. An important issue, therefore, is the question of secondary species. The Ivory Coast has been quite successful in commercializing some species that were formerly unknown to the market. In 1972 the government began to tax primary species at higher rates than secondary species and lowered the taxes on some species new to the market. Since 1969 tax rates have almost tripled on high-value species, increased moderately for medium-value species, and remained constant or even diminished for the low-value species. As a result the proportion of lesser known species in total log exports increased from 24 percent in 1960 to 47 percent in 1973. The share of major redwood species in log exports diminished from 54 percent in 1960 to 24 percent in 1973. If the secondary species are included, the reserves of the Ivorian forest could amount to some 300 million cubic meters.

The forestry sector, including wood processing, has been and still is very important for the Ivorian economy. In the early 1970s the sector represented on the average 7 percent of GDP, 8 percent of total wages, 8 percent of total tax revenue, and about 25 percent of exports. Logging operations, which are relatively capital intensive, are largely owned by foreigners who supply mills abroad, frequently their own, with high quality logs. Still, it is estimated that net foreign currency earnings have amounted to some 70 percent of gross earnings and as such the forestry industry has played an important role in earning the foreign currency required to develop other sectors. It is difficult to say whether in this respect government policy has been the most effective. It could have refused to export timber in unprocessed form or could have waited to export logs until a higher price could be obtained. Other sectors, especially agriculture, have benefited greatly from the opening up of land by forestry activities. It is probable that at the level of income experienced at independence, and given the general orientation of policy, the government has followed a logical forestry policy. Moreover, it was established in a World Bank regional study on forestry that the Ivory Coast has been able to command by far the highest export taxes on logs of any West African country. These taxes averaged about 20 percent of the f.o.b. (free on board) value for 1965–74, compared with 11 percent for Cameroon and 6 percent for Ghana. New tax regulations introduced in March 1974 in the Ivory Coast should raise the tax rate to about 26 percent.

The government (now with a separate Ministry of Forestry) has been trying for several years to create a viable forestry industry on a sustaining basis. One of the objectives of the 1971–75 plan was to limit the production of logs to 3.5 million cubic meters in 1975 and to 4.0 million cubic meters in 1980, an upper ceiling which obviously has been exceeded. Furthermore, local processing, which has oscillated around 25 percent of total production since 1960, would have to go up to 37 percent in 1975 and 42.5 percent in 1980. To stimulate local processing, export of unprocessed wood products was discouraged by a tax penalty: the average total forest tax on exported logs being about CFAF2,500–5,000 for a cubic meter; for processed wood in roundwood equivalent it is about CFAF750–1,500 for a cubic meter. As a further incentive, and to assure a supply of logs to the processing industry, the Forest Service has established quotas for logs to be supplied by logging firms to local processing plants. Logging firms have to deliver two units to local processing plants for every three units exported; for the logging companies with large concessions local deliveries have to equal exports. Here again, relatively unknown species have been left out of the quota and, as a result, local processing reached 35 percent of total log production in 1974.

Over the years the country has been innovative in its forestry policies. Despite its shortcomings the sector has made an extremely important contribution to the Ivory Coast's development in a direction that could be used as an example for other countries in the area. The Ivory Coast's most critical need in the sector is a determination of the size and location of permanent forest reserves. Next, efficient forest industries must be developed that are supplied by natural and, if feasible, plantation forests. Reforestation by SODEFOR has thus far been limited and, apparently, rightly so; other investments have been given priority over reforestation. Since all the forest area is allocated under concessions, the development of an efficient industry will require the review and revision of existing concession arrangements with a view to guaranteeing long-term supplies for integrated local forest industry complexes.

Ivorianization of the sector is another problem. Because of the capital intensity of logging activities and the link between logging and processing capacity located abroad, the logging industry is mostly foreign-owned, while the labor consists mainly of other Africans. This is another example of the use of foreign in combination with local resources (the latter being the forest), to yield a net revenue that can be used to create infrastructure, other services, and jobs acceptable to the Ivorian population. The Ivory Coast should benefit from the growing coordination of forestry resources among African countries by using it to Ivorianize the sector, to acquire more processing capacity, and to export this resource increasingly in processed form.

Policies and Results in Industry

The government is well aware of the key role agriculture will continue to play in the future. But it has also understood that industry would have to play an increasingly important part in the Ivorian economy. With an increase in population and improved productivity in agriculture, jobs would have to be created elsewhere. The local processing of raw materials and the expansion of local demand would serve as a sound basis for a diversified industrial sector. The government has had to reckon with the fact that many Ivorians, especially the increasing number with some education, get no satisfaction from hired employment in agriculture, while the number of jobs offered by the public sector has been limited. Consistent with the high standards in education, modern industry has been encouraged, while small-scale industry and the informal sector have been left without much help.

At independence the manufacturing subsector accounted for only 4 percent of GDP. Most manufactured products were imported from France. The government realized the problems involved in creating an industrial sector without a local tradition or skill in manufacturing, but it deemed such a sector an indispensable part of a balanced economy in the long run and devised a policy to achieve this. The open-door and liberal policy toward direct investment by foreign firms is an example. The government concluded that in the beginning the industrial sector would have to rely heavily on factors from abroad. This policy is closely related to the government's emphasis on political stability, membership in the franc area, free transferability of profits and capital, and the general policy of creating confidence abroad. A recent survey of the motivations of foreign investors in establishing industry in the Ivory Coast revealed that market and political factors rated highest. Investment code incentives ranked fifth, which could indicate that these industries would have come to the Ivory Coast even without the investment code.

Tariffs and the investment code

Although the unmodified tariff structure would have provided most import-replacement, industries with effective protection of 20 to 40 percent,[10] measures under the investment code have greatly increased the effective protection available. The World Bank calculates an effective protection of 1.42 for manufacturing as a whole. Broken down into fifteen subsectors, the values range from 0.56 for beer and soft drinks, 0.81 for board and paper articles, 1.03 for rubber products, and 1.05 for cement, to as high as 2.82 for footwear and 3.75 for flour and grain milling. In several instances the incentives have been excessive.

As an instrument of industrial policy, the investment code can be seen to have had certain advantages. If protection had not been given in this way, quantitative measures might have been used more frequently, and such measures have many undesirable aspects. The duty-free import privilege of priority firms enabled them to buy on the best available terms in world markets, in effect abolishing tariff preferences given to the EEC and other countries. The privilege at the same time removed an obstacle to the establishment of firms relying on imports from non-EEC sources.

---

10. Effective protection means the amount of protection necessary to enable local processing costs to exceed the price of imported goods that incorporate these same processes. As an indication of incentives, the effective rate of protection given to a firm replacing imports is equivalent to its value added, measured in border prices, divided by the net loss of customs revenue resulting from its existence. An effective protection of 1.42 means that the effective protection is 42 percent.

The code has also had a number of disadvantages. A ten-year exemption from duties on current inputs gave a very high—but disguised—effective protection to the import-replacement production of a number of firms. Moreover, with this exemption even quite low or moderate, duties on finished products could and did support high effective protection when domestic value added was low in relation to the value of the finished product. Behind such high effective protection some firms were established that were unsuited to circumstances in the Ivory Coast and therefore were unable to compete with imports at any acceptable level of protection. Other firms, behind the shelter of protection, earned profits that were excessively high. In other cases, protection led to excess capacity and overcrowding and to a diminished incentive to reduce costs during the period of the ten-year agreements. The exemption from duty on machinery and equipment also gave a bias in favor of capital-intensive techniques and industries, despite the existence of urban unemployment. Finally, the code was geared to the requirements of the relatively large foreign firms and therefore was of little assistance to the development of smaller firms and the artisan sector.

In 1970 a number of the weaknesses in past policies began to become apparent as priority agreements from earlier years began to expire. Over the period 1970–73, special additional concessions were given to most of the firms involved in these agreements, particularly reductions in tariffs on current intermediate inputs. One of the problems in building an industrial sector behind tariffs is that it takes most infant industries more time to mature than is anticipated, and in many cases the cost will continue to be high for some time. In 1973 the tariff schedule was revised so as automatically to meet the protective requirements of firms whose priority agreements would expire in the future. This was achieved by a general reduction in duties on most intermediate goods. Recently two basic reorientations of existing policies have been proposed. First, a plan for a revised investment code would make the granting, the extent, and the period of import duty privileges discretionary. Import duty reductions on materials would be granted in exceptional cases, and the privileges would be regressive over a fixed time period in order to impose steadily increasing pressure on the firms concerned to improve their performance. Second, in recognition of the high cost of supporting import-replacement industries that depend on the relatively small domestic market, means of promoting manufactured exports to developed countries, particularly the EEC, have been actively discussed and implemented. At present such promotion has taken place in the textile industry.

Industrial sector growth and problems

Manufacturing has developed rapidly in the Ivory Coast as a result of industrial policy. With a growth rate of about 15 percent over the last fifteen years, its share in GDP rose from 4 percent in 1960 to over 12 percent in 1974. Growth has been based on carrying out the simple processing of agricultural raw materials and the final stages in the processing of imported semifinished products. Industries based on local raw materials, which may be termed agro-industries, include canned foods, coffee and cocoa processing, edible oils and fats, tobacco, textiles (mainly cotton), rubber, and wood products. In the early days, import-substitution industries grew more rapidly than agro-industries, but more recently this trend seems to have reversed. The following are the average growth rates a year in manufacturing, based on value added in current market prices:

Category	1965–70	1972–74
Agro-industries	15.8	36.5
Import-substitution industries	20.7	18.5
Total manufacturing	18.2	27.5

Manufacturing employment has shown sizable increases as well. With a growth rate between 1965 and 1975 of about 10 percent a year, the total modern sector labor force in manufacturing amounted to about 45,000 in 1975, which is equivalent to 13 percent of all salaried employment in the modern sector.

The development of an industrial sector has not been without problems. Apart from being quite expensive, the emphasis on import substitution has tended to lead to concentration of industry in Abidjan, where in 1974 about 65 percent of the value added, and 53 percent of employment in manufacturing, was concentrated. It also made real industrial integration difficult because many industries imported semifinished products that did not need much processing. Furthermore, the optimum production unit often had a capacity that exceeded local demand. Export of the surplus was in many cases not possible since neighboring countries had the same problem and sometimes even the same foreign investor; therefore underutilization of capacity became a common phenomenon. Since the country had to rely on foreigners to get its industrialization started, it should not come as a surprise that production is relatively capital intensive and that foreign ownership amounted to 68 percent in 1975. Three-quarters of the local ownership is in the hands of the government, reflecting the reluctance of private

Ivorians to invest in industry. One reason for this is that large amounts of capital are needed. Another is that many establishments are parts of foreign firms and Ivorians hesitate to participate where their share is too small to exert a significant influence. Moreover, there are other sectors, such as real estate, in which it is possible to recover capital more quickly. Although it is still too early to draw firm conclusions, there may be a gradual change in this attitude as shown by the fact that Ivorian buying of shares on the recently opened stock exchange has been increasing. Wider market and industrial investment opportunities are likely to develop in the context of such regional economic groupings of countries as CEAO and ECOWAS.[11]

The government is aware of these and other problems and is trying to devise a policy to solve them. The most promising element is the government's view that the time has come to reconsider its import-substitution policy. Better opportunities seem to be presented by the processing of local raw materials. Industrial exports have already increased from 15 percent of total exports in 1965 to 32 percent in 1974. In 1973 about 60 percent of industrial exports went to Europe and 20 percent to the West African market. A changing attitude in developed countries toward raw materials producers in developing countries would help to implement a policy aimed at processing a bigger share of raw materials locally. Successful implementation of such a policy may cure some problems inherent in continuing the import-substitution type of industry. For instance, production techniques for integrated processes have a tendency to be less capital intensive than import-substitution processes and much of the processing would necessarily have to be done in the area of cultivation. This would counterbalance the dominance of Abidjan and would not require expensive incentives. To promote this change in emphasis in its industrialization program it is recommended that an export subsidy be introduced and that preferential treatment be granted more selectively to import-substitution industries. Agriculture and forestry would be able to supply to the industry a wide range of raw materials such as coffee, cocoa, logs, oil palm, fruits, coconuts, cotton, rubber, pineapples, and sugarcane.

11. The CEAO developed out of the UDAO (Union Douanière entre les Etats de l'Afrique Occidentale) established in 1959, which was transformed into UDEAO (Union Douanière des Etats de l'Afrique de l'Ouest) in 1966. The Economic Community of West African States (ECOWAS) is a grouping of fifteen states, including the Ivory Coast, set up by the treaty of May 28, 1975, which aims at achieving a full common market in the future.

Tourism—A Change in Policy

The tourism sector is another example of the government's diversification efforts. The potential of this sector is limited, but from a policy standpoint it is noteworthy that after a period of relatively heavy direct investment, the government has decided to leave tourism much more to the private sector. Such a change is significant and indicates that the government is continuously reconsidering its position and policies and is responding to changing conditions.

The tourism sector in the Ivory Coast is still small, but has grown rapidly since 1970, the first year for which statistics were kept. The number of international tourists increased by 17 percent annually between 1970 and 1974, when it reached approximately 86,000. During the same period, the number of guest-nights increased by 23 percent a year, reaching 460,000. The results for 1975 virtually met the ambitious objective set by the 1971–75 plan of 100,000 arrivals (as against 22,000 in 1968), which is an encouraging development.

The direct contribution of tourism to the economy of the Ivory Coast is marginal. The hotel industry's direct contribution to GDP is between 0.5 and 1 percent. Net foreign exchange earnings, estimated at only 40 percent of gross exchange earnings, are also about 0.5 percent of total exports of goods and nonfactor services, while about 3,000 people, or 1 percent of the modern sector work force, are directly employed in the hotel industry. Although the impact on the total economy is small and will remain so for a considerable time, the government is correctly arguing that the tourism sector is a welcome diversification of the economy.

If foreign hotel arrivals are broken down into business visitors, conventioneers, and vacationers, about 80 percent of the arrivals fall into the first two categories; clearly, vacation tourism in the Ivory Coast is still in its infancy. The government is optimistic about the future development of tourism, particularly in the latter category. The 100,000 or more vacationers expected by the government in 1985 would not, however, make the kind of contribution to economic growth that this sector provides in some other countries.[12] Even these figures, which seem optimistic, reflect the fact that the potential for leisure

12. The number of foreign arrivals in Kenya, for instance, was 380,000 in 1974, of which only 11 percent came on business.

tourism in the Ivory Coast is evaluated as moderate at best by the government. A market study is under way to determine whether a change in policy from elite to mass tourism would be feasible. The country does have assets that could be developed. For example, historic areas near Abidjan, tribal culture and folklore, handicrafts (particularly in the northern part of the country), and the tropical flora and fauna have not yet been exploited to any great extent. Unfortunately the climate, with its high humidity, is not as favorable as, say, that of Dakar, and the beaches have limited potential as a result of dangerous ocean currents in many places. But Abidjan itself, with all it has to offer in terms of high-quality facilities, services, and entertainment, could be a valuable asset and could develop into a "must" in West African package tours.

The Ministry of Tourism, created in 1971, has assumed the functions of several former agencies and supervises three semipublic organizations, the Ivorian Agency for Tourism and Hotel Promotion (SIETHO), the Ivory Coast Travel Agency (ICTA), and the National Handicrafts Office (ONAA). The Ministry of Tourism shares with the Ministries of Planning and Finance the task of establishing policies and objectives for the sector and administering the incentive system. Because of its relative inexperience and limited staff, the Ministry of Tourism has so far carried little weight in major policy decisionmaking. From independence in 1960 to the end of 1975, about CFAF28 billion was invested in hotels and tourism infrastructure. Roughly 60 percent was financed by the government, and private Ivorian and foreign interests financed 20 percent each. In addition, by the end of 1975 the government's accumulated operating expenditures for the Ministry of Tourism and the three semipublic companies it supervises amounted to about CFAF2.5 billion.

As a result of such investments, the Ivory Coast now has a sizable inventory of tourism facilities. In Abidjan, the number of hotel accommodations doubled between 1970 and the end of 1975, when they amounted to about 1,450 rooms of luxury and international standards. In the interior of the country such rooms number about 490, altogether representing about 50 percent of the country's 3,800 hotel rooms. Of the remainder, about 700 rooms are in vacation villages located mainly on the beach. Because of the fast-growing economy and the business-oriented character of tourism, occupancy rates have kept abreast of the rapid expansion of accommodations; 1974 occupancy rates for three- to five-star hotels in Abidjan averaged 85 percent.

With major infrastructure in place, the government decided in 1973 to reduce its direct involvement in the sector and to attract private promoters for hotel construction. Secondary infrastructure (access roads, public utilities) would still be financed by the government, and the users generally would be charged. To further encourage private investment, a tourism incentive code was introduced in 1973. This policy appears to be sound and will free public resources for pressing needs in other sectors of the economy.

Mobilization and Allocation of Savings

The Ivory Coast is a member of the West African Monetary Union (Union Monétaire Ouest-Africaine, UMOA). The treaty establishing the union was signed in 1962 by Benin (then Dahomey), the Ivory Coast, Mauritania, Niger, Senegal, and Upper Volta; Togo joined in 1963, while Mauritania withdrew in 1973. An agreement on cooperation between France and the members of the UMOA was also signed in 1962. The treaty established a common central bank, the BCEAO (Banque Centrale des Etats de l'Afrique de l'Ouest), which issued a single currency and assured its free convertibility into French francs at the rate of CFAF50 to one French franc with the guarantee of France. The member countries also agreed to centralize their reserves in an operations account with the French treasury and to maintain the free circulation of capital within the union. Since its creation in 1962, the reserve position of the UMOA countries as a whole has always been positive.

The UMOA system has been restructured several times to provide member countries with central banking operations more responsive to their changing needs for economic development, integration, and Africanization. The modifications introduced should be seen in the context of a gradual shift toward monetary autonomy. In 1973, for instance, a new level of authority, the conference of the heads of state, was added above the council of ministers. The former decides on matters related to membership in the union, and the latter formulates monetary policy. Both make their decisions unanimously. The decisions of the board of directors are made on the basis of a simple majority in most cases. France, which had one-third of the board votes previously, now has only one-seventh. An African, in fact an Ivorian, has become governor, and headquarters of the BCEAO will be moved from Paris to Dakar as soon as offices are ready.

Rather far-reaching changes in the UMOA were introduced in July 1975. They are designed to (a) ensure better utilization within the

UMOA of the member countries' financial resources; (b) facilitate financing for the economic sectors that are given priority in national development objectives; and (c) increase the role of nationals in the management of their economies. With regard to the first objective, UMOA's liquidity level will be based on the needs of economic development and on the monetary and foreign reserve position of each member country and of the UMOA as a whole. Solidarity within the union makes it easier for a member country to cope with balance of payments problems at a particular moment than if it were not a member. Nevertheless, should the gross foreign reserve position of a member country cover less than 20 percent of demand deposits for three consecutive months, consultations within the UMOA have to start in order to work out corrective measures. Furthermore, a member government is now entitled to a BCEAO permanent credit line equivalent to 20 percent of its tax receipts during the preceding budgetary year. In the past, the credit line was set at 10 percent for a limited period, but was changed to 15 percent in 1966. The credit line can now be granted automatically with no time limit.

With regard to the two other objectives, the BCEAO is provided with new policy instruments to direct credit allocation. In January 1976, the control on volume of credit by the BCEAO was changed from a system based on discount ceilings for banks and individual enterprises to a system based on allocating to each country a ceiling for each country's recourse to BCEAO resources, and within this ceiling, allocating specific ceilings for the treasury and other public institutions and the private financial institutions. In addition, BCEAO's prior approval of all lending in excess of CFAF100 million is now required. The BCEAO may determine minimum sectoral ratios for each commercial bank's lending and minimum ratios for credits to be extended to enterprises run by nationals. There is no difference in interest rates on loans to national and foreign enterprises, with the exception of small- and medium-sized enterprises with debt outstanding of less than CFAF20 million. Therefore, there is no interest rate incentive for lending to foreign firms.

Medium-term discountable loans, which are generally used to finance local costs and cover the import component of an investment when external long-term loans and supplier's credits are not available, cannot represent more than 50 percent of the project cost (as a general rule), or 65 percent for industrial enterprises, or 90 percent for loans to national small- and medium-scale enterprises. Loans for purchase of existing foreign enterprises can also be discounted. The BCEAO indirectly influences the allocation of long-term loans through its direc-

torship in development banks' boards and through ceilings on medium-
and long-term commitments for each bank; for development banks,
these ceilings are defined by BCEAO as 150 percent of the sum of the
bank's equity (minus fixed assets and equity investments), and its long-
and medium-term resources. Medium-term rediscountable loans guaranteed by the government are not included in the ceiling.

Interest rates

Interest rates were increased in December 1972 and in July 1975.
The interest rate range changed from 3.5–8.5 percent to 5.5–11.0 percent, to the present 8.0–13.0 percent, with a preferential discount rate
of 5.5 percent for special operations. Small industrial and agricultural
Ivorian borrowers now pay 5.5 percent plus a spread of 1 to 3 percentage points for a total of 6.5 to 8.5 percent a year. Large, mostly
foreign, borrowers pay 8 percent plus a maximum spread of 5 percentage points for a total of up to 13 percent a year. In the early 1970s
the interest differential with France was so large that foreign enterprises found it particularly profitable to borrow to the limit in the
Ivory Coast while keeping liquid funds abroad.[13] It is estimated that
over the last five years about 70 percent of the credits extended by the
banking system went to foreign-owned enterprises. This ready supply
of local resources, coupled with a generally large cash flow, made
recourse to foreign borrowing unnecessary for the private sector. The
increase in interest rates indeed may alleviate the anomaly of low interest rates for all members of the UMOA while at the same time maintaining free capital movements between the BCEAO and France. The
increase in the interest rates to the level prevailing abroad should discourage the transfer of funds by enterprises in the Ivory Coast. Previously, excess liquidity could be profitably invested abroad. In addition, commercial banks, which are no longer allowed to maintain
more than working balances in foreign exchange, should place their
excess liquid resources in sight deposits with the central bank. Deposits
with the BCEAO are paid a call-money interest rate of 7 percent and will
be reallocated within the union depending on needs. Thus, the BCEAO
will be able to operate a regional call-money market within the union.
All this may help change the pattern of investments and savings in the
private and public sectors as it has developed for several years, whereby
the public sector compensates for the transfers of private savings and

13. The discount rate in France increased from 7.0 percent to 13.0 percent in 1974,
while the BCEAO's rate remained fixed at 5.5 percent during the same period. Call money
in France fluctuated from 8.68 percent in 1970 to 12.91 percent in 1974.

the lack of borrowing abroad by the private sector. Reduced financing from the local banking system may force the foreign-owned enterprises in the country to borrow from abroad and to retain a larger portion of profits for investment purposes.

Interest rates on deposits were raised as well. Prior to 1973 deposits of less than CFAF200,000 earned no interest at all, regardless of term. Larger deposits earned interest, differentiated according to amount and term, up to a maximum of 4.5 percent in amounts exceeding CFAF5 million if held for more than six months. In January 1973 small deposits began to earn 2.5 percent a year, and the top rate was raised to 6.5 percent. In mid-1975 the minimum rate was increased to 3.25 percent and the maximum rate on large amounts became subject to negotiation. Unfortunately, inflation accelerated while these adjustments were taking place. It rose from an average of 3 to 4 percent a year between 1960 and 1972 to 13 percent in 1973, and to around 20 percent in 1974. With an economy as open as that of the Ivory Coast, future inflation will depend very much on inflation in the rest of the world and developments in world market prices for its main exports. Even so, it seems likely that most savers may be earning negative returns on their financial deposits. Despite this, the higher nominal rates appear to have had considerable impact on depositors. Time deposits in the banking system rose by 55 percent a year in 1973–75, compared with only 19 percent for demand deposits and with rates of 25 percent and 16 percent respectively in the 1962–72 period. It may be that price expectations are still influenced by the stability that prevailed through 1972, but the increased income after substantial producer price increases has probably played a role as well.

The banking system and the recent reform

Banking and credit institutions in the Ivory Coast include four commercial banks, five development banks, two financial institutions operating in a specific area, and two leasing corporations.[14] An American

---

14. *Commercial banks*: Banque Internationale pour le Commerce et l'Industrie en Côte d'Ivoire (BICICI); Société Générale de Banque en Côte d'Ivoire (SGBCI); Société Ivoirienne de Banque (SIB); and Banque Internationale pour l'Afrique Occidentale (BIAO).

Development banks: Banque Ivoirienne de Développement Industriel (BIDI); Crédit de la Côte d'Ivoire (CCI); Banque Nationale pour le Développement Agricole (BNDA); La Compagnie Financière de la Côte d'Ivoire (COFINCI); and La Banque Nationale pour l'Epargne et le Crédit (BNEC).

Special fields and leasing: La Société Africaine de Crédit Automobile (SAFCA); La Société Ivoirienne de Financement (SIF); La Société Africaine de Crédit-Bail (SAFBAIL) and La Taw Industrial Leasing Corporation.

bank opened offices in the Ivory Coast in 1975. In addition, there is a public institution, Caisse Autonome d'Amortissement (CAA), which manages the public debt, holds and manages public deposits, and mobilizes local resources through issuance of tax-free bonds. Another public institution, Société Nationale de Financement (SONAFI), was set up in 1962 to take direct participation in undertakings of national interest; it became involved in the Ivorian small-scale enterprise sector in 1972 when the government established within SONAFI a participation fund to make quasi-equity available to small Ivorian enterprises. The government also established in 1968 a guarantee fund to provide guarantees for credits granted to small Ivorian enterprises. Finally, a stock exchange was established in April 1976. Ivorianization of the banking world is progressing steadily; at the end of 1975 local participation in the equity of commercial and development banks was 54.5 percent, about one-fifth of it in private Ivorian hands.

The present banking system tends to serve the still largely foreign-owned industry well. In many cases foreign firms have been able to rely for most of their long-term capital needs on a mother company abroad. With the high liquidity preference in savings in the Ivory Coast, commercial banks apply the rule of risk diversification in their credit allocation, which means that short-term credit is granted strictly against short-term funds and medium-term credit against medium-term funds. The Ivorian banking system in this way has hardly played its role of intermediation, but this has been no problem for most foreign firms. Lending to local businesses, usually on a small scale, has been relatively costly for the banks in terms of dossier preparation, risks, and defaults that cannot be recovered because of fixed interest rate ceilings. Furthermore the demand of larger-scale firms in general has matched their means. About 70 percent of the short-term and medium-term credit has been granted to foreigners. The new BCEAO regulations are obviously designed to improve the situation for local initiative while harming foreign initiative as little as possible. This seems a difficult objective, but considering the Ivory Coast's circumstances it is the best road to follow.

In agriculture much of the development credit is channeled through the public enterprises charged with the development of the main crops. This seems to work reasonably well. Furthermore, the intermediaries who collect and prepare the crop for export probably provide certain banking services to the local farmer. Such services could include financing his crop and providing him with needed imported goods. The interest rates and prices for these services are unknown. In this way and also in financing informal sector activities, there is probably substantial banking activity of an informal nature that escapes the official circuit and is not included in the statistics. In general the established banks had little reason or incentive to meet the requirements of small-scale entrepreneurs and therefore confined themselves to rather unimaginative and conservative banking, which had little risk and comfortable profits.

It is difficult to evaluate the consequences of the latest monetary reform since it took effect in July 1975, but some comments can be made. The assets of the commercial banks show a pattern of optimal profitability and minimum risk. The reform, however, may compel the banks to modify the structure of their assets. If the pressure to finance the national enterprises is high, the banks may try to specialize by the nature of credit to offset the extra risks they may have to take in financing national enterprises. Thus, the existence of sectoral coefficients can lead to bank specialization and a loss of competition. In addition, with the relatively high cost and risk involved, which is probably not covered by the spread allowed the bank between borrowing and lending rates, banks will be reluctant to lend to national enterprises, at least up to the level required. Thus, they may prefer to deposit their extra funds at the central bank. In this case, credit to the private sector would decrease, whereas more public funds would become available. The transfer of savings would then benefit the government instead of the foreign sector as it did previously. Although the banks' response to the reform is not yet known, a simple computation shows that the cost of being compelled to finance national small-scale enterprises is reportedly 18 percent on the average. If a better appraisal of the projects could bring this rate down to about 10 percent, then the cost of risk would be 10 percent. If, using the rediscounting facility, the bank can make a return of 15 percent on the loan before risk, this leaves only about 5 percent if the risk is taken into account. Such a return can be easily obtained in the money market unless the government decides to lower this rate to below the international rate, which would lead to capital leaving the country.

Obviously, the risk represented by small-scale enterprises is a major obstacle to a successful development of this reform in terms of encouraging local initiative. Maximum effort should be put into assisting the local private entrepreneur during the preparatory stages of his business. A system of extended guarantee, for which existing government-owned guarantee funds can be used, should be set up. Initially a government subsidy may be required, but this would seem quite justified and in many cases preferable to the substantial protection that is frequently given to foreign private enterprises.

Mobilization of savings

In order to devise adequate instruments for the mobilization of savings, a number of characteristics of the Ivorian saver would have to be established more fully. It has been established, however, that the saver has an unusually high preference for liquidity and that the interest he earns seems of secondary importance. Part of the explanation for this probably lies in the fact that the large foreign community has made the decision to transfer some of its earnings regardless of the interest rate in the Ivory Coast. Also, there is little private interest in bonds, which are floated periodically by SONAFI and the CAA, although the interest rate after taxes is 10 percent. It also seems that many Ivorians are active investors. About 70 percent of Abidjan's inhabitants are renters. They are mostly foreigners and many live in Ivorian-owned property. Employers make substantial transfers of their employees' funds to creditors at the end of the month, and these are not just payments for consumer goods. It is also known that many who can afford the down payment enter the trucking business. The BNDA, realizing that most savers want to become active investors, has had reasonable success in proposing an investment plan to its customers. The saver must provide a minimum savings account, which can be built up slowly and unevenly, and as soon as the predetermined minimum is reached, the bank provides the difference between the savings accumulated and the total investment.

Other ways of increasing savings and improving their mobilization are to maintain high producer prices, which the government seems determined to do, and to pay higher interest rates on deposits. The latter again would be a matter for the Monetary Union to decide. Also, diversification of financial instruments in general has the effect of increasing the mobilization of savings. Several foreign banks from outside the franc area have shown interest in establishing branch offices in the Ivory Coast. This will introduce more competition into the banking system, which is a healthy development provided the new banks bring in their expertise in mobilizing local savings and do not concentrate solely on acting as financial agents for the government in such big projects as the iron ore and paper pulp projects in the southwest. An indication of the increased potential for mobilizing savings in the interior is that the number of windows has increased from thirty-five in thirteen locations in 1964 to ninety-five in thirty-seven locations in 1974.

A promising initiative in savings mobilization was the creation in 1975 by the government of the Banque Nationale d'Epargne et de Crédit (BNEC). The main thrust of this national savings and loan bank will be the mobilization of local savings for relending on long-term mortgages. This type of bank is similar to a savings and loan association and provides the customer with a highly liquid savings instrument.

Some of the new saving in the economy is used to Ivorianize capital invested earlier by foreigners. The government is participating increasingly in existing and new enterprises. Its shares are managed by SONAFI and the intent is to disseminate participation among Ivorian nationals by means of the stock exchange, which started operations in 1976. The exchange is a logical development but caution is needed. Sales of shares to Ivorians have been rather successful, rising from CFAF1.3 billion in 1975 before the stock exchange opened, to CFAF2.5 billion in 1976. Careful supervision of the stock market is necessary since, especially in the beginning, it will be a rather narrow one that could easily be manipulated. A failure in this market could impair the confidence of savers for a long time. The government, aware of these dangers, has therefore appointed high quality management for the stock exchange.

CHAPTER FOUR

Fiscal Policy and Public Financing of Development

PUBLIC FINANCING HAS PLAYED A MAJOR ROLE in the Ivory Coast's economic development and has generated substantial investment by the private sector. In many instances, the government has not hesitated to step up its involvement when it found its objectives jeopardized by a reluctant or skeptical private sector.

General Aspects

One of the most powerful of the government's incentives has been investment in supportive facilities and services. In the early 1960s, public investment in infrastructure, basic to any successful development policy, already amounted to 40 percent of total investment. With total investment going from 15 percent of GDP in the early 1960s to 21 percent in the first half of the 1970s—a rise deemed necessary by the government to meet its ambitious growth objectives and to put its impressive economic potential to work—the public investment share grew to 60 percent of total investment in the early 1970s. This does not mean that the private sector was inactive; private investment rose by 8.1 percent a year in real terms between 1960 and 1974, but over the same period public investment increased by an average of about 12.5 percent per year.

This phenomenon put an extra burden on public sector financing, and it is on this aspect that the present chapter concentrates. Table 4.1, which identifies the main issues, compares investment and its financing for three four-year periods. Average total investment a year in current prices amounted to CFAF24.5 billion in 1960–63, CFAF49.5 billion in 1965–68, and CFAF119.9 billion in 1971–74, representing an increase of about 11 percent a year in real terms between 1960 and 1974. The following will be noted:

- Gross domestic savings (GDS) have consistently exceeded gross domestic investment.
- The line giving factor services and other transfers abroad indicates that the foreign community claimed a substantial price for its efforts and transferred part of its remuneration for labor and capital abroad.
- Gross national savings (GNS) have always had to be complemented by substantial capital inflows from abroad because GNS has only covered about 80 percent of investment on the average.

The columns representing the public and private sectors show clearly their changing roles: the proportion of public to private investment reversed over the years from 40–60 to 60–40. The proportion of total investment financed by net transfers decreased from 35 percent in 1960–63 to 25 percent in 1971–74. In the latter years the public sector made no contribution because its interest payments offset an inflow of public transfers by the French government. Capital inflow for the private sector exceeded capital inflow for the public sector in the beginning, but later the deficit was almost entirely financed by inflows on the account of the public sector. The private sector's net inflow was reduced to almost zero, not so much as a result of lower inflows but rather as a result of growing outflows.

Foreign capital grants to the public sector increased roughly from a level of CFAF3 billion to CFAF4 billion a year between 1960 and 1974. Therefore, the bulk of foreign capital in the public sector is loan capital with fixed debt service obligations that have to be met irrespective of the success of the investment. The annual gross inflow of public loan capital increased from CFAF8.5 billion in 1963–66 to about CFAF40 billion in 1971–74, and the terms on which the public sector has been able to obtain this capital have hardened considerably in the recent past. In itself, this is not alarming as long as the investments pay off and are able to service the debt. Problems arise, however, from the coincidence of a substitution of loans for grants, the increase of foreign borrowing on commercial terms, an increase in the share of public investment in total investment, and a rising capital-output ratio. A further disproportionate increase in debt service payments would

TABLE 4.1 PUBLIC AND PRIVATE INVESTMENT AND ITS FINANCING AS A PERCENTAGE OF TOTAL INVESTMENT

Item	1960-63			1965-68			1971-74		
	Public	Private	Total	Public	Private	Total	Public	Private	Total
Gross investment[a]	42	58	100	50	50	100	60	40	100
Gross domestic savings	30	80	110	40	75	115	40	65	105
Factor services and other transfers abroad	-3	38	35	2	30	32	0	25	25
Gross national savings	33	42	75	38	45	83	40	40	80
Net capital imports	9	16	25	12	5	17	19	1	20
Average annual investment[a] (current CFAF billion)	10.9	13.6	24.5	24.7	24.7	49.4	72.0	47.9	119.9

Source: Statistical Appendix Table 5.
a. Including changes in stocks.

drive up the transfers abroad and thus lower national savings and increase the need for foreign capital. Moreover, a declining efficiency of investment would slow income growth and therefore slow gross domestic savings even more in comparison to investment. A crucial variable in this picture is the public sector's ability to generate revenue and save in order to finance its investments.

Features and organization of public sector finance

There are three dominant features in public sector finance. First, the overall tax rate is comparatively high, and with average revenue at 25.4 percent[1] of gross domestic product (GDP) in 1970–75, fiscal performance is remarkable. Second, in spite of this, net public savings as a percentage of public investment have declined continuously—from 60 percent in 1960–65 to 37 percent in 1975. And, third, public investment outside of the government proper (BSIE)—that is, by public enterprises and extra budgetary programs—as a proportion of total public investment increased from 30 to some 60 percent between 1965 and 1975, amounting to some CFAF80 billion in the latter year, while government control over these enterprises was inadequate until recent reforms were adopted. The well-prepared investment budget of the government proper, therefore, covers less and less the overall public financial situation, the soundness of which becomes difficult to assess.

Although politically and geographically the government is centralized, public sector finance is both decentralized and rather complex. An important part of the government's economic and financial policy is exercised through the following administrative machinery: (a) an ordinary budget and an investment budget (Budget Spécial d'Investissement et d'Equipement, BSIE); (b) some 60 public and semi-public organizations, among which are the Debt Amortization Fund (Caisse Autonome d'Amortissement, CAA), the Producer Price Stabilization Fund (CSSPPA), and the Price Equalization Fund; and (c) eight municipalities having financial autonomy. An assessment of the contributions of these components to development finance is given below along with a brief background of each.

The central government operates an ordinary budget and an investment budget that are financed through well-determined fiscal and non-fiscal revenue sources. The investment budget (BSIE) has two parts,

---

1. Includes Social Security Fund and Price Stabilization Fund (see Statistical Appendix Table 30).

which are distinguished by the source of financing. The so-called BSIE-Trésor relies on domestic financing (earmarked fiscal revenue, transfers from the Stabilization Fund and some other public enterprises, and local borrowing through bonds issued by the CAA), whereas the so-called BSIE-CAA is entirely financed through foreign borrowing.

Public and semipublic enterprises have proliferated rapidly as a consequence of greater direct public sector participation in the country's development. The government operates twenty-six state enterprises, contributes through budgetary transfers to the operation of twelve public institutions, and holds a majority participation in nineteen mixed companies.[2] Unfortunately, data on these undertakings are inadequate. The government recently embarked on a reorganization of this sector, but because of its political sensitivity, this is proceeding at a rather slow pace. Reorganization of this sector is strongly endorsed. Data are available on two major public institutions: the Debt Amortization Fund and the Stabilization Fund. The data on these two organizations, on the budgetary transactions of the government proper, and on the other public enterprises for which estimates are rough, have been consolidated as the public sector.

The Stabilization Fund, under the Ministry of Agriculture, stabilizes prices paid to producers of agricultural export products. Cocoa, coffee, cotton, and vegetable oils are the most important. Profits are made when the difference between the export prices and export costs is positive. The profits are used to make up for deficit years, to increase the fund's reserves, and to participate in the financing of the government's diversification policy. During the last decade, the Stabilization Fund has also transferred considerable excess profits to the BSIE and to the Treasury. The Price Equalization Fund stabilizes the prices of such basic consumer products as sugar, rice, and gasoline.

Earmarked taxes are used to finance parts of the investment budget as well as activities that are carried on independently of the budgets. Earmarked taxes incorporated in the investment budget benefit the National Park Services and the State Reforestation Agency (SODEFOR). Four quasi-public organizations that benefit from earmarked taxes are the Office of Support to Low-Income Housing (OSHE), the National Office for Professional Training (ONFP), the National Council of Ship-

2. A 1976 study by the Ministry of Finance reportedly shows the following numbers: state enterprises, 75; majority participation, 45; indirect participation by the state in other enterprises, 80. Thus, the state participates directly or indirectly in 200 of an estimated 2,000 enterprises.

pers (CIC), and the National Council for Export Promotion (CICE). Parafiscal revenue is also allocated to the National Investment Fund (FNI), to be returned to the taxpayers who invested matching funds locally.[3]

The Debt Amortization Fund, under the Ministry of Finance, manages the foreign borrowing of the central government and, through earmarked fiscal revenue, services the public debt. Through the fund, the government also guarantees the foreign borrowing of public enterprises, while it also functions as a development bank by receiving deposits of public institutions that are used to finance investments of public enterprises and municipalities.

Declining net public savings

Table 4.2 shows the decline of the public sector's ability to finance the public investment program. In the 1970s a steady increase in public investment as a proportion of total investment coincided with a continuous decrease, to about 35 percent in 1974 and 1975, in the proportion of public investment financed by public savings. This is a low

TABLE 4.2 PUBLIC INVESTMENT AND ITS FINANCING
AS A PERCENTAGE OF GDP

Item	1960–65	1965–67	1970–71	1973–74	1975
Public investment	6.9	8.9	11.6	13.0	15.2
Private investment	8.9	8.5	9.7	6.9	8.8
Total investment	15.8	17.4	21.3	19.9	24.0
Current budget surplus[a]	5.1	4.4	4.8	4.7	4.2
Stabilization Fund contribution	0.9	0.6	2.6	0.0	1.8
Other public enterprise savings		2.1	1.8	3.3	3.6
Gross financing capacity of public sector	6.0	7.1	9.2	8.0	9.6
Public debt service payment (interest and repayments)	−1.8	−2.1	−2.6	−3.4	−4.0
Net financing capacity of public sector	4.2	5.0	5.5	4.6	5.6
Proportion of public investment financed by public sector	61	56	57	35	37

Source: Statistical Appendix Table 27.
a. Before debt service.

3. Entrepreneurs are required to invest 10 percent of annual profits in FNI certificates.

proportion. If it is assumed that, for a number of reasons, 15 percent of public investment does not lend itself to foreign financing, on the average 75 percent of each remaining project would have to be financed from abroad, which is a high percentage and in most cases much higher than the foreign currency component of projects. In 1974 and 1975 these percentages applied to the Ivory Coast and led to gross public capital inflows of CFAF60 to CFAF70 billion a year. In recent years less than 50 percent of these capital requirements has been obtained on concessionary terms, hence debt service payments are increasing rapidly. Moreover, investment has been growing more rapidly than income, and the proportion of public investment in total investment is increasing as well. Under these conditions, it becomes crucial to analyze the underlying reasons for the deterioration of public savings performance.

The Central Government

Central government transactions pass through either the Treasury or the Debt Amortization Fund, the latter pertaining specifically to the

TABLE 4.3 PUBLIC SECTOR REVENUE
AND ITS ALLOCATION
(CFAF billion)

Revenue	1965–67	1970–71	1973–74	1975
Ordinary budget	38.4	63.1	98.7	126.9
Investment budget	7.6	13.6	17.5	17.1
Debt Amortization Fund	4.4	9.5	13.4	16.6
Earmarked taxes	0.0	2.1	3.4	6.9
Central government	50.4	88.3	133.0	167.5
National Investment Fund	1.7	2.1	3.6	4.0
Stabilization Fund	0.3	13.3	24.0	18.1
Social Security	2.6	4.2	6.9	9.4
Price Equalization Fund	n.a.	n.a.	1.1	2.6
Municipalities	n.a.	2.2	3.1	3.5
Total public revenue	n.a.	n.a.	171.7	205.1
Central government revenue (percent of GDP)	19.7	20.7	20.5	20.3
Total public revenue (percent of GDP)	n.a.	n.a.	26.1	24.8

n.a. Not available.
Note: The revenue of most public enterprises is excluded.
Source: Statistical Appendix Table 29.

public debt of the central government. The accounts of the Treasury not only permit budgetary control, but also enable financial management of public and nonpublic funds. According to these accounts for the 1965–74 period, the growth rate of current public expenditure above that of current public revenue (15 percent growth a year for expenditure, as against 13 percent for revenue), indicates that the relatively rapid growth of current expenditure was partly responsible for lower current budgetary savings.

Current revenue

Table 4.3 enables calculation of two tax pressure indexes. The current revenue of the central government, which amounted to 19.7 percent of GDP in the 1965–67 period, represented 20.5 percent of GDP in the 1973–74 period. If all quasi-tax revenue is considered, this share rises to 26.1 percent for the 1973–74 period. Although international comparisons of such indexes should be carefully interpreted since they attempt to compare observations that differ in many respects, it is interesting nevertheless that the Ivory Coast was found to have the seventh highest ratio of taxes to GDP in a sample of forty-seven countries.[4] It is concluded that the tax revenue performance has been very good.

During the past decade income tax proceeds have grown considerably faster than overall revenue; all other taxes have grown more slowly (see Table 4.4). Wealth taxes, already very low, dropped further to a 1.6 percent share, while commodity taxes continued to account for about three-quarters of total revenue.

To enable a better understanding of the factors responsible for the development of tax revenue, the buoyancy and the elasticity of the present tax system as a whole and of its components have been calculated (see Table 4.5). Buoyancy registers the relation between the change in tax revenue and aggregate income. Elasticity measures the relation between the change in tax revenue, corrected for discretionary changes that took place in the tax system, and aggregate income. The taxes for which these calculations have been made comprised 97 percent of total tax revenue in 1973, and thus provide a rather comprehensive picture of the overall buoyancy of the fiscal revenue system of

4. Its tax revenue for the 1969–71 period was 43 percent higher than the sample average. (Raja Chelliah, Hessel Baas, and Margaret R. Kelly, "Tax Ratios and Tax Efforts in Developing Countries, 1967–71," Ivorian Ministry of Finance *Staff Papers*, vol. 22 [March 1975], pp. 187–205). The tax revenue for the Ivory Coast used in this paper refers to the central government revenue.

TABLE 4.4. CENTRAL GOVERNMENT REVENUE
AS A PERCENTAGE OF TOTAL
CURRENT REVENUE

Source	1965–66	1969–70	1974–75
Income taxes	11.6	15.3	19.9
Wealth taxes	2.5	1.6	1.6
Commodity taxes			
Taxes on production			
and consumption[a]	34.6	21.6	22.1
Import taxes[a]	23.9	37.6	36.1
Export taxes	20.4	18.7	17.4
Subtotal	78.9	77.9	75.6
Other	7.0	5.2	2.9
Total government revenue	100.0	100.0	100.0

Source: Statistical Appendix Table 30.
a. Since 1968 the value-added tax on imports has been classified under import taxes; prior to that it was included in taxes on production and consumption.

the central government over eight years. The table gives the buoyancy of tax-to-income; the buoyancy of tax-to-base, indicating how tax revenue reacts to an expansion of its tax base; and the buoyancy of base-to-income, indicating how the tax base reacts to an increase in income. The buoyancy estimate for the overall tax system is 1.11. It is 1.19 if export taxes are excluded. This means that fiscal revenue has grown faster than GDP. Taxes on domestic alcoholic beverages and on fuel and the general income tax are buoyant. In the case of the tax on domestic alcoholic beverages, this is mainly due to an increase in the tax base with an increase in income, while for fuel and the general income tax the buoyancy is primarily due to the increase in the tax base itself. The coefficients in the third column (buoyancy of base-to-income) show that the tax bases have been rather responsive to the growth of income. The second column (buoyancy of tax-to-base) indicates to what extent fiscal authorities have made use of the available tax bases. A coefficient exceeding one means that the fiscal burden has gone up over the period investigated.

An increase in the fiscal burden may be due to an elasticity greater than one or an upward adjustment of the tax rates or both. The coefficients in Table 4.5 do not enable separation of these two factors. Therefore a coefficient of built-in elasticity of the tax system was estimated that permits isolation of the revenue resulting from the discretionary changes that were introduced in the 1965–73 period. The

TABLE 4.5. BUILT-IN ELASTICITY AND BUOYANCY VALUES FOR
TOTAL TAX REVENUE AND MAJOR COMPONENTS,
1965–73

Tax components	Buoyancy of tax-to-income	Buoyancy of tax-to-base	Buoyancy of base-to-income	Built-in elasticity
Taxes on wages and salaries	1.40	1.15	1.22	1.05
Taxes on business profits	1.52	1.37	1.12	1.46
General income tax	1.81	1.96	0.92	—
Value-added tax	1.42	1.26	1.11[a]	0.94
Tax on domestic tobacco	0.94	0.73	1.26	—
Tax on domestic alcoholic beverages	1.88	1.05	1.74	—
Fuel tax	1.73	1.60	1.06	0.77
Timber tax	1.51	0.86	1.30	—
Import duties and taxes	0.95	0.84	1.10	0.87
Stamp duties and registration fees	1.10	1.10	1.00	0.96
Business licenses	0.38[a]	0.39[a]	1.00	—
Export duties	0.86	0.76	1.08	—
Total tax revenue	1.11	—	—	—
exclusive of export taxes	1.19	—	—	1.03

— Not applicable.
Source: Calculations based on data provided by the Ministry of Finance.
a. The t-values of these coefficients are not significant at the 5 percent level of confidence.

results are given in Table 4.5 for the taxes for which discretionary changes took place. In every case, the elasticity estimates are lower than the buoyancy estimates. This is to be expected because all the discretionary tax changes during the period have been revenue-raising changes. The shares of tax increases that resulted from discretionary changes introduced in the 1965–73 period have also been calculated. For taxes on wages and services this was 11.4 percent; for the business profit tax, 1.6 percent; for the value-added tax, 5.9 percent; for the fuel tax, 35.4 percent; and for import duties and taxes, 5.0 percent. The built-in elasticity of 1.03 for total taxes indicates that the tax revenue over the past decade would have increased at about the same rate as GDP if no discretionary changes had been made.

As indicated earlier, tax revenue performance has been very satisfactory. Some further increase in the tax burden, gradually introduced, is still feasible, but possible adverse effects on further economic de-

TABLE 4.6. CURRENT BUDGET EXPENDITURE
BY FUNCTIONAL CLASSIFICATION
(Percent)

Item	1965	1970	1975
General services	37.1	26.4	19.7
Defense	8.1	7.3	7.3
Social services	28.4	30.2	33.4
Education	18.0	19.7	23.4
Health	9.6	9.3	8.1
Economic services	21.2	20.9	17.9
Agriculture	4.6	4.8	3.3
Public works	13.0	9.5	6.1
Other	13.6	14.3	20.9
Current expenditure/current revenue	73	80	83
Current expenditure/GDP	14.6	16.1	16.6
Total (CFAF billion)[a]	34.5	66.6	136.7

Source: Statistical Appendix Tables 33 and 34.
a. Including Debt Amortization Fund interest payments and annex budget.

velopment should be given due attention. For instance, import tariff levels have recently been raised in the Ivory Coast by aligning duties on imports from the EC countries with the "most favored nation" tariff.[5] Notwithstanding the revenue aspect of this tariff increase, it is advisable for the government to take measures to eliminate the effect of increasing protection. Improvements in budgetary savings performance will have to come mainly from the expenditure side.

Current expenditure

Current expenditure has grown more rapidly than GDP and current revenue (see Table 4.6). During 1965–75, current expenditure as a proportion of GDP increased from 14.6 to 16.6 percent, and as a proportion of current revenue went up from 73 to 83 percent. As the functional classification of current expenditure in Table 4.6 shows, after the administrative infrastructure was established, the outlays for general services declined considerably, while the expenditures for defense remained moderate. Of the social services, education increased greatly, reflecting the priority given by the government to this sub-

5. The European Community (EC) comprises the European Economic Community (EEC), the European Coal and Steel Community (ECSC), and the European Atomic Energy Community (EURATOM).

TABLE 4.7. CURRENT BUDGET
EXPENDITURE BY ECONOMIC
CLASSIFICATION
(Percent)

Item	1966	1970	1975
Wages and salaries	43.5	47.2	50.9
Materials and maintenance	35.5	31.1	28.1
Subsidies and transfers	. . .	19.3	20.0
Contracted debt payments	21.0	0.8	1.0
Other	. . .	1.6	. . .
Total	100.0	100.0	100.0

. . . Zero or negligible.
Source: Statistical Appendix Table 35.

sector. In economic services, expenditures for both agriculture and public works decreased relatively. The data given are not consolidated, however. For instance, the increase in current expenditure by the Stabilization Fund on agriculture, and the numerous public enterprises created in the agricultural sector in the 1960s, is not included. The category "other" includes the increased Ivorian contribution to the salaries of foreign technical assistants, interest on foreign debt, and payments due on buildings rented by the government.

The economic classification of current expenditure indicates that from 1966 to 1975 expenditure on wages and salaries increased 7 percentage points to 50 percent of total budget expenditure, while expenditures on material and maintenance dropped seven points (Table 4.7). To demonstrate the problems inherent in curtailing current expenditure, the next sections will focus on three categories: wages and salaries, education, and housing.

Expenditures on wages and salaries

The share of wages and salaries in total government expenditure rose from 43.5 percent in 1966 to 50.9 percent in 1975.[6] This has resulted from the increase in the number of government employees, promotions of the existing staff, general salary increases, and the increase in the Ivorian contribution to foreign technical assistance. The number of employees paid by the ordinary budget rose annually by approximately

6. Correcting for the increase in the Ivorian contribution to the cost of technical assistance from CFAF3 billion in 1970 to some CFAF8 billion in 1975, gives an increase of 4 to 5 percentage points. About 75 percent of foreign technical assistance personnel are engaged in education.

8 percent during the 1965–75 period; the annual cost of in-service upgrading and promotions is estimated at about 3.4 percent. As total wage and salary costs increased annually by 16.1 percent, the average general wage increase has been 4.2 percent a year. With an average price increase of some 6 percent a year, the average real employment cost to the government decreased by close to 2 percent a year. Recent salary increases have been differentiated, and range from 7 percent for higher-paid workers to 25 percent for the lowest paid. For the former this means a substantial decrease in real wages. This policy seems to reflect the government's concern about income inequalities and also its awareness that wages are comparatively high and that this has a negative effect on the country's competitive position.

With the number of those leaving school increasing, the government will be under pressure to devote a larger share of its ordinary expenditures to wage and salary payments. These pressures result partly from its role as "employer of last resort." Although signs of this phenomenon are apparent, it has not yet assumed the proportions it has in several other developing countries because the emphasis on growth has created many opportunities elsewhere in the economy. With the increased numbers being turned out by the education system, however, a long-term easing of the situation can only come through more relevant education in combination with continued growth and manpower planning. (See Appendix D on "Education.")

Current public expenditure on education and training

Since independence in 1960, the educational system in the Ivory Coast has experienced rapid expansion. Starting from a very low base at independence, when only 33 percent of the primary school age group was enrolled, the country now has about 55 percent of this group enrolled, and there are prospects of achieving universal primary education by 1985. During the same period of time, enrollment in secondary schools grew from about 15,000 to nearly 90,000, and enrollment in the university, which was established in 1959, was about 6,000 in the academic year 1975–76. This rapid numerical growth in the system of formal education is a very real accomplishment.

Taking into account the cost of technical assistance in education and of educational programs run by noneducational ministries, total budgetary costs rose from 23 percent to 33 percent of total ordinary budget expenditures between 1965 and 1975. An examination of comparable World Bank data from sixty-nine countries reveals that the Ivory Coast spends a larger proportion of its budget on education (32.6 percent in 1973) than any other country in the world; 3 percent was the lowest and the median was 18.2 percent. The high share of education in the budget is associated with the very high rate of growth in enrollment over a long period and the high cost per student that is perhaps twice as high as for most other African countries. This high student cost is, in turn, attributable to the heavy reliance on expatriate teachers, the provision of comfortable scholarships for students in secondary schools and universities, the high cost of teaching materials, the additional cost of introducing educational television in primary schools, and the fact that education is free.

The World Bank has calculated the implications of Ivorian planning for the recurrent cost of education and training until 1980. This calculation shows an increase in constant prices of 11.5 percent a year. Thus, the share of education and training in the budget could probably rise even further over the remainder of the 1970s. Reducing the share of education and training in the budget will depend on: (a) reductions in the rate of growth in enrollment; (b) the use of less costly educational technologies; (c) the introduction of a curriculum scaled to the country's needs; and (d) a more intensified use of the available resources—for example, more intensive use of educational television for other than primary education.

Even a vigorous implementation of these recommendations might not have immediate cost-reducing effects. It is therefore advocated that part of the social cost of university education and perhaps part of the cost of secondary education be passed on to the students; a system of loans to students could be developed. The pressures for expansion of education and its escalating costs to the government are largely attributable to the fact that private costs are near zero (or even negative) for individuals, while private benefits are substantial. Passing on part or all of the social costs of education to students and their families is theoretically the correct policy to follow. The distributional effects of the tax system are discussed in Chapter 6. Such a policy would accomplish two desirable objectives: It would raise revenue for education and would reduce the excess demand for education. The implementation of such a policy in a country that has traditionally provided free education will certainly be unpopular. Nevertheless, the government should consider that the alternative is a continuing rapid increase in the cost of, and demand for, secondary and higher education and the growing dissatisfaction of graduates provided with job opportunities that fall short of expectations.

Current public expenditure on low-cost housing

High standards are a common feature of urban services provided by the government and public housing is no exception. A logical consequence of adopting such standards has been the need for public subsidies to reduce private costs. These subsidies have been financed through various public institutions and in some cases have reached 30 percent of the rent. It is felt, however, that in many instances occupants are capable of contributing more. The financial situation of the public housing sector has reached the point where a costly salvage operation by the government is necessary. The government's objective was to build a large number of houses of high standard to be given to occupants at subsidized rents. The government underestimated the cost of this program and therefore failed to provide the public agencies with the necessary financial means; in trying to meet ambitious construction targets the public agencies had to turn increasingly to expensive suppliers' credits and the Eurodollar market. By the beginning of 1975 two public companies had built about 45,000 units and one of the companies (SOGEFIHA) had accumulated debts totalling CFAF36.8 billion by mid-1975, much of it on hard terms.[7]

Reorganization of the housing sector and reconsideration of policies in this sector have been given high priority. It is recommended that more appropriate standards be applied to housing, that the number of units built a year be cut, that existing urban areas be densified and upgraded rather than expanding into new areas, that attention be shifted to those really in need, and that in general the private sector should shoulder a great share of the cost, however difficult this may be politically.

The examples given above—salaries and wages, education, and housing—demonstrate that there are ways to lower expenditures. None of them is easy, however, and the pressure on government current expenditure will continue to be great. With the recent tendency to

---

7. A rehabilitation plan has been approved by the Ministry of Finance. Its main features are: (a) immediate increases in payments on the government's installment-purchase units and in rents on private rental units, with further increases in the future; (b) billing of construction supervision costs to projects under construction and of maintenance costs to tenants; (c) selling rather than renting existing and future commercial and higher-priced residential properties. These resources should not only improve SOGEFIHA's cash flow but also lead to more economic pricing of its units, reflecting construction and financing costs. Similar measures will be imposed on SOGEFIHA's future programs.

spend more on social investment, an additional impetus is given to increasing expenditure and to slowing down revenues. Fairly drastic policy decisions and strict budgetary discipline by the central government will be needed to generate future savings.

Public Enterprises

The proliferation of public enterprises, and the government's difficulties in getting sufficient control over them, have already been mentioned. The government's policy with these enterprises reflects its desire to further the economic development of the country, especially in those sectors where the private sector is thought to be insufficiently active; to create employment for Ivorian workers and management; and to orient Ivorian savings (by forced savings, if need be) toward productive investments. In 1974 the share of the Ivorian government in the equity of these enterprises amounted to more than CFAF20 billion. Direct investment contributions by the government amounted to CFAF5.2 billion in 1974, and were expected to rise to CFAF7.3 billion in 1975.

Classification of public enterprises

The public enterprises fall into four major categories: (a) quasi-administration, such as those in charge of regional development, for example l'Autorité pour l'Aménagement de la Vallée du Bandama (AVB), or those giving technical assistance to farmers such as the Société d'Assistance Technique pour la Modernisation Agricole de la Côte d'Ivoire (SATMACI); (b) research centers such as the Bureaux Nationaux d'Etudes Techniques et de Développement (BNETD); (c) financial institutions such as the Crédit de la Côte d'Ivoire (CCI); and (d) enterprises that are engaged in management or production such as the Société de Gestion Financière de l'Habitat (SOGEFIHA). The first and second groups of enterprises are in fact agencies that, for one reason or another, have been detached from the central administration and depend almost exclusively on budgetary transfers for their revenue. Their function is not to make a profit but to attain certain social and economic objectives, and their performance should be evaluated according to the same criteria used to analyze the public expenditures of the government. In contrast, the performance of financial institutions and public enterprises engaged in production and management can in principle be

TABLE 4.8. ANNUAL AVERAGE PUBLIC ENTERPRISE
INVESTMENT AND ITS FINANCING
(CFAF billion)

Item	1965–67	1974–75
Investment	7.3	44.2
Portion financed from internal resources	5.6	27.0
Deficit	−1.7	−17.2
Gross foreign borrowing	3.0	28.7
Debt service	−1.3	−11.5
Net foreign borrowing	1.7	17.2

Source: Statistical Appendix Table 26.

analyzed using criteria similar to those applied to the private sector, although these enterprises are often required to implement social objectives that act as constraints on profit (such as construction of low-cost housing at subsidized rent).

Investment and financing

In 1965 investment in public enterprises amounted to less than half that of the investment budget of the government proper (BSIE), but exceeded it in 1974 (CFAF44.6 billion compared with CFAF37.7 billion for the BSIE). The dynamic growth of this investment (25 percent a year between 1965–67 and 1974) was made possible by extensive foreign borrowing and the substantial internal resources of these enterprises. While internal resources financed a decreasing proportion of investment in public enterprises, gross foreign borrowing went up from 41 percent to 65 percent of public enterprise investment between 1965–67 and 1974–75 (see Table 4.8). The total outstanding debt of public enterprises[8] (including undisbursed debt) has risen at a rapid pace during the last few years, from CFAF42 billion in 1971 to CFAF164 billion in 1975, and commitments continue to grow.

Organization

Public enterprises are institutions with a certain financial autonomy. The economic, technical, and financial aspects of their operations are supervised by the government, as represented by a technical ministry and the Ministry of Finance and Economic Affairs. In several cases,

8. This includes debts contracted by mixed enterprises and guaranteed by the government. See Statistical Appendix Table 23.

however, this control is not effective. In addition, the objective of these enterprises is not necessarily to be competitive or to maximize profit, which does not always create the most efficient economic environment. As a result, the performance of many public enterprises is mediocre. In some cases there is no coordination with other government agencies, a situation which reflects the powerful position of the managers of these enterprises. Because of a lack of information, investments of the public enterprises, and especially their financing, are sometimes only partially inserted into overall development plans. In general, the reporting on past and future investment is inadequate. Foreign borrowing by these enterprises, which in theory must be cleared by the Caisse Autonome d'Amortissement, has in fact often been disclosed in an end-of-the year report.

This sector should be closely followed by Ivorian policymakers in view of the sheer size of the public enterprises, their importance in implementing national economic goals, and the level of and increase in their foreign debt. Closer scrutiny would not only provide the Ivorian authorities with the information needed for planning, but would also permit the government to coordinate the activities of this sector with others and to insure that company objectives coincide with national economic goals. Too many public enterprises currently escape such supervision and coordination. In addition, the government has allowed certain public enterprises (most notably in the housing sector) to expand their activities even though sound financial policy would have argued against such an investment policy. The government realizes that this uncoordinated policy in the public enterprise sector should not continue and has initiated actions which, although politically sensitive, could remedy the situation.

Improvements under way

Two developments are now under way to improve the situation with regard to the public enterprises. First, all public and private enterprises are required to keep their business accounts according to a detailed and uniform accounting system and to report regularly and systematically to the Ministries of Finance and Planning. This system was instituted in 1973, and about half of the enterprises have submitted detailed business accounts, which were published for the first time in early 1975.[9] Second, the central government in 1975 issued several decrees that would permit better coordination and stricter control over

9. Ministère de l'Economie et des Finances, Direction de la Comptabilité Publique et du Trésor, *Centrale de Bilans, Banque de Données Financières.*

the activities of public and mixed enterprises. In essence, it was decreed that the enterprises in which the state has a majority participation would be supervised by an interministerial committee composed of the Ministers of Finance and Planning and the ministers from the relevant technical ministries. The committee will define government policy with regard to public and mixed enterprises. To reinforce government financial control and to harmonize the development policies of these enterprises with the national development plan, it was decided to create several sectoral committees. These committees are intended to be the operational link between the boards of directors of the enterprises and the newly established interministerial committee. The members of these sectoral committees, who represent the above ministries, are also members of the board of directors of the public and mixed enterprises of their sector. They form a small committee to carry out day-to-day surveillance of the business decisions taken in their enterprises, and they report periodically to the interministerial committee on the implementation of the programs established. They must also give their approval on all foreign borrowing by the enterprises. Although much improvement is needed, controls and the pooling of profits in a special account in the treasury should not be allowed to impair the ability of public enterprises to build up their own reserves for the replacement and expansion of capital assets. Depending on the type of activity of the public enterprise, its management should be left an important yardstick for financial policies, that is, the measure of whether or not the cost-price structure allows a reasonable degree of self-financing of investments.

The amounts of capital involved are large, and if financial information on these enterprises does not improve, any forecast of public sector savings will be highly uncertain. It must be stressed, however, that these initiatives can bear fruit only if the government itself implements its chosen policy in a coordinated manner. Insufficient control has been due not so much to a lack of regulations as to a failure to implement them. The government has initiated a program for independent auditing of public enterprises that could lead to considerable improvements in this area.

The Stabilization Fund

The Stabilization Fund obtains its resources from the net price difference between export cost and export price in economically favorable periods and from earnings on its investments. A minimum purchase price guaranteed to all producers is set each year by presidential decrees on the recommendation of the Ministry of Agriculture. Among the elements that influence this decision are the following: the international market situation; the reserve position of the Stabilization Fund; the government's revenue requirements; the income distribution policy of the government; and the relative incentives that the government intends to give to the producers of various crops. Legal codes regulate all intermediary activities such as collection, bagging, and transport, for which the Stabilization Fund sets margins.

Revenue of the Stabilization Fund

The proceeds from selling coffee and cocoa in the world market are divided among the farmers, those involved between farm and port (such as processors, traders, and transporters), the central government (in the form of taxes), and the Stabilization Fund. The various shares are shown in Table 4.9.

Cocoa and coffee farmers have received an average of about 50 percent of the f.o.b. price. This assures them a higher income for a working day than that of any other crop grower. As mentioned in Chapter

TABLE 4.9. DISTRIBUTION OF THE EXPORT EARNINGS
FROM COCOA AND COFFEE
(Percent)

	1965–66		1974–75		Average 1965–66 to 1974–75	
Recipient	Cocoa	Coffee	Cocoa	Coffee	Cocoa	Coffee
Farmers	80	50	53	65	50	54
Traders, trans- porters	36	17	10	15	12	15
Government (export tax)	33	15	13	19	22	16
Stabiliza- tion Fund	−49	18	24	1	16	15
F.o.b. price	100	100	100	100	100	100
Public sector[a]	−16	33	37	20	38	31

Note: Years are crop years.
Source: Statistical Appendix Table 37.
a. Government export tax plus Stabilization Fund.

3, producer prices over the last ten years have been adjusted only upwards. Tax income is stabilized because export taxes are levied on posted prices, which are below export prices and have stayed the same for years. The tax rate of 22.5 percent of the posted price, which is the same for coffee and cocoa and which had not changed since 1960–61, was increased to 23 percent in 1972–73 for coffee and in 1974–75 for cocoa. Price fluctuations mainly affect the financial situation of the Stabilization Fund. Out of twelve seasons between 1963–64 and 1974–75, the fund had to pay out of its reserves three times, and in total earned CFAF130.6 billion, or an average of CFAF10.9 billion a year.[10] CFAF64 billion, or about 50 percent, was earned in 1973–74 and 1974–75. The earnings of the fund were high in these years because: (a) world prices for cocoa and coffee were high and producer prices were adjusted with a lag; (b) adjustment of taxation lagged even more, especially for cocoa; and (c) in crop year 1973–74 some 50,000 tons of coffee, which had been held in stock by the fund and for which producer prices and other costs had been paid earlier, were exported out of stock and most of the export proceeds accrued directly to the fund. Except for 1973–74 and 1974–75, the average earnings of the fund since 1963–64 have been CFAF6.3 billion a year.

Uses of revenue

The revenues noted above had been used to pay administrative costs of the fund of about CFAF1.5 billion a year. The Ivory Coast also contributed CFAF1.5 billion a year to the international organizations managing the various commodity agreements. In addition, there are expenditures for subsidizing experiments in diversification of the agricultural sector and of the processing industries. These expenditures have increased greatly in recent years and amounted to about CFAF7 billion in 1974–75. The allocation of these expenditures is decided in many cases by the president. This is another instance in which proliferation of funds makes it difficult to practice consistent financial and economic policies. It would be preferable to channel such funds by way of the budget and to subject the projects they finance to standard

10. Statistical Appendix Table 38 (Financial Results of the Stabilization Fund). The fiscal year of the Stabilization Fund follows the crop year (October to September). The government's fiscal year follows the calendar year. There are plans to let the government's fiscal year coincide with the crop year.

budgetary procedures. Following such procedures, about CFAF36 billion in earnings was transferred to the BSIE over the past twelve years, with a high of CFAF13.5 billion in 1969–70; in five years during this twelve-year period no contribution could be made. Also, the reserve position of the Stabilization Fund has been strengthened. These reserves stood at CFAF10 billion in 1964–65 and were increased to CFAF14.3 billion in 1974–75. None of the high net profits of 1973–74 and 1974–75, however, was used to increase the reserves.

The recent rapid increase in earnings in the Stabilization Fund is partly responsible for the fast growth of the public investment program. When the government found itself with this extra income in 1974, it decided to make a serious start on investment in the north, a region which until then had received relatively little in public funds. Programs for over CFAF20 billion were quickly developed and disbursements are expected to take place rapidly. These recent investment decisions will have longer-term consequences. A considerable part of the investment in the north is for social rather than directly productive purposes. For instance, schools being built with this money will require teachers and thus will have recurrent expenditures. Therefore, expenditures will catch up with revenue.

Since a frost damaged part of Brazil's coffee producing capacity in July 1975, world coffee prices have increased considerably and forecasts indicate that they may not come down to a normal level until the end of the 1970s. Also, world cocoa prices have been revised upward for the 1977–78 period. For the Ivory Coast, with an annual production of about 300,000 tons of coffee and 200,000 tons of cocoa, this is good news. It means that producer prices can be increased further, while at the same time the earnings of the Stabilization Fund will stay at a high level for a few years at least (see Statistical Appendix Table 38). At the same time, the situation will permit the strengthening of the reserve position of the Stabilization Fund, which, compared with the high producer prices paid and the large volumes produced, has become rather weak. It will also be possible for the government to continue to implement its investment program in the north. These price developments will enhance the savings role of the Stabilization Fund over the next few years, and its contributions to the financing of the public investment program are expected to be substantial.

Under such circumstances it becomes crucial that the government integrate the revenues of the Stabilization Fund into the usual budgetary process. As the public investment program will to a certain extent have to continue to rely on foreign capital, the Stabilization Fund's net profit should be used in such a way that, in a better-than-average year, foreign borrowing could be cut back. In a below-average year it could be stepped up. Thus the reserves of the fund could be used to stabilize not only the income of the farmers but also the investment program, and this could have a strong stabilizing impact on the entire economy. A unit should be created in the Stabilization Fund organization to work with the Ministry of Finance to establish guidelines for each party's share of export earnings. A concept such as "average year," based on the considerable amount of historical data available, could be defined. The government should not hesitate to use the reserves of the fund in a deficit year. There is no reason reserves should always be high if the average policy is followed conscientiously. The average concept has to be revised periodically, and international price stabilizing actions, such as those undertaken by the EC as part of the Lomé Convention, have to be taken into account as well. The more these actions put the burden of a guaranteed income for raw materials producers on the international community, the less local intervention will be needed. Also, as a result of the government's diversification policy, the output of more products (copra, palm oil, cotton, rubber) is rising to respectable levels, and with increased local processing of these products an automatic tendency toward more stable export earnings could develop.

Integration of Stabilization Fund earnings into the usual budgetary process should lead to lower expenditures on hastily developed extra-budgetary programs. This certainly would contribute to better allocation of these funds and to improved budgetary discipline.

Municipal Governments

The low-profile municipal governments in the Ivory Coast do not save. Their responsibilities include such activities as operating the municipal administration and maintaining their urban roads. Current revenues in 1969–71 average CFAF2.1 billion, equal to 2.7 percent of the current revenue of the central government over that period. The city of Abidjan accounted for about 70 percent of this total. Eight percent of this revenue is obtained from surcharges on real estate taxes and business licenses. The remainder is levied through a special rental income tax, service charges, and other minor taxes and fees. The municipalities also obtain revenue through transfers from the central government. These averaged CFAF787 million in 1969–71, part of which was earmarked for investment purposes. In addition, local governments engage in foreign and domestic borrowing. Current expenditures in 1969–71 constituted 86 percent of total municipal expenditures. The remaining 14 percent financed various investment projects. Road construction and maintenance absorbs one-third of total expenditures, provision of water and maintenance of the sewerage systems take up about one-fifth, and general administration accounts for 28 percent of the total.

The centralized administrative structure of the Ivory Coast assigns the municipalities relatively few functions and correspondingly few resources. The fact that municipal government budgets must be approved by the central government and municipal current revenue is supplemented by central government transfers further strengthens the control of the central government over the allocation of these resources. Local governments are not considered agents for the mobilization of investment funds, a fact that is illustrated by the excess of central government transfers over municipal investments. A strengthening of the fiscal bases of the municipalities could reverse this situation. While taxation at a local level is difficult and competent tax personnel may be scarce, real estate taxes are often better administered by the local authorities, especially if they rely on this revenue for the financing of expenditures. Their knowledge of local circumstances has proven a valuable asset. Local government should be given the necessary powers to collect the taxes due and should be required to exercise them. Some effort in this field in the Ivory Coast should pay off handsomely. In view of the fact that the central government has appropriated the most productive tax bases, it seems advisable for municipalities to concentrate their efforts on better implementation of a few taxes, rather than on instituting a range of new taxes and levies.

One of the objectives of the government is to improve living conditions in rural areas. Upgrading secondary centers is part of that policy. It should be clear that the municipalities themselves will have to play a major role in implementation, and they will need an improved tax base to generate the resources required to execute this new role. In view of all the needs of the rural areas, no savings to finance the national investment program are expected to come from the municipalities. It would be a welcome improvement if in the future they were able to take care of their recurrent expenditures. Such a policy would also be consistent with the government's aim of upgrading secondary centers and rural areas.

Public Debt

With public investment increasing and public savings lagging, foreign borrowing has increased substantially over the past decade.[11] Consequently, the level of outstanding public debt and the need for domestic resources to service this debt have risen considerably. Consolidated gross foreign capital drawings (including grants) of the central government and public enterprises rose from an average of about CFAF10 billion in 1965–67 to about CFAF80 billion in 1975, reflecting a 26 percent annual growth rate. The share of public borrowing in the financing of total public investment rose from 30 percent in 1965–67 to more than 50 percent in both 1974 and 1975. Public debt service also grew rapidly, from CFAF5.5 billion in 1965–67 to about CFAF33 billion in 1975.

Total public external debt, repayable in foreign currency, has developed as indicated in Table 4.10. Annual increases between 1969 and 1975 are as follows for the different categories: debt outstanding, including undisbursed, 26 percent; commitments, 38 percent; disbursements, 38 percent; and service payments, 29 percent. Future debt service payments are expected to continue to increase more rapidly than exports. As Table 4.10 indicates, the debt service payments based on existing commitments should exceed disbursements by 1977 unless new loans can be contracted, which they undoubtedly will be.

It is difficult to indicate exactly what level of foreign debt service payments the economy of the Ivory Coast could sustain since this depends on many factors. Because of the openness of the economy—exports (including nonfactor services) constitute about 40 percent of GDP—a debt service ratio of 15 percent should be considered high. The country could rapidly exceed this level if recent policies with regard to foreign borrowing are continued.

11. Because information on the local debt of the public sector is incomplete, this section concentrates on foreign debt. Medium- and long-term local debt of the central government is very small. Efforts to borrow large amounts of funds locally have not met with great success. Despite the increase in interest rates granted on the bonds issued by the Caisse Autonome d'Amortissement (CAA) in 1974 to a tax-free 10 percent, an annual amount of only CFAF500 million was floated in the Ivory Coast. The shallowness of the capital market and the availability of investment outlets that promise large returns (for instance, real estate) are given as reasons for the limited success of domestic borrowing so far. Since 1976 the bonds also have to compete with shares offered by the recently established stock exchange.

TABLE 4.10. DEVELOPMENT OF EXTERNAL PUBLIC DEBT, 1969–77
(Millions of U.S. dollars)

Year	Debt outstanding as of December 31, 1975		Developments during the period			Debt service ratio (percent)
	Disbursed only	Including undisbursed	Commitments	Disbursements	Service payments	
1969	207.7	388.5	66.1	48.9	29.7	5.9
1970	256.1	424.3	68.9	76.4	38.6	7.4
1971	351.7	539.3	119.6	107.3	44.7	8.5
1972	399.9	702.9	198.4	82.7	57.9	9.3
1973	578.6	923.4	274.9	228.0	72.3	8.2
1974[a]	738.0	1,200.3	328.8	218.8	115.1	9.1
1975	973.8	1,536.0	448.6	335.6	137.8	10.9
(1976)	n. a.	n. a.	n. a.	226.1	188.4	n. a.
(1977)	n. a.	n. a.	n. a.	148.9	187.9	n. a.

n. a. Not available.
Source: World Bank, External Debt Division.
a. Service payments in 1974 went up to an artificially high level, as US$20 million of a Eurodollar loan was rolled over before it was due.

TABLE 4.11. PERCENTAGE DISTRIBUTION OF EXTERNAL
PUBLIC DEBT OUTSTANDING
AS OF DECEMBER 31, 1975,
BY ORIGIN OF DONOR

Donor	Official assistance[a]	Suppliers' credits and private banks	Total
Multiple lenders	0.0	9.6	9.6
France	11.4	13.1	24.5
Germany	3.2	0.9	4.1
Italy	0.0	6.1	6.1
Lebanon	0.0	6.6	6.6
Norway	0.0	3.5	3.5
United States	4.6	11.1	15.7
Other countries	1.5	3.7	5.2
International organizations	24.7	0.0	24.7
World Bank	16.4	0.0	16.4
Total	45.4	54.6	100.0

Note: Includes undisbursed funds.
Source: World Bank, External Debt Division.
a. From international organizations and governments.

Origin of external public capital

As the Ivory Coast has moved out of the post-colonial period of
reliance on France as its main source of capital, the origin of foreign
capital has become much more diversified (Table 4.11). In 1975 only
25 percent of the Ivory Coast's debt was owed to France (of which 46
percent was owed to French banks and contractors), compared with
more than 80 percent during the early 1960s. The share of debt owed
to other donors, particularly international organizations, has increased
considerably.

With increased diversification has come a continuous hardening of
the terms of the aid blend. Although earlier financial assistance of the
EC consisted entirely of grants, loans represented 23 percent in the
second FED[12] and further increased to 39 percent during the third FED.
The same observation can be made for aid from France, in which the
proportion of loans increased from 52 percent in 1968 to 79 percent in
1970, and to 85 percent in 1974. Also, borrowing on commercial terms
increased considerably (Table 4.12). At the end of 1968, 50 percent of
the Ivory Coast's external debt was held by bilateral donors. Suppliers'

12. The development fund of the European Communities (EC).

TABLE 4.12. COMPOSITION OF EXTERNAL PUBLIC DEBT, 1968–75
(Percent at end of period)

Source	1968	1969	1970	1971	1972	1973	1974	1975
Suppliers' credits	29.4	25.8	23.6	22.4	20.1	20.6	23.9	26.6
Private banks	10.2	12.5	12.4	17.3	21.5	28.1	28.7	26.5
Publicly issued bonds	6.5	4.8	4.8	3.9	2.7	2.9	2.0	1.5
International organizations	3.8	11.2	15.3	18.4	19.4	19.7	20.3	24.6
World Bank	1.6	5.9	9.8	12.7	12.5	10.7	10.0	16.4
Governments	50.1	45.7	43.8	37.9	36.3	28.7	25.1	20.8
Total[a]	100.0	100.0	100.0	100.0	100.0	100.0	100.0	100.0
Total (CFAF billion)[a]	88.9	94.1	117.1	141.9	180.0	218.4	269.6	359.4

Source: World Bank, External Debt Division.
a. Including undisbursed and debts contracted by mixed enterprises and guaranteed by the government.

credits and private banks accounted for 40 percent and international organizations for about 4 percent. By the end of 1975, the share held by bilateral donors had fallen to 20 percent, while those of international organizations on the one hand, and suppliers' credits and private banks on the other, had increased to 25 percent and 53 percent respectively.

Hardening of terms of foreign capital

As a consequence of the changing pattern of foreign sources of capital, terms hardened from 1968 to 1974:

Item	1968	1974	1975
Average interest rate (percent)	5.3	7.1	7.9
Average maturity (years)	15.8	14.2	12.6
Average grace period (years)	4.7	4.6	3.1
Grant element of loans (percent)	29	17	10

Among countries at the same level of development, the Ivory Coast borrowed on the hardest terms during the period 1969–72.[13] Since

13. World Debt Tables, World Bank Report No. EC-167/74, December 15, 1974. Between 1969 and 1972, most of the countries in the $300–$400 per capita income bracket contracted loans with an average grant element in the range of 35–40 percent, compared with 23 percent for the Ivory Coast.

TABLE 4.13. GRANT ELEMENT OF LOANS PROVIDED
BY VARIOUS SOURCES, 1968–75
(Percent)

Year	Suppliers' credits	Private banks	International organizations	Governments	Grant element of total debt
1968	23	13	36	47	27
1969	11	13	24	38	25
1970	9	15	25	43	26
1971	13	−5	27	36	18
1972	15	10	21	34	20
1973	14	−1	39	47	15
1974	20	−1	28	45	17
1975	8	2	11	27	10

Source: World Bank, External Debt Division.

then, the grant element[14] has declined further (Table 4.13). While the deterioration in the average terms of loans resulted from a hardening of all sources, most of it was the result of the considerable increase in borrowing from private sources. Indeed, the proportion of hard-term loans in annual debts contracted on a commitment basis almost doubled between 1969–70 and 1974–75, increasing from 35 percent to about 65

TABLE 4.14. SHARE OF CENTRAL GOVERNMENT AND PUBLIC
ENTERPRISES IN EXTERNAL PUBLIC DEBT, 1968–75
(Percent)

Category	1968	1969	1970	1971	1972	1973	1974	1975
Central government	79.2	71.8	73.1	71.4	61.4	53.3	51.5	53.6
Public enterprises[a]	20.8	28.2	26.9	28.6	38.6	46.7	48.5	46.4
Total	100.0	100.0	100.0	100.0	100.0	100.0	100.0	100.0

Source: World Bank, External Debt Division.
a. Including debts contracted by mixed enterprises and guaranteed by the government.

14. The grant element of loans is the face value of loan commitments less the discounted present value of the future flow of amortization and interest payments. The customary rate of 10 percent is used. The grant element thus computed is expressed as a percentage of the face value of the loan. The lower the grant element, of course, the harder the loan terms.

percent. In absolute terms, these loans jumped from US$35 million in 1969–70 to US$240 million in 1974–75. With a limited supply of concessionary aid, the Ivory Coast accepted the terms dictated by the private capital market to finance an increasing part of its investment program. Capital grants, for instance, coming in at about CFAF3 billion in the early 1960s increased to only around CFAF4 billion in the early 1970s.

Foreign debt contracted by the central government and public enterprises

The proportion of public foreign debt contracted by public enterprises has increased rapidly (Table 4.14). Expressed as a proportion of central government revenue, foreign debt service increased from 8.4 percent to 10.7 percent between 1966–68 and 1973–75, as indicated below:

Period	Average annual government revenue (CFAF billion)	Average annual debt service payments of government (CFAF billion)	Ratio of Column 2 to Column 1 (percent)
1966–68	55.7	4.7	8.4
1970	83.2	6.9	8.3
1973–75	141.7	15.2	10.7

As far as the central government is concerned, debt service has grown more rapidly than revenue, especially in the 1970s, and more than 10 percent of total revenue is now needed to pay debts.

The available data on public investment suggest that capital financing from abroad has increased steadily. The percentages of total investment financed from abroad are as follows:

Period	Central government	Public enterprises	Total
1965–67	35.9	41.1	37.6
1973–75	63.8	54.2	58.3

Thus a higher proportion of rapidly increasing public investments has been financed from abroad, and this has been accompanied by a hardening of terms for the borrower. The resulting ever-increasing debt service payments absorb more revenue, leaving proportionately less net local savings to finance investments, which in turn leads to the need for more foreign capital. With only limited possibilities for increasing the tax burden, with the cost of development going up, with the debt service ratio related to exports going up, with public savings after debt service down to 35 percent of public investments, and with no clear indication of a dramatic acceleration of concessionary aid, some policy changes will be required to safeguard future development while maintaining internal and external equilibrium. Favorable forecasts for world coffee and cocoa prices for the coming years will create the conditions to introduce such changes gradually and should increase the chance for success.

Avoiding the Resource Constraint

Proposed improvements have already been discussed with regard to the financial management of public enterprises, the handling of Stabilization Fund profits, and the role of municipalities. Suggested improvements in two other areas are discussed in this section.

Improved control of expenditures

The present levels of taxation are high, and although some increase in tax revenue is possible, controlling the growth of current expenditure will be necessary to restore the level of current savings. Examples of ways to control expenditures in wages, education, and housing have been given. Technically, budgetary expenditures are annually reviewed and voted upon. But, as in the case of many other developed and developing countries, budgetary forecasts have a tendency to concentrate on investment expenditures. This concentration provides a kind of built-in inflexibility as far as reductions in current expenditures are concerned. Particular attention should be paid to investment-induced recurrent expenditure. Until very recently, the investment budget was drawn up with little concern given to the recurrent expenditures that would be needed to operate or maintain new facilities. The Loi Programme for 1975–77 did try to take this aspect into account, yet the information was not available for most of the investment projects retained. The annual recurrent costs of investments are thus only vaguely known, and it is doubtful whether the information available is being used in the preparation of the ordinary budget.

Abandoning the earmarking of tax revenue

All fiscal revenue in the Ivory Coast is earmarked for a budget or a special fund. During the last decade, earmarking of revenue for more organizations was instituted. Four new organizations were financed through earmarked funds between 1967 and 1971. In addition, there are the two programs for SODEFOR (the state reforestation agency) and the national parks; the road fund receives a portion of fuel taxes from the general budget. The revenues of the Stabilization Fund and the Price Equalization Fund are also earmarked in a special way. The orthodox theory of public finance condemns earmarking because it makes the budget process less flexible and prevents the optimal allocation of resources. This theory seems, however, to ignore the political context of budget formulation. Earmarking of taxes may be a practical solution to allocating funds to areas that are economically deserving but politically less appealing. Such a procedure may make the best of a suboptimal situation in which a government lacks farsightedness or the political ability to persuade the lawmakers to adopt its views on budget allocation. This does not seem to be the case with most tax earmarking in the Ivory Coast. Therefore it is recommended that earmarking of funds for CIC (Conseil Ivoirien des Chargeurs), CICE (Centre Ivoirien du Commerce Extérieur), ONFP (Office National de Formation Professionnelle), OSHE (Office pour le Soutien de l'Habitat Economique), SODEFOR, and the national parks, be terminated. Earmarking complicates budgetary procedures and limits budgetary control over the expenditures of these organizations.

A decision to earmark a given share of total fiscal revenue for a limited number of users (for instance, BSIE and CAA) would seem an improvement over the present practice of earmarking proceeds from specific taxes. First, it would assure that there would be no automatic erosion of the revenue allocated to a priority use. Any redistribution of such revenue would have to be explicit. Second, it would facilitate the introduction of tax changes that are desirable for economic or fiscal reasons but unrelated to the revenue needs of the beneficiary of a particular tax.

In conclusion, some firm policy decisions must be made and implemented to keep the debt service within reasonable limits and to safeguard the financing of future investments. Net public savings have fallen to a low level, although the public sector may be able to improve its savings performance with high earnings of the Stabilization Fund. Nevertheless, with too ambitious an investment program, the proportion of foreign financing in public investment may still increase to a level where foreign sources may become reluctant to provide capital. The volume and terms of the foreign debt to be contracted, as well as the earning power of the projects in which the capital will be invested, have become crucial matters. In Chapters 7 and 8 several ways are suggested to reduce future public investment without suffering a substantial drop in the growth rate. To maintain balanced growth with internal and external equilibrium, the future public investment program must be rigorously checked. With regard to the intended investment program for 1976–80, an effective arbitration procedure must be established and priorities set.

CHAPTER FIVE

Economic Relations
with Other Countries

FROM ITS COLONIAL PAST, the Ivory Coast inherited strong ties with
France and other members of the former French colonial empire in
Africa. A kind of regional economic framework existed even before
national considerations began to affect political and economic decisions.
Consistent with its choice to pursue an outward-oriented development,
the government decided in 1960 to continue to cultivate its existing
relationships abroad and also to diversify its contacts with the outside
world. The government has never left any doubt that it valued highly
the relationships inherited from the past and that it considered any
sudden disruption of them as undesirable, inefficient, and to the country's disadvantage. At the same time, the government indicated firmly
and unequivocally that its policy would be eventually to outgrow,
rather than discard, historically established patterns and arrangements.
No time limit was set for this process. It will be seen in the following
discussion that impressive progress has been made over the past fifteen
years in changing old structures. In certain instances a price had to be
paid. For example, as noted earlier, the diversification of sources of
foreign capital has led to a substantial hardening of terms. In its increased operations in world markets the country has been confronted
with a less generous attitude than it had become used to. The country
is still an active member of several organizations that have their roots
in the past. The most important ones are discussed below.

Memberships in the Franc Area

Mention has been made of the West African Monetary Union (UMOA), the common central bank (BCEAO), the free convertibility of the CFA franc into French francs with the guarantee of France, the centralization of the members' reserves in an operations account with the French treasury, and the free circulation of capital within the region. Since creation of the union in 1962, the consolidated reserve position of the UMOA countries as a whole has always been positive, as can be seen in Table 5.1. The share of reserves of the Ivory Coast in the reserves of the union decreased in the 1970s, and the Ivory Coast's reserves became negative for the first time in the course of 1975.

As part of the 1973 changes in the UMOA, a new common development bank, the Banque Ouest Africaine de Développement (BOAD) was established. The broad aim of the BOAD is to promote overall economic development of the union with a view to realizing the potential benefits of economic integration. The initial capital of the BOAD was CFAF2.4 billion, of which half was provided by the BCEAO and the remaining half by member states, each contributing equally. The operations of the BOAD are expected to cover four areas: the provision of credit for the financing of economic development, the mobilization of financial savings, the organization of a broader money and capital market for the region as a whole, and the provision of technical assistance in the training of banking personnel and in the appraisal of various project proposals.

Other major francophone regional organizations of which the Ivory Coast is a member are (a) the Organisation Commune Africaine et Mauricienne (OCAM),[1] which became responsible for harmonizing the activities of member countries in the economic, social, technical, and cultural fields, for coordinating their development programs, and for promoting discussions in the foreign policy sphere while respecting the sovereignty and freedom of choice of individual members; (b) the Conseil de l'Entente,[2] whose purpose is the promotion of political, social,

---

1. Members: Benin, Central African Empire, Gabon, Ivory Coast, Mauritius, Niger, Rwanda, Senegal, Togo, and Upper Volta.
2. Members: Benin, Ivory Coast, Niger, Togo, and Upper Volta.

TABLE 5.1. NET FOREIGN RESERVE POSITION OF THE WEST AFRICAN
MONETARY UNION, 1968–76
(CFAF billion)

Item	1968	1969	1970	1971	1972	1973	1974	1975	Aug 1976
Net foreign assets	40.5	47.9	73.0	76.2	58.2	45.1	73.7	34.4	n.a.
Share of the Ivory Coast	22.4	28.1	38.6	34.7	13.9	10.1	21.7	−7.8	−24.8

n.a. Not available.
Source: International Financial Statistics, published monthly by the International Monetary Fund.

and economic coordination among the member states (in recent years, it has increasingly concentrated on the latter element); and (c) the Communauté Economique de l'Afrique de l'Ouest (CEAO), which became effective in 1974.[3] The CEAO provides for the elimination of quantitative restrictions on the circulation of goods among member countries, for the tax-free circulation of locally produced agricultural products and materials, and for the establishment of a preferential tariff for manufactured goods produced in member countries. A jointly financed community development fund has been established to compensate members for revenue losses arising from the special preferential regime and to promote economic development throughout the community.

The fact that Benin and Togo are only observers in the CEAO is important. Togo was one of the main promotors of ECOWAS (Economic Community of West African States), a grouping of fifteen French- and English-speaking African countries. With its economic power, Nigeria, one of the members of ECOWAS, is a powerful pole of attraction in today's West Africa. Nigeria is an important trading partner for some of the CEAO members, accounting for almost 20 percent of exports in the case of Niger, for example. It is also the principal source of petroleum imports for Senegal and the Ivory Coast. Therefore, although many political as well as economic and technical problems remain to be resolved, the formation of ECOWAS seems to reinforce the trends toward cooperation between West African countries and overcoming language and cultural barriers.

3. Members: Ivory Coast, Mali, Mauritania, Niger, Senegal, and Upper Volta. Benin and Togo have the status of observer. See Chapter 3, note 11.

Relations with the European Community

The creation of the EC (European Community) has had significant implications for the Ivory Coast.[4] In contrast to many francophone countries for which association with the EC amounted to an exchange of a lower degree of preference for a larger preferential market, the Ivory Coast gained on both counts. By the early 1960s, major Ivorian exports no longer enjoyed much tariff preference in the French market. French tariffs favoring cocoa bean and timber imports from the franc area were suspended in 1957. Only coffee enjoyed a 20 percent tariff preference in addition to an effective price support scheme. However, Ivorian production of coffee[5]—as well as cocoa and timber—already exceeded by far the needs of the French market. Association with the EC opened up new markets and, indeed, was a major factor behind the rapid growth of exports. Financial assistance from the EC has also greatly contributed to diversification of the economy.

At the expiration of the Second Yaoundé Convention, the EC negotiated a new agreement with forty-six countries in Africa, the Caribbean, and the Pacific (ACP countries). The new convention signed in Lomé in February 1975 differs from previous ones in several ways. The main differences are that the tariff preferences granted to the ACP countries are nonreciprocal, a system of stabilizing the export earnings of these countries was established, and arrangements for industrial cooperation were developed that are intended to contribute to diversification of the ACP economies. Of special significance for the trade arrangements of the Ivory Coast is the fact that two other cocoa producers, Ghana and Nigeria, also received free access to the EC market. Furthermore, although Ivorian manufactured goods are covered under the Lomé Convention—as they were under the Yaoundé Conventions—and protected against competition from nonassociated countries in Eastern Europe and the Far East, they will now have to compete with many more exporters for the same markets. Financial assistance from the EC will continue to be important, but because the Ivory Coast is one of the more prosperous countries in the region, the terms will tend to harden.

4. See Chapter 4, note 5.
5. The Ivory Coast produces robusta coffee, which has distinct advantages in the production of instant coffee for which demand grew rapidly in the 1960s.

Tariff Structure

At independence, the tariff structure the Ivory Coast inherited from the French administration was maintained without major alterations. Roughly speaking, it distinguished between imports from France and imports from other countries, with tariff preferences given to imports from France. The role of the Ivory Coast was to provide raw materials, while France supplied the country with finished products. With the formation of the EC, the tariff preferences given to France were extended to the other EC countries. This has resulted in a diminishing role for France as a trade partner.

By comparison with the import tariffs of many other countries, the tariff schedule is relatively simple (most duties are an ad valorem percentage of the c.i.f.—cost, insurance, freight—price). It is fairly uniform for particular categories of goods and applies low-to-moderate duties on most imports (0–30 percent for franc area and EC countries, 5–45 percent for others). In July 1975, the Ivory Coast took advantage of the nonreciprocity clause of the Lomé Convention and raised tariffs on EC imports. Virtually all imports from the franc area and the EC are free from general quantitative import restrictions. Quantitative measures have, however, been used with increasing frequency in recent years for specific products. These measures must be seen in relation to a relaxation of general quota restrictions on imports from non-franc area and non-EC countries. Importation from non-EC countries outside the franc area is done in accordance with an annual import program and requires import licenses. The import program does not involve a commodity-by-commodity quota system, but is rather in the nature of an exchange budget specifying broad limits for imports from different regions or for different purposes. Under the program, special quotas are established for imports from countries with which the Ivory Coast maintains bilateral trade agreements. The quotas are decided in accordance with overall balance of payments considerations and the protection needs of local industries. The import program accounts for only a small part of the Ivory Coast's total imports, however, and is administered in a flexible manner. Recently, the Ivory Coast introduced a system of checking imported goods in their country of origin, reportedly to assure proper invoicing. In case of need—for instance, for balance of payments reasons—an effective general import control system could be executed relatively easily.

Direction of Trade

Diversification of contacts with the rest of the world, already shown in the sources of capital, is also indicated by the change in direction of trade. In the early days of independence, the orientation was largely toward France since other countries, especially neighboring ones, offered few trade opportunities. Language is a barrier with Liberia and Ghana. The Liberian-Ivorian border is sparsely populated on both sides and is covered with heavy, inaccessible tropical rain forests. Also, the regionally oriented political ambitions of Ghana in the early 1960s did not favor close relations with the Ivory Coast. Differences in Guinea's political regime and economic system have reduced economic relations between the two countries virtually to zero; Mali's interest was at first directed more toward Dakar, the capital of French West Africa (Bamako, the capital of Mali, is connected with Dakar by rail). Finally, the trading potential of landlocked and sparsely endowed Upper Volta was limited. Moreover, in all countries, subsistence agriculture was very important at the time of independence. The monetary sector was small, and because of the similarity of production, opportunities for exchange were few. There were no navigable rivers, and except for the coastal areas, trade in surplus production and the monetizing of the individual economies had to wait for the construction of transport infrastructure. When this happened, the Ivory Coast was able to start benefiting from its relatively favorable position, not only its ecological advantages but also its location in relation to landlocked countries like Upper Volta, Niger, and Mali.

Although still small in absolute terms, the CEAO has developed into an important market for Ivorian manufactured goods (Table 5.2). In 1974, sales to these countries accounted for 22 percent of industrial exports. Senegal has been the most important customer for Ivorian cotton fabric, absorbing more than 55 percent of exports during the 1968–71 period. Recently, the export destinations of manufactured goods have become more diversified, with Senegal's share decreasing to about 30 percent and that of Mali and France increasing to 25 and 15 percent respectively. Sales of petroleum products and mechanical and electrical equipment have also been largely concentrated in this market, particularly in Upper Volta and Mali. Upper Volta, Mali, and to a lesser extent Niger, are the main sources of livestock imports for the Ivory Coast. The trade balance shows a surplus for the Ivory Coast

TABLE 5.2. TRADE WITH THE WEST AFRICAN ECONOMIC
COMMUNITY, 1970–75
(CFAF million)

Trade[a]	Senegal	Mauritania	Mali	Niger	Upper Volta	Total
1970						
Exports	2,880	122	802	501	1,477	5,782
Imports	2,855	1	200	168	61	3,285
Trade balance	25	121	602	333	1,416	2,497
1973						
Exports	3,487	40	3,408	999	3,881	11,817
Imports	2,987	30	270	95	144	3,526
Trade balance	500	10	3,138	904	3,737	8,291
1975						
Exports	4,892	288	11,339	2,830	7,242	26,591
Imports	3,946	97	494	210	359	5,106
Trade balance	946	191	10,845	2,620	6,883	21,485

Source: Central Bank of the West African States, Abidjan.

a. Exports to the West African Economic Community (CEAO) amounted to 4.2 percent of the total commodity trade in 1970, 6.2 percent in 1973, and 6.9 percent in 1974. Imports from the CEAO amounted to 2.7 percent in 1970, 2.1 percent in 1973, and 2.0 percent in 1974.

in its trade with each of the individual CEAO members; the overall surplus has increased considerably.

The principal markets for Ivorian exports, however, lie outside Africa and are primarily in Europe. Furthermore, for equipment goods and other manufactured products the country depends on the industrial nations. Of particular importance are the roles of France and the EC. During the last fifteen years, the major change has been a shift of trade away from France toward other EC countries (Table 5.3).

Between 1960 and 1974, the proportion of exports to France was cut in half, while exports to other EC countries more than doubled. This process seems to be continuing. The proportion of exports to the United States decreased during the 1970s, but this proportion increased to the group of other developed countries. The EC external tariff on cocoa of 5.4 percent gave the Ivory Coast an edge over its competitors, Ghana, Nigeria, and Brazil. Palm oil received a tariff preference of 9 percent in the EC and has been successfully exported to this market. The effect of these preferences is striking, and the impact of the enlarged community after the Lomé Convention, which extends the same favors to many more countries, is difficult to predict, but it certainly increases the competition for some major Ivorian ag-

TABLE 5.3. PERCENTAGE DISTRIBUTION OF EXPORTS
TO VARIOUS COUNTRIES, 1960–74

Country	1960	1965	1970	1974
France	51	38	33	26
European Community (excluding France)[a]	15	23	30	36
United States	14	16	19	7
Other developed countries	4	9	9	12
West African Customs Union	6	4	4	7
Other franc area countries	5	5	2	5
Other countries	5	5	3	7
Total	100	100	100	100

Source: Customs statistics.
a. Excluding the United Kingdom, Ireland, and Denmark, which became
members of the European Community as of January 1, 1973.

ricultural export products. In an effort to expand further and to diversify its markets, the Ivory Coast is also trying to intensify relations
with some of the Eastern Bloc countries.

Although France's share of imports to the Ivory Coast has dropped,
it has remained important. The EC (excluding France) has been unable
to capture a proportion of the market comparable to the exports it
absorbs from the Ivory Coast (Table 5.4). There is, in fact, a major
imbalance in the trade between the Ivory Coast and France and between the Ivory Coast and the rest of the EC, which may be based on

TABLE 5.4. PERCENTAGE DISTRIBUTION OF IMPORTS FROM
VARIOUS COUNTRIES, 1960–74

Country	1960	1965	1970	1973	1974
France	65	62	47	45	39
European Community (excluding France)[a]	10	14	23	18	18
United States	3	5	8	9	6
Other developed countries	5	5	7	9	8
West African Customs Union	4	3	3	2	2
Other franc area countries	5	6	7	3	4
Other countries[b]	8	5	5	14	23
Total	100	100	100	100	100

Source: Customs statistics.
a. Excluding the United Kingdom, Ireland, and Denmark, which became members
of the European Community as of January 1, 1973.
b. In 1974 imports from Taiwan and Japan amounted to 4.3 and 3.5 percent of
total imports, respectively.

the comparative advantage of each of the trading partners. The situation in 1974 changed dramatically for the "other countries" group, mainly as a reflection of higher oil prices. The Ivory Coast may be able to expand exports to its oil suppliers; a bilateral trade agreement was recently concluded with Iran.

Because most import-substitution industries in the Ivory Coast are directly linked to French parent companies, it is not surprising that the proportion of imports from France remains high. France continues to supply the total demand for wheat and about 50 percent of the demand for dairy products and sugar. With regard to intermediate inputs and equipment goods, more than 60 percent of the basic metal products, 70 percent of electrical components, and 30 percent of mechanical equipment still come from France. The rest of the EC was able to expand its share in products of a more general character such as foodstuffs and plastics. Furthermore, diversification of aid enabled the EC countries to increase their sales of equipment goods; in the early 1970s the EC accounted for about 15 percent and 30 percent of Ivorian imports of electrical and mechanical components respectively.

Developments in the Balance of Payments

The Ivory Coast's relations with other countries, as recorded by the changes in its international reserves position, is shown in Table 5.5.

TABLE 5.5. INTERNATIONAL
RESERVES AND NET
FOREIGN ASSETS
(CFAF billion)

Year	International reserves	Net foreign assets
1968	19.8	22.4
1969	19.0	28.1
1970	33.0	38.6
1971	24.9	34.7
1972	22.0	13.9
1973	19.7	10.1
1974	15.8	21.7
1975	22.0	−7.8
1976 (August)	13.3	−24.8

Source: *International Financial Statistics* of the International Monetary Fund.

There is a striking difference between the comfortable position of the early 1960s when reserves were at a level equivalent to three to four months of imports, and the deterioration of the early 1970s to less than one month of imports in 1974–75. During the second half of 1975 and the first half of 1976, the Ivory Coast experienced a negative net reserve position for the first time in its history. It appears that the Ivory Coast has not only substantially increased its borrowing abroad to finance development, but in the process has also drawn down its reserves.

Table 5.6 shows that the deterioration in the external position, in spite of substantial trade surpluses, was mainly the result of considerably higher factor payments (debt payments, transferred profits, and workers' remittances) and a nonincreasing (and therefore proportionately diminishing) inflow of long-term private capital. The impact of such developments can be mitigated, as they were in 1974 when coffee was exported out of stock and short-term price movements were favorable for the country's main exports. Nevertheless, these trends reflect the cost of foreign services. Ivorianization of these services has high priority in the government's development program, but implementation will take time and require capital, and the situation may well become worse before it gets better. To be able to afford these substantial numbers of foreign factors, the economy will have to continue to grow rapidly. In addition, the foreign exchange saving or earning power of a project will have to be one of the important criteria in evaluating future investments. Many not directly productive investments will score low in this respect. It should be remembered in this context that a substantial part of the money leaving the country

TABLE 5.6. BALANCE OF PAYMENTS SUMMARY, 1963–75
(CFAF billion)

Item	1963	1965	1970	1971	1972	1973	1974	1975[a]
Trade balance	9.0	7.6	17.8	15.3	22.2	20.3	60.0	16.7
Net services and transfers	−13.5	−18.0	−33.8	−44.4	−52.4	−67.8	−89.3	−102.4
Net private capital inflows[b]	4.3	4.5	5.7	0.9	−2.6	2.9	6.1	3.0
Net public capital inflows	4.7	7.6	16.5	24.6	14.9	42.4	49.2	47.1
International Monetary Fund Special Drawing Rights	0.0	0.0	0.9	1.5	1.5	0.0	0.0	0.0
Errors and omissions	−0.1	2.8	−0.2	−0.2	−0.8	−0.1	−5.0	0.0
Reserve movements[c]	−4.4	−4.5	−9.4	3.2	18.9	2.3	−21.0	35.6

Source: Statistical Appendix Table 13.
a. Preliminary.
b. Taking into account reinvested profits.
c. The minus sign (−) denotes an increase.

as workers' remittances stays within the monetary union and therefore still has some positive value to the Ivory Coast, especially under the new monetary arrangements. Workers' remittances are also a very important revenue for the receiving countries and in that way directly affect the purchasing power in some of the Ivory Coast's export markets for manufactured goods.

Foreign exchange earnings from trade

Foreign trade is very important in the Ivorian economy, and commodity exports at an average level of 35 percent of GDP during 1970–75 accentuate the outward-oriented development of the economy.[6] As can be seen from Table 5.7, exports have indeed served as a powerful source of foreign exchange earnings. The value of exports increased six times over the 1960–75 period. This performance is mostly due to the

TABLE 5.7. BALANCE OF
TRADE
SUMMARY,
1960–75
(CFAF billion)

Year	Exports (f.o.b.)	Imports (c.i.f.)	Balance
1960	40.2	36.9	3.3
1963	58.6	49.6	9.0
1964	74.9	64.6	10.3
1965	70.5	62.9	7.6
1966	80.2	68.6	11.6
1967	80.2	73.5	9.8
1968	110.0	84.3	25.7
1969	123.9	95.2	28.7
1970	138.0	120.2	17.8
1971	137.3	122.0	15.3
1972	150.2	128.0	22.2
1973	191.9	171.6	20.3
1974	301.4	241.4	60.0
1975	266.3	249.6	16.7

Source: Statistical Appendix Tables 16 and 17.

6. Exports and imports are recorded by customs statistics and adjusted by the central bank for coverage (mostly unrecorded trade with neighboring countries), timing, and value. Since the breakdown of these adjustments by product is not available, the discussion in this section relies on customs statistics.

growth of the main exports (cocoa, coffee, and timber), whose earnings accounted for 80 percent of the total value of merchandise exports and for about 75 percent of annual real growth of commodity exports over the past fifteen years. Export receipts have climbed steadily, declining only three times in the fifteen-year period. Generally, only one product was affected at any one time by adverse weather or market conditions. When coffee exports decreased and timber exports stagnated in 1965, however, export earnings fell 6 percent. In 1971 when export earnings from both coffee and cocoa fell, exports dropped 0.5 percent. Exports fell about 10 percent in 1975 because of lower revenue from cocoa and timber. In general, these trends accentuate the fact that a degree of diversification already existed during the 1960s, and to some extent this sheltered the economy from the stop-go syndrome experienced by monoculture countries.

The degree of export product diversification in the Ivory Coast is best shown by the steady decrease in the share represented by the traditional exports (Table 5.8). Unprocessed coffee, cocoa, and timber, which represented 87 percent of commodity exports in 1960, accounted for 62 percent in 1974. Among the three major products, a better balance has been achieved as well. If processing is included, each accounted for about 25 percent in 1974, while in 1960 coffee earned 50 percent of total export earnings. The increase in "other" reflects several developments. First, in the agricultural sector, diversification has led to impressive growth in the exportation of bananas, palm oil, and rubber. Second, in manufacturing, the textile industry has been the most dynamic sector; it is now exporting 40 percent of its production and has become one of the driving forces behind the growth of indus-

TABLE 5.8. PERCENTAGE COMPOSITION OF
EXPORTS BY PRODUCT, 1960–74

Product	1960	1965	1970	1974
Coffee beans	49	38	34	22
Coffee processing	...	...	1	1
Cocoa beans	23	16	20	21
Cocoa processing	...	2	5	5
Timber logs	15	22	18	18
Timber processing	2	5	4	5
Other	11	17	18	28
Total	100	100	100	100

. . . Zero or negligible.
Source: Statistical Appendix Table 16.

trial exports. With the extension of productive capacity, the real future of the industry lies with exports to developed countries and particularly to the EC, where the Ivory Coast enjoys tariff advantages as a result of the Yaoundé and Lomé Conventions. Third, among the other important industrial products, exports have expanded rapidly for petroleum products and mechanical and electrical equipment.

Imports grew about 8 percent a year in constant terms between 1960 and 1974, and the import elasticity was about 1.1 percent. With a growth rate of about 10 percent, importation of raw materials and semifinished products has increased proportionally (Table 5.9). This has been the result of expansion of manufacturing activities based on the processing of imported inputs and on important infrastructure works undertaken during the 1969–72 period for the construction of the Kossou hydroelectric scheme and the deep-sea port at San Pédro. Capital goods have increased steadily at about 8.5 percent in real terms.

In 1974 consumer goods represented 24 percent of total imports, compared with about 34 percent in 1963. Most of this relative decrease may be attributed to the implementation of import-substitution policies. For example, the dependence on imports for textile products has been reduced to about 40 percent, whereas in the early 1960s imports constituted 80 percent of total textile consumption. The food industries have also expanded at a fast rate (about 22 percent a year during 1965–72) and have contributed substantially to limiting imports of foodstuffs. Rice practically ceased to be imported in 1975. The major foodstuff items still imported are sugar (the first local sugar mill recently started production), wheat (for processing) which cannot be grown in the country, meat, and dairy products. Further investments anticipated in sugar, foodstuffs, livestock, and food production in gen-

TABLE 5.9. PERCENTAGE COMPOSITION OF IMPORTS
BY PRODUCT, 1963–74

Product	1963	1965	1970	1973	1974
Foodstuffs	17	18	15	19	17
Consumer goods	34	34	29	27	24
Petroleum	5	6	5	5	14
Raw materials and semifinished products	17	17	22	21	18
Equipment goods	27	25	29	28	27
Total	100	100	100	100	100

Source: Statistical Appendix Table 17.

eral indicate that the Ivory Coast may reduce its dependence on food imports in the coming years.

Besides the textile, wood processing, and food industries, most of the import-substitution industries use imported materials to a substantial degree. These materials include chemicals, fertilizers, crude oil, steel, mechanical and electrical components, and clinker. Therefore, although many products have been replaced by domestic production, this has not resulted in a reduction of total imports. While the share of consumer goods in total imports decreased, imports of raw materials and semifinished products have increased to meet the requirements of the manufacturing industry. Of course, ideally, investments in import substitution should only be made in those activities in which the country has a comparative advantage. As noted in Chapter 3, some activities, especially in industry, are carried out at high cost using the infant industry argument, and in many cases the learning process has taken longer than anticipated. In view of this, further development in import substitution should be given a proper economic evaluation, using cost estimates based on available experience.

The year 1974 and the impact of the oil price increase

The impact of the oil price increase and other developments affecting the trade balance in 1974 deserve some special attention. It is remarkable that the same year the Ivory Coast had to pay CFAF15 billion more for its oil due to price increases, it had a record trade surplus of CFAF60 billion, or more than twice that of any previous year. Although the price increase for crude oil was by far the largest increase for any single commodity, some of the export products of the Ivory Coast also did very well. Price and volume increased by some 25 and 15 percent respectively for total exports. In one single year, 1974, the volume of coffee went up 35 percent, cocoa 39 percent, and palm oil 300 percent, while timber remained the same, all compared with the volume average for 1970–73 (Table 5.10).

In evaluating the 1974 export performance, a number of points should be kept in mind. Exports of palm oil should grow more moderately now that most plantations have reached full production. Log exports are not expected to go much over 3 million cubic meters a year owing to depletion and to conservation measures. Some 50,000 tons of coffee were exported out of stock in 1974. Finally, unrecorded cocoa was reportedly coming from Ghana, probably in response to the 1974 producer price increase in the Ivory Coast of 60 percent to CFAF175

TABLE 5.10. EXPORTS OF MAJOR PRODUCTS, 1970–75
(Thousands of tons)

Product	1970	1971	1972	1973	1974	1975
Coffee beans	195	185	189	213	264	255
Cocoa beans	143	147	159	143	205	170
Timber logs[a]	2.5	2.9	3.2	3.5	3.0	2.4
Palm oil	12	28	47	50	102	114

Source: Statistical Appendix Table 18.
a. In millions of cubic meters.

a kilogram as compared with CFAF110 a kilogram in Ghana.[7] This trade may not be completely unrelated to the high Ivorian cocoa exports in 1974. In conclusion, although prospects for agricultural production are good and the Ivory Coast may benefit from adverse developments affecting coffee production in Brazil and Angola, future exports should not be extrapolated from the 1974 bonanza.

Moreover, crude oil prices are not coming down and the development of potentially available hydroelectric power will take time. Thus large outlays for future energy imports are certain. With an elasticity with respect to GDP of 0.95, petroleum imports grew at an average annual rate of 7.2 percent in real terms during 1960–73. Since 1965, as a result of the establishment of an oil refinery in Abidjan, imports of refined products have been reduced considerably. Imports of crude oil have increased rapidly and reached the capacity of the oil refinery (1 million tons a year) in the early 1970s. Investments undertaken in 1972 and completed in September 1973 brought the refinery capacity up to 2 million tons a year. Currently, most of the crude oil imports come from Nigeria and Iraq in about equal proportions. The Ivory Coast exports about 40 percent of its refined petroleum products directly (the Ivory Coast is a major supplier to Mali and Upper Volta) and as bunker fuels. During the 1970–73 period, net oil imports averaged CFAF4 billion, or about 3.3 percent of imports, but jumped to CFAF22.2 billion in 1974 (7.6 percent of imports) as a result of price increases. The net loss resulting from the oil trade in 1975 will be equivalent to about half the public debt service or half the workers' remittances, which are both considered to be major claims on foreign exchange. It is also equivalent to 70 percent of the local public savings available to finance the central government's investment budget (BSIE) in 1976.

7. Calculated at the official exchange rate.

Claims on foreign exchange earnings from trade

The liberal and open policy of the government has been successful in attracting foreign capital, management, and labor, and has been instrumental in the country's economic growth. These foreign factors are not free of charge, however, and the effect of this policy on the outflow of earnings as registered by the balance of payments is discussed below.[8]

Nonfactor services. The nonfactor services (NFS) account has always been negative. In the 1970s (with the exception of 1974), it has been so to such an extent that it has exceeded the trade surplus and resulted in a resource gap rather than the surplus of the 1960s (Table 5.11). The main categories of nonfactor services are freight and insurance, travel and other transport, and "other services"—a miscellaneous group consisting mainly of commissions, fees, and nonmerchandise insurance. In transport, two shipping lines, one privately owned and the other a public enterprise, realize considerable revenues. Both companies have, however, a high proportion of foreign officers and crew, a situation that substantially reduces net foreign exchange earnings for the time being. The government has ambitious plans for the extension of its shipping line, but much of the financing would have to come from abroad. Promotion of tourism is another way in which the government is trying to reduce the services deficit. Prospects for tourism are moderately bright, although net foreign exchange earnings are expected to remain relatively small. Ivorianization of jobs would have a healthy impact on the deficit of nonfactor services. Both management fees and agent fees have increased rapidly, and in 1973 the net deficit on the balance of payments for commissions and fees stood at CFAF14.2 billion, compared with CFAF1.6 billion in 1963. In 1973, net payments to foreign agents by exporters and importers in the Ivory Coast represented about 15 percent of the foreign exchange earnings derived from trade, which seems high. Also, it appears that the gov-

8. Changes in the balance of payments presentation were made in 1973 by the BCEAO. The appendix to this chapter provides detailed explanations of these changes. To make a discussion of trends possible, the historical series had to be adjusted. It should be noted, however, that the net impact of these changes on the overall balance of payments is negligible. For example, higher estimates of direct investment income are partly compensated for by a larger inflow of capital on the account of undistributed earnings. Also, the change in residence status for technical assistants cannot affect the current account balance; their transactions are merely distributed among more items in the services and transfers accounts.

ernment has been very liberal about approving payments of management fees to parent companies, which, in some cases, include repatriation of investment profits. Such fees should be considered imported inputs and be taxed accordingly.

Factor services and current transfers.   The balance of payments items, factor services and current transfers, have developed as shown in Table 5.12. The interest payments in Table 5.12 stem almost entirely from the public sector and have been dealt with as public debt service earlier in the report. Direct investment income has to be balanced with a capital item of the balance of payments, namely, reinvested earnings which were about CFAF1.5 billion in the mid-1960s but increased to CFAF7.8 billion in 1973, suggesting that foreign-owned firms retained a higher proportion of earnings in the country for investment purposes. The net repatriation of profits is still substantial, however, especially in comparison with private capital inflows, which have never been high. Since the capital stock is not known, it is impossible to relate the

TABLE 5.11. DEVELOPMENT OF
THE RESOURCE
BALANCE, 1963–75
(CFAF billion)

Year	Trade balance	Net nonfactor services	Resource balance
1963	9.0	−3.6	5.4
1964	10.3	−0.6	9.7
1965	7.6	−4.4	3.2
1968	25.7	−7.4	18.3
1969	28.7	−9.0	19.7
1970	17.8	−13.0	4.8
1971	15.3	−18.2	−2.9
1972	22.2	−20.4	1.8
1973	20.3	−25.4	−5.1
1974	60.0	−41.0	19.0
1975	16.7[a]	−48.6	−31.9

Source: Statistical Appendix Table 13.

a. To cope with 1975 balance of payments problems, the International Monetary Fund agreed to the Ivory Coast's purchase of Special Drawing Rights 10.35 million (US$12.1 million) under the 1975 oil facility and in early 1976 agreed to its purchase of Special Drawing Rights 26 million (US$30.4 million) under the International Monetary Fund's compensatory financing facility. (1 SDR = US$1.17.)

TABLE 5.12. DEVELOPMENT OF THE CURRENT ACCOUNT BALANCE, 1963–75 (CFAF billion)

Item	1963	1964	1965	1968	1969	1970	1971	1972	1973	1974	1975
1. Resource balance	5.4	9.7	3.2	18.3	19.7	4.8	-2.9	1.8	-5.1	19.0	-31.9
Interest payments	-0.4	-1.3	-1.4	-2.3	-2.9	-4.3	-5.2	-6.0	-7.3	-9.2	-12.0
Direct investment income	-4.7	-5.6	-5.1	-7.3	-8.0	-8.4	-11.5	-10.7	-17.9	-17.2	-20.0
Workers' remittances	-6.3	-9.2	-9.8	-12.2	-13.1	-15.4	-18.8	-23.3	-27.5	-33.5	-34.9
Debit factor cost	-11.4	-16.1	-16.3	-21.8	-24.0	-28.1	-35.5	-40.0	-52.7	-59.9	-66.9
Credit factor cost	0.0	0.0	0.0	0.3	0.9	2.4	2.1	1.9	1.8	3.8	4.0
2. Net factor services	-11.4	-16.1	-16.3	-21.5	-23.1	-25.7	-33.4	-38.1	-50.9	-56.1	-62.9
3. Net current transfers	1.5	2.0	2.7	1.4	2.6	4.9	7.2	6.1	8.5	7.8	9.1
4. Current account balance (1+2+3)	-4.5	-4.4	-10.4	-1.8	-0.8	-16.0	-29.1	-30.2	-47.5	-29.3	-85.7

Source: Statistical Appendix Table 13.

net repatriation of profits to capital invested. It is estimated, however, that in the early 1970s, an average post-tax profit on equity of 12.2 percent was made. This is certainly not excessive. (See Appendix B on Industry.)

The outflow of money on the account of workers' remittances is by far the largest drain on foreign exchange reserves. This represents for 1973–74 on the average close to 14 percent of commodity export revenue, which is not surprising given the large and rapidly increasing foreign community in the Ivory Coast. It is estimated by the central bank that about 60 percent of the remittances are made by non-Africans, the rest by non-Ivorian Africans.

During 1970–75 an average of 24 percent of the net current transfers was private (75 percent of it pensions); the rest was public and was almost entirely for the financing of technical assistance, in which France plays a major role. The number of technical assistants under the direct supervision of the French Ministry of Cooperation came to 3,250 in 1973;[9] 79 percent of these were teachers, the rest were technicians assigned to different ministries and other public agencies. The composition of French technical assistance since independence is as follows:[10]

	1960	1965	1970	1972	1973
Teachers	405	994	1,969	2,487	2,571
Other	855	598	507	628	679
Total	1,260	1,592	2,476	3,115	3,250
Teachers as a percentage of total	32.1	62.4	79.5	79.9	79.1

From 1960 to 1965, the Ivorian contribution to the cost of technical assistance averaged CFAF1.3 billion a year (see Table 5.13), based on a lump sum payment of CFAF65,000 a month per technical assistant. After 1966, it was mutually agreed to limit the cost to France to CFAF2.1 billion, the difference being made up by the Ivory Coast. Although France raised her contribution to CFAF2.6 billion in 1973 (excluding some 0.2 billion not covered by the agreement), the cost to the Ivory Coast has become substantial as a result of the steady increase in the size and cost of technical assistance. Although in 1960 the Ivory Coast contributed CFAF0.8 million per technical assistant, the cost averaged CFAF3.1 million in 1973. Given the concentration of technical assistance in education, a rapid reduction of this burden would

9. Excluding experts recruited directly by the Ivory Coast and volunteers, such as the Peace Corps (United States) and Volontaires du Progrès (France).

10. Mission d'Aide et de Coopération, Abidjan.

TABLE 5.13. COST OF TECHNICAL ASSISTANCE, 1960–73
(CFAF billion)

Contribution	1960–65	1966	1970	1972	1973
France					
Lump sum	0.0	2.1	2.1	2.4	2.6
Other	0.0	0.0	0.0	0.2	0.2
Subtotal	2.2	2.1	2.1	2.6	2.8
Ivory Coast					
Payment to French treasury	1.3	1.4	3.5	5.5	6.6
Housing	0.0	0.0	2.1	2.5	3.2
Other	0.0	0.0	0.2	0.2	0.2
Subtotal	1.3	1.4	5.8	8.2	10.0
Total	3.5	3.5	7.9	10.8	12.8

Source: Mission d'Aide et de Coopération, Abidjan.

be inconsistent with the government's objectives for education and training, which are aimed at reducing reliance on foreign factors in the longer run. Import substitution in this area could pay off handsomely, provided efficiency can be maintained (see Chapter 6).

Creditworthiness of a country is conventionally measured by the debt service ratio, defined as the external public debt service as a percentage of export earnings from goods, nonfactor services, and workers' remittances. As the discussion above indicates, there are other claims on foreign exchange earnings in the case of the Ivory Coast. These claims come not only from imports, but also from foreign private capital and labor. Taking into account the cost of foreign private capital (direct investment income, net of reinvested profits) would add about 5 percentage points to the public debt service ratio for the year 1973 and would bring the total public and private debt service ratio to some 13 percent of export earnings.

Expressing the various items of the current account as a proportion of commodity exports reveals some interesting trends (Table 5.14). First, because of favorable export prices the trade balance was strong in 1968–70. The balance for the 1973–75 period qualifies as only average, in spite of the exceptional year, 1974. The results of 1974 were necessary to balance out two less favorable years, 1973 and 1975. Second, nonfactor services have increased rapidly and the resource balance, the difference between exports and imports including nonfactor services, has become negative. In other words, over the 1973–75 period the trade surplus has not been able to compensate for negative net

TABLE 5.14. CURRENT ACCOUNT ITEMS
AS A PERCENTAGE OF EXPORTS

Current account	1963–65	1968–70	1971–73	1973–75
Export of goods	100	100	100	100
Trade balance	13	19	12	13
Nonfactor services	−4	−8	−13	−15
Factor services	−21	−19	−26	−23
Current transfer	3	2	4	3
Current account balance	−9	−6	−23	−22

Source: Statistical Appendix Table 13.

nonfactor services. To do so now, the trade surplus would have to be approximately CFAF50 billion, although in the late 1960s and early 1970s a trade surplus of some CFAF20 billion was enough to end a year with an increase in reserves. Factor services and current transfers have remained at more or less the 1960s' proportion. The position of the current account may well become worse in view of the problem of keeping up export performance, the permanent character of the increased oil bill, the import effects of a stepped-up investment program, the long-term character of Ivorianization, the hardening terms on borrowed foreign capital, and the fixed nature of current transfers in which the inflow of pensions can only decline. Since reserves are at a low level, capital inflows will have to continue to be substantial. There is much discussion of changing the international economic order; plans are afoot for stabilizing the world prices for raw materials and for helping developing nations in other ways. For the time being, however, the amount of concessionary capital available for underdeveloped countries remains limited. Developing countries face many structural problems, whose solution will require considerable amounts of capital. The Ivory Coast will have to compete with these demands and it is unlikely that terms will soften in view of the magnitude of the investment program it wants to implement.

The capital account

The amounts, origins, and terms of foreign public capital have already been discussed. The rapid increase in this category is shown in Table 5.15. Because of hardening terms, the net inflow as a proportion of the gross inflow is expected to diminish, a phenomenon that had started in the early 1970s. In this respect, it should be realized that for

TABLE 5.15. DEVELOPMENT OF THE CAPITAL ACCOUNT, 1963–75
(CFAF billion)

Item	1963–65	1968–70	1971	1972	1973	1974	1975ᵃ
Current account balance	−6.4	−6.2	−29.1	−30.2	−47.5	−29.3	−85.7
Capital grants	3.5	4.5	3.6	3.8	3.8	3.5	4.0
Private capital (net)	4.4	1.9	0.9	−2.6	2.9	6.1	3.0
Public capital (gross)	3.8	15.5	29.8	20.8	46.5	52.3	72.0
Repayment	1.9	6.0	7.6	9.3	9.2	18.4	19.0
Public capital (net)	1.9	9.5	22.2	11.5	37.3	33.9	53.0
Errors and omissions, other	1.0	−0.5	−0.8	−1.4	1.2	6.8	−9.9
Reserve movementsᵇ	−4.4	−9.2	3.2	18.9	2.3	−21.0	35.6

Source: Statistical Appendix Table 13.
a. Some items are estimates.
b. The minus sign (−) denotes an increase.

a line of credit on commercial terms (interest rate 10 percent, maturity seven years, and a two-year grace period) to disburse $100 million annually on a net basis, the gross inflow has to increase to $204 million after five years, $471 million after ten years, $895 million after fifteen years, and $1,576 million after twenty years.

Grants have increased only slightly over the past fifteen years. Total private capital inflow, taking into account reinvested earnings, has continued but has diminished proportionally and has been rather volatile. Over the last five years, less than 7 percent of total net capital inflow was private, as compared with an average of about 25 percent during the 1960s. The twentyfold increase in the net inflow of public capital in fifteen years, and the depletion of reserves during the same period, show the increased involvement of foreign capital in the Ivory Coast's economic development. It appears from an analysis of the balance of payments that gradually, but at an accelerated pace, the reliance on foreign factors is tending to become excessive compared with the results obtained earlier with this mixture of local and foreign resources.

In summary, it seems clear that although export performance has been good, the direct cost of foreign involvement has rapidly increased; there is evidence that the indirect cost of foreign production factors may be going up as well. In the next chapter the problems of Ivorianization, which have a direct bearing on these costs, will be discussed. The discussion will be mainly in the context of employment and income distribution, but it is obvious that the impact of Ivorianization on the balance of payments is also an important consideration.

Appendix: Balance of Payments and National Accounts Estimates: Changes in Definition and Reconciliation

The Ivory Coast reports balance of payments data using the International Monetary Fund principles of balance of payments accounting. These differ in some respects from the United Nations system of national accounts. To make reconciliation with national accounts estimates easier, a number of changes in definition were introduced by the central bank in the 1973 balance of payments. This appendix describes the reclassification of transactions that resulted from the modifications of definition and attempts to adjust the series backward in order to have consistent data for analysis. It also defines nonfactor and factor services as these terms are commonly used in the World Bank; these differ slightly from the Ivorian definitions.

Definition of concepts and content of categories

In the balance of payments, services are classified by type, such as transportation, travel, and investment income, whereas in the national accounts a distinction is made between nonfactor services and factor services in order to derive GDP and GNP. Nonfactor services are defined as services produced in the domestic economy or imported from abroad, and factor services are defined as payment for the services of foreign factors considered to be engaged in production in the domestic economy and receipts from the services of domestic factors considered to be engaged in production in the rest of the world.

Therefore, with the exception of investment income, nonfactor services include all services as recorded in the balance of payments, including freight and merchandise insurance, other transportation, travel, government transactions not elsewhere included (n.e.i.), and other services. In the Ivory Coast the item "freight and merchandise insurance" is mostly composed of receipts from domestic carriers (COMARAN and SITRAM) since imports are recorded in terms of their c.i.f. prices. The item "other transportation" covers mainly port disbursements, particularly sales and purchases of bunker oil, and passenger fares paid by residents. The item "travel" includes, on the credit side, receipts from tourism and, on the debit side, mostly home leave expenses of expatriates. The main components of "government transactions (n.e.i.)" are operating expenses of embassies and diplomatic personal expenditures. Finally, "other services" covers mostly nonmerchandise insurance, agents' fees and management fees paid by foreign-owned firms to parent companies, and imports of construction services (which have been substantial, particularly during 1969–72 because of the construction of the San Pédro port and the Kossou hydroelectric scheme).

Factor services and current transfers are presented in the Statistical Appendix Tables 13 and 15. The items are self-explanatory. Workers' remittances and transfers by technical assistants are included in factor services to reflect properly, when deriving GNP, the drain on national resources represented by the repatriation of savings by foreign workers. The other difference from the standard presentation is the exclusion of capital grants from current transfers. These changes in the classification of transactions increase the deficit on goods and services by the amount of workers' remittances and the current account deficit by the amount of capital grants. Reconciliation with the standard presentation is provided in Statistical Appendix Table 13.

In the standard presentation, public enterprises are regarded as belonging to the private sector since most of them acquire foreign assets and liabilities for the same reasons as private enterprises. The changes in their foreign assets and liabilities can, therefore, from a behavioral standpoint, be attributed to the private sector. To have an overall view of the public sector, however, it is necessary to separate public enterprises from the private sector. Using the data provided by the CAA, loan transactions of public enterprises are reclassified under the public sector (see Statistical Appendix Table 13). In this classification, the central government is defined to include only foreign borrowing of central government agencies. Loans received by public enterprises and managed by the CAA are allocated to the public enterprise sector.

Changes in definition of transactions

Until recently technical assistants were considered nonresidents. The estimated cost of the aid program was therefore included under imports of services and was counterbalanced by a figure of the same amount on the credit side under public transfers. The net impact on the balance of payments was represented by purchases of goods and services generated by the aid program and local expenditures of technical assistants. To coordinate more closely with the national accounts statistics, it was decided to consider technical assistants residents of countries where they are assigned. Although this change cannot affect

TABLE 5.16. TECHNICAL ASSISTANCE: CLASSIFICATION OF
TRANSACTIONS ACCORDING TO RESIDENCE STATUS
(CFAF billion)

Transactions	Nonresidents (until 1972)		Residents (since 1973)	
	Credit	Debit	Credit	Debit
Travel	—	—	—	2.0[a]
Government transactions, n.e.i.:				
Services under aid programs	—	12.1	—	—
Personal expenditures of technical assistants[b]	5.9	—[c]	—	—
Government transfers	12.1	—	12.1	—
Private transfers (workers' remittances)	—	—	—	4.2[d]
Technical assistance (net)	5.9	—	5.9	—

—Not applicable.
Source: National accounts.
a. Estimated to equal two months' salary.
b. Often included in diplomatic personal expenditures.
c. Disregarding small amounts of services imported in connection with technical assistance.
d. Estimated at 35 percent of the technical assistant's salary.

the current balance, the transactions of technical assistants are now distributed among more items in the services and transfers accounts. To adjust historical series, it has been assumed that the technical assistant has the same consumption pattern as the expatriate working in the private sector, that is, that he spends two months' salary for travel, repatriates 35 percent of his salary, and spends the rest in the Ivory Coast. The example in Table 5.16 illustrates for the year 1972 the difference in the classification of transactions because of the modification of definition.

The change to nonresident status for Air Afrique[11] poses a more difficult problem since it affects the whole balance of payments. Current transactions of Air Afrique represent more than 25 percent of receipts on freight and insurance, 80 percent of net receipts on transportation, and 15 percent of imports of other services. Its capital transactions can also be substantial, particularly with the acquisition of new aircraft during fiscal year 1970–71.

11. Twelve countries (Ivory Coast, Senegal, Togo, Benin, Niger, Upper Volta, Chad, Gabon, Central African Empire, Congo, Mali, and Mauritania) each have 6.7 percent of the equity in Air Afrique. The rest is held by UTA (Union des Transports Aériens). Headquarters of Air Afrique are in Abidjan.

The last change introduced in the 1973 balance of payments concerns insurance companies, which are now considered resident in the Ivory Coast. The net impact resulting from the reclassification of transactions is, however, negligible.

Method of adjustment

In order to adjust the data on the transactions described above to conform to the new definition, it is necessary to start with national accounts figures for goods and services on which adjustments have already been made to take into account the change of residence status for technical assistants, Air Afrique, and the insurance companies. Since the Ivorian national accounts figures exclude receipts and expenditures in "travel," "government transactions," and "other services" (they are considered as transfers), these categories are added to get exports and imports of goods and nonfactor services as defined earlier. Since technical assistants are now considered residents of the Ivory Coast, corrections have been made to (a) exclude their expenditures from the credit side and the value of technical assistance from the debit side of government transactions, and (b) include the estimated amounts they spend on travel in the total expenditure for travel. (See Statistical Appendix Table 14.) As noted above, the change of residence status for technical assistants cannot affect the current account balance, which therefore differs from the basic data only by the current transactions of Air Afrique. These fluctuated between CFAF0.9 and CFAF2.4 billion a year from 1963 to 1972.

Long-term capital transactions of Air Afrique have been separated from the private capital flows using the data provided by the CAA. Because of the lack of information, it has not been possible to make the same adjustments on short-term capital flows.

CHAPTER SIX

Employment, Income Distribution, and Ivorianization

IN ITS ECONOMIC POLICY, the government has had to deal with three interrelated issues: employment, income distribution, and problems arising from the pressure of a large foreign population, both European and African. The discussion that follows attempts to evaluate the situation at the present time and to deal with the implications of current and proposed policies affecting income distribution and the employment of Ivorians.

Interrelated Issues

The government of the Ivory Coast has stressed growth of total and per capita production as its major goal. The very success of this policy lends urgency to questions of equity. The government has been criticized for paying insufficient attention to income distribution and for tolerating foreign domination of the economy at both ends of the spectrum: European expatriates in the decisionmaking positions in the economy, and non-Ivorian Africans, mostly unskilled, in the least desirable positions at the bottom of the income scale. No doubt many policies and decisions could be improved, but on examination it seems that in comparison with many other countries, the Ivory Coast has done well not only in growth but also in the specific areas explored in this chapter. With the general increase in incomes, the income of the poorest segment of the population has risen as well. The large number of foreigners from other African countries testifies to the attractiveness of the Ivory Coast to others. Farm price and wage policies show neither the overwhelming urban bias so frequently found, nor an overconcern for the upper income strata. Effective protection studies do not show tremendous distortion on the average. Income distribution calculations show a distribution similar to, or more equitable than, those found in comparable countries. Farm price policies and regional investment plans not only show an active concern with equity but also indicate that growth and equity are to a large extent consistent.

The Ivory Coast is nevertheless faced with a number of complex problems. The success of rapid economic growth and an improved situation for the country's poor have been associated with a policy of opening the Ivory Coast to the outside world and of favoring private enterprise. This had led to a large inflow of Europeans and Africans whose presence, though without question benefiting the economy, is also creating social tensions that raise the question of where the limit of tolerance, and therefore of efficiency, lies. The number of foreign Africans is so large that it would not be feasible simply to send them home. It would also be against the spirit of regional cooperation and solidarity with neighboring countries that has developed over time. The Ivory Coast is therefore faced with the issue of how much the employment policy should take into account the employment situation in neighboring countries. At the same time, increasing numbers of Ivorians leaving school compete with skilled foreigners for jobs. In certain sectors of the economy there will be less and less need for these foreigners, and it must be expected that Ivorians will increasingly take the place of foreigners, provided they have the skills and are willing to work at competitive wages. This situation affects the non-African expatriate and, in some sectors, the immigrant from a neighboring country if he holds a job in which Ivorians have become interested.

The present compromise between regional (in the sense of Ivory Coast and its neighbors) and national priorities in employment policies will probably be weighted more toward national considerations in the future. The problem of the balance between these priorities has its domestic counterpart in the disparities of per capita income in the different regions of the country, the differences in the ecologies of different regions, and the choice of moving people to the more favored regions or encouraging them to stay where they are.

Ecological differences among regions account for much of the discrepancy in income distribution. Many northerners have gone south in response to the job opportunities there, particularly in plantation agriculture. Not everybody is willing to leave his region and become a migrant worker, however. Furthermore, in the south, especially in Abidjan, employment cannot be created fast enough to absorb the influx. In fact, Abidjan has grown so fast that there is now unemployment and underemployment.

Ecologically disfavored regions are capable of providing a better living for their people if technological change can overcome the areas' disadvantages. The savannah of the Ivory Coast is a case in point. Improved methods of cotton cultivation have not only enabled the production of raw materials for a local textile industry, but have also made cultivation of other products in rotation with cotton a paying proposition. Food crops and livestock production are integrated parts of such a scheme. The government's regional distribution of planned investment shows that it recognizes these opportunities for the savannah, which coincided with a time when greater concern for the welfare of the people had become a political necessity.

A reduction of both regional and urban-rural disparities should reduce the population drift toward the cities, in the Ivory Coast's case predominantly to the capital. It would also lessen the pressure on the urban labor markets where most problems of open unemployment arise. This in turn would avoid labor shortages in the rural areas that would hamper agricultural development, still the mainstay of economic development in the Ivory Coast. It is understood by the government, as indicated by the sector allocation of its investment program, that policies required to limit the differences in income extend beyond farm prices or measures to disperse directly productive investments over the country; investments in amenities of life such as water, health, electricity, and schools are also important. For income is not real until it can be spent on what people desire.

As already mentioned, employment creation is felt to be a major problem for Ivorians: The supply of labor comes mainly from the countryside or from abroad. It will be affected by income-earning expectations in rural as compared with urban areas. A farm price and wage policy that allows rural inhabitants to earn a decent living will reduce pressure on the urban labor market while improving income distribution and raising output. Such a policy also requires improved productivity in rural areas. This may or may not be associated with mechanization, but it will almost certainly require structural change. Finally, the training of larger numbers of Ivorians for all levels of work will allow an increasing substitution of Ivorians for foreigners. In this regard, all that is necessary or desirable, at least initially, is that the growing economy use relatively more Ivorians. The policies of the government seem to be directed toward a creative solution to these problems.

A discussion of income distribution in the Ivory Coast should take three main factors into account. First, the ecological differences among areas are important. Second, the problem is evidently quite different in countries where no one is starving, like the Ivory Coast, from that in countries such as Bangladesh or India. Finally, the dominant social structure of the Ivory Coast, particularly the extended family system and ethnic and village loyalties, provides a sort of social security and an effective income redistribution system that cuts across class and urban-rural distinctions.

Population and Employment

The first population census in the Ivory Coast was held in April 1975. It established that the total population was 6.7 million in mid-1975 (Table 6.1), about half a million higher than previously estimated. Population growth appears to have accelerated from a rate of 1.4 percent a year for the period 1920–45, to 2.8 percent for 1955–65, and to 4.0 percent for 1965–75. The increase in the indigenous population is estimated at 2.5 percent, the balance coming from heavy and apparently accelerating immigration. In 1973, it was estimated that about 25 percent of the total population was foreign-born. When children born to foreign parents are included (a definition of foreign population considered more in accord with the political-social realities of the Ivory Coast), the number considered to be in the foreign population would be 2 million, or 30 percent.

About 100,000 Lebanese and Syrians and some 50,000 Europeans live in the Ivory Coast.[1] The urban population, which was low in 1955, has increased rapidly; the population of greater Abidjan increased eightfold in twenty years and is now estimated to be about one million. The rural population has also grown substantially and only a few departments in the north have actually lost people. The regional distribution of the population, as estimated for 1975 by the Ministry of Planning before detailed census results were available, is shown in Table 6.2.

The high and accelerating rates of migration cannot, of course, be automatically extrapolated into the future. The figures for the last few

1. See Ministry of Planning, *La Côte d'Ivoire en Chiffres*, 1975 edition.

TABLE 6.1. GROWTH OF TOTAL
AND URBAN POPULATIONS
(Thousands)

Year	Total	Urban[a]		Abidjan
		Total	Percentage	
1955	2,662.2	346.0	13.0	125.0
1965	4,302.5	946.0	21.8	340.0
1970	5,125.0	1,435.0	28.0	590.0
1975	6,700.0	2,300.0	34.3	1,000.0

Source: Statistical Appendix Tables 1 and 2.
a. Settlements of over 4,000.

years, for instance, were undoubtedly inflated by immigration resulting from the Sahelian drought. The presence of such large numbers
of foreigners and their rapid increase has begun to generate social pressures, and, although the term Ivorianization is more directly related
to the highly visible non-Africans, the need for some form of official
policy regarding the numerous other Africans will increasingly be felt.
The problem is complicated by the fact that many Ivorians find employment as hired labor in agriculture unattractive. Therefore, most
immigrants are employed in agriculture, where they have accepted low
wages, supplemented by the revenues from sharecropping and other
benefits in kind. This has produced a situation in which there is unemployment among Ivorians in the city, while in several rural areas
there is a shortage of agricultural labor.

TABLE 6.2. REGIONAL DISTRIBUTION
OF POPULATION IN 1975

Region	Population (thousands)	Density (per square kilometer)
North	598	11
East	339	9
South (excluding Abidjan)	1,380	27
West	735	18
Center West	810	18
Center	1,633	29
Southwest	205	7
Abidjan	1,000	435
Total	6,700	20.7

Source: Ministry of Planning.

Population and rural investments

In the past, substantial tax revenue from the agricultural sector has been used to create employment in other sectors, particularly industry. To enable future growth in agriculture in the longer run, however, substantial investments have to be made in the opening up of new areas in the southwest and in the structural transformation of the savannah areas. Both operations, added to the intensification of activities in the more developed areas in the south, will require major inputs in terms of capital and manpower on a sustained basis for many years. It is conceivable that the government's preference for a rapid and concurrent development of many areas and sectors will run into shortages of production factors. So far, the solution has been to import scarce production factors. With more people and capital coming from abroad, however, direct and indirect costs have gone up. The higher direct cost of foreign production factors and higher indirect cost of social and economic infrastructure should be important considerations in determining future priorities and the pace of development.

In this context, some form of population policy seems desirable. It is not so much the absolute size of the population as its rapid growth and migration that have caused problems. The associated rapid urbanization has greatly increased the demand for investment in social infrastructure. The needs of the increasing population come on top of the growing demand from the existing population for schools, health services, water, and other amenities associated with development. It cannot be assumed that because there are still vast tracts of virtually empty land, or because the level of productivity of the labor force can still be raised substantially by technical change, the rapid rate of growth of the population is without danger. All change takes time and no change in productivity is conceivable without sizable capital requirements. A policy of simply letting excess population spill over into empty lands where the people would use traditional agricultural methods would rapidly run into difficulties.

At present, no explicit population policy has been formulated. Other policies, however, affect population and its growth. Investment and pricing policies are directed toward stemming the rural exodus, and Ivorianization policies are intended to do the same at a national level. In order to create sufficient opportunities that would produce acceptable levels of income, investments would have to be substantial and would have to increase even more rapidly with higher population growth. The problem again is one of timing. To avoid placing too heavy a burden on the producing generation, population growth should be spaced over time.

The supply and demand for labor in 1973 and 1980

As in most other developing countries, the concepts of employment and unemployment are difficult to define because relatively few people are employed on a regularly salaried basis in the modern or formal sector. Moreover, uncertainties about employment in the informal sector make it difficult to consider unemployment as simply the difference between the total active labor force and the numbers whose employment can be accounted for. Unemployment estimates are also extremely sensitive to relatively minor variations in the percentage of the population deemed to be in the labor force (those aged fifteen to fifty-nine) and to their assumed participation rates. The latest population estimates suggest that 53 percent of the population is of working age. On the basis of this figure and the balance sheet approach, and if an actual labor supply of almost 89 percent of the active population is assumed, unemployment for 1973 is estimated at 80,000 people, or 3 percent of the active population. If it is assumed that there is no rural unemployment, this is equivalent to about 15 percent of the urban labor force.[2] Projections for 1980 are subject to even greater margins of error. By extrapolating past trends for the future growth in employment and urbanization, these percentages may double by 1980 unless policy changes become effective.

The weaknesses of the balance sheet approach suggest that it should be used only as supplementary information. In fact, the employment that can be measured with some degree of reliability is a relatively small part of the labor force, mainly the salaried employment in the modern sector. The informal sector in urban centers provides substantial employment, as well as a form of social security through its receptiveness to newcomers based on the extended family system. It also is a sector that, according to all observers, pays quite well and should therefore be given due consideration in government policies. Although very little is known about it, a preparatory study carried out for the

2. See Statistical Appendix Tables 42 and 43.

1976–80 plan shows the importance of the informal sector even in salaried employment (1970 data):[3]

	Formal sector (Salaried)	Informal sector		Total
		Salaried	Nonsalaried	
Number of employees	255,800	334,730	1,590,710	2,181,240
Percent	11.7	15.3	73.0	100

The nonsalaried are self-employed and family workers in the informal sector. A census of this sector, planned by the government, should be carried out as soon as possible.

The influx of labor into the urban areas has produced pressure for job creation, but it also indicates that the urban situation must look relatively good to the migrant. It is sometimes assumed that the urban unemployed are supported by their rural relatives, but no hard information on this point exists. It is not very likely, however, that large numbers of foreigners are supported from abroad. In fact, it is estimated that in 1973 about CFAF6–8 billion was transferred to Upper Volta alone. Such large transfers are not consistent with the existence of large-scale unemployment in either the formal or the informal sector.

The troublesome dimension of unemployment may be not so much its absolute size as its nature. Of the job seekers in 1973, more than 31 percent were illiterate, another 28 percent had been unable to finish elementary school, and another 16 percent had finished only elementary school. Thus of the unemployed, more than three-fourths were either illiterate or barely literate, were not educated for traditional farm work nor for more specialized urban occupations, and were seeking jobs in more congenial urban surroundings in occupations manifestly less strenuous than farm work. Most of these unemployed wanted jobs in trade and other services, but the majority of offers were for manual labor in construction and public works. It appears that young people who have learned trades have much less trouble entering the labor market and may do so within the informal sector. The schools have been criticized for failing to prepare the students for jobs and for being too academically oriented. Most would agree, however, that the basic skills of reading, writing, and arithmetic should not be neglected, but also that students should be directed early in their education into channels where labor needs are foreseen. The unemployment problem is aggravated by unreasonable expectations raised in the minds of the job

3. Société d'Etudes Economiques et Financières (SETEF), *L'Image base, 1970* (Paris, 1973).

seekers by the attractions of the urban environment and perhaps by the high standard of living of expatriates and a small number of Ivorians and other Africans.

The employment situation in the Ivory Coast points to the need for a school curriculum that better prepares young people for the job market and gives them a more realistic outlook about opportunities. It is difficult to imagine that a more realistic outlook can be developed as long as there are large differences in living standards and amenities. The solution of the employment problems requires, therefore, a large number of conditions such as the following: a wage structure that guides people into desired occupations; investment criteria that make maximum use of the available resources; the avoidance of high rates of effective protection for a few favored industries; a distribution of infrastructural investment that makes life outside Abidjan more attractive; and a farm price policy that raises farm incomes. With respect to the last point, such a farm policy would reduce public revenue and would therefore have to be accompanied by a shift from public to private investment. It is encouraging indeed that many of the policies of the Ivorian government are directed toward making income distribution more even, reducing differences between urban and rural incomes, assisting the ecologically disfavored regions, particularly the north, and encouraging private saving and investment.

Table 6.3 shows that Ivorians occupy most positions in the secondary and tertiary sectors, but that in the primary sector other Africans are the most numerous, even increasing in proportion between 1971 and 1974.[4] This reflects the fact that most Ivorians in the primary sector are self-employed or are related to the persons for whom they work. The share of Ivorians in the secondary sector is increasing. The high salary payments made to non-Africans in all sectors is striking. Such salaries range from about twenty times the average African salary in the primary sector to ten times in the secondary sector, to five times in the tertiary sector. Non-Africans usually cost, in money terms, two to three times as much as Africans in the same job classification. The cost of expatriates is high indeed, and contracts of some US$50,000 a man year—excluding costs of housing, car, and other fringe benefits—are not exceptional. This should be, and is, quite an incentive for

4. The primary or agricultural sector includes crops, livestock, fisheries, and forestry; the secondary or industrial sector includes mining, manufacturing, construction, and public utilities; the tertiary or service sector includes transport, communications, trade, public administration, banking, and insurance.

TABLE 6.3. PERCENTAGE OF EMPLOYMENT
AND SALARY PAYMENTS BY SECTOR
AND NATIONALITY, 1971 AND 1974

Sector and nationality	Employment		Salary payments	
	1971	*1974*	*1971*	*1974*
Primary sector				
Ivorians	25.5	16.9	38.0	16.2
Other Africans	72.7	81.8	39.1	56.1
Non-Africans	1.8	1.2	22.9	27.7
Secondary sector				
Ivorians	55.8	58.8	40.4	41.3
Other Africans	38.4	36.8	23.3	23.3
Non-Africans	5.8	4.4	36.3	35.4
Tertiary sector				
Ivorians	54.6	53.6	40.9	36.9
Other Africans	34.1	35.1	22.3	18.0
Non-Africans	11.3	11.2	36.9	45.1

Source: Data for 1971 are from *Enquête 1971* and apply to the private and parapublic sectors; data for 1974 are from *Enquête 1974*, and apply to the private sector only, both published by the Office National de la Formation Professionelle (ONFP).

Ivorianization, but only in the long run. For the moment, many young Ivorian graduates do not yet have the experience necessary to execute top functions. One result is that many management positions have "double occupancy," with an Ivorian and an expatriate filling one position. This makes the management of many undertakings relatively expensive at present but may result in a faster rate of Ivorianization later on.

Income Distribution

Perhaps no subject in economics gives rise to more discussion based on as little factual information as does income distribution. Income distribution estimates published for African countries are a case in point. It would be desirable to have information on the income of individuals, who could then be grouped by income class. This is not possible. All estimates start with average incomes of certain groups, and these groups are then ordered accordingly to average income without any real indication of the dispersion within the group. Some further difficulties that are not adequately handled by present estimates, whether for the Ivory Coast or elsewhere, are discussed below.

Problems in estimating income distribution

Income distribution estimates frequently rely on Gini coefficients or Lorenz curves. Both are percentage distributions that by definition add up to 100 percent. If one group gets a higher percentage of income, another necessarily must get a smaller percentage. Yet it makes a considerable difference whether there is an actual transfer of income from the poorer to the richer, that is, whether the poor have actually become poorer, or whether all groups have benefited—but some more than others.

Rural-urban comparisons present other problems. Although the statistics for the Ivory Coast show wage earners in the primary sector, most are owners, family members, or sharecroppers. Some 69 percent of the total population is classified as agricultural. The people in this group make their living from agriculture. Their income comes predominantly from the production of goods, rather than from the sale of their labor. Much of this production does not go through the market, and all major export goods are sold at prices that have been reduced by what is in effect a taxation of income. Differences in rural-urban income are exaggerated when rural incomes, which are to a large extent post-tax incomes, are compared with urban incomes, which are pre-tax incomes.

It would be difficult to make the proper allowance for differences in the cost of living in urban and rural areas, even if satisfactory indexes existed. The reason is that certain amenities, such as electricity or water, are provided only in urban areas. They represent a real income difference even though, because of pricing policies, the urban population pays the whole cost of these amenities. This difference would still exist, even if the urban wage income, divided by some ideal cost-of-living index, showed the same real income as rural income, divided by its appropriate cost-of-living index. This situation is relevent to the Ivory Coast's regionalized investment projects, which are designed to make various urban services more widely available.

Another problem in developing accurate income data is that there are many nonmarket incomes, even in a market economy such as that of the Ivory Coast. Examples are subsidized housing and access to credit on favorable terms. It has not been possible to allow for this type of income. Also, the presence of large numbers of foreigners who generally do not own land or real estate suggests that rental income is important. There is not sufficient information available to determine the distribution of this income.

Under the special Ivorian conditions, a Gini coefficient may, under certain quite realistic circumstances, be misleading. Many of the top incomes go to expatriates who, category for category, cost two to three times as much as Ivorians. The substitution of cheaper Ivorian labor for more expensive expatriate labor would undoubtedly be a net gain for the Ivorian economy, provided that the efficiency of the economy does not suffer. If the marginal Ivorian (in the theoretical sense) is more efficient than the marginal expatriate he replaces, there is no doubt about the gain to the Ivorian economy. For Ivorianization to be beneficial to the economy, however, it is not necessary that the Ivorian be as efficient as the expatriate; it is only necessary that the difference in their efficiencies be equal to or less than the difference in their salaries.

Suppose, however, that the marginal Ivorian has a lower productivity. If salaries fall correspondingly, the efficiency and competitiveness of the economy will be maintained. If salaries are maintained or raised, the economy will become less competitive. This will appear in the balance of payments and also in a loss of output and Ivorian employment, which in turn will put pressure on all factor prices. If the sector that has employed the less efficient Ivorian succeeds in maintaining the salary levels, there will be some unemployment and pressure on other factor prices, mainly "other wages," and perhaps prices paid to farmers. If this happens, it is possible that income distribution could become more equal as Ivorians are substituted for more expensive expatriates. This would be a dubious gain, however, if at the same time the rest of the lower-paid Ivorians were worse off. Of course, the income distribution of the Ivorian population alone would show a more uneven distribution. This theoretical point is important because the awareness of these problems probably accounts for the caution with which Ivorianization is being tackled by the government. Of course, a short-run small loss could turn into a long-term gain, but this is a risk the government is apparently hesitant to take.

Income distribution, 1973–74

With these provisos, which in general apply to income distribution estimates for other countries as well, it is believed that the income distribution estimates for 1973–74 presented in this section provide a valid picture of the situation at that time as well as of the policies pursued by the government in the area of income distribution.

Wage and salary earners.   The available data permit an income distribution estimate for the salaried labor force in the private sector in 1974, which is given below:

Lowest 40 percent receive 13.8 percent of the total salary payments.
Middle 40 percent receive 32.7 percent of the total salary payments.
Top 20 percent receive 53.5 percent of the total salary payments.

The top incomes go to expatriates; the lowest incomes go mainly to other Africans. But the top African incomes go to Ivorians rather than to other Africans.

For salary payments in the public and parapublic sectors (without the civil service), the pattern is repeated in that the lowest-paid groups are other Africans and the highest-paid group expatriates. The distribution for 1973 is as follows:

Lowest 40 percent receive 12.0 percent of the total salary payments.
Middle 40 percent receive 32.0 percent of the total salary payments.
Top 20 percent receive 56.0 percent of the total salary payments.

For the civil service, the income distribution is substantially more even. The bottom 40 percent of the employees receive 27 percent of income payments, while the top 20 percent get 35 percent.

In order to make the above calculations comparable with the income distribution in agriculture, they have been converted to a per capita basis by department. It is necessary to recall the relative numbers involved. In 1973, 53,114 persons were employed in the public and parapublic sectors (excluding the civil service), 126,814 in the private sector, and 39,828 in the civil service, according to the statistical bases analyzed. Thus, the information on salary income, which is relatively reliable, refers to 219,756 income earners.

Agricultural income.   The basic calculations made by the Ministry of Planning for agricultural incomes refer to the money income of the African agricultural population by department in 1973. The agricultural population is defined as the rural population, excluding those engaged in nonagricultural activities, but including farming population living in urban areas. The population involved is 80 percent of the population of the country.[5] It is necessary to make allowance for subsistence income, which is of major importance in the agricultural sector, particularly in the ecologically disfavored areas without major export crops. Therefore, for each department the net values for food-crop production, livestock, and fishing have been added. The income distribution obtained for the crop year 1973–74 is as follows:

Lowest 40 percent receive 27.5 percent of the country's total agricultural income.

Middle 40 percent receive 40.5 percent of the country's total agricultural income.

Top 20 percent receive 32.0 percent of the country's total agricultural income.

It will be noted that agricultural income, including money and subsistence income, is much more evenly distributed than the income in other sectors.

Other incomes.   The data for the other income groups are much less reliable than those calculated above. The missing elements are (a) paid-out interest and dividends, insofar as they are not transferred abroad; (b) gross profits of nonindividual enterprises; and (c) the income of the informal sector outside of agriculture. The procedure for (a) and (b) was to take the figures given by the 1973 national accounts and allocate them to the top 20 percent of the income earners; and for (c) to take the figure given by the "gross revenue of individual enterprises" (Revenue Brut des Entreprises Individuelles, RBEI) and correct it for payments to the agricultural sector. The result has been allocated to the departments according to nonagricultural population.

Total income.   The outcome of these somewhat elaborate calculations is given in more detail in Statistical Appendix Tables 44 and 45 and is summarized here. The distribution of the total income of the Ivory Coast for the crop year 1973–74 is as follows:

Lowest 40 percent receive 19.7 percent of the total.
Middle 40 percent receive 28.7 percent of the total.
Top 20 percent receive 51.6 percent of the total.

The margin of error in these calculations may be considerable, but as

5. Because the agricultural population here includes farmers living in urban areas, it constitutes a higher proportion of the total population than the 69 percent figure given earlier, which is based on urban-rural distinctions alone.

explained before this would apply to estimates for other countries as well. The above results indicate a more even income distribution than some other investigators have found, especially for the Ivorian population, given the fact that the figures include foreigners at the top and at the bottom of the income scale.

International comparison.   The international comparison presented in Table 6.4 shows that for the Ivory Coast the lowest 40 percent receive 10.8 percent of the total income, the middle 40 percent receive 32.1 percent of the total income, and the top 20 percent receive 57.1 percent of the total income.

TABLE 6.4. INCOME DISTRIBUTION ESTIMATES
FOR THE IVORY COAST, VARIOUS
OTHER AFRICAN COUNTRIES,
AND INDIA

		Percentage of income received		
Country	Year	Lowest 40 percent	Middle 40 percent	Top 20 percent
High inequality				
Kenya	1969	10.0	22.0	68.0
Sierra Leone	1968	9.6	22.4	68.0
Senegal	1960	10.0	26.0	64.0
Rhodesia	1968	8.2	22.8	69.0
Tunisia	1970	11.4	53.6	55.0
Gabon	1968	8.8	23.7	67.5
Medium inequality				
Benin	1959	15.5	34.5	50.0
Tanzania	1967	13.0	26.0	61.0
Zambia	1959	14.5	28.5	57.0
India	1964	16.0	32.0	52.0
Low inequality				
Chad	1958	18.0	39.0	43.0
Niger	1960	18.0	40.0	42.0
Uganda	1970	17.1	35.8	47.1
Ivory Coast[a]	1970	10.8	32.1	57.1
Ivory Coast[b]	1973–74	19.7	28.7	51.6

Source: Hollis Chenery and others, *Redistribution with Growth* (London: Oxford University Press, 1974), pp. 8–9.
   a. Hollis Chenery, *Redistribution with Growth.*
   b. Figures given for the Ivory Coast, crop year 1973–74, are based partly on detailed data provided by the Ivorian government and partly on World Bank estimates.

These figures differ from the World Bank estimates primarily because the Bank had access to more complete data but also because there was an improvement in income distribution between 1970 and 1973–74 (see the discussion on producer price and investment policies later in this chapter). The dangers inherent in the lack of precision of international comparisons, particularly in the field of income distribution, should be recognized.

Farm price policies.   One reason income is more evenly distributed in the Ivory Coast than in other developing countries is that per capita farm income is not startlingly lower than per capita salary payments. Although the Ivory Coast has taxed farmers, for instance, by paying them less than world market prices for their produce, farm prices have been kept rather high and agricultural production has sharply increased. It may be difficult to say with absolute certainty whether income distribution became more even or less even between 1970 and 1973–74, but the fact that agricultural incomes have developed satisfactorily may be more important. For coffee producers the price increase between 1970 and 1973 was 15 percent; for cocoa producers it was 30 percent. Incomes rose even more with the increase in producer prices in late 1974; for coffee from CFAF120 to CFAF150 a kilogram and for cocoa from CFAF110 to CFAF175 a kilogram between 1970 and 1975. Cotton prices went up from CFAF34.5 to CFAF45 a kilogram between 1970 and 1973 and were increased further to CFAF70 a kilogram in 1974. In 1974 the government also raised the producer price for paddy rice from CFAF28 a kilogram to CFAF65 a kilogram at farmgate.[6] In most cases, the Ivory Coast paid its producers a price comparable to, or higher than, that paid in other African countries. Thus through the control of prices in this area the government has shown an active concern for the welfare of the mass of the people. These and similar figures for other agricultural products explain in large part the relatively even income distribution.[7]

6. Most farmers were not able to benefit from this price increase, however. In 1975 the public enterprise operating in the rice sector (SODERIZ) did not have sufficient capacity to process the entire rice crop or the financial means to buy it at the producer price. Most farmers had to sell their production on the private parallel market, reportedly at about 60 percent of the announced price.

7. Continuing to follow the same policy, the government increased most producer prices for the 1976–77 crop year. Examples are (all prices in CFAF a kilogram): coffee from 150 to 180; cocoa from 175 to 180; cotton from 70 to 80; tobacco from 190 to 200; pineapples for canning from 8.8 to 13 (at farmgate).

TABLE 6.5. PERCENTAGE INCREASES
IN AGRICULTURAL
AND NONAGRICULTURAL SALARIES

Date	Nonagriculture		Agriculture[a]
	Low income	High income	
January 1, 1970	25	7	0
August 1, 1973	26	5	0
February 1, 1974	20	7	0
August 1, 1974	5	5	25
January 1, 1976	25	8	0[b]

Source: World Bank estimates.

a. Applies only to coffee, cocoa, cotton, and rice growing. For other crops, livestock, and forestry, wages are higher. In November 1974 wages were CFAF25 an hour for coffee, cocoa, cotton, and rice; CFAF30 an hour for other crops; CFAF30.1 an hour for livestock; and CFAF37.5 an hour for forestry, with a minimum wage for the nonagricultural sector of CFAF92 an hour at that date.

b. The minimum wages in agriculture were raised by 25 percent as of October 1, 1976.

Wage policies.   Minimum wage legislation applies to the private industrial, banking, and commercial sectors and is generally followed by the public sector. Increases have been differentiated for nonagricultural activities to allow larger raises for lower income groups (see Table 6.5). During the 1970–76 period, nonagricultural minimum wages increased from three times to about four times agricultural minimum wages.

Purchasing power.   No reliable price indexes exist. By using the cost-of-living index for African families in Abidjan, an approximate development of the purchasing power of nonagricultural minimum wage income has been derived (Table 6.6). Low-income groups appear in general to have gained in real terms; high-income groups have suffered a loss.

Effect of government income policies

The government's income distribution and price policies have had the following general effects:

a. The government has raised farm incomes substantially in the past few years, certainly more than the incomes of the high-bracket salary earners who live mostly in urban areas. The beneficiaries of the policies have been mainly, but not entirely, Ivorian producers of export crops or import-replacing crops.

TABLE 6.6. DEVELOPMENT OF PURCHASING POWER OF NONAGRICULTURAL MINIMUM WAGE INCOME

Item	1965	December 1969	January 1970	July 1973	August 1973	January 1974	February 1974	August 1974	September 1974	September 1975
Income										
Low-income groups	100	110	138	138	172	172	207	207	217	217
High-income groups	100	110	118	118	124	124	133	133	140	140
Cost-of-living index	100	118	124	147	147	149	152	169	169	188
Purchasing power										
Low-income groups	100	93	111	94	117	115	136	122	128	115
High-income groups	100	93	95	80	84	83	88	79	83	74

Source: World Bank estimates.

138

b. Wages have been raised, but farm wages have been raised much less than nonfarm wages. The policy has benefited Ivorian producers of export products and the large Ivorian- and government-owned plantations employing foreign African labor. Given the wage developments, the Ivory Coast must have been considerably more attractive to foreign African workers five to ten years ago than it is today. Little is known, however, about inflation in rural areas and remuneration in kind. Moreover, with the Sahelian drought, circumstances at home may have deteriorated to such an extent that transfers of less money to the home country may have become acceptable. Wages in forestry have risen more than wages in the more traditional sectors. Wage differences within the farm sector appear to have increased.

c. Nonfarm wages have increased more than farm wages. This has primarily benefited Ivorians, who are the majority in nonfarm wage employment. With increased emphasis on export-oriented raw material processing, the competitive position of Ivorian industry in foreign markets has become an important factor and this position is directly related to the level of labor cost, which is high.

d. The difference between Ivorian and other African wages, at least in money terms, seems to have increased, but government policies have been clearly geared to improving income distribution for Ivorians. Another sign of the government's desire to narrow income gaps is its effort to establish uniform prices everywhere in the country for essential commodities. Recently, uniform prices have been established for petroleum products, for instance, as well as uniform rates for electricity and water supply. The cost of these commodities is usually higher in rural than in urban areas as a result of higher production costs in smaller units and added transport costs; uniform prices and rates therefore mean that rural areas are subsidized.

Taxation and Public Investment Policies

Taxation and public investment have served as key instruments in the implementation of income distribution policy in the Ivory Coast. These policies are not independent of one another, a fact that should be recognized by Ivorian authorities. Although little is known about price elasticities, it is conceivable that with a given f.o.b. price for export crops, a relative increase in farmer prices could reduce tax revenue. This would happen if a price incentive fails to lead to the higher production that would offset the initial loss in tax revenue. Tax revenue could also go down if higher production by one of the world's major producers, such as the Ivory Coast, were to affect negatively the world market price. In both cases, tax revenue, and therefore public savings (and the capacity of the public sector to finance the public investment program), would decrease. Under those circumstances, especially if the farming community had little opportunity or incentive to save, the public investment program would have to rely increasingly on foreign capital. Although there is not enough statistical information available to quantify these relationships, these forces are probably at work in the Ivory Coast in the way described. Also, the producer price paid should be seen in relation to costs borne by the public sector for a particular crop. In the coffee and cocoa subsectors, for instance, it was found that some of the incentives could probably be taken away from relatively well-paid producers without affecting present or future output. The savings could be used for pursuing objectives with higher priority.

Farm price policies affect about 80 percent of the population, specifically those engaged in the production of cocoa, coffee, palm and coconut oils, cotton, rubber, pineapples, bananas, tobacco, rice, and other foodstuffs. As mentioned earlier, taxes are highest on the products in which the Ivory Coast has the largest comparative advantage. Part of the tax income has been used to encourage diversification into other crops and into other sectors of the economy, such as industry and tourism. The latter two sectors are mainly associated with the south, and the subsidies have been justified in terms of creating viable sectors that, in the longer run, will have to play a much more important role in employment creation than they do at present. Part of the tax money has also been used to open up the southwest, where the agricultural technology that is familiar in the southeast can be applied. The southwest is sparsely populated, and arguments that development of the area will improve income distribution are valid only insofar as low-income people can be persuaded to settle there. As indicated earlier, the rate at which this area can be developed depends on the capital available and also on the ability of the area to attract manpower. Since the mid-1960s, tax revenue from agriculture and other sources has been increasingly used to develop the less endowed savannah areas in the north and center. Here the government has preferred a longer-term strategy and, by financing research and encouraging use of technological innovations, has made the north suitable for economically feasible projects, rather than leaving it to depend on social projects or charity.

Redistribution through taxation

Taxation cannot directly improve the living conditions of the poor; the most that taxes can do is to leave their income position unaffected. A tax system that is ideal from the standpoint of improving income distribution would thus exempt poor families and gradually increase the burden on the wealthier families. In this way the tax burden would be distributed according to ability to pay. In this section, the tax structure of the Ivory Coast is examined to see how closely it approximates such an ideal tax system.

In theory taxes on wealth could be used to control the concentration of wealth and ownership among the citizens of a country. Since ownership of tangible wealth accounts for a considerable part of the income concentration, policymakers would seem to have at their disposal a potent instrument for the redistribution of income. In the Ivory Coast, however, taxes on wealth occupy only a minor place in the overall revenue structure and so far have not affected income distribution. The revenue from such taxes (property taxes, inheritance taxes, annual taxes on the ownership of motor vehicles, and transfer fees) does not exceed 1 percent of total current revenue. Real estate taxes are levied on the rental value of improved real estate or on the assessed market value of undeveloped real estate. Agricultural land is excluded from the real estate tax, and only about 2,000 square kilometers out of a total of 332,000 square kilometers is registered in a properly kept cadastre. Such registration is a precondition for the levying of any real estate or land tax. Good progress has been made in the elaboration of cadastres in urban areas, but the success of owners in avoiding payment of this tax for long periods has greatly handicapped its use for redistribution purposes. Of the modest real estate taxes collected, most are paid by the business community, for which these taxes are a normal business expense and are reflected in the price of products sold. Inheritance taxes, an effective way to limit the intergenerational transfer of wealth, are progressive in the Ivory Coast with respect to the amount transferred and to the closeness of the blood relationship between the deceased and the recipients of the inheritance. Rates vary from 3 percent to 45 percent. Few taxpayers comply with these legal provisions. The possible implications of the tax for income distribution are therefore negligible.

It is impossible to assess with any degree of certainty who bears the burden of taxes on business income and profits. Either the investor or the consumer can be assumed to bear the burden, and therefore these taxes can be thought of as either quite progressive or regressive-proportional. Their distributional impact cannot be established.

Progressive personal income taxes are often considered the most potent tax instrument available from the standpoint of income distribution. Because they are assessed as a fraction of the income of the taxpayer, they should enable the authorities to modify the income distribution in the desired direction. Ivorian income taxes, however, differ from this ideal because the taxes apply only to some income elements of some taxpayers and because effective tax rates are much less progressive than would appear from an inspection of the legal rates. The group that is most effectively taxed are the wage and salary earners. They pay a slightly progressive tax on wages and salaries, which is deducted at the source, and a quite progressive general income tax. The overall burden of the latter tax can be quite high and rises with the level of income. Families with several dependents are, however, allowed to divide their income among the dependents (the split system), thus drastically reducing their tax liability. The split system in the Ivory Coast benefits the better-off taxpayer more than the poorer one. Income taxes do not reach agricultural income, a situation that favors the agricultural worker over the salary earner. But because many poor farmers would have been exempted from the personal income tax anyway, it is the prosperous farmer who receives most of the benefit. Although it is widely recognized that agricultural income is difficult to tax, the Ivorian authorities should be able to extend the income tax to wealthier groups in the agricultural sector.

Taxes on consumption such as import duties, value-added taxes, and excise taxes are all assumed to be reflected in the final price of the products on which they are levied. If all families consumed an equal percentage of their income and if the average consumption package for the families with different incomes were identical, consumption taxes would be proportional. But the consumption patterns of families differ along the income scale, with poor people consuming fewer imported goods than the rich. Also, the tax burden is not identical for all components of consumption; import duties are higher on luxuries than on necessities. Detailed empirical studies of the burden of taxes on consumption in other countries have shown progression for the lower-income ranges, and proportionality or slight progression over most of the income scale, and then regression for the high-income group. Another finding is that these taxes fall more heavily on urban than on rural consumers because urban families consume more imported goods than rural families with the same income. The Ivory Coast follows this general pattern. The burden of import duties (35 percent of current revenue in 1974) is probably distributed fairly progressively. The import tax cannot, however, put a progressively higher burden on wealthy families because the Ivorian import duty scale does not show very large differences among the duties paid on the various categories of products. Value-added taxes, which would be regressive if all consumption were to be subjected to such taxes, allow many exemptions, such as for locally grown food and bread products. The result is that a large fraction of the consumption of poorer families is exempt. Also, subsistence consumption and consumption of products that do not pass through the formal market structure are exempt. These forms of consumption represent a decreasing share of total consumption as family income increases, and they represent a larger share of the consumption of rural families than of urban families. Although detailed family budget data are not available, informed estimates lead to the conclusion that the value-added tax, which constitutes 12 percent of total current revenue, is slightly progressive for the lower to lower-middle income classes, after which it becomes proportional. Excise taxes on fuel products are probably slightly progressive, while the incidence of excise taxes on tobacco and alcoholic beverages is progressive for low-income groups, then proportional, then moderately regressive.

Export taxes on coffee, cocoa, and cotton have contributed about one-fifth of the total current revenue over the last decade. In addition, the Stabilization Fund has taxed these products effectively. The tax liability is a function of the price of the exported product and not of the total income of the farmer, with the result that these export taxes in fact are proportional taxes that burden the small producer as much as the large one or the producer on poor land as much as the one on rich land. These taxes fail to shift the tax burden toward the better-off farmers. They therefore score rather poorly from a vertical equity point of view. Nevertheless, the taxes on cocoa and coffee, which are grown in the ecologically more favored regions, are much higher than the taxes on cotton, which is grown in the savannah; thus export taxes tend to tax richer regions more heavily than poorer regions. Changes in agricultural taxation should be based on a careful weighing of the impact on producer incentives.

In summary, it can be stated that taxation has not been used as an important instrument in the redistribution of income in the Ivory

Coast, although the agricultural pricing system has shifted substantial financial resources from farmers to the public sector. Only the personal income tax, which primarily affects wage and salary earners, can be singled out as a progressive tax. Its contribution to a more equal income distribution is limited by its relatively small contribution to total revenue and by features reducing its progressivity. The other taxes are, on the whole, probably somewhat progressive at very low levels of income and then become basically proportional. Studies show that a lack of progressivity of the tax structure is a common feature in developing countries; the Ivory Coast is no exception. Efforts to increase the progressivity of the tax system should concentrate on widening the scope of its progressive elements and on reducing its more regressive ones. Eliminating the split system that adjusts the tax liability for the number of dependents and strengthening real estate and inheritance taxes should certainly be part of such a program. Studying the extension of the income tax to the agricultural sector would also appear to be desirable. The reduction of the most regressive elements in the tax structure should concentrate on the gradual exemption from value-added taxes and import duties of those basic necessities still taxed.

Redistribution through public expenditure

Public expenditure is a major tool in improving distribution of income. This aspect of a number of programs is discussed below.

Public education and housing. Education and public housing are two sectors in which government policy seems to have benefited the better-off more than the poor. Educational expenditures, as indicated earlier, are high indeed, and the results in terms of enrollment are impressive. The level of education is not uniform in the country, but this should not be expected in one as young as the Ivory Coast. With so many different languages being spoken, the national language, French, is an important unifier, and the government has been prepared to invest heavily to have it taught. The introduction of educational television will gradually give a better regional coverage; this is important because unemployment surveys show that unemployment is highest among the illiterate. It appears that the better-off families in particular benefit from higher education, which is heavily subsidized. Because the better incomes obtained by graduates are subject to a tax system with a low progression, the pressure on the budget for education could be alleviated by granting scholarships only in exceptional cases and by requiring students themselves to finance a much larger part of their educations. (See Appendix D on "Education.")

Public housing has been provided mainly in Abidjan and is generally of high standard. Standards are so high, in fact, that in many cases only the wealthier and middle-class segments of the population can afford to use these services, even at subsidized rates. Many of the tenants in public housing could pay more. This is another indication that the well-off families have benefited more than the poorer families.

The government is reconsidering its policies in education and public housing. Quite drastic changes will be necessary, however, to yield tangible results. Income distributional aspects should receive major attention in the reforms. In both areas, a lowering of cost by modifying the standards should be possible. At the same time, charging the wealthier families a higher proportion of the actual cost of the services provided would go a long way toward greater equity. In this way, public funds would be set free and could be directed to those who are really needy.

The Cotton Areas Rural Development Project.   The Cotton Areas Rural Development Project was specifically designed to raise the income of the lowest income groups in ecologically disfavored areas by inducing a combination of technical and institutional changes. The Ivory Coast started a cotton development program in 1964 with the support of the Caisse Centrale de Coopération Economique (CCCE), Fonds d'Aide et de Coopération (FAC), and Fonds Européen de Développement (FED). Since excellent progress was made with the initial project, the government invited CCCE and the World Bank to cofinance the next stage of agricultural and rural development efforts for the cotton areas. This includes promoting the combined expansion and improvement of cotton in rotation with maize, rice, and groundnuts, and the introduction of ox-drawn cultivation. The objective is to modernize farm systems in parts of the savannah region. Feeder roads and bridges, wells for village water supply, ginneries and storage facilities, training, and a maize seed farm are all integrated parts of the project now under implementation. At full development, six years after the beginning of the project, 84,000 families—about 600,000 persons—will benefit; the average per capita money income of the beneficiaries is expected to increase by 80 percent, and total per capita income should increase by 40 percent. The project will lay the basis for further improvements in

production techniques and will render further efforts toward mechanization and other forms of modernization more successful. Cotton is
thus a crop that promises to produce benefits for lower income rural
groups.

Income effects of past and present agricultural programs. In addition to
the cotton program, development activities have included a number of
rice projects, extension of cocoa and coffee production, experiments
with arabusta (a new coffee variety), experiments in soybean production, cattle projects (essentially for the north), and projects for oil palm,
coconut, pineapple, banana, sugar, and rubber production. Moreover,
the effect of past planting of crops such as cocoa, coffee, and oil palm
will be felt in the future, whether they were the result of specific
projects or of the reaction of farmers to price policies. Two calculations
of the impact of these developments on money income in agriculture
in 1980 have been made. The first assumes that the population increases will be distributed in the same way as was the population in
1973 (Assumption 1); the second, that the rural population by department will continue to change as it did between 1965 and 1973 (Assumption 2). The results are given in Table 6.7. Regardless of which
population figures are taken, a substantial change toward more equality
in the regional distribution of income is implied. The policies of the
government are in part designed to stem the flow of population into
the cities and, if possible, to reverse this trend. It is likely that the
combination of rising incomes and job availability in poorer areas,
together with social expenditures to make life more pleasant, will in
fact induce people to stay. At the same time, a falling per capita income
in other areas would induce people to look elsewhere for opportunities.
Thus, migration movements could be substantially modified as a result
of changes in per capita income.

A word of caution is required concerning the interpretation of the
results. First, the calculations partly reflect actual implementation of
government programs but often they reflect only the government's
intentions; they assume that everything will go according to plan.
There have been and there will be slippages, perhaps very substantial
ones. The introduction of new technologies in the north will, in the
absence of substantial experience, take time. Second, some of the price
policies may turn out to be inconsistent, as discussed above in the case
of rice. A high producer price involves the government in substantial
subsidies, which in turn reduce public savings. If many nonagricultural
projects are undertaken and if their payoff is either too little or too
late, the government may feel compelled to delay some of the prom-

TABLE 6.7. REGIONAL AGRICULTURAL PER CAPITA MONEY
AND SUBSISTENCE INCOME AS PERCENTAGES
OF INCOME IN THE SOUTH

Region	Assumption 1			Assumption 2	
	1970–72	1975–76	1979–80	1975–76	1979–80
North	47	57	74	62	97
East	86	81	77	85	92
South	100	100	100	100	100
West	50	48	55	51	67
Center West	71	84	98	84	94
Center	83	64	72	68	89
Southwest	50	51	59	51	60
South (in CFAF)[a]	27,839	49,872	58,563	45,819	43,324

Source: World Bank estimates.
a. 1970–72 (the average of two crop years) is in producer prices of 1973; the rest
is in 1975 prices.

ising agricultural projects or to reverse some farm price policies in
order to raise public savings. The encouraging point is that the government has apparently identified a number of projects with favorable
growth and income distribution features. It is not always necessary to
choose between the two; both can be pursued at the same time. The
danger is that the government may commit itself to the implementation
of too many projects within too short a time span. To remain within
the limits of the available resources, priorities will have to be set.

The regionalized investment program. In the last two Ivorian development plans, regionalization has received increasing emphasis. The
objective of the regionalization policy is the reduction of regional disparities in income and development. The use of public investment
programs and special incentives to achieve this aim is an important
aspect of the development strategy of the Ivory Coast. In the years
immediately following independence, the outward-oriented policy led
to investment in areas that were already well endowed and productive,
primarily Abidjan and the cocoa area known as the Boucle du Cacao.
These areas would produce the most rapid growth for the least effort.
But a number of factors caused increased attention to be paid to areas
other than the south. These included the pressure of large-scale migration to the south, especially to Abidjan, population pressure in the
developed areas, technological change, the need for increased food production, and political pressure from the underprivileged regions. In

the late 1960s an ambitious program began to develop the potentially rich but sparsely populated southwest, while the Kossou hydroelectric scheme was coupled with a rural development program to transform the agricultural system in the center region. This program became increasingly important when most of the persons displaced by the lake behind the Kossou dam decided not to resettle in the sparsely populated southwest.

The 1971–75 plan recognized regional problems and began to identify investments by area as well as by sector. The efforts at regional planning have been conducted by a central planning office with a national orientation and with central control of the allocation of funds. In 1972 the Direction de l'Aménagement du Territoire et de l'Action Régionale (DATAR) was created in the Ministry of Planning to coordinate the regional aspects of the plan and to develop specifically regional programs. DATAR's primary efforts to date have been the regional classification of the government's investment program and the identification of regional problems. DATAR will ultimately develop a coherent program of regional planning based on the regions, as distinct from a national plan broken down into regional components. Local groups lacked the staff and expertise to contribute effectively to regional aspects of the national plan. The result is that consultation with regional bodies has been largely perfunctory. A major exception was the Programme du Nord, a largely impromptu program drawn up following the president's visits to the north in 1974 and in response to the Sahelian drought and expressions of social discontent in the area. The program led to the allocation of over CFAF20 billion to investment programs in the northern and central regions. It took shape largely outside of the regular planning process and involved the political bodies in the provinces to a meaningful extent. Local officials were able to stress regional goals and to exercise greater control over the allocation of funds. This program has also had the effect of involving a large number of small entrepreneurs in the implementation of local investment projects. In this way much of the direct income benefits of the investment remained in the region. It is not yet clear whether the greater local participation in regional planning will be continued, but the eventual outcome of the program may have important political and economic consequences for the future of regionalization and regional planning.

An analysis of the government's realized and projected investments by region for the 1970s reveals inequalities in the government's own investment program and also shows how this program has changed over time. The country has been divided into seven regions plus the greater Abidjan area, and the allocation of investment expenditure has been calculated according to this division (Table 6.8). But there are some disparities both within and among regions. The variation in expenditure between different parts of an area can be very large, for example between Bouaké and Yamoussoukro, both in the country's center. Abidjan gets the lion's share of public investments, but large shares go to the north, south, center, and southwest. The majority of planned investments in the north go for economic development (57.8 percent) and economic infrastructure (27.0 percent). This is in striking contrast to the other regions, where most investments go for economic infrastructure. Only in the city of Abidjan are more than two-fifths of investments spent on social infrastructure and only in the southwest are economic development and economic infrastructure about equally important. In the 1976–80 plan the proportion of investment for the north and the southwest is expected to stay at a high level. The large investments are the result of an ambitious sugar program in the north, as well as the further development of infrastructure and agriculture, and plans for an iron ore mine and a paper pulp plant in the southwest.

Table 6.9 gives a breakdown of per capita public investment by region. It is based on a series of Loi Programmes, and although it is incomplete for the later years the proportions still indicate priorities. The increases in the north and the southwest stand out clearly. On a per capita basis, the southwest has received very high levels of investment in the recent past. These levels are associated with the selection of San Pédro as a new pole of development. Abidjan, continuing to benefit from high levels of investment per capita, is second only to the southwest and is substantially above the national average.

The government's regional development strategy is basically determined by a particular region's growth potential. When it has identified a vehicle for growth, the government seems prepared to direct substantial resources to the area, even though the benefits may not accrue for many years. The authorities realize that for the development of a region a balanced approach is required and that investments in production have to be complemented by expenditures for social and cultural development. Although no regional breakdown of 1976–80 public investments is yet available, there are indications that the government is prepared to invest more in such areas as the east, west, and center west. These investments would be in addition to an already sizable public investment program, rather than the result of a reallocation of investments within an existing program. But given resource con-

TABLE 6.8. PERCENTAGE DISTRIBUTION OF PLANNED PUBLIC INVESTMENT
BY MAJOR PROGRAM, 1975–77

Program	North [a]	East	South	West	Center West	Center	South-west	City of Abidjan	Total allocated	Grand [a] total
Economic development	57.8	0.0	18.8	28.2	11.9	23.2	39.2	10.9	26.9	26.9
Economic infrastructure	27.0	58.4	76.2	68.6	34.0	39.7	41.8	26.4	41.1	39.6
Social development	9.2	30.8	2.8	0.4	31.6	18.6	14.9	41.5	20.2	19.6
Cultural development	5.4	5.1	2.0	2.9	22.5	17.2	3.7	11.3	8.3	7.8
Central government [b]	0.7	5.7	0.2	0.0	0.0	1.2	0.4	9.9	3.4	6.1
Total (percent)	17.8	0.4	18.2	2.8	1.7	14.8	14.0	30.3	100.0	100.0
Total (CFAF billion)	46.9	1.0	47.8	7.4	4.5	38.8	36.9	79.6	263.0	378.7

Source: Loi Programmes 1975–77; Ministry of Planning.
a. Does not include all expenditure for the Programme du Nord.
b. Includes defense.

TABLE 6.9. PUBLIC INVESTMENT PER CAPITA BY REGION, 1971–77
(CFAF thousands)

Region	1971	1972	1973	1974	1975 [a]	1976 [a]	1977 [a]	1971–77	1973 population [b]
North	1.3	10.8	21.3	18.4	27.0	28.8	29.4	137.0	554.6
East	5.3	0.4	0.4	1.1	1.5	1.1	1.5	11.3	266.5
South	6.5	7.7	6.3	8.2	12.3	13.2	13.6	67.9	1,193.6
West	0.3	3.4	2.3	3.7	4.6	2.8	3.1	20.2	701.9
Center West	0.3	0.1	0.1	0.7	2.5	3.2	0.6	7.6	712.0
Center	10.8	11.5	9.2	11.0	13.5	10.4	4.3	70.7	1,490.4
Southwest	49.4	17.9	13.5	33.3	60.3	75.0	102.6	351.9	156.0
Abidjan	11.7	14.5	23.0	31.1	41.4	33.0	22.4	177.0	840.0
Nonallocated	2.3	2.8	3.0	4.2	6.2	6.8	6.9	32.2	—
Total	9.6	11.0	12.4	16.1	22.9	22.1	19.8	113.8	5,910.0

— Not applicable.
Source: Ministry of Planning.
a. Projected.
b. In thousands. The 1973 population was used for all years. Thus, figures for the later years are biased upward in comparison with earlier years.

straints, the authorities should set priorities among the many economic, social, and cultural investment opportunities. If resource constraints force a delay in the implementation of some investments, which is likely, income inequalities for some areas may persist for a longer time than anticipated.

Ivorianization and employment policy

The blend of foreign production factors with local factors in Ivorian economic development has been mentioned. It is only logical that as more and more graduates have become available, the pressure to Ivorianize the top positions has increased. Government policy stresses that Ivorianization of positions in government and business should proceed as quickly as possible. It is realized that Ivorianization of capital and labor should be pursued concurrently since the two are linked on both the Ivorian and the foreign side. It would be difficult, although not inconceivable, to Ivorianize one without losing the other. At the same time, it is recognized that the presence of foreign labor and capital has allowed more rapid growth and probably a faster increase in productivity than would otherwise have been possible. Without the continued benefits of foreign production factors, the government realizes, development will not continue as it has in the past. Therefore, Ivorianization will probably be carried out gradually (a trademark of Ivorian policies) and selectively. Positions in which the comparative advantage of the expatriates has disappeared will be Ivorianized and other expatriates will be called in to support new government initiatives, such as the increased emphasis on the export of locally processed raw materials. Ivorianization is not meant to force out foreign production factors that can still be used advantageously; however, for a continuation of sound growth, the economy should utilize relatively more Ivorian production factors, labor as well as capital.

Ivorianization of capital

Agriculture is almost completely in the hands of Ivorians. Foreign ownership is still widespread, however, in forestry, industry, and modern commerce, although steady progress in Ivorianization is being made. At the end of 1975, national participation in the equity of commercial and development banks was 54.5 percent, of which about one-fifth was owned by private Ivorians. At the beginning of 1975 the government held 25 percent of the equity in the industrial sector and private Ivorians held an additional 9 percent; the rest was in the hands of foreigners.

When national savings fell short of investments, part of the capital needs had to be provided by foreign sources. The Ivory Coast deliberately offered incentives to foreigners to invest in forestry, industry, and commerce. The response was such that these sectors are now largely controlled by foreigners. Because this was deemed unacceptable in the long run, measures were taken from the outset to regain control eventually. In 1962 the government set up SONAFI (the Société Nationale de Financement) to acquire equity in foreign-controlled enterprises. This equity is to be disseminated by means of a stock exchange, which started operation in 1976. SONAFI's resources are about CFAF12.5 billion. Nine bond issues[8] provided 65 percent of this amount and the government provided 35 percent. The savings of most Ivorian nationals are still low, the preference for liquidity is high, and many savers apparently find other uses for their capital such as in agriculture and real estate. The success of the stock exchange will

---

8. Largely subscribed by FNI certificates, which each firm receives in return for the 10 percent of its annual net profit it has to pay to the government. This is not a tax; the certificates are reimbursed against an investment considered appropriate by the government.

depend on establishing confidence in investments in negotiable financial instruments and on providing these instruments with liquidity, security, and after-tax returns. The stock exchange should try to capture new savings rather than compete for existing savings. Perhaps the stock market could be a means of reducing investments abroad by Ivorians and expatriates (although the latter in principle can only buy bonds). By limiting investment abroad, it would be a useful instrument in increasing local savings that should have high priority in government policy. This point will be discussed further in Chapter 8.

Ivorianization of capital, that is, increasing the proportion of Ivorian-owned capital, should be pursued strongly by encouraging the establishment of national enterprises. Government policy thus far has concentrated much more on relatively sophisticated, capital-intensive industrialization. In several instances it has discriminated against the informal sector and small-scale enterprises. These enterprises have great difficulty obtaining capital. Existing banks have no incentive to lend to them. The new (1975) central bank regulations favor credit to small national enterprises; they enable changes to take place in the right direction and are an important step in Ivorianizing the economy.

Ivorianization at the top

The Ivorianization Commission, which consists of representatives of the government, industry, and workers, is primarily concerned with Ivorianization at the top of the professional ladder. Policies state that Ivorianization should proceed as fast as possible without disrupting production or growth. It is also stated that policies should favor the employment of Ivorians, that decisionmaking processes should be transferred to nationals, and that policies should try to foster the growth of Ivorian enterprises. It is understood that more is involved than simply replacing expatriates with Ivorians. A change in expectations and attitudes must take place as well. The approach is to try to build up Ivorian enterprises in addition to, not merely in place of, foreign businesses.

Ivorianization at the supervisory and managerial level is seen as essentially a matter of the proper education and training of Ivorians. Manpower planning must determine the needs of the economy, the number of people who should receive certain types of education, and the means of channeling them into certain fields. At the university level scholarships are already being used to influence students. Formal education has to be supplemented by on-the-job training, and there must be a change from a civil service to a private enterprise attitude. In the government itself, decentralization is under discussion and ways are being explored to receive more input directly from the people, as was done in the case of the Programme du Nord. But it is realized also that Ivorianization must not endanger the hitherto successful open-door policy. The Ivorianization Commission, in cooperation with the private sector, has prepared an Ivorianization plan for the next five years. The results, given in Table 6.10, propose for 1975–79 doubling the number of Ivorians at the top, reducing the number of expatriates by a third, and maintaining essentially the same number of other Africans. This plan is subject, however, to certain limitations: A limited number of Ivorians with adequate experience is coming into the labor market; the ages of existing Ivorian supervisors and managers are such that they will not retire for some time; and the efficiency of the enterprises must be preserved.

Provided the efficiency of the enterprises does not suffer, businesses have every economic interest in Ivorianization. Category by category Ivorians cost less than expatriates. If efficiency suffers, Ivorianization could be costly to the economy. If efficiency does not suffer, or suffers only briefly—the time element here is important and a short-term loss may well justify a long-term gain—any delay in Ivorianization would be costly to the economy and would, of course, also exacerbate domestic political problems. It would be felt that qualified Ivorians were being deliberately held back and that expatriates were extracting a disproportionate share not commensurate with their contribution. That profits and expatriate savings are transferred cannot in itself be considered a drain on the economy. Most expatriates have in all likelihood

TABLE 6.10. PROPOSED IVORIANIZATION OF
SUPERVISORS AND MANAGERS IN
PRIVATE INDUSTRY, 1975–79

Nationality	1975	1976	1977	1978	1979
Ivorians	1,423	1,874	2,339	2,499	2,750
Other Africans	199	195	192	192	190
Expatriates	2,305	2,144	1,959	1,815	1,665
Total	3,927	4,213	4,490	4,506	4,605

Note: For purposes of comparison, in 1974 a sample of 346 enterprises employing 84,000 workers had 3,617 supervisors and managers, of which 1,018 (28.1 percent) were Ivorians, 179 (4.9 percent) were other Africans, and 2,420 (66.9 percent) were expatriates.
Source: Ivorianization Commission.

contributed more to the output of the economy than their pay. Once efficient Ivorians are available, however, the cost of expatriates to the economy becomes substantial. The crux of the Ivorianization policy is to see that Ivorians are efficient and that they replace those foreigners who have lost their comparative advantage. The relatively slow rate of substitution that results from this process must, of course, be politically acceptable.

Ivorianization at the bottom

Over the past decades the availability of low-cost immigrant labor from neighboring countries has been a major factor in the growth of the Ivorian economy. This is especially true in the agricultural sector: Land and foreign and private capital were available while local labor was scarce. The immigration of foreigners has become a problem, however, because the number of foreigners and the number of schooled Ivorians have increased rapidly. The latter now compete for jobs with immigrants who are working in industry and services. More generally, the question has been raised as to whether it is socially and politically tolerable for a third of the population to be foreign, and the proportion is increasing. There is no formal government policy covering this situation. The Ivory Coast's borders have always been open and, in light of the relations developed with francophone neighbors before and after independence, it could not be otherwise. In the 1960s the introduction of double nationality was proposed, but this idea was not pursued. Some form of a more permanent integration of other Africans into Ivorian society may develop in the longer run. The problem is of central political importance and must be dealt with by the Ivorians themselves. Within the regional context, however, no purely legal or administrative solutions would be really workable unless they were supported by economic policies.

Since mid-1975 a new element has entered into the problem of other African workers in the Ivory Coast. The government of Upper Volta has asked that it be given a financial compensation directly from the Ivorian government for every citizen of Upper Volta working in the Ivory Coast. Thus far, the Ivorian government has refused to do this. It seems to have affected the flow of labor; since mid-1975 several areas and projects have suffered from labor shortages. The low wages in agriculture may also play a role, but even projects willing to pay a substantial premium have had labor problems. It would be difficult to predict the outcome of the negotiations between the governments, but an increase in the cost of agricultural labor seems likely. This could have a profound impact on employment in agriculture. First, it would enhance mechanization. It is hoped that this would take place gradually because rapid mechanization and motorization in the absence of sufficient experience invariably leads to high costs. Second, the higher remuneration may encourage young Ivorian families to work their own plots, although it might not be enough to lead many more Ivorians to accept positions as hired laborers.

If the Ivorian government, under the pressure of the demand from its own labor force, were to favor a national rather than a regional (in the sense of the Ivory Coast and its neighbors) employment policy, it could take many forms. For example, in industry and services management could be informed that the government prefers to see Ivorians employed rather than other Africans. Non-Ivorians could be left out of housing and other service schemes. It is interesting to review the characteristics of developments in the north and the southwest from the standpoint of the two employment policies. Investments in the north and center—in the parts that are relatively densely populated by Ivorian smallholders—are aimed at transforming the farming system. In the sparsely populated southwest a fair amount of foreign labor will be needed to make the development program a success. Because of the low density of Ivorians in the latter area, the proportion of foreigners may reach a high level indeed. Both regions will no doubt be developed at the same time; the question is at what pace and in what mix will the development take place. More emphasis on the southwest would tend to favor a regional employment policy, while emphasis on the north would tend to favor a national one. As indicated earlier, more is at stake here. On the one hand, it may be that if market prospects, investments in infrastructure, and remuneration of foreign factors are taken into account, investment in agriculture in the southwest could be better than investment in agriculture in the north. On the other hand, considering the income distribution aspects of investment in the north, such factors as the political cost of not investing in the north, together with the possibility of intensifying the nationality issue by investing in the southwest, may lead the government to decide that the north is a better investment after all. If, with all costs taken into account, the benefits of investment in the southwest are large and come fast enough, the government could decide to give priority to this area and use the proceeds to continue to subsidize the creation of employment in other agricultural areas and in other sectors, implementing policies similar to those followed thus far. The final mix should depend on both costs and benefits and on how the government evaluates its priorities.

Employment policies

A policy aimed at employment creation in general will best serve the Ivory Coast and its neighbors. In this respect, three measures are theoretically possible: (a) a devaluation of the CFA franc to induce, where technologically possible, a substitution of domestic Ivorian factors for imported factors; (b) an increase in interest rates to substitute, where technologically possible, labor for capital; and (c) a reduction in wages with the same effect. All these policies involve institutional problems. A devaluation of the CFA franc by the Ivory Coast alone is inconsistent with membership in the franc area. The advantages to the Ivory Coast of belonging to the franc area are still great and probably outweigh any advantage to be gained from devaluation at this time. Although second best, a policy of manipulating tariffs and subsidies would be a reasonable substitute for devaluation, while preserving the convertibility of the CFA franc. Such a policy, in fact, is already being followed by the government. Although effective protection rates have on the whole not been excessive, in a number of cases value added in the world market and even in domestic prices was negative, which implies that in the domestic economy more resources were spent to produce less. A reconsideration of the tariff structure should therefore be a part of an employment policy. With it would go a reconsideration of the investment code and any special privileges that make foreign capital particularly expensive. The use of foreign capital is economically justified in terms of growth and employment only if, measured in world market prices, it creates more resources than it uses up. It should also be realized that if labor costs (especially those in industry, which are presently high because of the number of expatriates and the relatively high local wages in this sector) could be brought down, for instance by not fully compensating for inflation, a major reason for costly protection of industry would have lost some of its relevance.

Like devaluation, the use of interest rates to induce changes in factor proportions and capital formation runs into obstacles. As a member of the West African Monetary Union (UMOA), the Ivory Coast must follow regional policy. In spite of the obstacles, changes have continuously been introduced in the monetary system, an important one being the alignment in 1975 of Ivorian interest rates with those prevailing in

France, which meant an increase of 2 percentage points in nonprefer-
ential rates—from a maximum of 11 to 13 percent.[9]

The additional institutional changes needed for a policy that gen-
erates employment are on two different levels: improving the actual
price structure and ensuring that the price signals are actually followed.
A buildup of savings institutions on the one hand, and of institutions
to disburse funds to wider groups of people on the other, might nom-
inally raise interest rates, but real rates would in fact be reduced for
those who previously had to go into the "unorganized" capital market.
Neither devaluation nor higher interest rates would necessarily reduce
total investments since these investments depend essentially on the
imports that can be financed. Import potential would remain determined by export earnings plus what could be financed by capital imports. How investments would be distributed would change, however;
the same amount of imports would employ more domestic resources.
With higher nominal rates of interest, more domestic savings would
become available, but as real rates to borrowers would fall at the same
time—except to the lucky few who had access before—demand would
not fall, and allocations would be different.

There are limits to what can be done by price policy alone, that is,
by simply changing the product mix. Ivorians envisage a modernization
of agriculture by mechanization. But this is much more easily said than
done. First, increased production can be achieved without going
quickly into a highly mechanized agriculture, as demonstrated in the
Cotton Areas Rural Development Project. It is fairly obvious, however, that the strategy employed for this project can be only part of a
long-term development one, which may result in quite a different form
of modernization. Second, the regionalized investment program should
in the longer run shift more toward the provision of amenities. This
would be especially true if it is found that farmers are willing to produce more and to reside in the countryside once life there is made
more attractive.

Third, a long-term development and employment effort would involve a reconsideration of factor proportions. There is on the one hand
a call for mechanization and modernization and for a change in attitude,
while on the other hand the complaint is made that methods developed
in the labor-poor industrialized countries are not really adapted to
(supposedly) labor-rich Africa. At the same time, it is argued that the

9. The basic discount rate has changed from 3.5 percent before 1973 to 8 percent
after July 1975.

Ivory Coast is really labor-poor, as proven by the large foreign labor force. The point is that even apart from cultural differences, labor in industrialized countries embodies a large element of investment in education and training, which has led not only to the widening of horizons but also to an increased capacity for cooperation with other factors. A machine will increase production, but only if used and maintained properly. The required change in attitude includes knowledge not only of how to be a better farmer and how to use a machine, but also of how to make better use of a government agent. Such labor takes time to create, and machinery is not really a substitute for it but a complement. Mechanization could be seen as an Ivorianization policy. Here again a comparison of the north and the southwest is interesting. Although the farming system in the north has to be transformed first in order to make mechanization possible, the annual crops that are and can potentially be grown in the north lend themselves in principle to a certain degree of mechanization. This is much more difficult or even impossible with the tree crops grown in the southwest. Here again, investments in the north would seem to emphasize a national employment policy, while investments in the southwest have stronger regional employment aspects.

CHAPTER SEVEN

The Econometric Model: Favorable Prospects with Policy Changes

TO MAKE A LONG-RUN ANALYSIS of the Ivorian economy and to investigate the implications of policy decisions, the World Bank developed a macroeconomic model. By design the model always projects a growth path with all the accounts balanced and the appropriate identities satisfied. This equilibrium, however, is not necessarily an economic equilibrium because balances may be struck at levels that are not feasible or sustainable. Thus, analysis of the model provides a consistency check on both the exogenously projected variables and the structural parameters and also gives projections of the economy. The model is able to show the long-term effects of a number of policy decisions on the development of the economy. Alternative tests with different policy options can then be made in so-called sensitivity runs to compare policies with respect to their effects both on target variables, such as growth rates, and on the equilibria constraints such as foreign borrowing potential.

In the short run the economic prospects of the Ivory Coast are greatly influenced by transitory events. These can be internal, such as crop failures or surpluses, or external, such as world price changes. In the longer run, however, the conscious policy decisions of the Ivorian authorities have a much greater impact on development than do these temporary fluctuations. Because this report is concerned with the basic strategy choices that face the Ivorian economy, some of which can have an effect only over the longer term, the projections have been extended from 1976 to 1990. It should be emphasized that these projections are not intended to predict the future in any exact way, but rather to suggest the kind of coordinated policy action that should be taken in order to implement an ambitious investment program without running unacceptable risks or resorting to unsustainable levels of foreign borrowing. The shortcomings of this approach are many. The assumptions are based on data that are sometimes far from adequate. For instance, the projections of the future resource gap are very sensitive to difficult-to-predict import and export prices, to changes in productivity, and to import elasticity. Nevertheless, the model is considered a useful tool in making possible future constraints explicit and in investigating how policy changes can affect these constraints.

The model itself is relatively simple, but it permits the investigation of the implications of a broad range of policy actions on the part of the government. The model is used to analyze the effects of the 1976–80 plan in light of the World Bank's evaluations of Ivorian and world economic prospects for the next decade. Since the results suggest that some aspects of the planned program are probably not feasible, the model is used to investigate alternatives that are feasible. Several policy changes are presented that move the economy toward a feasible growth path. The whole exercise is indicative rather than precise, but it does outline the constraints faced by the Ivorian economy over the long term and the kinds of policy changes necessary to remove them.

The Model

The Bank's Ivory Coast model is a two-gap macroeconomic model that is run in either a trade-gap or savings-gap version. In the trade-gap version, with a given level of investment, the export and import flows are forecast and the savings adjust automatically to the realized accounting equilibrium: Investment minus savings equals imports minus exports. In the savings-gap version, levels of investment, exports, and savings are forecast exogenously and imports are adjusted. An important constraint is the availability of funds from abroad to finance the gaps that are projected. The Ivory Coast is forecast to have a net resource or current account deficit that must be financed by inflows of external capital. The gap cannot be allowed to grow larger than can reasonably be expected to be financed from abroad. Basically, the model provides a means of testing hypotheses in three fundamental areas: (a) the consistency of hypotheses relating to growth, savings, and investment; (b) the consistency of hypotheses relating to imports, exports, and the balance of payments; and (c) the implications of these hypotheses with respect to foreign borrowing and future debt service payments.

The model consists of two parts: first, an accounting structure that keeps track of external public debt and, second, a projection model for the national accounts and the balance of payments. For convenience in dealing with the model and in presenting it, the structural equations are divided into several blocks that are developed in detail.

In the "foreign trade" block, exports are projected exogenously, imports are projected in relation to the growth of the rest of the economy, and most other flows are projected exogenously. These projections are made in both constant and current terms using the relevant World Bank price projections. The "national accounts" block disaggregates production of value added into eight sectors for projections and then reaggregates them into primary, secondary, and tertiary production of gross domestic product (GDP). Levels of investment of the administration, the parapublic enterprises, and the private sector are also projected in this block. At this stage it is possible to establish a full set of national accounts in the case when the trade gap is assumed binding and saving is treated as a residual. In the "government and saving" block, a simplified government account is projected, including revenue, expenditure, and saving of the administration and the public enterprises. Private saving is also projected so that total planned or intended saving can be calculated and the investment-saving gap derived. In addition to these blocks, which relate to the economy as a whole, there are blocks for two special projects currently being considered in the Ivory Coast, the iron ore and the paper pulp projects, which will have a great effect on the economy. They are treated separately so that their impact can be analyzed directly. The output of these blocks is integrated into the rest of the model. In addition to separate analysis of the two projects, the use of these blocks allows varying the time of project implementation and testing what would happen if they were not undertaken at all.

The strategy is first to present a base run that represents the Bank's interpretation of plan objectives. Parameters projected from historical data have been modified where recent events or policy changes seemed to warrant it. Because of the Ivorian government's demonstrated ability to implement policy and also its relative efficiency, the parameters selected have in general been optimistic; this selection tends to offset biases in the model in the opposite direction that result from the model's inherent structural rigidity. Even with relatively optimistic parameters, the pattern of development described in the base run was not feasible without major structural changes in the Ivorian economy.

Because there are many policy parameters as well as alternate assumptions about the exogenously projected variables, an exceedingly large number of alternatives could be tested. To prevent the number from becoming too large, a strategy of testing alternatives was developed that focuses on the most interesting questions about the future prospects of the Ivory Coast. The most important of these questions clearly concern the availability of resources needed to undertake the volume and variety of investment projects desired by the authorities. To evaluate resources and investments, a package of policy changes was assembled that reduces the major economic constraints without imposing too great a burden. These changes are not proposed as optimal in any sense, but rather as indicative of the kinds of actions needed to move the economy to a feasible growth path. Alternative mixes within the package or different tools with similar results could be tried for the same effect. Because the model is not sensitive to differences among policy tools, however, tests based on different tools were not run. Of course, the model could be used at any time to test other options.

Once a feasible package of policy options was analyzed, a series of tests was run to determine the effects of the two special projects on the economy. The base run, which includes the two projects, was repeated without them, and then the effects on the economy of the suggested policy package without the special projects was tested. The values of the major variables in each run discussed in this chapter are given for each year for the period 1976–85 in Tables 47–53 of the Statistical Appendix.

A number of indicators are helpful in analyzing, interpreting, and comparing the implications of each sensitivity run. The following indicators are used: (a) growth of gross domestic income (GDY); (b) investments as a proportion of GDY; (c) domestic savings as a proportion of GDY; (d) national savings as a proportion of GDY; (e) the shortfall in national savings needed to finance investments; (f) public savings after debt service as a proportion of public investment; (g) the debt service ratio, defined as public debt payments as a proportion of exports of goods, nonfactor services, and workers' remittances; (h) import elasticity; (i) incremental capital-output ratio (ICOR); and (j) the terms of trade. The various runs using these indicators are summarized in Table 46 of the Statistical Appendix.

The Base Run

The base run is a projection made with generally optimistic values for the various parameters.[1] Initially, the trade-gap option is used, which makes the run unconstrained as far as savings are concerned. At the time of the Bank's field visit in mid-1975, a public investment program for 1976–80 of some CFAF1,350 billion (in 1975 prices) was under discussion. In the expectation that the authorities would be able to scale down this program through arbitration, a public investment program for 1976–80 of CFAF860 billion is assumed for the base run, plus an additional CFAF60 billion (all in 1975 prices) in public investment directly related to the two special projects.

Savings unconstrained base run

The base run projections show a continuing deterioration of the current account. This is the result of rather high imports related to the construction phase of the special projects, moderate export growth, and rising interest payments and workers' remittances. The terms of trade improve to the 1973 level (1973 as 100) in 1978 as a result of better prices for coffee and timber, but thereafter gradually decline year after year to a value of 95 in 1985. Capital inflows are large for the years 1978–82 when most of the investment in the two special projects is assumed to take place. This investment includes both direct investment and borrowed capital. Recourse to foreign financing beyond that available from traditional lenders and that associated with the special projects is moderate through 1980 and is in line with what the country has been able to borrow and should be able to borrow in the future. Additional borrowing needs of the economy increase sharply after 1980, however, as the capital inflow for the special projects begins to slow down. Total gross disbursements of publicly guaranteed debt reach about US$800 million a year in the early 1980s.

The characteristics of the base run are best expressed by the macroeconomic indicators in Statistical Appendix Table 46. They are compared with historical performance in Table 7.1. The projected GDY

---

1. The assumptions underlying the base run are spelled out in the appendix to this chapter. The results for major aggregates and indicators are shown in Table 47 of the Statistical Appendix.

TABLE 7.1. HISTORICAL PERFORMANCE OF VARIOUS
INDICATORS COMPARED WITH BASE RUN
(SAVINGS UNCONSTRAINED), 1965–85

Indicator	Historical performance		Base run (savings unconstrained)	
	1965–70	*1970–75*	*1976–80*	*1981–85*
Annual growth in gross domestic income (percent)	9.9	3.9	8.6	7.0
Investment/gross domestic income	19.9	22.9	29.1	28.1
Domestic saving/gross domestic income	23.0	23.2	29.2	27.8
National saving/gross domestic income	16.4	17.0	22.8	21.2
Investment minus national saving/gross domestic income	3.5	5.9	6.3	6.9
Net public saving/public investment	55.0	40.0	43.7	26.4
Debt service ratio (percent)	6.9	8.9	10.8	12.8
Import elasticity	1.1	1.1	1.2	0.8
Incremental capital-output ratio	2.7	4.1	3.8	4.3

Source: Statistical Appendix Tables 47–49.

annual growth rate, a satisfactory 8.1 percent from 1976 to 1980 and
6.7 percent in the subsequent five years, compares favorably with past
performance. Much of the growth during the period 1976–80 is due
to the investment boom caused by the construction of the special
projects. Real growth of the construction sector is 25 percent a year
in 1978 and 1979 and 13 percent in 1980. It remains constant for the
next two years, and then drops in 1983 as construction of the special
projects is finished. This slack is taken up by the paper pulp and iron
ore projects themselves as they begin operation in 1981 and 1983 respectively. Because their combined total share of GDP in 1985 is less
than 2 percent, the impact of the special projects on the overall growth
rate is less marked than was the investment boom of the late 1970s
associated with the two projects. The investment share of GDY rises
from 22.9 percent in 1970–75 to 29.1 percent, which suggests a major
structural shift in the economy in the coming plan period. In spite of
the considerable increase in investment, growth is not faster because
the ICOR values are above long-run historical levels. These values are
consistent, however, with recent rising costs of investment for a unit
of growth in the Ivory Coast. The debt service ratio rises during the
whole projection period to 12.0 percent in 1980 and to 12.6 percent in

1985, but this growth is not alarming. It should be noted that this ratio does not include direct investment income payments, which should be considered if the Ivory Coast is going to continue its policy of free capital movement. If these payments were included, they would add 4 to 5 percentage points to the debt service ratio. The capacity of the public sector to contribute, in terms of net savings, to the financing of the public investment program decreases from 43.7 percent in 1976–80 to 26.4 percent in 1981–85, and in fact falls constantly from 53 percent in 1976 to 21 percent in 1985.

The most striking feature of the base run, with its open-ended savings assumption, is the level of savings that the economy will have to generate. Domestic savings have to go up from 23 percent of GDY, the historical level, to around 28 percent; for national savings the figures are from about 17 percent to 22 percent. The obvious implication of the base run projection is that there will have to be an important shift in the savings behavior of the Ivory Coast economy in the next five years. The government's plan has not explained how this will come about. In fact, one of the implications of the base run is that the share of the public sector in total domestic savings will decline over time. Because of high interest payments, the decline in the public sector's contribution to national savings is even sharper. The government has traditionally been a major source of savings and is planning to undertake an increasing share of total investment. In the past the ability of the government to carry out its ambitious investment programs and to borrow abroad has been based on its proven ability to generate and save significant amounts of resources. If it cannot maintain its share in the total saving effort, this raises questions not only about the investment program but also about the continued ability of the government to mobilize the necessary foreign resources.

The major conclusions to be drawn from an analysis of the base run relate to the availability and use of resources during the next five to ten years. Most important is the inadequacy of national savings to meet the investment demand and the increased dependence on foreign resources. The base run gives an accurate estimate of the gross borrowing necessary, but only if the required national savings are generated. The situation when they are not generated is described in the sensitivity runs.

In the final analysis, the development pattern shown in the base run does not seem feasible in the short run without major structural changes. Given the structure of the Ivorian economy and its foreseeable growth path, it will not generate enough resources to finance the investment targets and to continue its past consumption growth. Foreign borrowing, especially on commercial terms, cannot be used in large quantities to finance the level of structural disequilibrium in the savings-investment balance that is implicit in the projections covering the next ten years. The rising levels of gross disbursements and debt service cannot be sustained. In effect, investment projections in the base run considerably exceed the historical trend; national savings substantially higher than the historical trend would have to be generated quickly and this does not seem feasible.

Savings constrained base run

In applying the savings constraint to the base run (see Statistical Appendix Table 48), savings are no longer calculated as a residual of the projected trade gap and investment program of the economy. Instead, savings are calculated from projections of revenues and expenditures for the public sector and from past savings behavior for the parapublic and private sectors. Any gap between projected savings and planned investment must be financed by net foreign resources, primarily by borrowing. The independent estimation of savings gives projections that are more realistic than those presented in the unconstrained base run, which implicitly assumes that any level of savings needed to satisfy the investment program can be generated.

The effect of applying the savings constraint is startling, as can be seen from Table 7.2. The growth rates and investment shares remain the same as in the base run, but because saving is now forecast independently, the share of domestic saving falls from about 28 percent in 1976–85 in the unconstrained base run to 20.8 percent in 1976–80, and 18.5 percent in 1981–85 in the constrained run. The burden of financing is now on capital from abroad. The investment gap (investment minus national saving) to be financed by foreign resources rises to 16.1 percent of GDY in 1976–80 and to 20.7 percent of GDY in 1981–85. The debt service ratio rises from a 16.1 percent average in 1976–80 to an unsustainable 45.9 percent in 1981–85 and continues rising through the end of the decade. Gross borrowing would have to be about US$2 billion in 1980 alone to finance investment needs plus debt service requirements. The participation of the public sector in financing the public investment program vanishes completely. This means that instead of being able to finance 40 to 50 percent of its investment as it did historically, the public sector would have to obtain foreign financing in 1981–85 for part of its current budget. The accom-

TABLE 7.2. HISTORICAL PERFORMANCE OF VARIOUS
INDICATORS COMPARED WITH BASE RUN
(SAVINGS CONSTRAINED), 1965–85

Indicator	Historical performance		Base run (savings constrained)	
	1965–70	1970–75	1976–80	1981–85
Annual growth in gross domestic income (percent)	9.9	3.9	8.6	7.1
Investment/gross domestic income	19.9	22.9	29.0	28.0
Domestic saving/gross domestic income	23.0	23.2	20.8	18.5
National saving/gross domestic income	16.4	17.0	12.9	7.3
Investment minus national saving/gross domestic income	3.5	5.9	16.1	20.7
Net public saving/public investment	55.0	40.0	32.8	−45.0
Debt service ratio (percent)	6.9	8.9	16.1	45.9
Import elasticity	1.1	1.1	2.1	0.6
Incremental capital-output ratio	2.7	4.1	3.8	4.3

Source: Statistical Appendix Tables 50–52.

panying rise in imports, which accomplishes the real resource transfer, increases the import elasticity to 2.1 in 1976–80. It falls sharply in the following period as imports for the special projects are phased out.

There are two important implications of this constrained run. First, investment programs that greatly and continually exceed the savings potential of the economy are not feasible unless large and growing amounts of external resources are available. Second, foreign borrowing on anything approaching commercial terms is not satisfactory for long-term investments because commercial borrowing builds debt service too rapidly to be feasible in the medium to long run.

Sensitivity Runs

In this section, several alternative means of bringing the economy into balance are investigated. First, some simple changes are introduced. Then a combination of policy changes is employed that increases savings and reduces the investment program to a point at which, given the error inherent in this kind of projection, a feasible path is approached. Finally, a series of sensitivity runs is made in which the special projects are not included. These runs help to describe the net effects of these projects on the economy and to answer the question of whether they are necessary or even beneficial to the stable growth and development of the Ivory Coast.

More rapid growth

Because the Ivorian authorities have been considering alternative projections with higher growth rates, a sensitivity test was made with the savings unconstrained base run, in which the overall GDY growth rate was increased to 9.3 percent a year in 1975–80 and 8.0 percent thereafter. In particular, undefined manufactured exports were assumed to grow more rapidly than in the base run, thus increasing both exports and the value added in that sector. In addition, it was assumed that domestic agriculture and domestic manufacturing grow slightly faster than they do in the savings unconstrained base run. Statistical Appendix Table 49 shows the major aggregate projections; the comparison indicators are shown in Statistical Appendix Table 46. Compared to the base run, the higher growth rate lowers both the investment and savings shares of GDY. Implicitly assumed are more efficient use of investment capital and more successful agricultural programs. The crucial factor, the investments-savings gap, is nearly as large as it is in the base run. The national savings required would still have to be approximately 21 percent of GDY, or about 5 points above the level achieved historically. A major structural change in savings performance would still be required, and such a change would be unlikely in a short period of time. Thus, merely achieving a higher growth rate by improving efficiency somewhat would not solve the problem of the savings gap.

Lower public investment program

Another alternative considered was to bring the public investment program down from CFAF860 billion to CFAF700 billion (1975 prices), excluding the CFAF60 billion public investment directly related to the special projects. Since part of the planned investment is not directly productive and could be delayed or canceled without harming the short-run growth prospects of the economy, the proposed investment program was pared to a minimum level consistent with the growth target of the plan. The lower level of investment leads to a somewhat lower growth rate, primarily because of slower growth in the investment-dependent construction sector. The investment and savings shares of GDY both fall about two to three percentage points compared with the savings unconstrained base run. Foreign resource requirements also fall on the basis of either domestic or national savings when compared with the base run. Incremental capital-output ratios, import elasticities, and debt service ratios are also slightly lower. Required domestic savings fall no lower than an average of 27.7 percent of GDY for the next five years, which is still well above the projected savings rate of about 21 percent. Cutting the public investment program to the bone apparently is not, in itself, a feasible policy either. In other words, if cutting investments were the only policy option, balanced growth could be achieved only by reducing public investments to a level below CFAF700 billion. This would seriously affect the future growth rate, which would drop below 6 percent a year.

A package of policy changes

In order to see what policy changes would be necessary to achieve a feasible growth path, a number of such changes were tested in a series of sensitivity runs. Rather than present a large number of single parameter changes, each of which would have only a small effect, a package of four policy changes was assembled. The package brings the economy much closer to equilibrium. It is not claimed to be an optimal package; to specify an optimal policy package would imply exact knowledge of how much value the government puts on each of its goals. To say the least, it would be presumptuous to assume such knowledge. The package was designed rather to show the kinds of adjustments needed to achieve the external and internal balances that are implicit in the 1976–80 plan and following plans over the next decade.

The four policy changes are as follows: (a) a level of public investment that lies between that of the base run and the lower investment run discussed above; (b) higher retained earnings and savings by public enterprises and the private sector; (c) slower growth of current expenditures by the public sector; and (d) larger tax revenues. In quantitative terms, the changes are given in Table 7.3.

The level of public investment. A public investment program of CFAF810 billion for 1976–80 would, in the opinion of the Bank, enable the economy to continue to grow satisfactorily and at the same time make meaningful progress in improving the living conditions of the

TABLE 7.3. PACKAGE OF POLICY CHANGES
IN QUANTITATIVE TERMS

Item	Base run	Policy package
Public investment, 1976–80, in CFAF billion[a]	860 + 60[b]	750 + 60[b]
Percentage growth of public enterprise saving in real terms	5	8
Private domestic saving as a percentage of disposable income	12	15
Percentage growth of government expenditure in real terms	8	5
Tax burden in percentage of GDP[c]	19	20

Source: World Bank.
a. 1975 prices.
b. Public investment directly related to the two special projects.
c. Excluding revenue of the Stabilization Fund.

poor. A careful project-by-project examination by the mission of the tentative sector proposals put forward by the Ministry of Planning results in the conclusion that investment in agriculture of 61 percent of the amount proposed, and in transport of 56 percent of the amount proposed, seems feasible. With these two sectors taken as indicative of what is feasible in the 1976–80 period, the level of future public investment is placed at 60 percent of the CFAF1,350 billion discussed in an early planning stage;[2] this is equivalent to CFAF810 billion in 1975 prices.

Public enterprise and private sector saving. To achieve the higher saving rate, the growth rate of public enterprise savings is raised to 8 percent and the savings propensity of the private sector is raised to 15 percent of projected disposable income. The increased growth in savings by public enterprises assumes that they will be able to improve their economic performance. It also assumes that improved financial management and more effective control over their investments will yield results; both goals are recommended and the government is taking steps to meet them. Many of the public enterprises operating in the agricultural sector are implementing ambitious programs at high cost, and in several cases a reexamination of policies and objectives seems

2. A May 1976 draft of the 1976–80 plan indicates a public investment program of CFAF1,020 billion (in 1975 prices).

opportune. In the development of new products, the successful oil and coconut palm development company (SODEPALM) is now taken as a model, but it should be remembered that one of the main reasons for SODEPALM's success was the favorable world market price for its products. Moreover, the expenditure pattern of a successful company—especially if it is public—has a tendency to adjust itself to high profits. The development of a new product (such as sugar and to some extent rubber) can certainly benefit from experience elsewhere, but in the end has to be justified on its own merits. For instance, a reexamination of plans for rice and sugar production could improve public enterprise performance. In rice, the level of subsidy could be lowered and objectives could still be met. In sugar, the pace of development could be slowed in order to gain more experience. Such a cautious policy would probably also pay off with regard to the ambitious investment program envisaged for the national shipping line.

The increase in the savings propensity in the private sector is much less subject to analytical justification. The private sector has been an important saver in the past and can continue to be so in the future. Several steps taken by the government indicate the importance authorities give to an improvement in private savings. Interest rates on deposits have been increased, a stock market has been established, and producer prices have been increased regularly. Producer price policies and wage policies are, of course, crucial in this respect. An expansion of the banking system to enable effective mobilization of savings would also be important. A continuation of foreign interest in the Ivory Coast is essential, and the increased emphasis on an export promotion scheme may attract new foreign private capital. There are prospects for increased investment from the private sector if the government continues its liberal policy and if economic conditions in the Ivory Coast and the rest of the world continue to improve. As indicated earlier, Ivorianization, a liberal policy toward foreign investment, and, at the same time, stimulation of local initiative are feasible. If these measures are successful, it will be easier to attain high growth and still achieve the country's official goals for improved regional distribution of investment and development.

Growth of current expenditure.   To increase government savings, it is assumed that the rate of increase of government expenditures on salaries and goods and services will grow by only 5 percent. This is a considerable reduction and assumes that the government will be able to achieve important economies in the use of materials and that there will be an increase in employee productivity. In order to achieve this, the government will have to forego its role of employer of last resort for the large number of secondary school leavers and graduates who are coming into the job market. Part of the economies in wages and salaries could come from increased Ivorianization of the government; this would also reduce the private transfers abroad by expatriates. In addition, to bring its generally high level of labor cost more in line with its competitors, the government should consider undercompensating salary and wage earners for inflation. In some areas, such as housing and education, the government should give more initiative to the private sector and should be less generous in its subsidization. There is a potential danger that cutting back government expenditures may lead to deterioration of services and infrastructure; however, applying more appropriate standards and making better use of existing infrastructure would certainly allow a slower growth of expenditure. Careful consideration during the planning stage of current expenditures by new investments would help to achieve this goal.

Tax revenue.   The last part of the policy package is an increase in government revenues from 19 to 20 percent of GDP, exclusive of the contribution of the Stabilization Fund. Although the current level of taxation is high by both regional and international standards for countries at the Ivory Coast's level of development, the analysis of elasticity and buoyancy indicates that some increase is possible. Some duty levels have already been increased. Some taxes, for instance, those on real estate, have low collection rates and more vigilance in collection would increase government revenues. The possibility of increasing revenues from other taxes also exists.[3]

It should be emphasized that making the policies yield the results indicated here would be a severe task indeed. Scaling down an investment program by means of arbitration would be difficult. Applying more appropriate standards in implementing projects involves a structural change and requires a change in the attitudes of the planners and managers. Many tasks have to be undertaken, the benefits of which will accrue only in the long run. The financing of these tasks has to

3. In March 1976 the government announced a number of tax increases. Profit tax was increased from 35 percent to 40 percent as of November 1, 1975. Payroll tax for locals was increased from 2 to 4 percent, and for expatriates from 7 to 9 percent as of January 1, 1976. Value added tax was increased from 16 to 17 percent as of March 12, 1976. A preliminary estimate of the tax revenue generated by these increases is 0.6 percent of the GDP.

come from revenue earned elsewhere. The base run indicates that satisfactory future growth cannot be achieved by following past trends;
insurmountable debt problems would arise even if foreign capital
sources were not limited. Recent tax increases, the start that has been
made in reorganizing public enterprises, and the effort made to increase
local savings are all very encouraging.[4] These actions are consistent
with the tradition of responsive management that Ivorian authorities
have shown in the past. They strengthen the belief that, although the
proposed policies are tough, they can be implemented successfully.

Statistical Appendix Tables 46 and 50 present the results of applying
these four policy assumptions, combined with the "more rapid growth"
alternative discussed above, and the savings constraint. These results
are summarized in Table 7.4. Growth in this run is very satisfactory.

TABLE 7.4. HISTORICAL PERFORMANCE OF VARIOUS INDICATORS
COMPARED WITH BASE RUN (POLICY PACKAGE AND
SAVINGS CONSTRAINED), 1965–85

	Historical performance		Base run (policy package; savings constrained)	
Indicator	1965–70	1970–75	1976–80	1981–85
Annual growth in gross domestic income (percent)	9.9	3.9	8.9	7.8
Investment/gross domestic income	19.9	22.9	27.3	25.5
Domestic saving/gross domestic income	23.0	23.2	25.5	24.9
National saving/gross domestic income	16.4	17.0	18.8	17.8
Investment minus national saving/gross domestic income	3.5	5.9	8.5	7.7
Net public saving/public investment	55.0	40.0	63.2	51.1
Debt service ratio (percent)	6.9	8.9	11.1	18.2
Import elasticity	1.1	1.1	1.5	0.4
Incremental capital-output ratio	2.7	4.1	3.5	3.6

Source: Statistical Appendix Tables 56–58.

4. World prices for the Ivory Coast's main products, coffee and cocoa, were revised
upward during 1976 and are forecast to stay at a rather high level. The earnings of the
Stabilization Fund for the next two to three years will therefore be substantial; it will
help generate the savings, directly or via the policy package, required for the successful
implementation of an impressive public investment program of roughly CFAF800 billion.

The key factor in this test is that the projected level of savings generated in the economy has risen significantly. This sharply reduces
reliance on foreign resources in comparison with the base run. The
lower level of borrowing leads to debt service ratios that average 11.1
percent in 1976–80 and 18.2 percent in 1981–85. In 1985 the ratio
reaches over 19 percent, which is probably still too high. The challenge
of such a course is twofold—to maintain a strong economy and to
convince foreign lenders that it will remain so. Given the current world
economic situation, this will not be an easy task.

Unlike the constrained base run, without the policy package this run
does not have a sudden greatly expanded need for foreign financing.
The overall effect of the policy package is to bring the economy to a
new, nearly feasible growth path. This path is different from that
followed in the past and does involve structural transformation of the
economy. The need for such a transformation has been recognized by
the government since the beginning of its planning exercises. The implied path is one of high saving and high growth and involves major
investments in infrastructure and diversification as well as in the development of productive capacity itself. This run shows the sort of
policy changes that are needed to get the economy on a feasible growth
path for the next decade. It is the savings constrained runs that are
valid for the analysis since they project what will happen based on the
levels of savings that the economy is likely to generate, not on the
savings that would be required.

The higher incremental capital-output ratios (ICORS) reflect a number
of factors, including the shift from traditional to more modern agriculture, the greater capital intensity of new industrial projects, and the
longer gestation period of investment in structural changes in urban
and rural areas. The increased emphasis on industrial expansion, particularly the emphasis on large-scale units, will absorb large amounts
of capital for each unit of increased production. It is argued that large
size is necessary to achieve economies of scale that will be required in
the longer term as demand increases and as the economy begins to
compete more effectively on world markets. This argument is valid
only if real demand does grow sufficiently and if the Ivory Coast does
enter world markets. Development in the agricultural sector is also
becoming more industrial and is using more capital. This is true of
both some smallholder schemes involving irrigation investments and
of plantations, where investment per unit of output or per employee
can be as high or higher than that in industry. This shift in the agricultural production function may not always be avoidable. If, however,

that sector is to maintain its important role as a primary engine of growth in the Ivory Coast, the margin between costs and benefits will have to be worked out carefully. Rapid urban growth is already a reality. High levels of investment will be required to provide the expected amounts of housing and urban services even if the standards are reduced.

The projections presented so far are optimistic. They assume that no major external crises—caused by adverse world price changes, weather, or otherwise—will occur and that the assumed policy changes will be implemented quickly and efficiently. To the extent that the levels projected are not attained, the economy will face serious problems, which will be evident first as abnormal declines in foreign exchange reserves and sharp increases in foreign borrowing. This will lead to higher debt service payments, harder terms for credit if indeed external credit remains available, and fewer resources available for investment. The investment program will be delayed, if not seriously damaged, and real growth will fall. The danger of following a strategy that makes few provisions for unexpected difficulties is that although potential gains are larger, so are the potential losses. That is the wager now implicit in the Ivorian development strategy. A fair assessment of the policy package projections is that if they are feasible, and they are just barely, a major effort in both the public and private sectors will be required. Implicitly, goals would not be reached when conditions are not met, and consequently it would be necessary to reexamine priorities and objectives. If there are advantageous unforeseen developments, like the upward revision of world price forecasts for coffee and cocoa, the severe policy package might be relaxed somewhat and the economy would still be able to generate the savings to implement the ambitious public investment program of about CFAF800 billion in 1975 prices.

No special projects

In the projections discussed thus far it has been assumed that the two special projects would be implemented. In this section the effect on the economy of not undertaking the special projects will be projected and a determination will be made of whether it is possible to achieve a feasible growth path without them. Since the model has treated them as separate blocks, excluding them from the runs presents no technical difficulty. First, the model was run with the base run assumptions but without the special projects. Then the policy package was introduced with and without the saving constraint. And finally, a test was made with only the paper pulp project and the policy package (excluding increased taxes) with the savings constraint. Before turning to these runs, the major aspects of each of these two projects will be summarized.

The iron ore mine and paper pulp projects were included in the 1971–75 plan for partial implementation during that period, but no start had been made at the end of the period. Activity around these projects has gradually intensified, however, and the government now intends to start both in the 1976–80 planning period. Although information is rather sketchy, the investment involved is so huge that an attempt has been made to gauge the impact on the Ivorian economy in terms of a change in major macroeconomic parameters. Sensitivity runs were made using the macroeconomic model with and without these two projects.

Both projects are located in the southwest. The iron ore deposits are about 350 kilometers north of San Pédro, and the idea is to upgrade the 40 percent ore content to 65 percent and transport the pellets by rail to the port of San Pédro at a rate of 12 million tons a year. The paper pulp project would produce 250,000 to 400,000 tons a year based on the utilization of mixed tropical hardwood or pulpwood or both. These projects are receiving considerable attention from the government; they would make the Ivory Coast the most industrialized country in West Africa and might improve its chances of attracting other export-oriented forms of industry.

As Table 7.5 indicates, both projects are very capital intensive and

TABLE 7.5. ECONOMIC IMPACT
OF THE SPECIAL PROJECTS

Item	Iron ore project	Paper pulp project
Direct investment in project (CFAF billion)[a]	220	100
Investment in infrastructure (CFAF billion)[a]	100	10
Value added/GDP (percent)[b]	1.4	0.8
Gross export revenue/total exports (percent)[b]	8–9	6–7
Net export revenue/total exports.(percent)[b]	3	2
Number of jobs[b]	3,350	1,000[c]

Source: World Bank.
a. 1975 prices.
b. At the time of full production.
c. Excluding another 2,000 on plantations.

need substantial investments in supporting infrastructure. They contribute relatively little to employment and growth. Furthermore, they have a limited net effect on the balance of payments when debt payments are taken into account.

The overall impact on the economy in terms of contribution to GDP, or net foreign balance, is not large, nor is the projected effect on employment. In the model it is assumed that iron ore production would begin at a level of 2 million tons in 1983 and rise to 8 million tons in 1985. A second pelletization plant, to be built in 1984–86, would allow production to rise to a maximum of 12 million tons in 1987. At that time the project's share in total GDP would peak at 1.4 percent and decline thereafter as production remains constant. The mine and related operations are expected to provide permanent jobs for about 3,300 Ivorians, which is a significant number, but not if compared with the investment required. The borrowing terms assumed are twenty years maturity, five years grace, and 9 percent interest. These terms, in particular the maturity, are generous. Harder terms would considerably reduce the net value of the project to the economy and to the balance of payments. The project does have a positive effect on the economy, but it is not nearly as large as would be expected from the size of the investment.

The paper pulp project would begin production in 1981, and its value added share in GDP would peak at 0.8 percent in 1985. Although investments and production levels would be much lower than for the mine, the paper pulp project's contribution to the balance of payments would be up to 75 percent as large. This is a result of the lower capital intensity of the paper pulp project and the much lower requirement for additional public infrastructure investment. Compared with the iron ore mine, this project appears to be more immediately profitable to the Ivory Coast. It would increase production in the southwest and better utilize the investment that has already taken place there. It has lower capital requirements, would employ as many Ivorians, and has the potential for integrating forestry activities in general in the Ivory Coast, especially in the southwest.

Before starting implementation, the economic impact of both projects should be investigated fully and a proper phasing worked out. Total investment in both projects would be equivalent to about 50 percent of the country's GDP in 1975. Both projects should be considered export-oriented enclave projects, initially contributing relatively little to industrial integration, employment, Ivorianization, growth, and income distribution. The projects are of such a size that they should obviously only be undertaken after the government has obtained sufficiently attractive contracts with financiers and buyers. Also, the projects should not be allowed to absorb a major share of the concessionary capital allocated to the Ivory Coast. This capital will be needed in the coming decade to bring about structural changes in other sectors. The mere size of the projects could create serious problems for the entire economy and jeopardize growth for more than a decade unless sufficient guarantees are obtained from the outset.

Table 7.6 presents a comparison of three runs: (a) the base run, savings constrained; (b) no special projects, savings unconstrained; and (c) no special projects, savings constrained, with the policy package. An inspection of the macroeconomic indicators for the three runs shows the following trends:

- Investments fall from about 29 percent of GDY to a more reasonable 24 percent; annual growth drops, but less than proportionately as values of the incremental capital-output ratio improve slightly.
- Domestic and national savings drop to levels that seem attainable although they are still high compared with those achieved in the past.
- In the savings constrained (with the policy package) run, the debt service ratio reaches manageable averages of 11 percent in 1976–80 and 15 percent in 1981–85 (17.1 percent in 1985).

The runs in which the special projects are not included describe an economy that has some room to maneuver. If there are shortfalls in production or exports or there are external crises, it would not be necessary to take immediate policy action. When the special projects are not undertaken, public investment funds are freed to pursue other government goals. Because the growth assumptions are not changed, investment would implicitly be shifted into the projects that improve income distribution, contribute to social welfare, and reduce regional disparities.

In the final sensitivity test (Table 7.7), the paper pulp project was reintroduced because it appeared to be the better of the two special projects in terms of capital requirement and contribution to growth, employment creation, and net export revenue, although these advantages would depend on the terms of any arrangement between the Ivory Coast and foreign investors. Furthermore, since chances for an early implementation of the iron ore project had diminished at the end of 1976, the run with the paper pulp project seemed the more realistic of the two.

TABLE 7.6. COMPARISON OF VARIOUS INDICATORS: RUNS WITH NO SPECIAL PROJECTS, 1976–85

Indicator	Base run (savings unconstrained)		No special projects (savings unconstrained)		No special projects (policy package; savings constrained)	
	1976–80	1981–85	1976–80	1981–85	1976–80	1981–85
Annual growth in gross domestic income (percent)	8.6	7.0	7.6	6.7	7.2	6.5
Investment/gross domestic income	29.1	28.1	25.4	26.0	24.0	24.3
Domestic saving/gross domestic income	29.2	27.8	27.4	25.7	25.3	24.7
National saving/gross domestic income	22.8	21.2	20.8	19.4	18.4	18.1
Investment minus national saving/gross domestic income	6.3	6.9	4.6	6.6	5.6	6.2
Net public saving/public investment	43.7	26.4	44.1	22.8	61.9	50.3
Debt service ratio (percent)	10.8	12.3	10.5	13.4	11.0	15.5
Import elasticity	1.2	0.8	1.0	0.9	1.2	0.8
Incremental capital-output ratio	3.8	4.3	3.9	3.7	4.1	3.6

Source: Statistical Appendix Tables 47–49, 59–64.

TABLE 7.7. COMPARISON OF VARIOUS INDICATORS:
RUNS WITHOUT SPECIAL PROJECTS
AND WITH PAPER PULP PROJECT, 1976–85

Indicator	No special projects (policy package; savings constrained)		With paper pulp project (policy package minus tax increase; savings constrained)	
	1976–80	*1981–85*	*1976–80*	*1981–85*
Annual growth in gross domestic income (percent)	7.2	6.5	7.5	6.9
Investment/gross domestic income	24.0	24.3	26.0	24.1
Domestic saving/gross domestic income	25.3	24.7	24.5	24.6
National saving/gross domestic income	18.4	18.1	17.4	17.3
Investment minus national saving/gross domestic income	5.6	6.2	8.6	6.8
Net public saving/public investment	61.9	50.3	53.4	33.6
Debt service ratio (percent)	11.0	15.5	12.1	20.1
Import elasticity	1.2	0.8	1.4	0.5
Incremental capital-output ratio	4.1	3.6	4.1	3.6

Source: Statistical Appendix Tables 62–67.

The policy package in this run was not applied in its entirety; the tax increase component was left out. This shows up in lower savings and a higher debt service ratio than the previous run (no special projects, policy package, savings constrained). If the tax increase is introduced, both these indicators would change for the better, but by 1985 the public debt service ratio would still be close to 20 percent, which is very high. This last run shows that any additional investment would strain the situation and make it necessary to take something out of the program. In line with priorities seen by the government, choices would have to be made.

All things considered, the last two runs indicate reasonably acceptable development paths. They maintain satisfactory rates of real growth over the next decade. During this time major structural changes in the economy can be completed. Investment and savings propensities are sufficiently balanced that reliance on foreign resources will be within the borrowing ability of the economy. In fact, the creditworthiness maintained in these projections implies that not only will it be possible to achieve the required borrowing on acceptable terms, but also that the economy will continue to be attractive for private foreign investment, a factor that will remain important for future development in the Ivory Coast.

The basic message of this analysis is that in order to achieve a feasible growth path, policy adjustments need to be made. These include reduction of investment targets from the very high level proposed, the delay of projects, increased savings in both the private and public sectors, and better control of current government expenditures. In several instances, the exact means of achieving these policy changes have been specified. The next chapter contains a further discussion of these methods and describes the elements on which the Ivory Coast's future development strategy should be based.

Appendix: Assumptions Underlying the Base Run

The model uses 1973 as a base year because at the time it was constructed, 1973 was the last year for which complete data were available. As further data became available, the 1974 and 1975 projections were "tuned" so that the projections replicate the actual data at the end of 1975 to a reasonable degree. The projections of national accounts and trade are both made in constant 1973 CFA francs. National accounts are also projected in current CFA francs, as are trade and balance of payments variables. The exchange rate used for 1976 and after is CFAF230 to the U.S. dollar.

The specific parametric assumptions used in the base run are derived from econometric estimations where possible, but adjusted to reflect policy or structural changes assumed to occur in the plan period. In the production or GDP block, value added in export agriculture is derived from the export projections. It is assumed that total production is exported either in raw or processed form, with the exception of some stocking of coffee. Value added is estimated to be 80 percent of total production for unprocessed exports and 24 percent for textile exports representing the value of cotton inputs. At this stage, current production is evaluated at free on board (f.o.b.) prices; the surpluses of the Stabilization Fund are deducted later in the aggregation into three sectors. Domestic agriculture is assumed to grow by 4 percent a year on the basis of the World Bank's evaluation of prospects in that sector. In mining, it is assumed that the current level of value added will continue in the future for miscellaneous mining. This will be augmented by the contribution of the iron ore mine when it comes into operation. From available financial estimates, value added is assumed to be 44 percent of total iron ore production. Value added in export manufacturing is estimated at 24 percent of production, and it is assumed that import-substitution manufacturing will grow by 10 percent in real terms on the basis of the estimates. Value added in construction is calculated to be 27.5 percent of fixed investment expenditure. Services, transport, and commerce are assumed to grow at the same rate as the industrial and agricultural sectors, and the government wage bill is assumed to grow at 8 percent (which is about the actual rate from 1966 to 1973). Projections are made in both current and constant terms, but most of the analysis is, of course, done with the constant value projections. Once the external sector variables and investments are projected, consumption and savings (based on the trade gap) are derived from the standard accounting identities.

In the government and savings block, government revenues are the sum of fiscal receipts plus the contribution of the Stabilization Fund, which for this purpose includes the export taxes collected on the products it handles as well as its operating surplus. Rather than estimate revenues from specific taxes, it is assumed that the overall tax burden will remain at 19 percent of GDP exclusive of the Stabilization Fund profits. This is on the high side of the historical range. The contribution of the Stabilization Fund is based on World Bank projected world prices for the commodities and on the assumptions that the producer price will remain at its current share of the f.o.b. price, that handling charges will remain the same in real terms, and that the Stabilization Fund will continue its current subsidy program at the same level in real cost. Recurrent expenditures of the government are the wages and salaries (projected in the production block) plus expenditures on goods and services, which are assumed to grow at 8 percent in real terms—somewhat below the historical trend. Revenues minus expenditures represent the government's domestic savings. Interest payments abroad on the government's foreign debt are subtracted to arrive at national savings. Because the Ivorian national accounts treat almost all foreigners as residents, the repatriation of earnings of nonnationals employed by the government is included in the calculation of private sector national savings.

It was difficult to obtain sufficiently detailed data on public enterprise and private sector savings as separate entities in a form applicable to this model. Instead, global projections of savings were made for each sector, which seem optimistic in comparison with available data. Public enterprise domestic savings (excluding the Stabilization Fund) are projected to grow by 5 percent, reflecting the troubled financial situation of several major public enterprises. Private domestic savings, which act as a proxy for disposable income, are projected to be 12 percent of GDP minus government revenues. National savings are also calculated for each sector, and total domestic and national savings are calculated from these three sector projections. These totals constitute the savings projections when the savings constraint option is used.

Investment is projected for each of these sectors. Public investment is taken from the plan projections by major program, and investment by the public enterprises is taken from the plan on the basis of the Loi Programme definitions extended through the plan period. After the plan period, investment is assumed to continue growing at about the same rate in real terms. The base level of investment for the plan period by the public sector (government proper plus parapublic) is about CFAF860 billion in 1975 prices plus an additional CFAF60 billion directly related to two special projects, the iron ore mine and the paper pulp projects. Public capital invested in those projects in 1976–80 will vary with the phasing of implementation. This package corresponds roughly to an overall total investment of 29 percent of GDY. Private investment is assumed to be about 9 percent of GDY, and investment in the special projects is given exogenously.

The two special projects are treated as separate subsectors with their own projections of production, imports, exports, investment, and debt service. These projections are added into the appropriate sectors for aggregation. Production is assumed to be equal to exports and value added to be 44 percent of production for iron and 46 percent in pulp and paper. The borrowing, direct investment, and total investment, including related public investment, are given exogenously in constant terms. Their current value depends on the year the project is brought into production. Imported capital goods are exogenously determined in constant terms from the technical data, while intermediate goods imports are assumed to be 50 percent of all intermediate inputs. Direct investment income is assumed to be 10 percent of value added. The share of each project in GDP, as well as three measures of the impact of the projects on the balance of payments, is calculated in current dollars. The first is the direct impact, exports plus direct investment minus direct imports; the second is the direct impact minus the debt service on the direct borrowing and the investment income payments; and the third is the preceding minus debt service on the public investment relating to the projects. The latter is calculated assuming that the additional public investment entailed additional borrowing in the same proportion as overall government borrowing for other public investment. Since the starting year of each of these projects can be varied, their net impact will be different depending on when they are begun. In the base run the iron ore mine is assumed to start production in 1983 and the paper pulp project in 1981.

The export projections are given exogenously for twelve specific products, two miscellaneous categories, and nonfactor services. These are specified in either volume or value terms and converted to constant or current value by applying changes in the World Bank commodity price forecasts to the export unit values of the base year. Five import goods categories are projected. One, foodstuffs, is projected exogenously on the basis of the Ivory Coast's self-sufficiency program in a number of commodities. Imports of consumption goods are assumed to grow with an elasticity of 0.9 with respect to private consumption in 1976 and 0.8 thereafter (continued import substitution assumed). This elasticity is below recent historical levels. In the cases in which the savings constraint is binding, the additional imports flow into consumption goods and the assumed elasticity is no longer binding. Petroleum and fuel imports have been forecast exogenously. The installation of hydroelectric generating capacity has been taken into account. Imports of intermediate goods grow with an elasticity of one with respect to growth in the industrial sector plus 50 percent of the intermediate inputs of the special projects. This is consistent with the historical relations. Imports of capital goods are assumed to remain at about 30 percent of fixed investment in the economy, plus the specific capital imports of the special projects. This is comparable to the historical share of 32 percent. Nonfactor service imports are exogenously specified. Imports are also calculated in both constant and current prices on the basis of World Bank price projections.

For the rest of the current account, workers' remittances in current prices are projected to grow by 9 percent until 1980 and 7 percent thereafter, reflecting the approach of a balance between Ivorianization and the need for more foreigners. Net direct foreign investment and net investment income payments are assumed to grow at 12 percent. The investment and investment income of the special projects is calculated separately and added in. Net transfer levels are specified exogenously. In the capital account, new commitments from traditional lenders are given exogenously, and reserve buildup is assumed to keep reserves at an average level of about two months of imports. Any additional borrowing needed comes from commercial sources in what the model calls GAPFIL. Current average terms are assumed for each category of commitment. Current and capital account projections are in current terms.

Most assumptions in the base run are generally optimistic in terms of the evaluations of the World Bank's experts in the field and in terms of empirically estimated historical relationships where it has been possible to estimate them. Thus, the base run already assumed a high level of performance on the part of the government and the economy as a whole in savings and efficient use of resources.

CHAPTER EIGHT

Elements of Future Development Strategy

IN THE PREVIOUS CHAPTER it was determined, with a fairly simple macroeconomic model, that by investing about 25 percent of GDY an annual growth rate of 6 to 7 percent could be obtained for the next ten-year period. If public investment is assumed to be some 65 percent of total investment, the public investment program would amount to about CFAF800 billion in 1975 prices. The tentative public investment program prepared on a project-by-project basis by the government in mid-1975 was considerably higher—CFAF1,350 billion. Local planners in their macroeconomic projections must have realized that such a program cannot be implemented in its entirety in as short a period as five years (1976–80).[1] Thus it becomes essential to set priorities and to design policies that use scarce resources to satisfy priority needs in the best way.

The Need for Policy Change

The challenge facing the Ivory Coast is to maintain the high rate of growth and, at the same time, to improve the income distribution, all within the resources likely to be available. The government is correct in its understanding that this cannot be done simply by continuing

1. In a May 1976 draft edition of the 1976–80 plan, the public investment program had been scaled down to CFAF1,020 billion. The plan, which should have become effective January 1, 1976, was not published until early in 1977.

past policies. Structural changes are required. These changes are difficult to implement for political and other reasons. The essential flexibility of the Ivorian economy and the record of its management suggest, however, that it will be able to find adequate solutions. Some of the main issues the Ivory Coast has to address in the next decade are as follows: (a) the balance between growth and income distribution; (b) the increasing cost of future development; (c) the possibility and desirability of importing foreign production factors while at the same time strengthening the role of local production factors; (d) the balance between public sector involvement and private initiative; and (e) the financing of public investment.

The magnitude of the public investment program

The procedure of planning by objectives, which has led to some imaginative programs and well-prepared sectoral approaches, is one of the reasons why the public investment program has become so large. The technical ministries have the tendency to want to see long-term objectives, which are formulated at the beginning of the planning process, implemented in a relatively short time.

The magnitude of the program also reflects the government's increased concern for the poor, as well as its determination to maintain a high rate of growth. There are programs to increase production in the relatively developed areas, to transform the less favorably endowed savannah area in the north, and to accelerate the opening up of the southwest. For the rural areas, substantial investments are proposed to improve the quality and the quantity of services and to provide the people with a production base for a decent income. The same approach is planned for the urban communities. Diversification in agriculture will continue to be pursued vigorously, as will industrial development. A third growth sector, mining, will be added to the economy. The investment policy acknowledges the need to address new problems that have gained in urgency, but at the same time maintains the existing program. Thus, it is a policy of addition rather than of shift. The preliminary program, while it has many excellent elements, lacks a ranking of priorities.

The Ivory Coast has successfully implemented public investment programs that were considered too ambitious at the time. For example, when the output of the ambitious oil palm (80,000 hectares) and coconut palm (20,000 hectares) scheme started to reach the market in 1973 and 1974, the fats and oils market was booming. Similarly, less than a year after the controversial hydroelectric scheme at Kossou was completed, petroleum prices tripled. Also, the development of the port of San Pédro was expensive, but it enabled exportation of about 1 million cubic meters of logs in its first year of operation in 1973, earning CFAF16 billion in export revenue. These are probably the events the government refers to in the Loi Programme for 1976–78 when it states than an audacious investment policy has proved to pay off. None of these events is a guarantee, however, of the success of future programs and projects in the tentative public investment program. Some need much more research before their economic merits can be determined. The ambitious plans for local sugar production is a case in point. Although world prices for sugar in the 1980s are difficult to predict, the question of economic and financial feasibility should not be neglected on that account. Indications are that the investment cost will be about twice that in some other countries.[2] If the sugar is sold in the same export market, the Ivory Coast will seem to be placed at a distinct disadvantage.

The Ivory Coast has been very successful in supplementing its local resources with production factors from abroad. The planners seem confident that this policy can be extrapolated into the future without great difficulty. Moreover, rapid world inflation has moderated the burden of debt contracted in the past. Recent forecasts, however, take into account a rate of inflation considerably higher than was forecast some years ago. It would be dangerous to assume that future inflation will again be much higher than is assumed now. Also, a five-year maturity period on most Eurodollar loans does not give much time for inflation to have an effect.

Instead of being the difficult year that was expected as a result of the higher outlay for energy imports, 1974 was a very good one. The trade balance surplus of some CFAF60 billion was more than twice the 1969 record surplus. This surplus probably increased expectations of the planners. The results of 1975 have been quite different; the balance of trade showed a surplus of only CFAF16.7 billion, and although the net inflow of foreign capital continued to be substantial, the country that year lost CFAF35 billion in reserves and its overall net international reserve position became negative for the first time in its history. High world coffee and cocoa prices for 1976 and price forecasts favorable to producers for the next five years could change

2. A World Bank study estimates the capital investment costs in sugar-producing countries for new capacity at $950–1,200 a ton in 1975 prices.

the situation for the better. The same applies to the earnings of the
Stabilization Fund. To maintain internal and external balances, however, it is necessary to follow an "average" rather than a "maximum"
public investment policy.

The government believes that if it continues to manage the economy
well the goals it has set are realistic, and that the developed world has
a responsibility to help the Ivory Coast achieve them.[3] It hopes that
the discussions of the New Economic Order, schemes for guaranteeing
raw material prices, and other proposals will lead to quick, tangible
results. Such results require that the Ivory Coast set forth clearly what
it wants to achieve in the decades ahead. It would then be up to the
developed world to make a genuine effort to join local forces in meeting
the targets set. Finally, recent trends show an increase in the cost of
development; the incremental capital-output ratio is going up. This
means that a certain rate of growth can be obtained only with more
investment than before, which explains in part why the public investment program has become so large.

The increasing cost of development

There are signs that growth in the Ivory Coast is becoming more
expensive. First, the terms of trade are deteriorating. Second, locally,
the return on investment is decreasing. Third, the direct and indirect
costs of production factors are going up. All three elements are interrelated, but for the sake of clarity they will be discussed separately.

The terms of trade.   As discussed in Chapter 5, the terms of trade
have fluctuated in the last fifteen years, but there has been no systematic deterioration. Taking 1973 as 100, the values will hover around
100 for 1976–78. A gradual deterioration thereafter is forecast. The
deterioration of the terms of trade means that, relatively, the Ivory
Coast will have to export more to be able to import the same amount.
The Ivory Coast is trying to escape this adverse effect by diversification
of agricultural production and by exporting more raw materials in
processed form. The introduction of a variety of other crops contributes to the stabilization of the world price for cocoa and coffee. But
diversification has its costs as well. Exporting raw materials in processed form will be profitable only if the final product can be produced
efficiently enough to be competitive in the world market.

3. Mohamed T. Diawara, "Coopération ou Confrontation," *Africa* (March–April
1975).

Declining return on investment.   The incremental capital-output ratio (ICOR) and the domestic resource cost (DRC) give indications of the cost of investment in relation to return on investment. The ICOR of the Ivory Coast may have been as low as 2.5 in the 1960s, and it should not come as a surprise that this value is rising. The values of the DRC show the same trend. There are several reasons for this phenomenon.

First, the agricultural sector is diversifying into crops having lower comparative advantages. The DRC values have indicated that it was more profitable to grow cocoa than, for instance, cotton, since the comparative advantage of cocoa exceeded that of cotton. If all available money were put into cocoa production, however, many constraints would develop, particularly in marketing, and they would cause a dramatic change in the ranking of DRCs by product. This is one of the justifications for the government's policy of investing in products that have lower comparative advantages than cocoa and coffee. This policy naturally and unavoidably has led to lower returns on investment. As a result, the profit available for investment in other activities has shrunk.

Second, diversification into sectors like industry was necessary, but it is becoming more and more costly. Substantial investments were made, sometimes at very low or even negative returns to the national economy, especially in the short and medium term. Industrialization in the Ivory Coast, as in many other countries, started with import substitution. But after fifteen years of rapid growth in manufacturing, the Ivory Coast is running out of the more obvious possibilities for import substitution. It is an open question how long or to what extent the government wants to, or will have to, continue subsidizing industry. The question becomes particularly pressing if the profitable activities (coffee, cocoa, and timber production) have problems of their own.

Third, the Ivorian forest has contributed substantially to economic growth. Costs in logging have been relatively low because the most accessible areas were logged out first and almost no reforestation was done. Because of the depletion of reserves, output is probably at its peak. Costly reforestation will have to be carried out if the present level of production is to be maintained beyond ten to fifteen years.

A fourth issue relating to declining return on investment is the government's ambitious program to improve the living conditions of the people in the less favorably endowed rural areas. To provide a permanent improvement in conditions, a basis for earning an income is being developed at the same time. The program has many innovative aspects and deserves full attention. Unfortunately, at the time of the

World Bank's field visit, many details were still to be worked out. The impact of the program is potentially far reaching, as indicated in Chapter 6. The objective is to give the people in the north and the center an incentive to stay there rather than move to Abidjan. The national economic benefit of having somebody gainfully employed in the north instead of unemployed in Abidjan would be substantial. The costs of such a program are high, however, and because structural changes are involved, the gestation period would probably be quite long. This does not mean that it should not be tried, but to carry out the program on the scale proposed will tie up substantial amounts of capital for a long period of time. The same argument applies to programs encouraging people from other areas to settle in the southwest.

Fifth, there is increasing concern about the living conditions of the poor. Investments in this area do not always yield immediately traceable results. Apart from humanitarian and social considerations, such investments may be necessary to buy social stability, without which continued growth would be jeopardized, and in that sense returns could be high. This type of investment, however, increases the cost of growth.

Sixth, cost overruns have been substantial for a number of agricultural projects. The reasons given in Chapter 3 were: underestimation of the size of the public investment in buildings, roads, and social infrastructure necessary to reach project targets; insufficient control over the size of overhead and spending programs of state companies; the choice of what seems to be an oversophisticated production technology, at least in the case of sugar; delays in project execution; and insufficient project preparation. An issue that is related to most of these points is the cost level of, and the standards applied by, some public agricultural development companies (SODE). General standards of construction, facilities, and fringe benefits have a tendency to follow the example set by the most successful, and the successful company, in general, adjusts its standards and cost level upward.

Seventh, urban, educational, and transport infrastructure displays a tendency toward high standards, overdesign, and expansion rather than densification. In many cases densification would be the better solution economically.

The cost of foreign capital.   Along with the decline in the return on investment has come an increase in the cost of foreign capital. Foreign private capital has been an important factor in the economic development of the Ivory Coast. As calculated in Chapter 4, however, the net inflow has been reduced from 16 percent of total investment in 1960–63 to about 1 percent in 1971–74. This probably reflects the increased participation of the government in private enterprise in its effort to Ivorianize capital; the transfer of profits over a growing foreign private capital stock; and the fact that profitable import-substitution opportunities became harder to find. In the public sector, the demand for foreign capital far exceeds the level that donors of concessionary capital have been allocating to the Ivory Coast. Following independence, the Ivory Coast, along with its diversification of trade, began to diversify its sources of foreign capital. This diversification has been successful, but costs have increased as discussed in Chapter 5. Furthermore as a result of the excellent economic performance of the Ivory Coast, concessionary capital has tended to become relatively scarce. Several donors with both soft and hard forms of concessionary aid have allocated, or are shifting toward allocating, the hardest forms of their concessionary capital to the Ivory Coast. Countries or organizations allocating their aid by region, in this case West Africa, have reserved their softer terms more and more for the drought-stricken Sahel countries.

An important constraint on foreign borrowing is the proportion of public savings available to finance the public investment program. Net public savings as a proportion of public investment has dropped from over 50 percent in 1960–65 to around 35 percent in 1975. If it is assumed that 15 percent of public investment does not lend itself to foreign financing, an average of about 75 percent of the remaining program would have to be financed abroad. With a sizable investment program, this would be unsustainable for any length of time, as noted in Chapter 7.

The cost of foreign labor. The development of the balance of payments shows that the cost of foreign production factors in general has increased considerably. It was calculated in Chapter 5 that the payments abroad for foreign capital and foreign skilled and unskilled labor have increased to such an extent that the resource balance and the current account balance have deteriorated rapidly in both absolute amount and as a proportion of exports. Because the contribution of France in financing technical assistance is fixed at a level well below total cost, the full cost of any additional assistance must be borne by the government.[4]

4. In an effort to accelerate Ivorianization of teachers, many of whom are expatriates, the government in January 1976 increased salaries up to 70 percent, which will make the teaching profession more attractive to students.

Furthermore, there are indications that the limits to the capacity or willingness of the Ivorian society to absorb foreign labor are being approached. The number of graduates is increasing rapidly and demands for Ivorianization will become more pressing. The proportion of Ivorians in jobs of higher responsibility has been rising gradually and this process will probably accelerate. A certain pace of Ivorianization that takes account of efficiency, as discussed in Chapter 6, is economically advantageous; there is little doubt that, with increased pressure for Ivorianization, political realities will hasten this pace. At the other end of the scale, the number of Africans from neighboring countries has increased rapidly. Some Ivorians are questioning whether their society will be able to absorb more foreigners without creating conflicts. Furthermore, the government of Upper Volta has asked to be compensated for letting its people go south. The demand for this type of labor in other countries in west and central Africa has increased in recent years. Such demand can only raise the supply price of this factor of production for the Ivory Coast.

The real constraint: local participation

Until now, the country has successfully stretched the span of its own resources by complementing them with resources from abroad, a very sensible decision that has helped the Ivory Coast to improve the income of all its citizens. However, the community of foreigners has grown faster than the Ivorian population itself, the cost of foreign capital has increased rapidly, and today the Ivory Coast is employing more foreign production factors in its economy than ever before. There are clear indications, from the supply as well as from the demand side, that the boundaries of the possible and desirable are gradually being approached. There is no doubt that for a long time the Ivory Coast will continue to need, and be able to obtain, substantial amounts of foreign production factors, both labor and capital, but their proportion in the Ivorian economy cannot grow much more. Since participation of foreign factors is already substantial, future economic growth will depend increasingly on the successful mobilization and participation of local production factors and their integration into the economic process. The major constraints to further development lie within the Ivory Coast itself. The country's capacity to absorb efficiently more foreign production factors and, consequently, its capacity for further development depend on whether these local constraints can be alleviated.

The government realized from the very beginning that heavy reliance on foreign factors should be a temporary expedient. Deciding the right moment for a change in policy is a matter of judgment. Actually, the government has been making adjustments all along, but it is important to make the policy change more explicit as was done, for instance, with the decision in 1960 to favor an outward-looking policy. Then a host of decisions supported the choice of an outward orientation, and a favorable climate was created for the policy's success. Now more emphasis should be given to measures that mobilize and integrate local production factors more fully into the economic process. This is not to say that there should be a hostile policy toward foreign factors. Continued participation of foreign manpower and foreign capital in the economy of the Ivory Coast is vital to continued development. The government understands that foreign investment, local initiative, and Ivorianization all have to be promoted simultaneously. But such a course may sometimes lead to conflicts. Explicit policy statements, assuring that everybody knows what to expect, will reduce the risk of conflict. A continuous dialogue between the government and the local and the foreign private sectors is in the interest of all parties.

The need for an employment-based strategy

Protected by tariffs, local industry has been allowed to pass on its high cost to the consumer. And part of the profits made in agriculture has been used to create more sophisticated jobs of the type more and more Ivorians are seeking. This type of employment creation has been expensive, but it has given the Ivory Coast an industrial base. Management and higher skilled positions are now gradually being Ivorianized. If this process proceeds too quickly, efficiency will suffer. Efficiency is certainly below that of European countries. This is important because in the change in emphasis of the industrial policy from import substitution to an export orientation, Europe is expected to be the main export market. This policy will not, however, create the number of jobs required. The surplus profit from agriculture itself is going down, and the cost of the type of capital-intensive industry that is brought from abroad is going up. Therefore, policies in all sectors have to be examined from the standpoint of their capacity to generate employment. Indications are that unless recent changes have an impact and changes in policy continue to take place, there will be substantial unemployment in urban areas, especially in Abidjan, together with labor shortages in the rural areas. It is therefore important to realize the potential agriculture still has in terms of employment creation. The investment cost per job in agriculture in most cases is much lower than it is in modern industry, and although Ivorians are not eager to be employed as hired labor in agriculture, projects in which plots of land are given to Ivorian families have been very successful. One element of an employment-oriented strategy should therefore be to favor family-sized farms over industrial-sized plantations for which additional foreign labor would have to be imported. There are opportunities in other sectors as well. The informal sector, which in several instances has been obstructed by the public sector rather than encouraged, is another source of meaningful employment, as is the small-scale enterprise sector. The government recently started to give the latter more serious attention.

Private and public initiative

It has been mentioned that the government stepped up its direct investment considerably in the early 1960s when it detected a hesitation to invest in the private agricultural sector. The proportion of public investment in total investment has risen ever since then, lately to over 60 percent. There are good reasons, however, for making a start toward reversing this trend. The private sector has time and again shown a keen understanding of incentives, particularly price incentives. Producer prices for most products are at a relatively high level. The higher the producer prices, the lower will be the income for the public sector, given a certain price f.o.b. Abidjan. In other words, paying high producer prices and maintaining an ambitious public investment program at the same time leads increasingly to the foreign financing of such a program. High producer prices and improvements in instruments for the mobilization of private savings should go together. The government, of course, still has many ways of influencing what part of the income will be consumed, what part will be saved, what goods will be consumed, and how savings will be invested. This procedure would be a more sophisticated approach than paying the farmer a price for his product that covers only his direct consumption and letting the government take care of the rest of his needs. The public sector's role would still be an important one in terms of research, technical advice, and other forms of service. Limiting the role of the public sector to the areas in which it has a comparative advantage, however, should receive considerable attention.

It should also be understood that this approach cannot be followed indiscriminately. For instance, a person who settles in the southwest needs much more assistance than a good price for his product. Programs to provide this assistance should be developed and the public sector should play a major role in this field. The government should seriously consider the possibility of returning initiative to the people whenever feasible. This would be consistent with the government's own broad policy outline as developed in 1960.

Development Strategy by Sector

The previous discussion has stressed the need for greater emphasis on the mobilization of local resources and on economizing as much as possible in the use of foreign production factors. Whatever foreign capital is made available in the future should be used with as high a proportion of local production factors as possible. The maximum number of units of labor should be combined with a unit of capital and if there is an alternative, preference should be given to local labor. The public sector should encourage private initiative, rather than replace it. In pursuing such a strategy many options are open to an economy as buoyant as the Ivorian one. These options will be discussed by sector, and specific examples of projects consistent with this strategy will be given.

One longer-run option already discussed concerns population growth. Currently, there is no explicit program to limit the rapid growth of population and the heavy burden this places on resources. Even if efforts to reduce the birth rate were successful, the labor force would not be affected for fifteen years. Nevertheless, effective population policies could have a significant long-run impact on employment and on income distribution.

Agriculture

Investment in agriculture should continue to receive high priority. This sector in general creates more employment for each unit of capital and each unit of foreign skilled labor than any other sector. With appropriate techniques, productivity can be increased. This would lead to higher private earnings, which would in turn make employment in this sector acceptable to more Ivorians. Self-employment as farm owners would be more acceptable to Ivorians than employment as hired labor. The family farm is therefore a better way of employing Ivorians than the estate farm, which requires many unskilled foreigners and is generally more capital intensive. The creation of additional jobs in this sector will help slow urbanization, reduce the need for urban infrastructure, and reduce urban unemployment.

The regional distribution of agricultural investment is another consideration. Investment in the south, except for the southwest, should benefit from the availability of rather complete infrastructure, and the concentration of agricultural activities should bring good returns on investment.[5] The savannah areas in the north provide interesting opportunities, as mentioned earlier. The population density in some parts of the north is quite high. The crops that can be grown there lend themselves to simple forms of mechanization, and using these methods the farmer can earn a decent income and lay the basis for improved forms of mechanization and motorization. The southwest is sparsely populated and new ventures in this area require relatively high amounts of capital and non-Ivorian labor. This proportion can be reduced by the use of family-sized plots. It is expensive, however, to settle families from elsewhere. The best way to proceed may be to start with plantation agriculture with an outgrower component that can gradually be increased. In selecting crops, regions, and techniques for future agricultural development, such factors as the scarcity of capital, the problems of foreign labor, the availability of local labor, and marketing considerations should be systematically taken into account. Each of these factors should be weighted in accordance with the government's objectives. This can only be done in a full-fledged economic and financial evaluation, to which some investments in the Ivory Coast are, it seems, no longer subjected.

It is estimated that the agricultural sector will continue to grow by about 5 percent a year during the period 1975–85, provided the labor is available. As part of its plan to reduce regional disparities, the government is expected to place more emphasis on the savannah. Development of this area should involve a complete change in the traditional system of farming to achieve continuous use of the land through appropriate crop rotations. An intensive research effort should be made to design and test new farming systems that will lead to more sophisticated forms of mechanization.

Livestock production should be developed as an integral part of such

5. Recent calculations for a cocoa project in the Ivory Coast, financed with the help of the World Bank, show that the return on investment in new plantings was very satisfactory, but that the return on a rehabilitation component in the same project was about three times as high.

a program. The contribution of livestock to GDP is probably less than 2 percent and no significant growth has taken place during the past decade. Livestock development in the Ivory Coast is constrained by ecological and human factors. In the view of officials of the Ministry of Animal Production, the chief obstacle to development is disease. The human constraint to development is the almost total lack of any tradition of animal husbandry. This is true even of the savannah areas, where most of the cattle population is found. To some observers, this lack of livestock tradition is the most difficult constraint to deal with. It can be overcome only through a comprehensive and well-executed educational program, which should lay a solid basis for genuine and sustained livestock development. Government ranching schemes have existed for many years, but the results have been poor. Excessive reliance on expensive expatriate personnel has made operating costs high, while the spin-off in terms of training the local population has been low. The success of livestock projects, therefore, will rest largely on their close integration with ongoing agricultural operations that include animal traction, fattening operations, the introduction of fodder crops in the rotation, and utilization of crop by-products as livestock feed.

On the basis of existing research, ecological conditions in the forest region should be excellent for the expansion of cocoa, coffee, oil and coconut palm, and rubber. Priority should be given to crops that can be grown on family farms. Greater concentration of trees, rehabilitation and uprooting of unproductive trees, and the introduction of high-yield varieties in the already developed areas are all ways of increasing production at minimum cost. They also make maximum use of the existing infrastructure. Increasing production by these methods should be weighed carefully against increasing production by expansion into the sparsely populated southwest.

In spite of rapid urbanization and an increase in per capita incomes, the Ivory Coast has become less dependent on food imports. Food-crop production, an entirely Ivorian affair, has increased considerably over the past ten years. Food imports per urban inhabitant declined from 200 kilograms in 1965 to 115 kilograms in 1974. It is estimated that over the next ten years each rural food producer will have to nearly double his marketed surplus to meet future demand. The past performance of the Ivorian farmer indicates that this can be done. In fact, this should improve the incomes of farmers, especially in the north.

In the rice sector the government's price policy seems to have created overproduction at the cost of a high subsidy to the rice farmer. It seems likely that the country could produce the rice it needs without such a subsidy. Little is known about how the rice marketing and distribution system operates, what the consumption patterns are, and what quantities are marketed and imported. Rice is produced in different regions and with different techniques, some of which are distinctly more expensive than others. A better understanding of these issues is requisite to the shaping of a policy that provides the country with the food it needs at the lowest cost. The farmer should be able to meet this challenge, provided proper guidance is given by the government. On the basis of successful experience with private intermediaries in the past, it should be worthwhile for the government to remove direct price and marketing controls, at least for a trial period, to see whether market forces move in a direction compatible with, or perhaps even conducive to, government objectives.

It is generally accepted that to produce larger marketable surpluses of food and to increase per capita and family incomes, larger-sized family farms will be required. Farm size is reported to be constrained by labor availability, particularly at the time of land preparation. The use of animal and mechanical traction would largely alleviate this constraint and permit a considerable expansion in cultivated area for each family. Several institutions have experimented with both forms of traction and have concluded that at present animal traction is best for the Ivory Coast. Such a system could contribute much to the adoption of settled agriculture and the disappearance of shifting cultivation. In a later stage, small machines may be introduced to increase productivity further. Heavy machinery has proved to be unsuited to the conditions found in the small-scale agriculture of the Ivory Coast. Experiments should continue, however, because more sophisticated forms of mechanization will eventually become feasible.

The policy of diversification of agricultural production has been successful. It should be understood, however, that new products must be economically feasible. The same reasoning applies to the notion of self-sufficiency. When a country can produce a commodity only at a comparative disadvantage, it is economically feasible to import it. These remarks may be relevant for the production of sugar in the Ivory Coast. At the end of 1974 the government announced its decision to become a sugar exporter. The program aims at the installation of ten sugar complexes, each producing 60,000 tons annually, with a total investment cost of CFAF250 billion in 1975 prices. Inasmuch as local sugar consumption at the time of completion is estimated at about 100,000 tons, the remaining 500,000 tons would be available for export.

One sugar complex in Ferkéssédougou started production in 1975; the Loi Programme for 1976–78 indicates that the construction of five other mills will start during this period. Financing had been found for two of these mills by the end of 1976.[6]

There is no question that the savannah zones of the Ivory Coast are capable of producing sugarcane and that this would be consistent with the government's objective for developing the northern part of the country. But before it commits itself to further sugar investment, the Ivory Coast must find satisfactory answers to the following questions:

· What will be the cost of production? The production costs of the first complex are not encouraging, in part because the ecological conditions are less favorable than those in other sugar-producing countries.
· To what markets and at what price might the Ivory Coast export up to 500,000 tons of sugar during the 1980s?
· Is investment in sugar production an efficient form of employment creation in the north? The Ferkéssédougou complex expects to employ only about 2,500 unskilled workers (including field- and millworkers) at full production, implying an investment of nearly CFAF10 million a job. Moreover, because the sugarcane will be grown on plantations, many workers will probably have to come from neighboring countries.

Industry

The government knows that its import-substitution-oriented industrial sector is costly in terms of capital and foreign labor. Many import-substitution firms have earned healthy profits in a highly protected market at the expense of the majority of the Ivorian population. Although such firms were established with long-term rather than immediate national economic benefits in mind and may become less expensive as efficiency increases, some will continue to be expensive even in the long run. The government has therefore become much more selective in encouraging this type of activity and should be prepared to discontinue, or at least not renew on the same basis, agreements with firms that have proved unable to survive without excessive pro-

6. Total cost of one of these mills, which will be constructed during the next few years, has reportedly gone up to CFAF35 billion.

tection.[7] It is worth noting that one of the reasons for this protection has been the compensation of industry for the high costs of local and expatriate labor. If the government were to succeed in bringing local wages more in line with productivity (by not fully compensating employees for inflation) and at the same time make progress in Ivorianization, part of the reason for protection would cease. In this case contracts with these firms should be renegotiated. With regard to production for the domestic market, a case can be made for raising tariffs on imported intermediate goods.

The government is considering shifting the emphasis of its incentives to export-oriented, local raw material processing by introducing an export subsidy. Such a reorientation is a most desirable development and ought to be vigorously pursued. Incentives for import replacement have been substantial, whereas incentives for export have been zero or negative. Industrial expansion achieved by low to moderate rates of expenditure on export promotion is more desirable from the country's standpoint than further expansion of import replacement based on high effective protection. For example, it would be preferable to pay an effective export subsidy of 20 percent rather than to allow the creation of another import replacement project requiring effective protection at the level of the average for priority firms, that is, about 100 percent. The successful development of manufactured exports has certain other important potential advantages, including the possibility of operating on a large enough scale to exhaust most available economies of scale; the discipline of having to meet the standards of importers in other countries with respect to price, delivery, and product quality; and the possibility that for some firms the successful development of exports will allow lower levels of protection for their domestic sales. The availability of foreign markets is difficult to predict, however. This issue is less vital when a sizable local market exists, but even in the case of textile manufacturing, where the Ivory Coast is making impressive progress, effective protection is high.

A greater concentration on small-scale enterprises and the informal sector is also advocated. The informal sector is hard to define precisely but, in effect, it represents a transitional economy between the modern and traditional sectors. Its activities range from those of the artisan to small-scale entrepreneurs employing up-to-date technologies in man-

---

7. The firms benefiting from the investment code have to submit annual reports on activities and results to the Ministry of Planning. The ministry has contracted technical assistance to improve its economic evaluation of existing and prospective establishments.

ufacturing, trading, and services. Typical characteristics of the informal sector include: ease of entry, reliance on indigenous resources, family ownership, wages obtained outside the officially regulated labor market, skills acquired outside the formal educational and training system, markets that are unregulated and competitive, and an overhead that is often identical with the entrepreneur's personal living expenses.

The informal sector provides a great deal of employment that uses production functions closely related to the economy's factor endowments. Moreover it has a spontaneous dynamism that contains the entrepreneurial elements critical to the future growth and modernization of the Ivorian economy. The sector makes a significant contribution to total national employment and value added that is not fully reflected in the statistics (see Chapter 6). Socioeconomic studies indicate that many incomes in the informal sector are close to or even higher than the minimum official wage for lower-level workers in the formal sector.

Official policy, through a variety of controls and regulatory measures, has discouraged slum settlements where informal activity thrives. But because the informal sector is likely to continue to absorb a considerable part of the continued migration of peasant and rural youth, more emphasis should be given to finding out what steps can be taken to promote it and to reinforce the links between it and the organized modern sector. This could be done particularly through the promotion of small-scale enterprises as well as through such incentives as roads, marketplaces, and the provision of water and energy. The government is now changing its sometimes neglectful policy toward the informal sector. Much can be done to create an attractive climate, but the approach should be careful because "formalizing" of the sector should be avoided. The World Bank recently made a loan in support of public policy toward small-scale enterprises, which included upgrading and strengthening government institutions active in this area. It should be kept in mind that promotion of these enterprises and the informal sector will involve changes in both structure and mental attitude. For these reasons and because the institutions involved are inexperienced, major results should not be expected immediately.

In this context, two activities included in the government plan should receive a lower priority than they now do. These are the replacement of small-scale private operations in rice milling and coffee deshelling by capital-intensive, publicly owned industrial plants. Indications are that the private sector thus far has operated efficiently, and it is therefore not clear why the government would want to replace these operations, particularly when such action runs counter to what is believed appropriate for Ivorian circumstances. The major justification in the case of coffee deshelling seems to be the reduction in losses of coffee during the deshelling process. An investigation should be made of whether it would not be a more economic and appropriate approach to extend coffee production on Ivorian-owned family plots.

The discussion in the previous chapter dealt with the two special projects, iron ore mining and paper pulp production. Two additional points are relevant:

- Although the capital investments are enormous, it could be argued that a major share of this capital would be available to the Ivory Coast only for these two projects. The public funds to be invested would still be substantial, however. An evaluation should be made to determine whether such funds could be invested elsewhere more profitably, particularly from the standpoint of job creation.
- Part of the limited hydroelectric potential would have to be developed for the iron ore mine. Since this power would not be available for other uses, a proper evaluation of the cost of the project would have to include the cost of generating more expensive thermal power.

The desire of the government to boost the country's development by exploiting its iron ore deposits is understandable, but it is highly important that a full feasibility study be undertaken before final commitments are made. This study should take into account all elements, including infrastructure requirements, and give due consideration to what contribution the project will make toward achieving national economic goals.

Tourism

The tourism sector in the Ivory Coast is small (around 100,000 international arrivals in 1975), and it is expected to remain that way. The sector does offer an opportunity for diversification of the economy, however, and there was an interesting change in policy in 1973. With major infrastructure in place, the government chose in principle to leave hotel construction to private initiative. As part of its new policy, a tourism incentive code was introduced that had adequate but somewhat less advantageous incentives than those in the 1959 investment code for industry. The change in policy is an example of leaving more initiative to the responsive private sector and directing the public sector to the areas where it indeed has an advantage.

The transport, public utilities, and urban sectors

The government is convinced that in order to stem migration toward Abidjan, the rural community must be offered a complete package of services; secondary urban centers must be developed and at the same time services in the main urban center, Abidjan, must be improved. This concept is sensible, but it is clear that an investment program based on what is desirable could easily far exceed the means. Careful planning and the use of proper criteria are essential. First, an improvement in services without at the same time providing a sufficient basis for earning a decent income will have limited, if any, effect. Second, standards should be appropriate to local needs, and the tendency to overdesign should be avoided. Third, the principle that users pay for the services provided should be applied as much as possible. Fourth, in view of the fact that the different elements of such a program would be prepared by different ministries, close cooperation would be required in planning, programming, and implementation.

The substantial investments in the transport sector over a period of some thirty years have provided the country with a well-developed transport infrastructure. It seems time for a gradual reduction in the relative share of resources invested in this sector. The country is moving toward a situation in which the major infrastructure is in place, and more emphasis on feeder roads to make better use of earlier investments would be appropriate. A major issue in the transport sector is inadequate planning at the subsectoral levels and the lack of overall coordination and evaluation of transport policy and investments. These factors produced a tendency toward overinvestment during the 1971–75 plan period. The need to reinforce sectoral planning capabilities has been recognized by the government and a planning and research unit has been established. Also, a master highway plan and a general feeder road study were under preparation at the end of 1975. The rail, port, air, and maritime transport subsectors are still deficient in planning and policymaking capacity. This has led to high standards and ambitious proposals for these subsectors for the next planning period. Careful reexamination of these programs could result in substantial savings.

In the energy sector the country is fortunate to continue to have potential to generate hydroelectric power. Investment in this sector is being used to phase out obsolete thermal plants and small uneconomic thermal units in secondary centers and rural areas. In order to promote a new hydroelectric scheme, the government recently decided to on-lend to the energy company on softer terms than those on which it borrowed funds. It is questionable that the sector needs this subsidy.

The government has drawn up an ambitious scheme to improve water supply. Calculations show that, even at the present uniform national tariff, implementation of the entire program would require substantial subsidization. Because there is little room for further tariff increases in real terms and progress in this sector seems to be faster than in the other sectors, the government should consider bringing the program more in line with the other sectors.

Because of the huge potential demand for low-cost housing and other urban services, appropriate criteria should be developed to bring the public program within reasonable limits. Even if the 8,000 pro-grammed housing units a year are constructed between 1976 and 1980, this would leave a considerable proportion of the demand unsatisfied because the number of Abidjan residents is expected to increase by 600,000 during that period. A substantial part of subsidized housing has gone to income groups that are already relatively well-off and should be able to make larger contributions to the cost. It is therefore recommended that housing for certain income classes be left more to private initiative. It would be possible to help many more individuals if the given amount of resources were used to provide incentives that mobilize private initiative. Many residents of Abidjan should be able to improve their living conditions if the government provided the ap-propriate framework to guide private initiative. Another cost-saving measure would be to improve and densify existing living quarters. The alternative of expanding the area of the city would make transport and other services increasingly expensive. The government and the World Bank are undertaking an urban development project for Abidjan and San Pédro that takes these elements into account, makes the best use of what is already available, and tries to make the best use of new inputs.

Education

The remarkable enrollment achievements of the Ivorian educational system have been mentioned. The proportion of the budget absorbed by education has increased continuously and rapidly, and to do justice to other needs expenditure for education cannot continue at the same pace. Appendix D on education contains recommendations for a strategy aiming at providing the type of education the country needs at minimum cost. Costs are high for two major reasons: (a) The standards of education are high as are costs per individual student; (b) because of the system of incentives—education is free—the numbers enrolled are large and there is no direct relationship between the number of pupils and quality of education on the one hand and the economy's needs on the other. Substantial savings could be made by gearing the incentive system to the needs of the economy. Also, most buildings are constructed to high standards, and a simpler design would be appropriate. The use of the recently introduced educational television system in primary education should be extended to other stages of education, and in some instances the quality of inputs could be reduced. A saving of only 10 percent in the recurrent costs of financing a single student at the university would finance the cost of four places in a primary school. Furthermore, the bunching of pupils who fail to make the quota for secondary education and therefore stay in primary school for another try could be eliminated by providing more alternatives in secondary education, especially short courses that prepare pupils for a productive role in society in a relatively short time. This policy could provide students with incentives to enter such activities as the informal sector and small-scale enterprises. Finally, it is recommended that part of the burden of education be shifted to the private sector. The implementation of such a policy in a country that has traditionally provided free education may prove unpopular. In view of the fact that the tax system is not really progressive, it would be appropriate, especially for the higher forms of education, to let the graduate bear the social cost of education. To ease the transition while better serving society's needs, scholarships could be kept at current nominal levels with no adjustment for inflation and could be given as an inducement to students to go into priority fields. This would be consistent with a policy of providing more initiative to the private sector. The private individual would have to look at education as an investment rather than as a free good, which in a national economic sense it is not.

The level of cost is not the only problem in education. The increasing gap between expectations raised by the education system and what the real world can offer in terms of jobs has been discussed earlier. A change in the system would have to be based on a change in the appreciation of education itself. Education serves a purpose only if it can be applied in the real world. When education cannot be so applied, it leads to frustration, which is a negative return in the national economic sense. Too much dissatisfaction is harmful not only to the individual but to society as a whole. It is strongly recommended, therefore, that manpower planning be strengthened and that the educational system be viewed as a supplier of skills that the economy needs. Increased emphasis on local production factors and on creating an environment in which they can thrive would be consistent with such a policy.

Mobilization and allocation of local savings

For the mobilization and allocation of local savings, the most relevant points in the context of the discussion here are that: (a) the latest reform of the West African Monetary Union encourages the allocation of funds for local, private, relatively small-sized activities, for housing for nationals, and for agriculture; (b) the reform stimulates local savings through higher interest rates on deposits; (c) a stock exchange was established in April 1976 to stimulate local savings; and (d) an expansion of the banking system by bringing in new banks is hoped to improve the mobilization and allocation of national savings and at the same time should improve access to outside sources of capital.

As indicated in Chapter 3, the reforms of the Monetary Union will have to be followed by national measures. For instance, the interest rate incentive to lower the cost of credit will probably not be enough to enable small-scale enterprises to grow rapidly. Additional measures may have to be taken to limit the risk for commercial banks. One way of doing this would be to improve technical assistance to prospective small-scale businessmen. A project started in 1975 by the government and the World Bank is designed to do so. This method of creating employment would make maximum use of local private savings, skills, and initiative.

Private savings as registered by the banking system may well remain low for a variety of reasons, some of which the government might alleviate. First, the tax burden is relatively high, a situation that reduces the possibility of private savings.

Second, most of the savings and profits made by foreigners are transferred to the home country. The government is looking into this question but it may be difficult to keep people from transferring their savings abroad without violating the rules of the Monetary Union. Since the stock exchange is meant to be a device for the Ivorianization of capital, expatriates cannot buy shares, only bonds. Allowing non-

Ivorian Africans to invest in property in the Ivory Coast could keep savings in the country.

The Ivorian economy offers many investment opportunities, and private savers and private investors are often one and the same. If the banking system serves as an intermediary, it is usually so for a short period of time. This situation will continue as long as the private sector can find investment opportunities that earn a better return than interest rates on deposits. The Ministry of Finance is studying a system under which the saver makes an agreement with the bank on an investment, then starts to build up a deposit level until he reaches a predetermined minimum amount. He would then be eligible for a loan for the remainder of his investment requirement. The government would still be able, by means of various incentives, to direct the private investment into areas it considers to have priority. The investment decision would be basically that of the private person. This method is considered important as a means of turning over part of the investment initiative to the private sector.

It is clear from the high tax burden and the volume of public investment that the public sector has made and is making very significant decisions on saving and investment on behalf of the people. Frequently the public sector makes investments that use high standards but cost more than the users are charged or can afford. The cost of the government's ambitions as reflected in its tentative public investment program exceeds its means, and the level of foreign borrowing needed for full implementation would not be sustainable. With the appropriate set of policies, however, a balanced growth rate of 6 to 7 percent a year would be possible during the next ten-year period; it would allow a substantial economic improvement in the lives of all Ivorians.

APPENDIX A

Plans for Agricultural Development

THE PROSPECTS FOR CONTINUED SUBSTANTIAL GROWTH of the agricultural sector during the next five to ten years are good. It should, moreover, be possible to achieve overall growth while at the same time emphasizing the role of the savannah and markedly improving farming systems and standards of living in that region.

Development of the forest region should continue to be geared to expansion and improvement of the major export crops: cocoa, coffee, oil and coconut palm, and rubber. Ecological conditions are excellent for these crops, and research is producing a steady stream of improved varieties and techniques. The southwest offers new potential from several points of view. Land use planning, however, has not been particularly strong so far, and this should receive immediate attention.

Implementation of the 1971–75 Plan for Agriculture

Total agricultural investment (including livestock, forestry, and fisheries) over the 1971–75 plan period was expected to reach CFAF111 billion in current terms, equivalent to about CFAF75 billion in constant 1970 terms, which is very close to the plan forecasts. As a proportion of total public investments during the plan, however, agriculture has received a lower share than forecast (about 26 percent compared to 32 percent planned) because of delays in the implementation of some agricultural projects and an increase of resources in the volume being devoted to other sectors. Details of 1971–75 agricultural investment for each crop or activity appear in Table SA79.

In terms of volume of production, plan targets for commercial crops grown in the forest zone were all more or less reached or exceeded in 1975—coffee, cocoa, copra, rubber, oil palm (90 percent of target), bananas (85 percent), and pineapple (125 percent); for other crops such as cotton, sugar, rice, and industrial groundnuts the plan targets proved overoptimistic. Estimated production of traditional foodcrops appears to have kept pace with plan forecasts.

Taking the years 1970 and 1975 as points of comparison, it is estimated that the volume of commercial crop production (plus timber) grew by about 28 percent over the plan period as against a plan forecast increase of 21 percent. In effect, an increased rate of exploitation of timber resources has more than compensated for shortfalls in the realization of certain crop targets such as those for sugar, cotton, and bananas, and lack of diversification into new industrial crops such as kenaf,[1] tobacco, cashew, avocado, and groundnuts.

More disquieting from the standpoint of future production growth have been delays in the physical realization of certain expansion or replanting programs for perennial crops, combined with serious cost overruns in several cases. Thus planting targets for oil palm, coconut, rubber, and cocoa have been less than two-thirds realized as a result of delays or bottlenecks in implementation, while actual costs in real terms have invariably been higher than foreseen (Table SA80). The coffee replanting program has been only about 50 percent achieved, at more than twice the total cost in real terms foreseen in the plan. Establishment of the first sugar complex has suffered from a number of technical difficulties, and cost so far has been about double the original estimate in real terms. For cocoa, coconut palm, and rice, real unit costs of development have been more nearly in line with original estimates, but with some shortfall in physical realizations.

Among a variety of reasons for the high cost overruns in constant prices may be singled out the following: (a) underestimation of the extent to which public investment in buildings, roads, and social infrastructure would be necessary in order to reach project targets; (b) insufficient control over the size of state companies' (SODEs) overhead and spending programs; and (c) at least in the case of sugar, the choice of what seems to be an oversophisticated production technology. There is full awareness among government officials of these problems, and in some cases, such as control over the SODEs, corrective action is being taken.

---

1. This project was finally abandoned in 1974; the area developed will be used for rice and other crops.

The Draft 1976–80 Investment Plan

For the formulation of its 1976–80 plan the Ivory Coast has chosen planning by objectives so that the plan's component elements would reflect more faithfully the strategy choices made by the government. In practice, it is hoped that the new system will make it easier for the government to face up to these choices, to keep a better balance between public sector activities in different sectors and regions, and to involve the technical ministries more closely in the planning process.

Inevitably, the new planning process has engendered delays. In addition, the continuing world economic uncertainties have aggravated the delicate task of making some difficult decisions concerning, for example, pricing policy and subsidies, the extent to which Ivorian agriculture should (or can) remain dependent on foreign immigrant labor, and the cost of self-sufficiency in certain foodstuffs.

Overall framework and objectives

For 1976–80 the four main objectives for agricultural development, with their respective ancillary objectives, are:

a. Improvement of agricultural incomes, particularly of smallholder farmers, and reduction of regional disparities.
b. Modernization of the agricultural sector through the gradual evolution and deliberate transformation of traditional agriculture, and through the development of medium-sized modern family farms.
c. Ivorianization of agricultural employment, including technicians and managers as well as unskilled labor.
d. Improving the balance of payments by diversifying agricultural exports, increasing their volume, and reducing agricultural imports, particularly food products.

Generally speaking, these are individually well-defined objectives; what is more important is the relative importance that will be accorded to each in the final formulation and implementation of the 1976–80 plan. In fact, it seems doubtful that planning by objectives in the Ivory Coast can be made a full reality in an operational sense since the technical solutions and financial means to meet some of the objectives may begin to appear only during the course of the plan period. Discussed here are the investment and output forecasts included in draft documents to the plan available at the end of June 1975,[2] along with the

2. In the rest of this appendix called "the draft plan."

World Bank's estimates of probable agricultural investment, output, and exports, indicating where appropriate the choice of policy options that the government is assumed to have adopted.

The proposals of the draft plan (Table SA81) include total investment in publicly financed agricultural development (including self-financed investments of SODES) amounting to about CFAF343 billion (in 1975 prices). Government planners estimate that, based on a continuation of present policies, about CFAF60 billion of this investment cost would be generated within the various operations, leaving a net amount to be financed by the government of about CFAF283 billion over the five years. This amount includes both the capital costs of projects, strictly defined, and the part of operating costs not covered by project revenues. It compares with a total of CFAF111 billion spent during the 1971–75 plan, which is equivalent to about CFAF137 billion in 1975 prices. The proposed programs would imply an annual average of government agricultural investment of CFAF57 billion (in 1975 terms), compared with CFAF27 billion spent a year in the 1971–75 period (in 1975 terms). The draft plan proposals for agricultural investment are summarized in Table A1.

It is evident that a major reason for the large size of the proposed agricultural investment program was the government's plan for sugar development, which assumes the establishment of six new complexes of 50,000 tons sugar capacity each by 1980. For reasons given later, this target seems unrealistic and it is assumed instead that only two more sugar estates will be established by 1980. With this and other adjustments for likely rates of implementation, it is estimated that total investment in agriculture (in 1975 prices, and excluding the cost of pulpwood plantations) over 1976–80 will be of the order of CFAF212 billion, or about two-thirds of the sum presently being considered (Table SA81). Allowing CFAF60 billion for project-generated resources, which may be optimistic, the government financing requirements would amount to about CFAF152 billion, or an average of CFAF30 billion a year.

Individual programs

Oil palm. The draft plan foresees an increase in output from about 1.0 million tons of fresh fruit bunches in 1975 to 1.3 million in 1980 and 1.7 million in 1985 (Table A2). About 60 percent of these increases in output would come from modern plantations managed by SODEPALM and 40 percent from village plantations established with SODEPALM's

TABLE A1. DRAFT PLAN PROPOSALS
FOR AGRICULTURAL
INVESTMENT, 1976–80

Item	CFAFbillion
Agriculture	
Sugar	120.6
Cotton	28.0
Rice	21.0
Cocoa	19.2
Coffee	11.4
Rubber	13.8
Oil palm	11.2
Coconut	9.9
AVB/ARSO	23.8
Other	23.5
Subtotal	282.4
Forestry (excluding pulpwood plantations)	24.0
Livestock	29.2
Fisheries	7.0
Subtotal	60.2
Total (gross)	342.6
Possible cost recovery from project beneficiaries	−60.0
Total (net)	282.6

Source: Ministry of Planning.

assistance. No important increase in production is foreseen from other privately owned plantations or from the harvesting of wild palm. The program would increase the oil palm area controlled by SODEPALM from 73,000 hectares in 1975 to 109,500 hectares in 1980; with present plans the proportion of village plantations would increase from 37 to 43 percent by 1980. With industrial and village palm plantations estimated to cost about CFAF400,000 and CFAF200,000 a hectare respectively, the proposed planting program is expected to cost about CFAF11.2 billion. There is no reason to doubt that the proposed program can be carried out in full.

Coconut palm.   As of 1975, SODEPALM had about 18,000 hectares of coconut palm plantations under its control (11,300 hectares of industrial blocks and 6,600 hectares of village plantings) situated along the coastal belt to the east of the Sassandra River. Since 1973 all new

TABLE A2. ESTIMATES OF OIL PALM PRODUCTION,
1970–85

(Thousands of tons of fresh fruit bunches)

Item	1970	1975	1980	1985
SODEPALM plantations	95	473	613	901
Village plantations	40	161	288	441
Total SODEPALM	135	634	901	1,342
Private plantations	100	120	130	140
Wild palm	245	230	230	220
Total fresh fruit bunches	480	984	1,261	1,702
Industrial oil[a]	43	162	227	326
Industrial kernels[b]	11	34	46	67

Source: Ministry of Agriculture and World Bank estimates.
a. At a yield of 21.5 percent in 1975, 22 percent in 1980 and 1985.
b. At a yield of 4.5 percent.

plantings made by SODEPALM have been with a new high-yielding hybrid developed by IRHO. Moreover, the first plantings of coconut in the southwest have begun concurrently with an oil palm project. Present plans consist of the establishment of 7,500 hectares in industrial blocks and 2,000 hectares of outgrowers, for which suitable land has already been surveyed. Another coconut project involves planting 1,000 hectares annually in the southeast. Finally, an ambitious program for coconut palm in the interior has been suggested to SODEPALM by the Ministry of Agriculture with the aim of establishing coconut palm under smallholder management in the inland southern belt, which extends northwards as far as Touba in the west, Daloa and Bouaflé in the center, and Abengourou in the east. The target area for this interior program was recently raised by the government from 12,000 hectares to 30,000 hectares to be planted by 1980, although the physical factors affecting plant establishment and eventual copra yields have not yet been fully researched.

In projecting 1976–80 investment costs and future output, it was assumed that only about 12,000 hectares would be planted by 1980, with a further 18,000 hectares in 1981–85 if the program is successful. On this basis the total cost of new plantings during 1976–80 would be CFAF6.1 billion instead of the CFAF9.9 billion planned. Estimates of the future area and production of plantations established by or with the technical assistance of SODEPALM are given in Table A3.

TABLE A3. PROJECTED GROWTH OF AREA AND PRODUCTION
OF SODEPALM PLANTATIONS, 1970–85

Item	1970	1975	1980	1985
Area planted (hectares)				
Industrial blocks	4,600	11,300	20,200	25,500
Village plantations	2,500	6,600	26,500	44,500
Total	7,100	17,900	46,700	70,000
Production (thousands of tons of copra equivalent)				
SODEPALM	. . .	2.7	41	114
Other	10	12	14	16
Total	10	15	55	130

. . . Zero or negligible.
Source: Ministry of Planning.

Rubber.   The draft plan calls for planting 23,000 hectares of rubber between 1976 and 1980, and a further 25,000 hectares by 1985, bringing the total number of hectares planted to 40,000 in 1980 and 65,000 in 1985. Latex production would increase from 17,000 tons in 1975 to 21,000 tons in 1980 and 47,000 tons in 1985. The implementation of the full development program for rubber, however, is subject to a number of uncertainties. First, the project to create a plantation of 13,500 hectares of rubber at Grand Béréby in the southwest[3] has run into management problems and cost overruns, and project cofinanciers will have to decide whether the entire area originally envisaged should be planted. Second, a planting project in the southwest (north of San Pédro) seems to overlap with the 225,000 hectares of forest reserved for the pulpwood project, and indications are that planting will be limited to 2,800 hectares of rubber. Third, especially in the southwest, there is the potential difficulty of attracting sufficient labor during the planting period without unduly escalating costs. The cost of providing adequate temporary housing and services, for example, has already been one of the main factors contributing to increased costs at Grand Béréby. Here it is assumed that revised costs and construction standards agreed for the Grand Béréby project will be successful in attracting sufficient labor to meet project targets.

Other projects involve the establishment of a trial and processing station for rubber, trials of smallholder plantations, and prospecting

3. Being cofinanced by the Ivory Coast, CCCE, FED, and the World Bank.

for a new rubber estate in the extreme southeast. The total cost of the development program for rubber in 1976–80 is estimated at CFAF13.8 billion (in 1975 prices) by the government and the World Bank.

Coffee. The aim of the government as expressed in the draft plan is to improve productivity, product quality, and resistance to annual yield fluctuations of coffee without causing in the process an excessive increase in production. This objective provides the rationale for the SATMACI replanting program, which aims to replant about 15,000 hectares each year of traditional coffee bushes with stumps of a selected variety. Given proper maintenance the improved robusta variety may yield 1,000–1,200 kilograms a hectare of beans compared with an average of only about 300 kilograms a hectare on traditional plantations. Although only 22,000 hectares were replanted between 1971 and 1974, SATMACI expects to achieve the goal of 15,000 hectares in 1975, and this rate can probably be maintained during 1976–80. If properly maintained, it could result in an increase in production by 1985 of about 60,000 tons of coffee.

Taking account of this replanting–new-planting program, government planners forecast an increase of production from the 270,000 tons expected for 1975 to 336,000 tons in 1980 and 361,000 tons in 1985, thereafter falling off to 353,000 tons in 1990. They argue that the age-structure of the existing plantations—over 40 percent of bushes were planted before 1960 according to a 1973 survey—is such that by 1985 declining yields of traditional coffee will already begin to outweigh increases from new, more intensive plantations. Those figures seem to underestimate future growth in production, however. There is likely to be increasing pressure on the government in the next few years to go ahead with an expanded program of establishing new medium- or large-sized coffee plantations, either as inducements for the young or as rewards for the old.

The government is keen to expand further coffee production as is clear from other projects included in the draft plan. One project centers on arabusta, a new type of coffee developed by IFCC in the Ivory Coast that combines some of the qualities of arabica coffee with the ability of robusta to grow well in hot tropical conditions. Arabusta coffee could give the Ivory Coast an edge in case of weak or static markets for robusta coffee. The initial planting program, which started in 1975, amounts to 500 hectares. Yields of 1,600 kilograms a hectare are expected. The arabusta trials center (CEDA) will devise and test alternative farm models, experiment with different processing methods, and place samples of arabusta on the market. Assuming the pilot 500 hectares are followed by another 1,000 hectares by 1980, 1976–80 costs for this project are estimated at around CFAF700 million. The draft plan also includes about CFAF400 million for completion of a 1,000-hectare robusta coffee plantation, which is being established with supplementary irrigation, with the object of settling young farmers. Another project of 6,500 hectares along the same lines is in the planning stage.

The total costs of the coffee development program for 1976–80 (excluding the cost of processing plants) is estimated by the World Bank at CFAF12.8 billion if fully realized. With present policies the entire cost of this development would be borne by the government. However, we believe that the higher price paid for coffee and the improved yields available from the selected varieties should permit a good part of these costs to be recovered from planters. Planters settled on the new larger-sized coffee blocks should repay the direct development costs through, for instance, a BNDA credit. Such an arrangement need not run counter to the objective of providing profitable opportunities for young farmers, but would rather permit greater replicability of such schemes.

The level of production might be as high as 350,000 tons by 1980 and 400,000 tons by 1985, implying exportable amounts of about 335,000 tons and 375,000 tons, respectively. Whether such export levels could be achieved under an International Coffee Agreement is not certain. At present, however, it is clear that for a few years at least the export market prospects for Ivorian coffee have markedly improved.

Cocoa. Cocoa production has risen fairly steadily over the past fifteen years by an average of 10,500 tons or 6.5 percent annually. It reached a record level of 240,000 tons for the 1974–75 season. The draft plan tentatively forecasts a much faster increase in output for the next ten years, averaging 24,000 tons a year, which would double the size of the crop to 483,000 tons by 1985, with a production in 1980 of 350,000 tons.[4] The assumptions on which these forecasts are based have not been defined, but it would appear that most of the increase in production up to now has been attributable to extended area rather than higher yields. The first results of the agricultural census carried out in 1973–74 show a gross area planted in cocoa of 899,000 hectares,[5]

4. The International Cocoa Organization has recently estimated that Ivory Coast's cocoa production may possibly reach 500,000 tons by 1985.
5. Equivalent to 740,000 hectares of cocoa in pure stand (exclusively cocoa) at 1,357 trees a hectare.

compared with an estimate of only 490,000 hectares made as recently as 1971.

The draft plan foresees the area replanted in hybrid cocoa varieties increasing from the 58,000 hectares achieved by 1975 to over 160,000 hectares by 1980. The total cost of the 1976–80 program is estimated at CFAF19.2 billion or an average of CFAF180,000 a hectare planted, including the cost of SATMACI support of cocoa planters and the new planting subsidy of CFAF60,000 a hectare, which alone would represent a cost of CFAF6 billion for the five-year period. As in the case of the coffee program, with present policies the entire cost of replanting and support services will fall on the government; without the planting subsidy, which appears unnecessary to induce planting of new cocoa trees, and with a charge for improved planting material and chemicals, the cost to the government could be reduced to about CFAF8 billion for the same area planted. Allowing for past increases in planted area and for some yield improvement as a result of ongoing projects and the recent producer price increase, it is estimated that production may be about 320,000 tons in 1980 and 375,000 tons in 1985. This would represent an average annual increase of about 5 percent during 1975–85, which is below the 6.5 percent average a year during 1961–75, but which would still be above the linear trend of production established in recent years.

Cotton.   The draft plan expects that the area planted in cotton will increase from about 60,000 hectares in 1974–75 to 80,000 hectares in 1979–80, and that average yields which are already high, will gradually improve from around 950 to 1,150 kilograms a hectare of seed cotton, giving a production of 95,000 tons in 1979–80. This forecast seems reasonable. The expansion would come about mainly as a result of assistance with land clearance, intensive supervision by CIDT, adoption of ox-mechanization, credit for fertilizer and farm equipment, and provision of free planting seed and insecticides, all of which form part of the ongoing rural development project for the cotton areas being co-financed by the government, CCCE, and the World Bank.

The domestic textile industry absorbed 6,000 tons of cotton lint in 1974; the balance and most of the cotton seed was exported. A rapid expansion of the textile industry is under way that is expected to absorb at least 30,000 tons of cotton by 1980, or 80 percent of domestic production. An oilseed crushing plant is also under construction that may be processing most of the cotton seed by 1979–80. If cotton production is to continue to expand, it will be important to ensure that any subsidies provided to these industries are not made at the expense of cotton growers through a diminution in the effective producer price.

Sugar.   The sugar development program, as announced in early 1975 and included in the draft Loi Programme for 1976–78, aims at the installation of ten sugar complexes of about 6,000 hectares each plus mill by the mid-1980s. Altogether these projects would cost about CFAF250 billion in 1975 prices (about US$1.0 billion) and by 1985–90 would be producing about 600,000 tons of refined sugar annually. Since domestic consumption at present is some 60,000–70,000 tons, about 450,000–500,000 tons would be available for export.

The first sugar complex at Ferkéssédougou started production in December 1974, but as a result of delays in commissioning the mill, the production during the first season amounted to only 5,000 tons of sugar. Water demand for the irrigation system and energy requirements have both exceeded the original estimates, necessitating additional investment. At full production of the total 6,000 hectares, it is hoped to reach an average yield of 80 tons of cane and an extraction rate of 10 percent, which would give a production of about 48,000 tons a year by the 1979–80 season.

The rate at which the government's aspirations concerning sugar development can be realized, in view of the massive investment required, is still under discussion within the Planning and Finance Ministries. The plan for 1976–80 includes the construction of six new sugar estates plus a major sugar export terminal in the port of Abidjan and associated transport investment at a total estimated cost (in 1975 prices) of about CFAF120 billion. Such an investment on the part of the state (through SODESUCRE, its sugar development company) would absorb over one-third of planned (and over one-half of probable) public investment in the primary sector for the next five years.

There is no question that the savannah zones of the Ivory Coast are capable of producing sugarcane and that development of this capability would be consistent with government objectives for developing the northern region. The Ivory Coast, however, must find satisfactory answers to several questions before it commits itself to further sugar investment:

a. What will be the costs of production? If each new sugar complex will really cost CFAF23 billion, capital charges alone would amount to about CFAF40 a kilogram at full production,[6] suggesting a total

6. Assuming capital can be borrowed at 8 percent with a repayment period of twenty years.

production cost of at least CFAF100 a kilogram (US$0.23 a pound), while World Bank forecasts[7] indicate a 1980–85 free market price of only CFAF50 a kilogram (US$0.10 a pound).

b. Where and at what price might the Ivory Coast export up to 500,000 tons of sugar during the 1980s? There is little reason to suppose that new preferential markets will be granted by any of the major importing blocks, including the United States, European Community, and West African Economic Community.

c. Is investment in sugar an efficient form of employment creation for the north? The Ferkéssédougou complex expects to employ only about 2,500 unskilled workers (in field and mill) at full production, implying an investment of nearly CFAF10 million for each job created.

It seems likely that careful consideration of these factors will induce the government to proceed more cautiously with its sugar development program, and that it will establish at most two new sugar estates during 1976–80. It is also assumed that ways will be found to keep the cost of developing each 60,000-ton unit down to a maximum of CFAF20 billion (in 1975 prices), including all studies and SODESUCRE overhead.

Rice. On certain assumptions as to future consumption, government planners initially forecast sizable supply shortfalls and propose substantial investments aimed at reaching self-sufficiency in 1985. Projects costing about CFAF21 billion to develop 35,000 hectares with full or partial water control and 30,000 hectares of improved upland cultivation during 1976–80 are expected to yield an additional 350,000 tons of paddy by 1980, leaving a deficit of 65,000 tons of rice to be met by imports.

Because of recent developments following changes in producer and consumer prices, however, government officials are increasingly aware that rice development policies and projects merit close scrutiny. Indeed, the strong supply response to variations in producer prices since 1974 would seem to counsel a scaling down of rice development programs. This would permit a reduction in the most expensive form of rice production, that is, irrigated rice.

It is advisable that the Ivory Coast concentrate its agricultural development efforts in promoting improved types of farming in the savannah area, where stabilized agriculture should progressively replace shifting cultivation. In this context rice would be a basic commodity in a rotation that would also include cotton, groundnuts, sorghum, and a fodder crop.

7. In terms of constant 1973 U.S. dollars.

Bananas.   The draft plan foresees modest increases only. The main emphasis continues to be placed on reorganization and concentration of the industry so as to raise production efficiency, to reduce marketing costs, and above all to improve quality. The volume of banana exports is forecast to increase from 170,000 tons in 1975 to 200,000 tons in 1980 and 220,000 tons in 1985.

Pineapple.   Over the last four years production of pineapples for canning has met plan targets and is expected to reach 170,000 tons in 1975. Export of fresh pineapples has exceeded expectations, attaining in 1975 the 1971–75 plan target for 1980 of 80,000 tons. Ivorian pineapples now account for 70 percent of Western European imports, but competition from other suppliers such as Kenya, Cameroon, and even Latin America is a distinct threat. In 1973 and 1974 export prices failed to advance in line with production cost increases. There have also been some problems of oversupply and a decline in quality, in part because growers have attempted to sell their industrial fruit as a product of export quality, which brings a producer price about seven times higher than that for industrial quality. The problem is essentially one of educating planters in better growing techniques. This is the responsibility of SODEFEL, which up to now has received insufficient funds to recruit and train competent staff to provide adequate extension services. The draft plan sets ambitious targets for canned and, particularly, fresh pineapple production for export. The latter are forecast to increase from 80,000 tons in 1975 to 150,000 tons in 1980 and 230,000 tons in 1985. Increased production and exports at rates similar to those expected for bananas may be feasible, provided quality standards are not allowed to deteriorate and market promotion is effectively pursued.

Other fruit and vegetables.   Besides bananas and pineapple, the program of SODEFEL encompasses the development of a range of other horticultural products. Citrus for oil extraction currently covers 3,500 hectares, mainly in the Sassandra area, with a production of 50,000 tons of fruit. The draft plan foresees an expansion to 5,000 hectares and 80,000 tons of fruit by 1980, but pressing problems of quality and market outlets must be faced with expanding production.

Exports of avocado do amount to only about 600 tons annually. EC imports alone, however, are now at a level of 20,000 tons a year and are expected to double by 1980. Consequently, prospects are good for increased exports, especially since Ivorian avocados are ready for shipment from February to September when little is available from the main exporter, Israel. The draft plan projects avocado exports of 4,000 tons by 1980 and 10,000 tons by 1985.

Promotion on a limited scale by SODEFEL and further trials by IFAC will be continued for other fruit. Mango and papaya may begin to offer some possibilities of export to Europe during the next five years. Further ahead there may be possibilities of developing a trade in some of the more specialized tropical fruits such as guava, grenadilla, and mangoustan. In general, however, the development of a profitable export trade in tropical fruit faces many obstacles. The industry consists mainly of small and scattered producers whom it would be extremely difficult and expensive to reach and train to adhere to the severe quality standards and marketing discipline required by overseas buyers. The lack of significant domestic outlets for nonexportable production aggravates the problem.

A number of firms, mainly run by expatriates, are engaged in the production of flowers and ornamental plants for export; the value of these exports reached CFAF370 million in 1973 and good possibilities for growth exist. SODEFEL has created a company, HORTIVEX, in association with private shareholders, for the development of floral horticulture and export marketing. The draft plan also foresees public investment of about CFAF8 billion during 1976–80 for the development of vegetable production and processing. The program would be implemented by SODEFEL.

In general, the overall objectives of SODEFEL's programs for horticultural development are appealing and might offer interesting new possibilities for development of the north. It is precisely in these northern projects, however, that costs are exceedingly high. Careful study will be required to determine their financial and economic viability and the income levels that participating farmers might reasonably expect. In addition, the north is relatively far away from the main centers of consumption, and much will depend on the success of AGRIPAC and other marketing projects in ensuring regular and economical shipping of produce.

Regional programs. Currently only two agencies, AVB and ARSO, have statutory regional development responsibilities. AVB's activities are mainly in the agricultural field, while ARSO's have, or will have, a broader multisectorial scope. The draft 1976–80 AVB investment budget comprises three main activities with a total cost of about CFAF22 billion. Two operations would be geared to savannah farming:

(a) promotion of ox-drawn cultivation on 7,700 farms of about 4 hectares each, with cotton, rice, maize, and stylosantes planted in rotation, and cattle fattening introduced as part of the operation (cost: CFAF8.5 billion); and (b) semimotorized cultivation on 5,760 farms of 5 hectares each, with a proposed rotation of cotton, rice, maize, yams, and stylosantes (cost: CFAF7.8 billion). A third activity would improve traditional farming in the forest area. The average farm size would be 4 hectares, of which 1.5 hectares would be devoted to improved coffee and cocoa plantings, 0.5 hectare to plantain, and 2.0 hectares to other traditional foodcrops. The total cost would be CFAF5.8 billion, of which CFAF3.5 billion is designated for the coffee-cocoa component. It is included in the separate budgets for those crops and has been netted out in the consolidation of total planned government investment. The ARSO program includes a number of operations (oil palm, coconut, rubber, rice) that have already been described. The additional CFAF1.8 billion included in total investment represents mainly the estimated cost of establishing eight new villages along the middle Sassandra (seven have been completed so far) to provide adequate living conditions for new settlers.

The draft plan for 1976–80 tentatively advocates a large-scale program to develop motorized medium-scale modern farms in the savannah region. Only the broad features have been worked out, and much additional study and discussion are required. The basic premise of the program is that an annual net revenue of CFAF700,000 a family is required to make farming attractive to young, educated Ivorians. Accepting this premise, the planners are seeking a socially and economically efficient farming system that would be feasible to implement. According to current thinking, individual family farms of about 20 hectares each would be grouped together in a block of 100 farms (2,000 hectares). Each block would have a central unit of 100–200 hectares, which would, at least initially, work as a pilot farm, with properly trained management responsible for acquisition, operation, and maintenance of all major machines and equipment required for the block. For the most part, block size would be determined by considerations of efficient use of machinery. Deliveries, credit, and purchases would be channeled to individual farmers through the central unit. Management of this unit would eventually be done by the farmers themselves, who would receive training and advice to form cooperatives.

The total development cost is roughly estimated at CFAF250,000 a hectare, including clearing and developing the land and investing in machinery and equipment and central unit facilities. Planners estimate that net revenue per hectare would be around CFAF50,000, with a total for each farm of about CFAF1 million; net family income would be the targeted CFAF700,000, and the remaining amount would permit repayment of development costs in a fifteen- to twenty-year period. Basic studies are being carried out. A tentative target of developing 60,000 hectares (30 blocks) by 1980 at a cost of CFAF15 billion appears feasible to government planners. These figures seem overly optimistic to us, however, and even if the ongoing studies come out with acceptable models, we expect no more than a third of the targets mentioned would be achieved by 1980.

The draft plan contains eight main programs for livestock development with a total cost of about CFAF29 billion. At the Seminar on Agricultural Development held in Yamoussoukro in February 1975, livestock development emerged as a primary national objective, in fact, as the "priorité des priorités." Presumably, the final version of the 1976–80 plan will reflect this consensus in the form of increased emphasis and allocations. In the view of the authors, although considerable progress could be made in the livestock sector, not more than about CFAF15 billion in public investment could be absorbed in the 1976–80 period.

APPENDIX B

The Industrial Sector

THE MANUFACTURING INDUSTRY has developed rapidly in the Ivory Coast with an annual growth rate in real terms of about 15 percent over the last fifteen years. Its share in GDP rose from 4.0 percent in 1960 to 12.3 percent in 1974. Since 1972, however, the share of manufacturing in GDP has slightly decreased (see Table B1). This is mainly due to a slowdown of local demand, which reduced growth rates in manufacturing in 1973 and 1974 to 8 and 9 percent, respectively. Industries supplying the domestic market have been affected by high rates of inflation and a loss of purchasing power. In 1975 the manufacturing sector picked up again as farmers' purchasing power increased with higher producer prices.

TABLE B1. SHARE OF INDUSTRY IN GDP at CURRENT MARKET PRICES, 1960–74

Sector	1960	1965	1970	1972	1973	1974
Agriculture	43.7	35.9	27.2	26.5	28.2	26.4
Mining	0.8	0.7	0.2	0.3	0.3	0.2
Manufacturing	4.0	6.9	10.8	12.7	11.7	12.3
Crafts	4.0	3.2	2.7	2.5	2.4	1.9
Public utilities	0.6	0.9	1.1	1.2	1.1	1.1
Construction	4.8	5.4	6.7	6.9	6.1	5.4
Service sectors	42.1	47.0	51.3	49.9	50.2	53.2
Total	100.0	100.0	100.0	100.0	100.0	100.0

Source: National accounts. See also Tables SA82, SA83, SA84, and SA85.

Performance and Problems

The development of Ivorian industry has been based on import sub-stitution and processing of agricultural raw materials. In the early 1970s import-substitution industries developed more slowly than those for export, in contrast to the 1960s when they grew at about the same pace. Agro-industries that process raw materials from local agriculture and forestry include canned foods, coffee and cocoa processing, edible oils and fats, other food industries, tobacco, textiles (mainly based on local cotton), and rubber and wood products. The common character-istic of the nonagricultural industries is that they use imported mate-rials (chemicals, fertilizers, crude oil, steel, mechanical and electrical components, and so forth). Table B2 shows how the two categories have developed.

TABLE B2. GROWTH OF AGRO- AND IMPORT-BASED
          INDUSTRIES, 1965–74

Industries	Value added[a] (CFAF billion)				Compound annual growth rate (percent)		
	1965	1970	1972	1974	1965–70	1970–72	1972–74
Agro-industries							
Wood based	2.8	2.9	2.8	5.3	0.7	−1.8	37.6
Nonwood based	3.5	10.2	14.4	26.7	24.2	18.8	36.2
Subtotal	6.3	13.1	17.2	32.0	15.2	14.6	36.5
Import-based industries	5.5	14.1	19.0	26.7	20.7	16.0	18.5
Total	11.8	27.2	36.2	58.7	18.2	15.4	27.5

Source: World Bank estimates.
a. At current factor cost.

The acceleration in industrial growth rates during 1972–74 was mainly due to price increases. Nevertheless, it can be seen that al-though agro-industries and import-based industries developed at about the same rate over the whole 1965–72 period, the situation has been different in recent years. Since 1972 agro-industries have developed much faster than import-based activities. The latter have been affected by lower domestic demand, limited market opportunities, and the high cost of imported inputs. Should special efforts be made and succeed in the development of subsectors based on local agricultural and for-estry resources, a new pattern of growth may occur in the years to

TABLE B3. LABOR FORCE IN MANUFACTURING, 1966–74

Sector	1966	1970	1972	1973	1974	Increase 1966–74 (annual percentage)
Food, beverages, tobacco	5,908	8,842	10,328	10,962	11,806	9.1
Textiles, footwear	4,289	6,976	8,317	8,426	8,724	9.3
Wood products	6,300	9,320	9,800	10,844	11,820	8.2
Chemicals, oil products, rubber products	2,205	3,476	3,902	4,178	4,207	8.4
Building materials	398	865	821	908	845	9.9
Metals, machinery, transport	1,225	2,871	3,705	4,269	4,354	17.2
Other	455	1,002	1,255	1,382	1,487	16.0
Total	20,780	33,352	38,128	40,969	43,243	9.6[a]

Note: Labor force employment is at mid-year.
Source: Chamber of Industry.
a. It is not known how much of the growth is due to considerably improved statistical coverage.

come with more reliance on agro- and forestry-based industries and less on import-based activities.

In addition to the rapid growth in manufacturing output and its growing contribution to GDP, industrial employment has shown sizable increases. From 1966 to 1974 employment rose by almost 10 percent a year, although here again the rate fell below 7 percent in 1973–74. Despite the fact that the manufacturing labor force represents less than 2 percent of the total labor force, it now constitutes about 13 percent of all salaried employment in the modern sector of the economy (see Table B3).

Along with growing industrial production, there has been a sizable expansion of industrial exports amounting to 20 percent of industrial production in 1960 and 29 percent in 1973. Industrial exports are somewhat overvalued in relation to production because the figure for exports contains certain trading margins that are not included in the data on industrial production value. Nevertheless, results are impressive with industrial exports growing more rapidly than total exports, constituting 30 percent of the total in 1974. Table B4 shows the substantial increase in major industrial exports, which consist of eight groups of products based on primary commodities[1]: palm oil, wood products, cocoa products, pineapple products, ginned cotton, latex, instant coffee, and canned fish. These products represent about two-thirds of total industrial exports.

1. See Table SA93.

TABLE B4. INDUSTRIAL EXPORTS, TOTAL EXPORTS,
AND PRODUCTION VALUE, 1965–74
(Percent)

Category	1965	1970	1971	1972	1973	1974
Industrial exports/industrial production value	27.0	28.0	24.0	27.0	28.9	n.a.
Industrial exports/total exports	16.3	20.4	20.1	24.5	24.3	30.0
Major industrial exports/ industrial exports	54.7	72.2	72.6	57.0	61.4	63.5

n.a. Not available.
Source: National accounts and trade statistics.

Table B5 shows that, with the exception of cocoa butter and cocoa cake exports, both of which have stagnated since 1970, all other major industrial exports have grown substantially, the largest increase taking place in palm oil. Many of the so-called industrial exports are produced by relatively simple industrial activity, as in the case of cocoa butter, palm oil, sawn lumber, and latex. Many of these outputs could go through more advanced stages of production locally before being marketed, and they therefore offer considerable potential for further growth of industrial activities and exports.

TABLE B5. VOLUME OF SELECTED INDUSTRIAL EXPORTS, 1965–74

Item	Metric tons				Percentage growth	
	1965	1969	1970	1974	1965–69	1970–74
Instant coffee	410	970	1,400	2,494	136.6	78.1
Cocoa liquor	n.a.	n.a.	10,000	10,958	n.a.	9.6
Cocoa butter	4,980	7,880	7,540	7,473	58.2	−0.9
Cocoa cake	n.a.	n.a.	11,000	8,277	n.a.	−24.8
Canned pineapple	12,880	21,920	27,280	59,257	70.2	118.2
Pineapple juice	7,820	9,820	12,460	15,551	25.6	24.8
Palm oil	...	...	12,440	101,618	...	716.9
Ginned cotton	1,690	11,670	11,680	16,151	590.5	38.3
Sawn lumber[a]	153	180	183	313	17.6	71.0
Veneer[a]	13	46	47	57	253.8	21.3
Plywood[a]	5	7	7	16	40.0	128.6
Rubber (latex)	2,760	7,130	10,870	15,197	158.3	39.8

n.a. Not available.
... Zero or negligible.
Source: External trade statistics.
a. Thousand cubic meters.

Reasons for growth

The successful development of medium- and large-scale industry can be linked to the rapid growth of agriculture, a stable political climate favorable to direct foreign investment and expatriate management and technicians, an ample supply of foreign capital, a relatively adequate infrastructure, and the convertibility of the CFA franc. This convertibility meant that there has been no restriction on the transfer of dividends or the repatriation of capital, and it has minimized the exchange risks of direct investments. Perhaps most fundamental to industrial growth was the successful expansion of the Ivory Coast's agriculture, mostly export-oriented, which created purchasing power. Agricultural exports also provided the foreign exchange earnings that have helped make the franc area arrangements viable and have enabled the country to increase its imports, including imports of equipment and raw materials required for industrial expansion. At the same time, the money supply has been steadily expanded by the provision of relatively uninterrupted credit to business and consumers without the imposition of significant quantitative or other restrictions on payments abroad in order to protect the balance of payments.

Despite these advantages, prospects for rapid industrialization did not look bright in 1960, mainly because of the lack of experienced indigenous labor. As a reflection of this scarcity and also as a consequence of minimum wage and labor regulations inherited from the colonial regime, African wages in industry have been relatively high compared with countries at similar levels of development. In addition, the Ivory Coast had to rely to a considerable degree on expatriate personnel at two to three times the cost of its equivalent in Europe. For these reasons, the country did not have a sufficiently decisive cost advantage to make manufacturing for export to Europe attractive, except in the case of some locally processed primary products. Moreover, the protection provided by the existing tariff structure seemed inadequate to attract many import-substitution industries.

In the face of this situation, the government opted for a policy of providing substantial incentives to import substitution under the 1959 Investment Code by exempting priority firms from duties on imported raw materials and other intermediate inputs. In addition, some quantitative restrictions were introduced to protect a number of local firms. Further, the code provided freedom of transfer of capital and remunerations and guaranteed the legal, fiscal, and social rights of enterprises being established in the Ivory Coast. The code certainly played a role in attracting industries. In a special survey to determine motivations for establishing an industry in the Ivory Coast, however, Investment Code incentives ranked only fifth among various motives, well behind market and political factors.[2] Although most industries that mentioned the code thought it had been critical or essential to their coming to the Ivory Coast, a number of enterprises that had benefited from the code did not mention it even as a secondary factor. This might indicate that, even without such incentives, these industries would have come to the Ivory Coast.

Problems of industrial development

The government's industrial policy to attract foreign manufacturers and to concentrate in the beginning on import substitution helps to explain some of the present characteristics of the industrial sector: inadequate integration (which may be partly linked to foreign dominance of ownership); a heavy concentration in the country's capital, Abidjan; a high proportion of foreign labor and ownership; underutilization of capacity; and a relatively capital-intensive form of production. Industrial protection has also resulted in domestic resource costs in manufacturing that are high compared with those in agriculture. Although the government's industrial policies have been successful in enlarging the industrial sector and in sustaining a high growth rate, problems of economic efficiency, employment, foreign ownership, regional concentration, and income distribution have now arisen.

Low level of industrial integration. Integration of Ivorian industry remains limited. The share of imported inputs in total inputs used by Ivorian industries rose from 56 percent in 1961 to 63 percent in 1966, but declined to 58 percent in 1971. National accounts data for 1973 indicate that this share has decreased further. The overall development of the industrial sector has not significantly reduced the dependence on imported intermediate inputs. A fall in the share of imported inputs for agro-based industries has been compensated for by increased reliance on these inputs in most other sectors, which is typical of an early industrialization process. In addition, of inputs domestically purchased by Ivorian industries, 25 percent came from the primary sector in 1971 and only 17 percent came from the industrial sector. This shows the close relation between strong industrial expansion and the government's agricultural policy, a relation that no doubt will be developed

2. Office de la Recherche Scientifique et Technique d'Outre Mer (ORSTOM), "Les industriels de la Côte d'Ivoire—qui et pourquoi?" (March 1975).

TABLE B6. SHARE OF INDUSTRIAL DOMESTIC
OUTPUT IN DOMESTIC DEMAND, 1970–73
(Percent)

Category	1970	1971	1972	1973
Domestic output in domestic final demand	45.0	48.0	52.0	52.5
Domestic output in domestic capital goods demand	8.0	13.0	14.0	14.9
Domestic output in domestic demand for industrial inputs by agriculture, forestry, and fisheries	51.5	50.7	54.3	52.4
Total	37.0	41.0	42.0	45.1

Note: Figures for domestic output include both manufacturing and mining. Percentages are practically the same for manufacturing alone because the mining sector in the Ivory Coast is negligible. Domestic demand is defined as domestic output for sale on the local market plus value of industrial imports, excluding those used as inputs for manufacturing and mining enterprises.
Source: National accounts.

further in the years ahead. But it also shows the weakness of industrial integration, as evidenced by the low rate of 17 percent for domestic interindustrial purchase in 1971, which, however, had increased considerably to 30 percent in 1973.[3]

The share of industrial domestic output in domestic demand was only 45 percent in 1973, as shown in Table B6. One reason for low integration is that industrial processes in import-based industries in most cases affect only the final stages of production. This is the case for building materials, metals, and vehicle assembly. And in the agro-industries, production frequently involves only the relatively simple and very first stages of processing, as with sawn timber, cocoa butter, and latex. Economies of scale have often prevented industrial integration—the Ivorian market is still too small in most cases to justify integrated production of many chemicals, steel products, or automobile parts. Another factor is that most Ivorian industries are owned by foreign-based firms with ample capacity abroad either to supply their Ivorian subsidiaries with imported inputs or to buy semiprocessed agricultural or forestry products for further treatment abroad. The Investment Code itself, of course, is partly responsible. The ten-year exemption from duties on current imports gave high—but disguised—effective protection to the import-replacing production of a number of firms. With this exemption, even quite low or moderate duties on

3. National accounts. Rates for 1961–71 are taken from a special study by ORSTOM.

TABLE B7. LOCATION OF MANUFACTURING
INDUSTRY, 1974

Category	Abidjan	Bouaké	Other	Total
Production value	64.7	8.8	26.5	100.0
Value added[a]	70.0	17.0	13.0	100.0
Wages and salaries	65.2	10.5	24.3	100.0
Employment	52.6	11.9	35.5	100.0

Source: Chamber of Industry.
a. Estimates by the Ministry of Planning for 1973 (Abidjan) and 1971 (Bouaké).

finished products did support high effective protection when domestic value added was low in relation to the finished product.

Industrial concentration in Abidjan.   About two-thirds of Ivorian industry is located in Abidjan as shown in Table B7. Throughout the 1960s, industry became increasingly concentrated in Abidjan. Despite some stabilization in this trend since the early 1970s, the 1971–75 plan target of reducing Abidjan's share of total value added in manufacturing from 65 percent in 1968 to 50 percent in 1975 has not been met. Large projects such as the paper pulp and tire plants, which were to be based outside Abidjan, could not be implemented, and the lack of effective incentives for decentralization further affected this target. Since the government's industrial policy has given priority to import-substitution industries, while market and infrastructure are in Abidjan, an unbalanced regional distribution of industrial activity is not at all surprising.[4]

A number of factors militate against moving industry outside Abidjan. The city is an attractive industrial pole in terms of market, infrastructure, and services; infrastructure is less developed in the interior, regional markets are small, and minimum labor wages are the same in and outside of Abidjan. Other factors, however, favor industrial decentralization. Industries linked to primary activities, such as agro-industries and fisheries, are often located near the source of raw material and consequently are usually outside Abidjan. Industries already located outside Abidjan[5] include: six wood product plants (both veneer and plywood) belonging to integrated complexes and aiming at maximum integration near the raw material source; ten well-established production units at Bouaké—originally set up there because of the

4. The Investment Code does not offer specific regionalization incentives.
5. Ministry of Planning (DATAR), February 1974.

railway—some of which are connected with the city's integrated textile plant; and two new textile complexes at Dimbokro and Agboville, also along the railway to the north. Some extra costs may have resulted from locating these new textile mills in the interior. To a large extent the government has absorbed these costs, but they have probably been low because the mills are on the railway and on the natural road from raw materials (cotton) to the consumer market.

The processing of local raw materials will, in many cases, continue to take place where the raw material is produced, that is, outside of Abidjan. Such a trend seems less costly, helps lessen the problem of migration to urban areas—especially to Abidjan—and contributes to a better balance in income distribution between Abidjan and the rest of the country. At the same time, most import substitution is now done in Abidjan, and to reverse this trend would be costly. Foreign investors cannot be forced to locate outside Abidjan. To induce profit-minded Ivorian investors to set up outside Abidjan, incentives would have to be high enough to compensate for extra costs incurred in moving to the regions. Incentives should also take into account the benefits provided to the economy as a whole for having an industry located outside the capital.

The DATAR (Direction de l'Aménagement du Territoire et de l'Action Régionale) has estimated that a minimum decentralization premium might range from CFAF0.5 to CFAF1 million for each job created, adjusted according to the remoteness of industries (maximum premium at Korhogo-Ferkéssédougou, Odienné, Bondoukou; minimum premium in the south, center and center-west) and to the desirability of developing certain industrial poles (average premiums for location at San Pédro, Gagnoa, and in the north, west, and east). Inasmuch as incentives provided to priority enterprises have averaged CFAF2 million a job over the ten-year duration of the priority agreement,[6] it is questionable whether a CFAF0.5 to CFAF1 million premium would be sufficient to eliminate resistance by industrialists to investing outside Abidjan and vicinity.

Processing of local raw materials should continue to take place in the countryside because in most cases it is more efficient economically, and outside of Abidjan most import substitution of industrial products could be undertaken only at substantial additional cost. Industrial decentralization should therefore not be overemphasized in industrial policies, at least at this stage of the Ivory Coast's industrial develop-

6. Ministry of Planning.

TABLE B8. PLAN TARGETS FOR INVESTMENT AND EMPLOYMENT
IN MANUFACTURING, 1971–75

Category	Target (1971–75)	Realization (1971–74)	Degree of realization (percent)
Employment	22,500	9,891	44
Investment (CFAF billion)[a]	76.5	42.5	56

Source: National accounts and Table SA88.
a. At 1968 prices. According to the Chamber of Industry, the total realized in current prices was CFAF62.6 billion. The deflator used in 1971, 121.1; in 1972, 126.3; in 1973, 138.8; and in 1974, 170.0.

ment. With more emphasis on the export-oriented processing of local raw materials in the government's industrial policy, a better regional distribution of activity will be arrived at more or less automatically and logically, without paying a premium for creating jobs outside of Abidjan. It should be remembered that within Abidjan itself the level of industrial integration of manufacturing firms is low. In 1971 Abidjan's industries contributed two-thirds of Ivorian manufacturing output, but supplied only about 15 percent of semifinished industrial products used as inputs by industry.[7] These inputs were not diversified very much. Consequently, despite the existence of a growing urban center where almost three-quarters of the manufacturing enterprises are located, it is difficult to speak of an industrial environment based on active interfirm relations. Incentives to decentralization should therefore probably be given in a very selective way. Perhaps one area that should receive priority is the new industrial zone of San Pédro, which may in the future offer an alternative to Abidjan in import-substitution industries.

Industrial labor. From 1966 to 1974 manufacturing employment rose by 9.6 percent a year, that is, from 20,780 to 43,243. As table B8 shows, from 1970 to 1974 fewer than 10,000 jobs were created, only 44 percent of what was anticipated by the 1971–75 plan.[8] A major lag has occurred in textiles, however, and since investments have already been made, a substantial increase in employment in that sector should take place from 1975 to 1977 upon completion of large new textile mills. Plan employment targets for industrial and automotive repair work were also overly optimistic. Excluding these two sectors, about

7. ORSTOM, March 1975.
8. See Table SA88.

TABLE B9. DISTRIBUTION OF EMPLOYMENT
IN MANUFACTURING BY NATIONALITY, 1969–74
(Percent of total)

Category	1969	1970	1971	1972	1973	1974
Ivorians	56.5	58.1	59.7	59.9	60.4	62.0
Other Africans	39.2	37.8	36.2	36.1	35.8	34.4
Non-Africans	4.3	4.1	4.1	4.0	3.8	3.6
Total	100.0	100.0	100.0	100.0	100.0	100.0

Source: Chamber of Industry.

two-thirds of plan targets were achieved by mid-1974. In general, creation of jobs has been slower than foreseen and has increased less than
output because of improved labor productivity and higher capital intensity of enterprises.

The proportion of Ivorians in total manufacturing employment rose
from 50 percent in 1965 to 62 percent in 1974 (Table B9). At the same
time, other African labor decreased, as did non-African labor, which
represented 3.6 percent of the labor force in 1974. In 1971 non-African
expatriates, mainly Europeans, held 87 percent of managerial and
professional technical positions and 48 percent of supervising jobs.
This high proportion of European cadres and technicians is linked to
a lack of qualified Ivorians and to the foreign structure of industry,
which, at least until recently, had encouraged the hiring of expatriates.
It must be recognized that demand for technical and supervisory staff
is limited; total employment in these two categories is about 1,500 in
the Ivory Coast, and only a small number of jobs are held by expatriates in manufacturing. In some cases it might be cheaper to send
people abroad for training rather than to set up costly local technical
training institutions for one specialty for which there may be very
limited demand from industry. More on-the-job training for semiskilled and skilled workers is in order. Regional technical centers (CTR)
and urban technical centers (CTU) are now starting to produce workers
who are better adapted to actual industrial requirements. These schools
are managed by ONFP (Office of Professional Training) and combine
training at the centers with work at the plant. The existing training
tax (0.5 percent of salaries) and external assistance are useful incentives
for making these programs effective.

Constraints on industrial employment include not only a scarcity of
qualified manpower and the use of imported techniques that minimize
labor use, but also labor wages that are relatively high in relation to

other countries. On the basis of a 1972 minimum Ivorian wage scaled at 100, equivalent minimum wages were 93 in Zaire, 87 in Senegal, and 67 in Cameroon and in Togo. Since 1972 none of these countries, except Senegal, has authorized wage increases as substantial as those made in the Ivory Coast.[9] In 1973 average monthly wages ranged from CFAF4,000 to CFAF5,000 in Taiwan and CFAF10,000 in Singapore. In the Ivory Coast average unskilled and skilled workers' wages amounted to CFAF20,700 a month in 1974. There is reason to believe that the level of wages for unskilled and semiskilled factory workers exceeds their opportunity costs to the Ivorian economy, that is, the output foregone by employing them in modern industry (or other sectors also subject to minimum wage laws) rather than elsewhere in the economy.[10]

Another reason for relatively high wages in manufacturing is the number of well-paid non-African expatriates, who received 41 percent of the total industrial wage bill in 1971 but accounted for only 4 percent of employment. According to a rule of thumb commonly used in the Ivory Coast, the cost for one expatriate is two to three times the cost of employing equivalent staff in France. Most managerial and technical positions are held by Europeans. Their salaries are much higher than those for Ivorians and other Africans in similar positions because of expatriation allowances and the fact that seniority or diplomas often place Europeans at the top of their grade.

In the ORSTOM study of the reasons why foreign industrialists settle in the Ivory Coast, labor cost comes at the bottom of the list. Many industrialists fully realize the need to hire more Africans, particularly for medium-level positions, in order to increase competitiveness. They have been reluctant to do so, however, either because of sheer conservatism, a desire to continue working with other expatriates, or, sometimes, unsatisfactory experiences with African labor. In addition, until now many industries received substantial protection and were able to sell at high prices in a protected market, which allowed them to compensate for the higher cost of labor. Although the government is liberal in its pursuance of Ivorianization of personnel in industrial firms (consistent with its general policy), the private sector has been asked to prepare progressive Ivorianization plans. Recently, increasing

9. The minimum wage rose from CFAF73 an hour in August 1972 to CFAF92 in August 1974, that is, by 26 percent (see also Table SA89). This just compensated for cost-of-living increases.

10. The actual wage cost may exceed the shadow price of labor by about 25 percent and by even more for unskilled and semiskilled wages.

numbers of Ivorians have been hired at the higher echelons of management and have been given preference for technical and supervisory jobs. What is needed for Ivorianization without loss of efficiency is systematic on-the-job training of Ivorian technicians and potential middle-level managers in existing enterprises.

The growth of the industrial sector in the Ivory Coast has been heavily based on foreign technology, capital, and expatriate skills, with relatively low rates of absorption of local labor. Policies that favored capital-intensive industries led to a demand for skilled labor of all kinds, and therefore tended to displace less-skilled African laborers who might have been employed in smaller-scale enterprises using simpler techniques. In addition, high effective protection enabled industries with relatively high labor costs to survive. If industrialization priorities were shifted to develop more labor-intensive industries and export-oriented activities subject to keen international competition, the problem of industrial labor wages would become more critical, as would problems with the entire framework of pricing and incentives related to the use and cost of factors complementary to labor.

Foreign ownership. Foreign ownership amounted to 67.6 percent of equity of manufacturing companies (wood products excepted) on January 1, 1975.[11] Three-quarters of Ivorian participation is in the hands of the government and one-quarter is in private hands. Private Ivorian participation is still limited for several reasons. Industry demands relatively large amounts of capital, which, in general has not been accumulated by individual Ivorians. Moreover, the processing of basic materials for export and the final processing of semifinished imported goods in the Ivory Coast are frequently carried out by an affiliate of a foreign enterprise with access to the markets and know-how. Private Ivorians have been hesitant to take part in this kind of operation where their share is too small to exert significant influence. And in other sectors such as real estate it is, for the time being, possible to recover capital more quickly.

Realizing that Ivorianization of jobs and capital should go together, the government has made Ivorianization of ownership an important goal for the past several years. The share of government investment increased from about 10 percent of total equity in industry in 1967–68 to 18 percent in 1971 and 24 percent by January 1, 1975.[12] Despite

11. See Table SA90.
12. Most government investments are in agro-based industries, the textile sector, petroleum refining, and fertilizer production.

this increasing ownership, the state usually does not intervene directly in the management of companies in which it has a share, but uses other means such as price control, fiscal measures, and tariffs. In accordance with its liberal policies the government has been reluctant to specify quantitative targets for its promotion program of Ivorian enterprises. It has, however, set up a program to promote small-scale Ivorian enterprises and facilitate their access to credit institutions; participated in banks and industrial and commercial enterprises through SONAFI, a public financial institution; established in 1976 a stock exchange that will help develop Ivorian shareholding in private enterprises; and encouraged changes in the Monetary Union so that certain local activities receive priority in the allocation of credit.

The capital needs of large industrial companies will probably continue to be met substantially by foreign enterprises over the next few years. Such enterprises are still mostly French, although other nationalities have been growing in importance as the Ivory Coast seeks to diversify its sources of foreign capital.[13] With the exception of the Blohorn Group, a vegetable-oil processing industry (comprising 20 percent of all French investments), most French capital comes from French-based firms. Most French affiliates are almost totally controlled by the parent company, although minority shares are now accepted more frequently because they offer certain advantages: outlets for semi-finished products produced elsewhere than in France by other production units affiliated with large industrial groups, a market in the Ivory Coast for such units located in France, and access to the sale of licenses and know-how.

Since the most logical or easiest opportunities for import substitution have already been used, this policy is becoming more difficult and expensive to implement, and priority is now being given to planning for export-oriented industrialization. Such industrialization includes agro-based industries as well as a highly capital intensive paper pulp project and an iron mining project. Many of these projects cannot be implemented efficiently without foreign capital, expertise, and markets. Consequently, to realize its plans, the government is more or less bound to continue its policy of attracting expatriate firms and of participating in the financing of large industrial projects. The present policy of attracting foreign capital is not necessarily inconsistent with

13. According to the Chamber of Industry, non-French foreign enterprises represented 6.6 percent of the value of industrial sales in 1961, but 20 percent in 1971. On January 1, 1975, French shares represented 70 percent of all foreign-owned shares and 47 percent of all equity in manufacturing.

the desire to promote Ivorian ownership and participation. In the past, however, the dominance of foreign elements, especially in manufacturing, has resulted in certain structures that suit foreign firms well but that are felt to be obstacles to the development of a significant class of local entrepreneurs. An example is the banking system, which has loaned short- and medium-term capital to local manufacturing. Foreign-owned firms operating locally could obtain long-term capital from abroad (headquarters), but this source has not been available to locally owned enterprises. Foreign-owned banks have considered the generally larger, foreign-owned enterprises a lower risk, and if they have been interested in lending to local firms, charges have often been higher than for foreign-owned firms. The government is eager to remove this kind of disincentive for local firms, and the new credit regulations, in effect since July 1975, clearly try to correct this bias.

Growing size of industrial firms.   Despite the fact that enterprises are for the most part of modest size (80 percent of the existing 204 firms had sales below CFAF1 billion in 1974), a growing share of production is provided by the larger firms. From 1971 to 1974 the number of enterprises with gross annual sales exceeding CFAF1 billion rose from twenty-six to forty, and their contribution to total sales increased from 69 percent to 85 percent. The size of firms in the Ivory Coast is increasing for a number of reasons. New industries such as the oil refinery and the fertilizer plant must be relatively large for technical and economic reasons, and several newly created export-oriented units had to be large to be competitive in the export market—cocoa processing, instant coffee, edible oil, pineapple canning, and textile plants, for example. This trend is likely to continue as high priority is given to export-oriented industrialization. Foreign capital and management will be needed to implement and run these larger plants as they have been needed for import-substitution industries, but at the same time training of local managers should receive high priority. Domestic smaller-scale enterprises should continue to satisfy the local market for products and services such as clothing, footwear, and automotive repairs, since economies of scale play a relatively minor role in these industries. Government policy in these cases should encourage training to overcome the lack of technical skills and should enable smaller firms to be competitive with larger ones by improving their access to credit.

Profitability of industry.   Financial profitability seems, on the average, comparable to European norms. The net profit on sales was 6.2

percent in 1973, and the ratio of cash flow to sales was 10.9 percent.[14] In several cases, however, protection is much higher than in industrialized countries, and direct taxation is lower. An analysis of 126 industrial enterprises showed an average post-tax profit on equity of 12.2 percent. A sample analysis by ORSTOM concluded that companies with headquarters in France show an above-average profitability ratio. The study also noted that in general the big undertakings seem to be more stable than the small enterprises, which are often forced to acquire equipment too large for their needs and to invest without sufficient planning. Another finding was that enterprises with government-owned shares—particularly agro-based industries where private entrepreneurs were reluctant to invest—have shown a low financial profitability in several instances. This gives rise to interesting questions regarding the need for technical assistance to small firms, especially for project identification and evaluation, and the danger to the state of engaging in industrial ventures, which sometimes prove more costly than originally foreseen, without sufficient preparation and control.[15]

Increasing industrial exports.   The processing of primary products for export is a major activity in the Ivory Coast. A group of eight products (cocoa, instant coffee, pineapple, palm oil, ginned cotton, wood, latex, and canned fish) represents more than 60 percent of all Ivorian industrial output. In addition, exports of refined petroleum products, produced in excess of local demand by the local refinery, amounted to CFAF10 billion in 1974, that is, about 10 percent of total industrial exports. Textile exports amounted to CFAF11 billion.[16] In 1973 about 60 percent of industrial exports went to Europe. The West African market is second in importance and represented 20 percent.

Despite significant protection granted to CEAO and potentially to CEDEAO exports, several negative factors seem to be at work, preventing the share of intraregional trade from rising rapidly: political and social differences; competition for the same projects in neighboring countries; high transport costs, including freight rates for coastal traffic; and disparities among regulations, tariffs, and institutions. Some progress has been made, however, with the creation of the CEAO as a tool of regional industrial integration. A new regional bank, the BOAD, was set up

---

14. See Table SA92.
15. Typical examples have been the fertilizer plant and the jute bag factory.
16. See Tables SA93 and SA94.

recently. A few regional projects are either in an advanced stage (a cement plant in Togo) or under study (a tire plant). Despite these encouraging regional initiatives, the Ivory Coast will inevitably have to continue to rely mainly on nonregional trade to promote industrial exports in the next few years.

Achievements in industrial development—a quantitative evaluation

The discussion in this section is based entirely on preliminary results of a World Bank research project on incentives and comparative advantage in the Ivory Coast, Senegal, Mali, and Ghana. The study uses the concept of domestic resource cost of foreign exchange (DRC) to quantify the comparative advantage of manufacturing in the Ivory Coast. The DRC values represent the value of domestic resources spent in saving or earning a unit of foreign exchange, expressed as a proportion of the actual exchange rate. Accordingly, a DRC greater than 1 shows that the "implicit exchange rate" in the processing activity, representing the amount of domestic resources spent to earn or save a unit of foreign exchange, is higher than the actual rate of exchange. Consequently, if the actual exchange rate represents the scarcity value of foreign exchange to the economy, it will be desirable to expand activities with a DRC lower than 1 and reduce or make more efficient those with a DRC exceeding 1.

With eighty-nine firms sampled, the study covers modern manufacturing almost completely, with the exception of wood processing and petroleum refining. Table B10 (column 1) gives the results of the DRC calculations by subsector, showing the difference between subsectors. The overall DRC for manufacturing is 1.34, which indicates that the domestic resource cost of earning French francs is above the official exchange rate of CFAF50 to one French franc and is equivalent to an exchange rate of CFAF67 to one French franc. This DRC compares with a coefficient substantially below unity for many agricultural activities, such as coffee and cocoa production.

Compared with agricultural activities, protection in manufacturing has obviously been high on the average. Compared with protection given to industry in other countries, it is moderate. Protection as expressed by the effective protection coefficient (EPC, column 2) is calculated in the same way as is the DRC, the only difference being that values are expressed in market prices in order to derive the EPC, while the DRC computations are done with shadow prices. As mentioned earlier, African wages in manufacturing are higher than in agriculture

TABLE B10. DOMESTIC RESOURCE COST AND EFFECTIVE
PROTECTION IN MANUFACTURING

Product	Domestic resource cost coefficient (DRC) (1)	Effective protection coefficient (EPC) (2)	Difference with shadow price for	
			African labor (3)	Capital (4)
Flour and grain milling	3.33	3.75	0.13	0.29
Canned and prepared foods	0.94	1.10	0.04	0.12
Beer, soft drinks	0.43	0.56	0.03	0.10
Edible oil, soap	2.08	2.48	0.07	0.33
Milk products	1.16	1.05	0.07	−0.18
Tobacco products	0.85	1.19	0.03	0.31
Textiles, clothing	2.31	2.47	0.19	−0.03
Footwear	3.16	2.82	0.24	−0.58
Lubricants	0.96	2.23	0.07	1.20
Chemicals	2.05	1.80	0.10	−0.35
Rubber products	1.52	1.03	0.14	−0.63
Cement	0.92	1.05	0.03	0.10
Transport equipment	0.99	1.17	0.06	0.12
Metal products, mechanical and electrical industries	2.15	1.75	0.11	−0.51
Board and paper articles	0.55	0.81	0.03	0.83
Total	1.34	1.42	0.08	0.00

Source: World Bank Research Project, preliminary results, June 1975.

or in the informal sector, and there is evidence that shadow wages may be some 25 percent below market rates. To obtain a shadow price for capital, the real cost of capital to the economy has been estimated. The main components of this estimate are: the marginal cost of borrowing foreign capital (debt and equity); the average productivity of capital in Ivorian industry and agriculture; and the weight of new foreign capital and of capital withdrawn from existing activities in the capital cost of new investments. A central discount value of 12 percent has been obtained and applied to net assets (defined as the depreciated book value of fixed assets, stocks, and net receivables). The next step was to adjust domestic value added by the difference between the actual earnings of capital and the earnings that would have been obtained at the shadow rate of return. The actual return on capital was defined as pretax profit plus interest and royalties. The results are shown in columns 3 and 4. Excess wages are equivalent to 8 percent of world market value added, but the actual average return on capital is exactly the same as the shadow rate of 12 percent. (Note that the figures for column 2 are equal to the sum of those for columns 1, 3, and 4.)

As shown in Table B10, there are wide variations in economic efficiency between sectors.[17] There is also a marked difference between firms granted priority status and the nonpriority firms, the median DRCs being 1.68 and 1.13 respectively, as compared with the overall median of 1.47. The difference between the median (1.47) and mean (1.34) for all firms is explained by the relatively low DRCs of certain large firms, notably food processing and drinks. The higher median for priority firms as compared with nonpriority firms indicates that priority firms had considerably higher costs and, on the average, were apparently less suited to Ivory Coast conditions than nonpriority firms. This is not surprising since the Investment Code granted special incentives to establish them in the country.

Although average domestic resource costs in manufacturing are high compared with most agricultural activities in the Ivory Coast, this does not mean that Ivorian industrial development should not be pursued any further. For one thing, over the longer term industry is bound to become more important in the Ivorian economy as arable land becomes more limited. Moreover, industry offers greater possibilities than does agriculture for external economies in the form of technological change and the training of labor. It should be possible, by appropriate policies, to increase production with the resources presently devoted to industry, given the need to improve efficiency and to expand in directions that are socially profitable. Low-cost activities could be expanded through greater utilization of capacity, at least in some branches, and some high-cost activities could be contracted. With the rapidly rising cost of import substitution in the small domestic market and the limitations of intraregional trade, these objectives can be served by providing inducements to the extraregional exportation of manufactured goods. The increased emphasis by the government on exporting locally processed raw materials appears to follow this line of reasoning exactly. This direction in policy may be worthwhile, since the processing of raw materials may have lower DRCs than the later stages of import substitution, and there is the possibility of adding consecutive stages of processing before the materials are exported, which also may favor-

17. This is also true between firms because Ivorian industry is still only slightly integrated and of limited size. As a result, factor costs affecting one large firm may heavily influence the average for a whole subsector.

ably affect DRCs. This type of industry is also expected to induce a better regional distribution of activities and better integration of the economy, and it may well facilitate the government's Ivorianization policy. To enable the government to become more selective in granting incentives to the industrial sector, it is recommended that project evaluation techniques be improved to indicate adequately the national economic value of a project before it is executed.

Industrialization Objectives

The industrial objectives expressed in preliminary documents for the Ivory Coast's 1976–80 development plan are numerous and general, which is consistent with the method of planning by objective followed in preparing this plan. The objectives range from maximum growth and integration to employment creation, Ivorianization of industry, contribution to foreign trade, increased competitiveness and dynamism, cooperation with other West African countries, and decentralization. An analysis of the draft plan for industry raises a question about its objectives: So long as they are not quantified in more detail it is difficult to see whether and how they can be met. From documents and discussions with government officials, it would seem that the present thinking aims at three main objectives: (a) export-oriented industrialization, which seems to offer better prospects for growth than does pushing import substitution much further, and which would increase competitiveness and dynamism, provide needed foreign exchange earnings, and help develop trade with other West African countries; (b) employment and income distribution—objectives that would be met through development of labor-intensive activities, manpower training, increased Ivorian participation in industry, and assistance to small-scale industry; and (c) better regional distribution of industrial activities, which would be achieved through the growth of export-oriented processing of local raw materials since such raw materials are usually processed outside Abidjan. Industries in the hinterland would also help achieve objective (b) by providing additional opportunities for employment and Ivorian participation.

Improvements in the import-substitution policy and emphasis on exports

Plan objectives are to develop export-oriented industries based on local raw materials, but of course there are still some import-substitution possibilities in the Ivory Coast, as evidenced by the high import dependence of most manufacturing sectors for their inputs and by the high share of imported final goods, machinery, and equipment. Moreover, the rapid population increase expected for the years ahead should result in continued demand for consumer goods and light equipment goods, some of which are already produced or will be produced in the Ivory Coast. The easiest opportunities seem to have been implemented, however, and the cost of import substitution seems to be rising,[18] thus necessitating a very selective industrial policy that encourages the establishment of efficient firms and improvements in the operation of existing ones.

An export-oriented strategy should accompany the development of an efficient industrial base, including import-substitution industries that may provide inputs for export industries.[19] In order to increase efficiency it would be desirable to:

a. Consider limiting the duty exemptions on imported materials for priority firms. The evidence is that these exemptions are the principal cause of excessively high protection and the establishment of high-cost import substitution. On the average, the adjusted domestic resource cost of priority firms is about 64 percent higher than that of nonpriority firms.

b. Avoid the use of quantitative import protection to the extent possible since this, too, tends to be associated with high-cost production, and in a number of cases the protected firms would be able to compete successfully with unprotected imports. The demand from local firms for quantitative limitations on imports seems to be increasing, however. Although there may be a need for import licensing in cases of balance of payments difficulties, it should remain temporary since it can easily lead to higher-cost operations and excessive profits.

c. See to it that profits do not exceed an acceptable level. In this context, price control could possibly be tightened, but it would be preferable to bring the firms concerned under increased competitive pressure from imports and from local production. This could be

18. DRC calculations (assuming full capacity utilization) show that the most recently established industries have the highest DRCs.

19. A typical example is agricultural machinery, which, if produced efficiently, can reduce agricultural production costs and thus decrease the cost of inputs used by industries exporting processed primary commodities.

done by reducing the effective protection available to them on their domestic sales and by encouraging local entrepreneurs.

In addition to a more selective application of incentive provisions to industry, including the Investment Code, the Ivorian authorities are now thinking of additional incentives for the export of manufactured goods. Export taxes already encourage domestic processing of agricultural products. Rates were very high for the major commodities—23 percent for coffee and cocoa and between 21 and 33 percent for timber—but were substantially lower or even nil when these commodities were processed before export. For example, instant coffee is exempted from export tax, plywood is subject to a 2 percent tax, and sawn timber is taxed between 5 and 10 percent. Additional measures would ensure that new industrial activities conform more closely to their social profitability for the Ivory Coast. This is of special importance since, with the limitations of import-substitution possibilities, the Ivory Coast will have to rely on exports in order to ensure the efficient development of its manufacturing sector.

Export subsidy.   The export of manufactured goods can be encouraged in many ways, for instance, by subsidized interest rates and special insurance coverage against unsuccessful prospecting of export markets and nonpayment of bills. An export subsidy granted on the basis of net foreign exchange earnings would be more effective, however. The authors' calculations indicate that such a subsidy may be set at 20 percent in relation to net foreign exchange earnings, a level that may be considered a target for import protection as well since in several instances the latter is considered too high.[20] Subsidies should be provided on all manufactured exports. Because of the difficulties of assessing the export prospects of various manufactured goods and the fact that subsidies would be paid only if exportation took place, it is not recommended that the scope of export subsidies within this sector be restricted. To avoid subsidies to firms that would export anyway, it would be desirable to set targets for firms that at present export manufactured goods outside the CEAO as a condition for obtaining a subsidy. Naturally, existing exportation outside the CEAO should be included in principle in the subsidy scheme, in part because these exports should receive equal treatment with new exports, and in part to avoid a decline in existing exports.

20. In 1972 tariff protection and exemption to priority firms provided on the average a 55 percent subsidy in relation to the net foreign exchange saved in replacing imports.

The budgetary cost of export subsidies should be less than the budgetary cost of attaining an equivalent increase of manufacturing output through import substitution. Our tentative calculations carried out by the World Bank indicate that, under certain conditions believed to represent the situation in the Ivory Coast, the budgetary cost of an export subsidy would be only one-third of the revenue foregone for further import protection. In addition, tax and tariff revenues should increase as a result of rising incomes and consumption associated with higher exports. These revenues should reduce the budgetary cost of the export subsidy. The latter could also be compensated for by lessening the preferential treatment of priority firms producing for the domestic market.

Tariff structure.   Tariff levels have recently been raised by aligning duties on imports from the EC countries with the "most favored nation" tariff. Although in some instances this change will permit the Ivory Coast to buy from low-cost "minimum tariff" suppliers, on balance it is bound to have undesirable consequences.

First, raising protection above present levels, which are already high, provides inducements to high-cost operations that make inefficient use of available resources or reap high profits that may in large part entail losses in foreign exchange through the immediate or future repatriation of savings. These adverse repercussions will be aggravated since, with tariffs higher on outputs than on inputs, the protection of domestic production will increase more than proportionately. Second, it is difficult to avoid increases in profits through price control because of all the differences in quality and product specifications. These difficulties are already apparent and have led to covert price increases through changes in product specifications and the lowering of quality in cases when the firm cannot obtain the desired increase in price. Since the prices of most products are adjusted on the basis of increases in various cost elements (*prix homologués*), historically high profit margins may be maintained and even increased. As suggested above, a case can be made for relying to a greater extent on domestic competition and on competition from imports that would necessitate lowering rather than raising tariffs. These considerations point to the need to reconsider the level and the structure of tariff protection at the first possible opportunity. To the extent that increases in tariffs have been dictated by budgetary considerations, an increase in the rate of the value-added tax would be preferable since it would affect imports and domestically produced goods equally.

In addition, it would be desirable to reduce the extent of tariff escalation, which at present leads to the high protection of processing activities in a number of cases. Reducing tariff disparities would also lessen incentives for capital-intensive production, which are now provided by low or nil duties on machinery, and provide incentives for the production of agricultural machinery.

Foreign markets.   In line with the development of industrial exports, industrial policy should seek to improve accessibility to foreign markets. Increased government activity may be required to open up regional, European Community, and other international markets. For instance, promotional offices could be set up in important EC centers (Cologne, Paris, Milan, and Brussels have been mentioned) in cooperation with the Bureau de Développement Industriel (BDI) and the Centre Ivoirien du Commerce Extérieur (CICE). The latter has been operational since 1972 and has been supervised by the Ministry of Commerce since 1974. The CICEs main task is to promote exports, in particular through a systematic search for new markets. Its role is crucial, since the priority given to industrial exports is not without the danger of heavy dependence on external markets and control of these markets by foreign interests. Absolutely necessary to promote Ivorian exports are marketing efforts such as advertising abroad, providing Ivorian industrialists with information on foreign markets, setting up external trade regulations, and ensuring access to credit. The CICE could also deliver a quality label and establish norms and controls.

The BDI does not appear to have sufficient financial and human resources to carry out aggressive promotion campaigns in the EC and elsewhere. These resources should be provided, especially now that more developing countries are associated with the EC through the Lomé Convention and are competing for the same markets. Project ideas and memoranda are prepared by the BDI and sent to potential investors or foreign organizations. To attract export-oriented industries, coordination might also be improved between BDI and the Ministry of Planning, which handles industrial matters at the ministerial level through the Direction du Développement Industriel (DDI) in cooperation with other planning departments. The trend seems to be to concentrate on a few large industrial projects under the supervision of DDI. Insofar as these projects use subcontractors or supply small industries, the BDI should be well equipped to give assistance since it has frequent contact with small- and medium-sized enterprises in the Ivory Coast and abroad.

Export industries based on processing of local raw materials may attract foreign investors interested in obtaining a regular supply of raw materials locally. Industries such as clothing, leather articles, toys, wood products (furniture and components, wooden frames, and the like) are all based on local materials and are labor intensive. The development of this type of industry appears to have been given priority by Ivorian planners, whereas the more limited concept of subcontracting (*industries de transfert*, that is, labor-intensive plants that use Ivorian manpower but are based mostly on imported inputs) seems to have been given less emphasis, at least for the 1975–80 plan period.[21] Subcontracting industries in fact face two main difficulties. First, products must be identified for which labor costs are low enough to compensate for extra costs in transportation, imported inputs, and equipment. Second, the number of expatriate technical and supervisory personnel has to be kept to a minimum in order to limit costs and remain competitive in export markets. Because of an inability to identify specific projects and to attract potential investors, and because of a lack of sufficiently skilled domestic labor at competitive cost, no subcontracting industry for export has been set up in the Ivory Coast so far. Industries that match Ivory Coast skills, aptitudes, and raw materials (forestry and agricultural output) with the specific needs of enterprises in developed countries would seem to stand a better chance than subcontracting industries that use local skills but import most of their inputs.

Employment and income distribution

Ways to increase employment and improve income distribution include the development of labor-intensive activities, manpower training, increased Ivorian participation in industry, and assistance to small-scale industries. These objectives may best fit into an export-oriented industrialization strategy based largely on processing domestic raw materials. New export industries should attract Ivorian private and public capital in association with foreign partners and thus increase Ivorianization. In addition, the creation of a local class of small-scale entrepreneurs is essential for longer-term growth.

Labor-intensive activities.   The priority given by the plan to agro- and forestry-based processing industries seems in accordance with the ob-

21. The 1971–75 plan had tentatively made provision for such subcontracting industries for the period 1975–80.

jective of developing labor-intensive activities, although there are noticeable exceptions. Investment in sugar refineries is very costly nowadays and creates little employment. Labor is relatively expensive in the Ivory Coast, and it may not always be possible to maximize its use to compete with Asiatic countries unless the desire for high employment for each unit of capital is coupled with a realistic wage policy. The projected number of school leavers and the expected continuation of urbanization both point to a need to create as many jobs as possible. Industrial policy as well as economic policy in its entirety should be geared to this objective.

Industrial training. It is crucial to improve the balance between the training of the labor force and the labor needs of the economy. The Ivorian education system has two major functions: (a) to prepare a minority of students for high, middle, and skilled positions in the modern sector of the economy; and (b) to provide the majority of young people with a basic education to equip them for jobs in the economy's informal or traditional sector. Given the requirements for economic growth and the desire to replace expatriate personnel, the education system has placed greatest priority on producing high- and middle-level manpower. Both primary and secondary schools have been oriented to prepare students for the succeeding education cycle, despite the fact that only a minority of the school-age population ultimately reaches the final year of secondary school, and the majority who drop out are not prepared to enter the labor market. Efforts have been made to create vocational training programs to produce skilled manpower, but these programs have met with limited success; the rate of growth of enrollments in vocational-technical training has been far below that for the classical education system.

Manpower estimates, although tentative, clearly indicate a need to step up the training of skilled labor. The efficiency of training could be improved by an optimal mix of general or theoretical education and more specialized skill training, combined with on-the-job training. Efforts now being made by the Office National de la Formation Professionnelle may contribute to solving this problem, in particular through better cooperation with industrial entrepreneurs. The training programs themselves should introduce students to the work environment as soon as possible. Programs of this nature will require much closer cooperation with employers in order to find places for students in industry. The Ivorian government has already established an industrial apprenticeship tax and subsidizes firms with training programs. A more integrated work-study vocational training system will entail higher costs than at present, but the expense will be well justified if it replaces expenditures on formal technical training and if the training is more closely linked to employer needs. It may well justify an increase in the apprenticeship tax.

It is understood that the 1976–80 plan will give priority to training, and considerable effort will go into seeing that training programs fill the needs of specific priority sectors, such as textiles and wood products, and meet the general requirements of mechanical and electrical maintenance and repair jobs in industry. Here again, the general attitude is essentially pragmatic in order to reconcile the continued need for foreign expertise with the legitimate Ivorian desire to participate actively at all levels in industrial operations.

Ivorian participation in industry.   The government will continue to participate through SONAFI in the equity of industrial and commercial enterprises and banks. It will also continue to require enterprises to present plans for the Ivorianization of personnel, and it will promote small-scale Ivorian enterprises and facilitate their access to credit institutions. Incentives to Ivorian enterprises should enable the latter to compete progressively with foreign-controlled industrial firms. New export-oriented industries will require Ivorian participation, desired both by the government and by foreign investors. The Ivorian authorities will continue to invest in a number of industrial projects for a variety of reasons, ranging from a desire to help develop priority sectors (such as textiles) to the need to supplement insufficient private Ivorian interest in this type of investment. The government is convinced of the need to encourage both foreign and local investors and entrepreneurs. It has lately increased its promotion of small- and medium-sized local enterprises, but at the same time it is careful to avoid the impression that foreign investors would no longer be welcome in the Ivory Coast.

Small-scale industry.   The role of small-scale industry in creating a local class of entrepreneurs and its potential for employment creation must be stressed. There are no comprehensive data on the status and activities of small-scale enterprises (SSEs) in the Ivorian economy, however, apart from some limited surveys on the activities of traders, craftsmen, and other small-scale enterprises in Abidjan and Bouaké and partial data from financial and technical assistance institutions. The government is planning to conduct a nationwide census of the sses in an effort to update and extend the 1967 Abidjan sample survey.[22] For the time being the role and importance of sses can be only roughly deduced from preliminary data on the traditional or informal sector, even though these figures are not complete, accurate, or fully comparable. Virtually all sses are in the informal sector. They are largely family run and are characterized by the use of predominantly local resources, a small scale of operation and turnover, rudimentary operating equipment and technology, a small number of wage earners, and low labor productivity. Workers' skills are generally acquired outside the formal education system, and the enterprises are concentrated in nonregulated, competitive markets. The importance of the informal crafts subsector in economic growth is probably not adequately reflected in the national accounts and GDP computations, since only estimates are available. The value added of the informal secondary sector in 1970 was estimated at CFAF18.1 billion, whereas value added in the crafts subsector amounted to CFAF10.6 billion (see Table B11). The most important crafts subsectors are found in grain milling, textiles, garages, and wood products.[23] Although palm oil processing, wood products, textiles, and clothing seem to have stagnated over the years (in the latter case because of competition from the fast-growing modern domestic industry), bakeries, rice milling, cattle slaughtering, fish smoking, and printing activities seem to have developed to a certain extent.

The government program to foster small Ivorian private enterprises consists of four main elements: (a) a National Office for the Promotion of Ivorian Enterprises (OPEI), which provides technical assistance to small-scale firms and develops lending proposals for them to present to financial institutions; (b) a Guarantee Fund, which guarantees a certain percentage of the loans extended to Ivorian businessmen by financial institutions; (c) special facilities under which SONAFI can provide quasi-equity capital to Ivorian enterprises to enable them to qualify for loans discountable with the Central Bank; and (d) the July 1975 modifications of Central Bank rules, which give certain priorities to the financing of small local enterprises.

According to OPEI,[24] over the 1968–73 period it assisted 602 enterprises, of which 159 obtained a total of about CFAF1.2 billion from

22. Ministry of Planning, "Recensement des activités commerciales, artisanales et des services dans l'agglomération abidjanaise" (Abidjan, 1967).

23. See Tables SA84 and SA85.

24. See Table SA95.

TABLE B11. VALUE ADDED AT CURRENT FACTOR COST
IN MANUFACTURING, 1965–74
(CFAF billion)

Sector	1965	1970	1971	1972	1973	1974
Large- and medium-scale manufacturing	11.80	27.16	29.52	36.21	39.09	58.72
Crafts	2.89	10.61	11.04	11.95	13.08	13.84
Total	14.69	37.77	40.56	48.16	52.17	72.56
Percentage of crafts in total	19.7	28.1	27.2	24.8	25.1	19.1[a]

Source: National accounts.
a. This percentage is abnormally low because of the extremely rapid price increase in edible oils and canned foods, which distorted the value added structure at current prices in 1974.

banks to finance investment programs totaling CFAF1.7 billion. Only 41 percent of these 159 enterprises were manufacturing establishments, which invested CFAF0.7 billion or 43 percent of the total. In general, the system is considered not to have operated very effectively.

In response to the government's request for technical and financial assistance, in 1975 the World Bank agreed to support a project that would finance 120 to 150 small enterprises, creating 1,600 jobs at a total investment cost of about US$8.3 million.[25] The project aims to: (a) improve the quality and focus of OPEI's technical assistance by streamlining and reorganizing the institution (this has already taken place); (b) provide capital to enterprises promoted by OPEI through a loan to CCI (Crédit de la Côte d'Ivoire), a majority government-owned development bank that will develop its capability to appraise small-enterprise projects during loan processing; and (c) develop cooperation between OPEI and CCI and foster better coordination among the other institutions involved in the promotion of small enterprises. To achieve those objectives, a new approach will be used in this pilot project. OPEI will promote specific enterprises such as woodworking, garages, and bakeries, where repetitive operations can be implemented under model projects, where suitable vocational training exists, and where efficient technical assistance can be provided. To allow flexibility in the project, however, part of the loan could be used to finance enterprises other than those in which OPEI specializes.

Further actions that should be undertaken soon include the creation of small industrial zones in the regions and the establishment of special

25. This is an average investment cost of CFAF1.2 million a job, compared with an average of CFAF5 million a job in modern manufacturing.

incentives, perhaps in the Investment Code. It would be logical to extend to artisans and small entrepreneurs the incentives already given to large industries, such as duty-free importation of machinery and other inputs and the proposed export subsidies. Central agencies for purchasing and selling in large lots would enable SSEs to lower production costs and would help them as a group to gain such advantages as credit facilities, insurance, and guarantees. Preferential purchase by ministries and state agencies might also be envisaged. Such measures are already under study by the government. In view of the government's Ivorianization goals, these steps should be implemented rapidly to support the financial assistance CCI will provide. As a prerequisite, however, there is an urgent need for more data. Without minimum information, it is extremely difficult to develop a consistent long-term strategy for small-scale industry in the Ivory Coast. The development of small-scale industry is likely to be slow, but more attention is being given to the issue of small industry itself and should reverse the declining trend of the sector.

Regional distribution of industry

Until recently the Ivorian administration did not have a regional industrial policy, and little was done to counterbalance the influence of Abidjan. Ivorian authorities now stress the advantage of setting up processing plants close to the supply of local raw materials. This policy will improve the regional distribution of employment and income and, in many cases, is the logical solution for technical and economic reasons. In addition, already existing clusters of manufacturing activities may promote the establishment of other industries. Although there is clearly a tradeoff between balanced regional growth and more rapid overall growth, the latter objective certainly receives higher priority in the 1976–80 plan. Industry as a whole is still of limited size in the Ivory Coast, and spreading industrial activity too thinly may endanger its vital role as a driving force for economic growth. Although decentralization is likely in such cases as wood products, cotton textiles, and agro-based industries, the lack of skilled labor in Abidjan will make it difficult to recruit qualified personnel to the interior unless substantial incentives are offered.

Small industries usually enjoy access to local or regional markets, and, in contrast to larger projects, they need equipped industrial land and technical assistance facilities on the spot. Some progress has already been made by OPEI, with UNIDO and World Bank Assistance, in the selection of priority fields for small industries such as tailoring, carpentry, bakeries, and garages. Preparations are also being made to develop small industrial zones in Odienne, Korhogo, San Pédro, Katiola, and Bouaflé.

It is expected that urbanization will continue in the Ivory Coast and that the pressure to create jobs in urban areas, especially in Abidjan, will be great. Consequently, rural areas cannot hope to get much large- and medium-scale industry beyond the processing of local raw material. Decentralization incentives[26] should be very selective and given only to industries for which a real advantage exists in setting up business outside Abidjan. Budgetary constraints are likely to preclude generous investment premiums to industrialists who will demand substantial compensation for the inconvenience and risk of moving outside Abidjan. Better regional distribution, should result primarily from choosing carefully the location of new local raw material processing plants rather than from forcing industries to establish themselves in illogical places at the expense of costly budget subsidies. So far the government has not considered it feasible to penalize industries for establishing in Abidjan, which might indeed have an adverse effect on industrial development itself.

Industrial sector planning and research

Industrial sector planning is now carried out in a specialized department of the Ministry of Planning (DDI). This department is essentially project oriented, however, and, in part because of staff constraints, it does not have the full capability to elaborate and implement a consistent industrial strategy.[27] Moreover, questions of industrial incentives, small-scale industrial development, and employment are covered by the Ministry of Finance, OPEI, and other departments in the Ministry of Planning. In the past, industrial policy was essentially implemented through the 1959 Investment Code and other general incentives. The government intervened only to accept or reject priority

26. Such incentives have been discussed in the beginning of this appendix. Proposals under study include an investment premium, low-cost industrial land, development of industrial land, lower water and power rates, reduced taxes on salaries, and above-average export subsidies for industries located outside Abidjan.

27. Various industrial sectoral studies were made as a contribution to the 1976–80 plan preparation. At the time the World Bank mission was in the Ivory Coast, only a few studies had been completed—electronics, textiles, wood products, leather—and they were in fact very preliminary summaries of various project ideas.

agreements and to participate in a few important projects (textile mills, fertilizer plants, oil refinery, and the like). Today more stress is put on (a) consistent export-oriented industrialization, which involves difficult decisions not only on projects but also on revision of incentives and tariffs and on promotion of exports and foreign investment; and (b) better distribution of employment and income, which involves the development of small-scale industry and appropriate training programs. Coordination among government agencies (DDI, Ministry of Finance, OPEI, BDI, CICE, ONPF) has so far been achieved on an ad hoc and personal basis that may no longer be sufficient to implement effective industrial sector planning and research. It would be useful to inventory the services available in the country, either public or private, to study markets, sources of supply, production processes, accounting and finance, and management. The government should then consider policies and programs to increase (not necessarily by direct intervention) the country's capabilities in support of longer-term research and development planning. The government might consider bringing together in a separate ministry the activities involved in and related to industrial development.

Future Industrial Development

According to tentative forecasts made by Ivorian planners in preparing the next five-year plan (1976–80), growth of value added in manufacturing could be 16 percent a year from 1975 to 1980, that is, slightly higher than the rate registered in the 1960s and the early 1970s. Growth would slow down to 12 percent annually during 1980–85. Some details by sector are given in Table B12. Forecasts for the industrial sector, as presented in preparatory documents by the Ministry of Planning, are still rather global at this stage, without detailed sector analysis and project preparation in many cases.

From 1965 to 1975 agro-industries' contribution rose from 30 percent of value added in manufacturing to almost 40 percent. The wood products subsector declined from 24 percent of value added in 1965 to 11 percent in 1975, and import-based industries[28] remained about constant, as shown in table B13. Thus, the plan anticipates that the share of agro-industries in total value added will increase at an accelerated

28. Chemicals, fertilizers, crude oil, steel, machinery, transport, equipment, and so forth.

TABLE B12. PRELIMINARY PLAN ESTIMATES OF VALUE ADDED
IN MANUFACTURING, 1975–85

Sector	Value added (billion CFAF)[a]			Growth rates (annual percentage)		
	1975	1980	1985	1975–80	1980–85	1975–85
Agro-industries[b]	6.2	13.0	21.5	15.9	10.6	13.2
Food processing[c]	11.0	19.0	28.0	11.6	8.1	9.8
Subtotal	17.2	32.0	49.5	13.2	9.1	11.2
Textiles, leather	10.0	26.6	44.5	21.6	10.9	16.1
Wood products	6.0	13.5	25.5	17.6	13.1	15.3
Petroleum products	2.5	4.5	7.0	12.5	9.2	10.9
Chemicals	6.0	11.0	20.0	12.9	12.7	12.8
Rubber products	0.5	1.5	2.0	25.0	5.9	14.9
Building materials	2.3	3.9	6.1	11.1	9.4	10.2
Iron and steel	...	...	2.0	...	...	...
Metals, mechanical and electrical industries	3.5	7.0	11.0	14.9	9.5	12.1
Transport equipment	2.5	4.5	8.0	12.5	12.2	12.3
Garages	3.7	5.5	9.0	8.3	10.3	9.3
Miscellaneous	2.0	3.2	5.0	9.9	9.4	9.6
Subtotal	56.2	113.2	189.1	15.3	10.8	13.0
Paper pulp	...	4.0	13.0	...	26.5	...
Tire plant	...	...	7.0	...	...	...
Total	56.2	117.2	209.1	16.0	12.3	14.1

... Zero or negligible.
Source: Ministry of Planning.
a. At estimated 1975 prices and at factor cost.
b. Coffee husking, industrial rice milling, palm oil and cake, ginned cotton, latex, sugar, pineapple canning.
c. Grain and flour milling, cocoa products, instant coffee, fish canning, beverages, tobacco products, confectionery, animal feed products.

rate for the 1976–80 period. At the same time, the wood product industry is expected to develop at a faster than average rate (17.6 percent a year from 1975 to 1980). As a result, the importance of import-based industries in industrial value added would decline. This intention to stress development of industries based both on local raw materials and on exports generally seems to be in accordance with the Ivory Coast's comparative advantage.

Assumptions and prospects for main subsectors

The growth rates anticipated for 1975–80, averaging 16 percent a year in real terms, seem overly optimistic. With the changes in indus-

TABLE B13. SHARE OF MAJOR INDUSTRIAL SUBSECTORS
IN VALUE ADDED, 1965–85
(Percent)

	Actual			Plan forecast	
Sector[a]	1965	1970	1975[b]	1980	1985
Agro-industries	29.7	37.3	39.3	45.6	43.8
Wood products	23.7	10.9	10.8	11.9	13.3
Import-based industries	46.6	51.8	49.9	42.5	42.9
Total	100.0	100.0	100.0	100.0	100.0

Source: National accounts and World Bank estimates.
a. At factor cost; crafts excluded as well as paper pulp and tire plant projects for 1980 and 1985.
b. Provisional.

trial policies that are taking or about to take place, making forecasts is
very difficult. A major unknown in the entire exercise is the foreign
market that has to absorb an export-oriented production. Nevertheless,
a growth rate for manufacturing of somewhere around 10 to 11 percent
seems reasonable.

In agro-industries, sugar production is not likely to expand to
200,000 tons by 1980; the coffee deshelling program is under review
because of its high capital intensity; and pineapple processing is facing
increasing competition in the preferential French market. The target
for cotton is considered to be too high by about 10 percent. On this
basis, value added for agro- and food-processing industries is estimated
at CFAF28 billion.

Cotton textile production will increase substantially in coming years
as a result of three large textile projects being implemented. The government policy is to encourage further integration of this sector
through clothing production and exportation. The domestic resource
cost of textiles has been high but should decline in the future with
integrated, more efficient firms, and an increase in grey cloth output
should eliminate imports from Taiwan. The difference in wage costs
will enhance the Ivorian textile industry's competitiveness in European
markets, although perhaps not in relation to some other developing
countries, particularly in Asia. In any case, the Ivorian textile industry
should be able to develop efficiently with large, modern plants integrated down to the clothing level, free access to the EC, availability of
domestic cotton, good management, and at least partially ensured export markets. There are, however, doubts regarding the three main
companies' abilities to realize their second-phase expansion plans after
1978. The leather shoe sector is expected to expand quickly when a

tannery opens in 1980, but this project is only an idea so far, and it is impossible to know what production will be, at what cost, and when. All these factors show how difficult it is to forecast textile and leather output for 1980, particularly since export possibilities will represent a critical part of the operation. The problem of access to international markets may indeed prove the most difficult.

The wood processing subsector is projected to grow by 17.6 percent from 1975 to 1980. Production would increase as follows (in millions of cubic meters of log equivalent):

	1974	1980	1985
Sawn lumber	1.1	2.0	2.0
Veneer	0.5	1.0	1.5

The plan rightly gives priority to the expansion of sawmilling and the manufacture of veneer and plywood, furniture, and other finished products that should progressively replace unprocessed logs as exports. The real problem is to ensure regular supplies of logs to the industries and to enforce forestry and export regulations before resources are depleted. A decree has been passed by the government that empowers the Forest Service to prepare forest management plans for each of twenty-six stipulated regional areas, including a general plan for forest industrialization to secure raw materials for existing and new processing units. Detailed inventories are required, and the Forest Service has to be strengthened to implement those decisions. To assure a supply of logs to the processing industry in the short run, the Forest Service was authorized to establish annual quotas for logging firms. The latter had to deliver 66 percent of the log export volume to local processing units, and logging companies with large concessions had to deliver 100 percent—meaning a local delivery equal to exports. A long-term solution in this sector is required, since integrated industries will be established only if a long-term supply of raw material is guaranteed. Industry representatives are in general agreement that wood processing can be doubled by 1980 and that substantial increases could take place in the veneer and plywood sector by attracting foreign investors and expanding existing units as soon as long-term supplies are secured.

For the other sectors, growth in general has been correlated with overall economic growth, which is assumed to be 8.7 percent for the 1976–80 period and 10 percent thereafter. The World Bank has suggested the following modifications: (a) a CFAF4 billion reduction in the value added projected by the plan for 1980 in agro- and food-processing industries; (b) a CFAF4 billion cut in value added for textiles, reflecting uncertainties about export markets, and a CFAF1.5 billion cut in the leather subsector; (c) a tentative 50 percent reduction in projected output of wood products, reflecting the current slowdown in the industry and the serious constraints on the log supply that discourage potential long-term investors; and (d) a reduction in the average growth rate of all other sectors from 12 percent a year during 1975–80 to about 8 percent, consistent with a growth rate of about 6 percent for the overall economy. On the basis of domestic resource cost indicators, the Ivory Coast seems to have a comparative advantage in export-oriented industries such as pineapple canning and shrimp fishing and freezing. Implicit subsidies may have been granted to exporters of instant coffee and cocoa products in the form of supplies of exportable primary products to these industries at below-export prices. But this is not to argue that production of such processed food products should not be undertaken or expanded. Rather, it should be emphasized that the extent of subsidies should be very carefully studied, and the narrow margins that often exist in world trade for export-processing activities should be taken into account. This obviously also applies to the growing production, mainly for export, of palm oil, palm kernel oil, copra oil, and groundnut and cotton seed oil. International competition is keen for vegetable oils and margins are narrow, but the Ivory Coast seems to have a comparative advantage in this sector. As a result of these considerations, total value added in manufacturing in 1980 would reach CFAF94.5 billion (excluding the paper pulp and iron ore projects), and manufacturing would grow by 11 percent from 1975 to 1980. The same order of magnitude would probably apply for 1980–85.

The paper pulp and iron ore projects

The Ivorian authorities are giving special attention to developing two particularly large projects, a paper pulp mill and iron ore mining. A detailed review of these projects is given in separate sections at the end of this appendix. Striking features of these projects are their relatively high cost, low employment intensity, and relatively low value added in relation to total value added in manufacturing projected by the plan for 1985.

The capital-labor ratios in both projects are obviously high. Forward and backward linkages may not be very numerous, at least in the first stage, and hence would contribute little to industrial integration. One

TABLE B14. MAIN CHARACTERISTICS OF THE PAPER PULP
AND IRON ORE PROJECTS

Item	Paper pulp project	Iron ore project	Total
Investment (CFAF billion in 1975 prices)	110	320	430
Employment in 1985 (number)	1,000[a]	3.350	4,350

Source: Ivorian government and World Bank estimates.
a. Plus another 2,000 on the forest plantations.

argument in favor of these projects is that they fit into the export-oriented industrialization strategy of the Ivory Coast, since one of their major goals is to increase foreign exchange earnings of the industrial sector. These projects will have to be financed mostly from abroad, however, and as a result net foreign exchange earnings may not be very high when capital (and expatriate labor) costs are included. Detailed information would be necessary in order to calculate economic rates of return, and the latter may well prove to be positive if good export prices for pulp and iron ore can be obtained and markets secured, ensuring full utilization of plant capacity. Both projects should be considered as export-oriented enclave projects, contributing relatively little to industrial integration, employment, and Ivorianzation objectives. Because of their size, the projects should be undertaken only after the government has obtained sufficiently favorable contracts with financiers and buyers. The magnitude of the projects proper and the infrastructure required could create serious problems for the entire economy and jeopardize growth for a decade or so unless sufficient guarantees are obtained from the outset.

Small-scale industries

The plan assumes an acceleration of the growth rate of the small-scale industry and handicraft sector from 3 to 5 percent a year during 1976–85.[29] The estimated value added would thus increase from CFAF15 billion in 1975 to CFAF24.5 billion in 1985. This growth rate for small-scale industries seems justified and reflects the priority being given to this sector. Success in this area would be entirely in line with many of the general plan objectives, and in this respect small-scale enterprises are quite different from the big projects. The govern-

29. A 3 percent annual growth rate has been estimated in the national accounts for 1960–75.

ment should therefore evaluate not only the inherent merits of the big projects but also their impact on alternative policies. Bringing the big projects to the state of implementation will absorb much of the time that the few qualifed local planners and other local authorities could spend probably more usefully on smaller projects that might better serve plan objectives. With sufficient attention, smaller projects would probably show higher growth than envisaged in the draft plan.

Paper Pulp Project

Preparatory work is under way on a large paper pulp project tentatively planned for the San Pédro area. The forest in this region is composed of mixed tropical hardwood, and in 1969 the government set aside 250,000 hectares for the pulp mill. In 1971 the French Centre Technique Forestier Tropical (CTFT) made an initial forest inventory, and in 1973 a more detailed one was done to determine how to supply the mill with raw material and guarantee a uniform quality of pulp throughout the year. Additional laboratory tests were then made, and the CTFT concluded that pulping of a heterogeneous mixture of tropical hardwood from the San Pédro area was possible. The results justified conducting industrial-scale tests to give potential investors positive proof of the uniform quality of the pulp produced. It was also established that the forest limits (250,000 hectares) could supply a mill with a capacity of 250,000 to 300,000 metric tons a year for a period of at least thirty years.

Following an agreement between the Ivorian government and a Taiwanese pulp corporation, a sample of 4,900 metric tons of wood, based on the 1973 forest inventory, was processed in Taiwan from October 16–27, 1974. Results were positive and confirmed the laboratory conclusions of the CTFT that it was possible to produce a bleached pulp of uniform quality equivalent to that of European and North American wood.

Samples of the pulp were tested at regular intervals in independent laboratories as a check on the Taiwanese firm's results. The Pulp and Paper Research Institute of Canada and the French CTFT confirmed the results of these tests. Several pulp and paper companies have requested pulp samples of 10 to 60 tons each for paper-making tests. These companies include two French firms and one each in Canada, the United States, Colombia, and Spain. Industrial tests by the Canadian and American firms gave favorable results; other reports are coming.

In addition to French aid, the government has obtained the assistance of the Canadian International Development Agency (CIDA) and Norwegian Aid Agency (NORAD) to make a number of studies.[30] CIDA is making a preliminary site study of the San Pédro, Sassandra, Bandama, and Kiloe rivers. Although the initial project is still planned for the San Pédro area, other rivers were included in the site study to evaluate the possibility of additional mills in those areas if conditions were found to be favorable. A detailed hydrological report of the San Pédro River indicated that at certain periods of the year it would not be able to supply both the mill and the neighboring region, including the town of San Pédro.[31] A new dam to regulate the river flow is now envisaged, with the understanding that the average annual flow will be considerably more than the requirements.

Other CIDA studies include one on the cost of wood delivered to the mill (including logging, transport, road, and other costs), either from the natural forest or from plantation wood. Another study will analyze the possibility of utilizing various species of wood in the perimeter to ensure the highest economic yield from the forest. The Canadian Pulp and Paper Research Institute will carry out additional tests on the pulp produced by the Taiwanese corporation and will also test paper and board samples produced by other companies from Ivory Coast pulp. Additional tests will try to improve the process used in Taiwan in order to decrease the cost of production if possible.

NORAD financed a prefeasibility study by a Norwegian firm, completed in mid-1976, which contained a market study and other information, to allow potential investors to assess the viability of the project. The Norwegian Pulp and Paper Research Institute will proceed with laboratory testing of Ivorian wood using the semichemical and thermomechanical processes. Eventually, industrial-scale trials will be done with the same processes. The purpose is to investigate all possible processes that could be recommended for other pulp and paper mills in the Ivory Coast.

Parallel with the tests on mixed tropical hardwood, the government has also explored nurseries and trial plantations of fast-growing coniferous or hardwood species. Even if a pulp mill were initially supplied with mixed tropical hardwood, it could not operate indefinitely without reforestation.

30. French aid amounts to CFAF80 million, Norwegian CFAF60 million, and Canadian CFAF50 million. Total study costs amount to CFAF600 million up to 1977, including CFAF60 million spent before 1974, CFAF181 million spent in 1974, and CFAF235 million budgeted for 1975. The balance is some CFAF100 million in 1976 and CFAF20 million in 1977.

31. ORSTOM, "Hydrologie de la région de San Pédro" (December 1972).

Plantation trials were done near Abidjan in 1964 and within the perimeter near San Pédro in 1970–73. Preliminary results have determined that: (a) climatic and soil conditions are favorable for the establishment of pulpwood plantations; (b) the annual average growth rate for hardwood is about 15 cubic meters a hectare for a rotation cycle of twelve to fifteen years, and the growth rate for pine is on the order of 30 cubic meters a hectare for a rotation cycle of seven to ten years; (c) 60,000 hectares of hardwood plantations and 100,000 hectares of pine plantations would be required to supply a pulp mill having an annual production of 250,000 to 300,000 metric tons.

It will be necessary to obtain or produce enough seed to create additional trial plantations and eventually semi-industrial and industrial-scale plantations in other areas of the forest. Semi-industrial trials were planned for approximately 400 hectares, if budget resources can be found, and would be extended to approximately 900 hectares over a three-year period.

The Ivorian authorities in April 1975 informed a number of pulp and paper companies about the results obtained and also about the remaining work program. The Ivorian government hoped to be able to negotiate agreements with potential partners soon after the prefeasibility study was completed by the Norwegian firm and reviewed by a Canadian consultant hired by the government. The plan was to form a company in which one or more private groups will participate, including at least one internationally known pulp and paper producer. The government was, however, unable to find technical partners willing to invest in this venture. It, thus, decided to proceed with the project anyhow by creating a state enterprise which would own 100 percent of the equity. Technical partners will still be needed. They would be remunerated on the basis of sales volumes.

The pulp plant project is estimated to cost CFAF110 billion in 1975 prices (about US$500 million), excluding the forest perimeter plantations, the main road to the plant and secondary roads, and the regulating dam on the San Pédro River. This investment is for a plant with a 400,000-ton capacity instead of the 300,000 tons initially envisaged.[32] Equity would be CFAF40 billion. The project would provide 1,000 jobs in the plant (excluding forest exploitation and plantations).[33]

It was originally assumed that construction work would start at the

32. This may require increasing the existing 250,000 hectare perimeter as well as the size of planned plantations.

33. A study by ARSO in 1973 envisaged a 300,000-ton unit that would employ 795 in the plant plus 2,000 on forest plantations.

end of 1977, with 40 percent of the work completed in 1978, 40 percent in 1979, and 20 percent in 1980. This plan has, however, slipped by about two years. Sixty percent of the cost of the project would represent imported equipment and foreign expertise. In the first year of production about 25 percent of the capacity would be used, that is, 100,000 tons of pulp would be produced. Capacity utilization would increase to 75 percent and 100 percent in the following two years. At the price of US$425 for one ton of pulp (CFAF230=US$1), the value of a 400,000-ton output would be about CFAF39 billion.

It is generally agreed that the above schedule is extremely tight. The success of the tests in Taiwan has speeded up the tentative construction schedule, and the longer-term alternative of using only plantation wood as raw material seems to have been abandoned. Once the rest of the studies and experiments are completed, a detailed feasibility study will have to be made, but only after one or several partners have been identified. Even if technical partners can be rapidly found, financial arrangements will have to be negotiated. Completion of the construction work in thirty months in a still remote and difficult area such as San Pédro may also be optimistic. This is not to deny the potential of the San Pédro area and the favorable industrial environment in the Ivory Coast. The pulp project might well prove justified to supply a growing demand for pulp in world markets, and it is generally acknowledged that this type of activity will move to tropical areas because of the fast growth of trees there. But substantial work will have to be done to complete existing studies and, above all, to find a suitable partner, which may be the most difficult task in the present international economic climate. There is also the threat of competition from other countries such as Gabon, which have plans for similar projects. So far the approach of the Ivorian government has been highly professional, but negotiations with potential technical partners may be difficult and should be handled carefully. Under certain conditions the project could be economically feasible for the Ivory Coast and an important impetus to further economic development.

Iron Ore Project

The Ivorian government succeeded in putting together in March 1974 a consortium, COMITERCI, which studied the possibility of exploiting the Bangolo deposits of magnetite ore. Mitsubishi was the largest shareholder with 27 percent; other Japanese interests (Sumimoto Shojo Kaisha, Nippon Steel, and others) held 18 percent, bringing the total Japanese share in the consortium to 45 percent. The Japanese have recently expressed reservations, however, and are understood to have withdrawn. The British had 22.5 percent; France's USINOR and Holland's Hoogovens had 11.25 percent each. Pickands Mather, the U.S. subsidiary of Moore McCormack Resources, which has been prospecting in the country since 1966, had a 4.5 percent stake. The Ivorian government, through the state company SODEMI, had a 5.5 percent ownership. A preconstruction study was completed in August 1976 at a cost of US$9 million.[34]

The project is estimated to cost about US$2.0 billion for an annual output of about 12.5 million metric tons of iron ore pellets. A slurry pipeline or railway would carry the magnetite ore (iron content of around 40 percent) found in Mount Klahoyo, near Man, to the distant pelletization plant in San Pédro. Four years before the start of the project, it is planned to achieve 10 percent of the necessary investment; for each succeeding year the percentages would be 18, 37, 32, and 3.

The preliminary schedule assumed that the mine would be ready for production at the end of 1979 and that, after a few months to build up stocks, production would start early in 1980. Replacing the Japanese sponsors might well delay the project for several years, however, and four to five years would be required to implement it. The project includes a workers' community, loading and unloading wharves near San Pédro (bentonite will be imported for the pelletization plant), and a power plant. In addition, a hydroelectric dam estimated to cost CFAF45 billion (including CFAF10 billion for power transmission lines) would have to be constructed.

Other problems include coordination among the various administrations concerned with power, other infrastructure, and the San Pédro port and the recruitment and training of 10,000 people for construction work in addition to the 3,350 who would be permanently employed at the mine. Despite the fact that Ivorian authorities have succeeded in interesting a number of steel companies in the consortium, no final decision has been made about participating. The project would supply ore to captive markets, but the latter will depend on the overall steel situation in Japan and Europe. The recent downturn in construction in Europe, competition from richer deposits in Africa, and increased production in Brazil and Australia will all affect the prospects for this

---

34. This study combined the prefeasibility study with the study of the site and the analysis of desired equipment specifications and industrial processes to be used.

project. Some of the main issues which remain to be settled are: (a) the European decision to invest in the project, depending on the assessment of their long-term requirements for iron ore and the availability of ore elsewhere; (b) replacement of the Japanese participants; and (c) the financing of the various components of the project, including the hydroelectric plant, the pipeline, and the port extension.

Besides such basic questions, the reliability of the production forecast will also have to be examined. It is now assumed that output could reach 8 million tons in the first year of production; at US$0.31 per ferrum unit it would bring a price of US$20.46 a ton (at least 66 percent iron content). At CFAF230 to the U.S. dollar, the value of the output would be CFAF37.6 billion for 8 million tons in the first year, and CFAF56.5 billion for 12 million tons five years later.

APPENDIX C

The Transport Sector

THE IVORY COAST'S RELATIVELY WELL-DEVELOPED transport infrastructure has been instrumental in the spectacular growth of the country's economy over the past twenty-five years. The government has placed major emphasis on transport investment and has provided reliable and efficient infrastructure for the shipment of the country's major export products.

The transport network of the southeastern region of the Ivory Coast links the area with the port of Abidjan. In this densely populated area, economic development took place initially in agriculture and forestry, whose products were first shipped to Abidjan by rail and later over a system of paved roads. Commercial agriculture logically followed forestry activity, and the increasing demand for export products resulted in the densification of the primary road network centering on Abidjan. A similar pattern of development is currently under way in the sparsely populated southwestern region where, in 1971, the deep-water port at San Pédro was opened. The program of road construction in that area is designed to tap potential resources there and boost development.

This pattern of growth has highlighted the regional imbalance between the south and the sparsely populated north, an area that has not been allocated comparable investment funds in the past. The government is now conscious of the need for a more balanced system of regional development and better income distribution, both of which have important implications for transport investment strategy.

Historical Developments

Over the years the government has made vigorous efforts to improve the country's transport system, upgrading and expanding a network that had originated in colonial times. In 1975 the network consisted of more than 38,000 kilometers of roads, of which some 2,200 kilometers were paved, 640 kilometers of railways, two major seaports, 400 kilometers of navigable lagoons (the rivers are not navigable), two airports of international standard, and eight domestic airfields.

The development of the transport sector of the Ivory Coast has been marked by four major events: (a) the construction of the Régie du Chemin de Fer Abidjan-Niger (RAN) railway, which began as early as 1905; (b) the opening of the Vridi Canal in 1950 and the development of a modern port in Abidjan; (c) expansion of primary roads centered around Abidjan; and (d) the inauguration of the port of San Pédro in 1971.

The RAN railway, built from 1905 to 1954, runs northward from Abidjan to Ouagadougou in Upper Volta and provides an important link with the interior. It contributed to the growth of small towns along its route, the development of agriculture and forestry in the southeast, and, ultimately, cotton production in the central region. Later, following the development of the port of Abidjan in the early 1950s, the upgrading and expansion of the road network and the clearing of the forest led to the expansion of export production of coffee, cocoa, palm oil, and other crops. Increased demand for the shipment of these commodities, particularly during the last two decades, has resulted in further upgrading of the road network. Paved roads now link Abidjan with all major centers of population in the southeastern and central regions of the country.

With the westward progression of forestry and cash-crop production during the 1960s, transport costs increased. A logical response was to provide an export outlet nearer to the new areas of production. The subsequent development of the southwest, encompassing a port, roads, and urban infrastructure, will be a major accomplishment for the Ivory Coast. San Pédro, the country's second deep-water port located some 300 kilometers west of Abidjan, started operations in 1971. Although general cargo traffic has not yet developed as expected, mainly because of delays in the construction of paved roads into the hinterland, the port project represents a major effort on the part of the government to tap the resources of the southwest, which include timber, cocoa, coffee, rubber, palm oil, and iron ore deposits near Mont Klahoyo (Bangolo), some 300 kilometers north of San Pédro. The similarity in potentials for development patterns between the Abidjan-Ouagadougou corridor and the area north of San Pédro is striking indeed.

As a result of these efforts, transport has provided a major stimulus to the rapid growth of the Ivorian economy. Furthermore, three land-locked countries—Mali, Upper Volta, and Niger—use the Ivory Coast as an outlet and have benefited from the well-developed road and rail system and an efficient seaport. An important share of transport capacity has been allocated to satisfying much of the foreign trade needs of these countries.

Recent Trends

Funds allocated to transport investment during the early 1960s amounted to about 30 percent of public investment, attesting to its importance in the development of the economy. More recently, in a rapidly growing public investment program, the overall share devoted to transport infrastructure decreased to about 20 percent, an indication that some of the basic needs in transport infrastructure have been met. Because of the wide dispersion of economic activity and the heavy transport requirements of forestry production, the contribution of the transport sector to GDP has been fairly high—8 percent during the early 1970s. The transport sector constitutes an important source of employment, and the well-developed trucking industry provides an entrepreneurial opportunity for Ivorians.

Roads are the principal mode of domestic transport, carrying about 78 percent of interurban passenger traffic and 70 percent of freight traffic (Table C1). Annual traffic growth has been rapid over the last decade—10 percent for passenger traffic and 7 percent for freight traffic.

With the improvement in the road network over the years, the role of the railway as a long-distance hauler has been accentuated. Road transport has now captured virtually all short-to-medium distance freight traffic between Abidjan and Bouaké. Except for points located directly on the rail route and for bulk transport, rail transport is no longer competitive in this area, but it is basically well suited to development in the north. Recent government policy has been to locate new raw material processing industries within the rail corridor. Moreover, RAN carries about 90 percent of Upper Volta's foreign trade to the seaport of Abidjan. The railway is also of importance to Mali, partic-

TABLE C1. INTERURBAN PASSENGER AND FREIGHT
TRAFFIC, 1974

Item	Road	Rail	Total
Passenger traffic			
Number (thousands)	18,000	2,384	20,384
Percent of total	88	12	100
Passenger kilometers (millions)[a]	3,100	850	3,950
Percent of total	78	22	100
Average length of haul			
(kilometers)	172	356	194
Freight traffic			
Amount (thousands of tons)	5,000	750	5,750
Percent of total	87	13	100
Ton kilometers (millions)[b]	1,200	515	1,715
Percent of total	70	30	100
Average length of haul			
(kilometers)	240	687	298

Source: RAN and World Bank estimates.
a. Number of passengers times distance traveled.
b. Number of tons times distance traveled.

ularly its southeastern region; in recent years, the Abidjan route has handled about 50 percent of Mali's foreign trade, about half of which was carried by RAN.

Faced with the growing dominance of Abidjan—the capital, port, and center of public administration and commerce—the government has become increasingly preoccupied with efforts to decentralize economic activities. With the major urban centers as development poles, it is hoped that greater regional specialization and market-oriented economic activity on a regional basis will be developed.

This policy will entail an important shift in emphasis in transport investment strategy. To support expanded production of cash and food crops, secondary and feeder roads will be needed to complement the existing primary routes. Because the planning of such transport projects requires considerable intersectoral coordination and because priorities are less apparent than in the primary network, the formulation of policies and programs and the selection of projects will require great care. The high cost of developing and integrating the northern region underlines the danger of spending large sums of money with little foreseeable economic return. Transport investment must therefore be planned as an integral part of specific development projects to maximize return. These demands will place an increasing burden on subsectoral planning capabilities and on overall coordination and policy formulation in the transport sector.

Implementation of the 1971–75 Five-Year Plan

In the transport sector, plan preparation was largely based on the recommendations of the 1969 Transport Survey—financed by UNDP with the World Bank as executing agency—which identified a pipeline of projects for implementation over the 1970–80 period. The main thrust of the program under the 1971–75 plan was in four areas: (a) upgrading the primary road network to meet increased transport demand; (b) construction of a deep-water port and supporting road infrastructure in the southwest; (c) further development of the port of Abidjan to handle increasing traffic; and (d) modernization of the RAN railway system with emphasis on rehabilitation and realignment of track between Agboville and Bouaké. All these priorities are sound and in line with the objectives of rapid economic growth. The 1971–75 plan, however, also included a few projects of questionable economic justification, such as the paving of low-priority secondary roads in the cocoa circuit and construction of an airport of international standards at Yamoussoukro, the president's hometown about 275 kilometers north of Abidjan.

On the basis of actual expenditures incurred between 1971 and 1974 and estimated expenditures for 1975, implementation of the transport plan exceeded the initial financial targets by over 20 percent. Sector investment as a whole during the 1971–75 period was estimated to be on the order of CFAF53 billion in 1968 prices as against the initial target of CFAF43 billion, or 22 percent higher. The financial targets were exceeded in all subsectors, with a notable 30 percent increase in the railway program. As a whole, the program represents about 22 percent of total public investment planned, with the road program accounting for 50 percent of total sector investment.

The increase in total sector investment has been due in part to cost overruns, but also to the addition of new projects. A detailed analysis of the road program shows that only about 50 percent of the original proposals were implemented during the plan period. The implementation of projects was held up by government indecision in the construction of the Man-Duekoue-Yabayo road, by the need to strengthen pavement, and by delays in construction of the Abidjan-N'Douci road. A number of projects, such as low-priority roads in the cocoa circuit, were not initially foreseen in the plan. With these additions, approximately 800 kilometers of road were upgraded, or about 75 percent of the total initially foreseen. Significant delays have also occurred in the railway subsector. Realignment of the Dimbokro-Bouaké line finally started in late 1974, and about 40 percent of the program will be implemented during the late 1976–80 plan. The fact that only part of the transport program was implemented, and at considerably higher cost than envisaged for the entire program, suggests a serious underestimation of costs during plan preparation.

In contrast to the progress made in implementing the investments identified by the 1969 Transport Survey, not much has been achieved in institutional improvements recommended for the transport sector. This state of affairs is evident in the recent escalation of investment proposals in the sector, which has resulted in premature investment in certain projects. The only substantive move in this direction has been the reorganization of the Department of Public Works (DPW) to strengthen maintenance operations. The capacity for sectoral and subsectoral planning and policy formulation needs to be greatly increased and overall coordination of the transport sector is also needed.

The 1976–80 Plan

According to the World Bank's analysis of investment proposals and priorities, public investment in the transport sector as a whole should probably be on the order of CFAF160 billion at 1975 prices during the 1976–80 plan. In constant prices, this would represent about a 60 percent increase in transport investment over that of the 1971–75 plan, and would amount to between 20 and 25 percent of total public investment for the period. The estimated distribution of investment among the different subsectors is shown in Table C2. Because of the large spillover from the last plan, primary roads will account for almost half the total sector program. Forecast investment for the Régie Abidjan-Niger railway is unlikely to exceed CFAF35 billion during the 1976–80 period, representing for the most part track improvement between Bouaké and Tafiré, and the procurement of locomotives and equipment. Investment in the port sector will be more modest than in the past, particularly at Abidjan where the development of container traffic will avert the immediate need for major investment and expansion. But during the 1980s port investment at both Abidjan and San Pédro may represent an important share of transport investment because of technical difficulties associated with possible longer-term expansion needs. Further development of airport facilities and government assistance in expanding the merchant fleet are not considered priority investments in the sector and, as a whole, they will probably account for less than 10 percent of the total program.

TABLE C2. ESTIMATED TRANSPORT SECTOR INVESTMENT, 1971–75 AND 1976–80
(CFAF billion at 1975 prices)

Subsector	1971–75 plan		1976–80 plan	
	Actual investment[a]	Percent	Forecast investment	Percent
Roads				
Primary[b]	38.9	38.9	73.3	46.8
Secondary	9.1	9.1	18.1	11.5
Feeder	1.0	1.0	5.0	3.2
Subtotal	49.0	49.0	96.4	61.5
Railways[c]	22.2	22.2	34.8	22.2
Ports	19.6	19.6	13.0	8.3
Maritime transport[d]	0.2	0.2	6.0	3.8
Airports	4.6	4.6	5.0	3.2
Aircraft	4.4	4.4	1.5	1.0
Total	100.0	100.0	156.7	100.0

Source: Ministry of Planning and World Bank estimates.
a. Implicit price index for investment of 100 in 1968 and 190 in 1975.
b. Including bridges and ferries.
c. RAN railway.
d. Government contribution.

Not included in the World Bank's investment estimates is the proposed contruction of a new 350-kilometer railway linking the port of San Pédro with a possible iron mining development near Bangolo in the west-central region. Although the government has decided in principle to construct the railway during the 1976–80 plan, the sources of finance at present remain unresolved, and a decision as to the development of the mining operation has not yet been made. Rough estimates put the cost of the railway at CFAF80 billion, about half of which might be financed by the mining consortium, and which is equivalent to the cost of a slurry pipeline, a more economic solution. If implemented during the 1960–80 plan, though unlikely, the railway would clearly represent the single most important project of this plan; it would increase public expenditure allocated to the transport sector by at least 25 percent.

APPENDIX D

Education

Since independence in 1960 the development of the educational system in the Ivory Coast has been one of the government's remarkable achievements. Enrollments have been rapidly increased at all levels, a university has been built, and the quality of teachers has been improved. At the same time, the country has undertaken a bold and innovative reform of primary education with the introduction of television into the classrooms of both public and private schools. In addition to improving the quality of primary education, particularly language training, educational television serves important social and political purposes by helping to provide a country with over fifty different languages with a means of communication through one common language, French. Currently the country is embarking on a reform of technical and vocational education that will not only expand the whole system, but will render it more efficient and more closely related to the needs of the economy in terms of skills and training. In order to accomplish these objectives the government has reorganized the Ministry of Technical Training and has secured greater employer participation in the planning, financing, and execution of training programs.

Objectives and Problems

In general, the achievements in education are consistent with or are exceeding, sometimes by considerable margins, the objectives that are stated in government plans or have been expressed in the policy pronouncements of senior government officials. In primary education these objectives include the achievement of universal primary education by about 1985, the improvement in the quality of education, and the phased introduction of a system of educational television by 1981. In the interim, targets are being reached as planned. From a narrow base at independence of only 33 percent enrollment of the primary school age group, enrollment has now reached 55 percent. At independence fewer than 40 percent of primary school teachers were fully qualified; by 1975 well over 80 percent were. By 1976 educational television was available for some classes in all six primary grades; by 1985 it will be available for all classes in these grades.

In secondary education the major objectives of the government have been to meet the nation's demand for high- and middle-level manpower, to satisfy the aspirations of the country's youth, and to maintain the quality of education. Numerically, enrollments in secondary schools have exceeded plan targets by nearly 29 percent. Current enrollments are approaching numbers sufficient to meet higher- and middle-level manpower requirements if the system is complemented by appropriate training programs.

In the realm of higher education the government's objectives have included an expansion in enrollments consistent with manpower requirements, a reduction in the high rate of repeating, and a reduction in the number of foreign students studying at the university. The current danger is that an overly ambitious expansion in enrollments during the next plan period may create a surplus of high-level graduates that the country will not be able to absorb.

Accomplishments in education have been accompanied by some new problems and an increased awareness of old ones. These problems include: the rapidly mounting burden on the government of financing education, the geographic maldistribution of educational facilities, a demand for suitable employment by secondary school graduates in excess of the ability of the economy to provide jobs, and a failure on the part of the education and training systems to meet the economy's needs for high- and middle-level manpower, with a consequent low degree of Ivorianization of economically and socially strategic positions in the country.

More fundamentally, the government has become increasingly aware that the standards set for the educational system may not be appropriate under Ivorian conditions. A system that is of high quality by French standards is not necessarily appropriate for the conditions prevailing in the Ivory Coast. Many Ivorians feel the system has not done enough to conserve and promote valuable features of their own culture.

Aside from the mounting costs of education, the rapid expansion in primary school enrollments has increased the pressure to expand secondary school enrollments beyond the country's manpower requirements. The government's efforts to restrain this growth by limiting enrollment and investment in secondary school facilities have been only partially successful. The average class size in secondary schools has increased rapidly in recent years to forty-five students. Restricted access to secondary schools has caused more students to repeat the last two years of primary school—a costly process—to improve their performances in competitive examinations for entrance into secondary schools.

In addition to inviting aid donors to study these problems, the government has performed its own internal assessment of the system through a National Commission for Educational Reform. A UNESCO survey of the education sector is now in hand, and the government is studying the report of its own national commission with a view to inaugurating important reforms. Studies are planned to develop new programs relating education and training to specific sectoral and regional needs and opportunities, and to reform the curriculum in secondary schools and improve the management of educational television.

The Growth in Enrollments and the Emergence of Structural Problems

The structure of the Ivory Coast's educational system follows the French pattern with six years of primary education followed by two cycles of secondary education lasting seven years in all. A full range of courses is offered at the University of Abidjan where the highest degree is the doctorate. Teacher training normally begins after the completion of the first cycle of secondary education, and includes a variety of programs, ranging from a one-year course for assistant teachers in primary schools to an eight-year course for teachers in the second cycle of secondary school. Technical training in the lycées and technical colleges begins after the first cycle of secondary school, and vocational training takes place in special centers after completion of primary education. All instruction is in French, and all qualifications normally have their French equivalents. The system has not been designed to conform to the social and economic conditions that exist in the country.

Total enrollments in the educational system have grown dramatically since the country achieved independence. Primary school enrollments have grown at a relatively steady annual rate of 7.2 percent. This rate of growth in public school enrollments has actually accelerated in recent years, but it has been offset by a rather sharp decline in the rate of growth of enrollments in private schools.

The growth rate in secondary education has been much greater than that in primary schools, partly because it started from a much lower base at independence. During the last decade total enrollments in secondary schools have grown at an average annual rate of 15.3 percent, but this rate has decelerated in recent years to approximately 12.6 percent a year. Private school enrollments in 1963–64 comprised only 18 percent of total lower secondary school enrollments, but by 1973–74 the proportion had risen to over 28 percent.

One important reason for this change is the officially restricted entry into the publicly financed *sixième*, or first year of secondary education, to 24 percent of enrollments in the last year of primary school. While this rate may be consistent with the achievement of the country's manpower planning objectives and the government's conception of the social rate of return to education, it is not consistent with private perceptions of the private rate of return. The policy has accelerated the growth in private secondary education and has distorted the structure of enrollments in both public primary and public secondary schools.

At independence the Ivory Coast had only 850 university students, and these were studying abroad. Today the country has almost 1,500 university students abroad in addition to its own university with over 6,000 students, some 30 percent of whom are foreigners. The growth in the University of Abidjan has been phenomenal since its creation as a center of higher education in 1959–60. During the last five years alone the institution has grown at an average annual rate of over 19 percent, and by 1981 total enrollments are expected to reach 10,000, which will be in excess of any demands placed on the system by the economy.

Major distortions in the structure of enrollments

A severe distortion has taken place in the structure of primary education. This was evident in 1965 when the survival rate (the ratio of enrollments in a given year to enrollments in the previous year) showed rather rapid increases after the third year of primary school, especially for male students. By 1970 enrollments in the last year of primary school were actually greater than enrollments in the previous year, and by 1973 the enrollments of boys in the next to last year were greater than in the grade before that.

The increasing survival rates and enrollments in the last two years of primary school are a result of the growing number of repeaters. High repeating rates in the last year of primary school restricts the number of new entrants into that grade and is at least partially responsible for high repeating rates in the preceding year. The total number of repeaters in the system was 26 percent of total enrollment during academic year 1973–74. This indicates a potential for lowering the total cost of sending a student through primary school as well as a way to increase the flow of students through the system at zero cost.

Aside from repeating the last year of primary school, students who can afford it may enter a private secondary school for the first year in the hope of gaining entry into a public institution for the second year. This is a relatively common procedure in the Ivory Coast. A very sharp drop in enrollments occurs in private secondary schools between the first and second year, but there is practically no drop in enrollments in public institutions in spite of an 11 percent repeating rate for the first year. Roughly 1,000 students repeat the first year in private secondary schools, and almost 1,700 transfer from private to public institutions after that grade. Moreover, over 2,000 unsuccessful students apparently leave school at this point.

At the university level, three major structural problems exist, which have great relevance to costs. First, the failure and repetition rates in most faculties are extremely high. For example, in the four-year law course, for every 100 students who begin, only 21 finish. In the faculty of letters, for every 100 students who begin a four-year course, only 36 finish, and more than 11 student years are required to produce a diploma. The problem is even greater in the economically important science faculty. For every 100 students who begin a four-year science course, only 4 finish, and nearly seventy-five student years are required to produce a diploma. In spite of very large enrollments, the university has little output and, as a consequence, its contribution to the amelioration of the country's high- and middle-level manpower problems is still limited. Furthermore, these attrition rates render what output is produced extremely expensive.

A second problem is that foreign students are a very large proportion of the total enrollment. Although this percentage is low compared with previous years when the University of Abidjan had a more important role in providing higher education for students from other French-speaking African countries, it indicates that a considerable amount of the capacity for higher education is not available for the production of high- and middle-level manpower for the Ivory Coast.

The third structural problem is that the distribution of students among the various schools of the university is not consistent with the country's manpower needs. Only 3 percent of those Ivorians who receive higher degrees are in the faculty of science even though 18 percent of total university enrollments are in that faculty. The relatively large percentage of total enrollments in the faculties of law, economics, and letters indicates a structural imbalance between faculties, which can be assessed only in the context of the country's manpower requirements and its Ivorianization policies.

The effect of educational television on the structure of education

Since its introduction in 1971 television has had a pervasive impact on the structure of primary education that will soon produce consequences in the secondary schools as well. Two systems of instruction have evolved in primary schools—the traditional one using television teaching materials but without access to actual television transmissions, and a full audio-televisual system. The latter is being introduced gradually grade by grade and is expected to be available to all classes in all grades by 1985.

Since the new curriculum was introduced, it has been a matter of policy to eliminate class repeating. This will increase the demand for places in the first year of secondary school, and because this demand is already considerable, educational reform at the secondary school level will be even more urgent.

Cost of Education and Training in the Ivory Coast

Recurrent budget expenditures on education have sustained a very high rate of growth since independence, with total expenditures doubling every four or five years. From 1960 to 1973 total recurrent public expenditures on education and training grew at an average annual rate of 17.5 percent, while total recurrent public revenues grew at a rate of only about 12.5 percent. As a result, the share of education and training in the total recurrent budget grew from 22 percent to 33 percent during this period. An examination of comparable data from 69 countries reveals that in 1973 the Ivory Coast spent a larger proportion

(32.6 percent) of its recurrent budget on education than any other country in the world.[1]

The comparison suggests that the government may be spending too much on education and training and that public resources may be more profitably used elsewhere in the economy. The unusual set of conditions responsible for these huge expenditures include the high rate of growth in enrollments and the high costs per student. These costs are, in turn, attributable to the heavy reliance upon expatriate teachers (75 percent of the total number of secondary school teachers); the provision of generous scholarships for students in secondary schools and universities; the high cost of teaching materials, and other costs associated with the introduction of educational television in the primary schools. Costs per student associated with different levels of education for 1972–73 are shown in Table D1.

TABLE D1. RECURRENT COSTS OF EDUCATION
PER STUDENT, 1972–73
(CFA francs)

Level of education	Cost	Index[a]
Primary	19,550	100
Secondary	104,160	533
Technical	247,840	1,268
Primary teacher training	229,930	1,176
Higher education	550,220	2,814

Source: UNESCO *Côte-d'Ivoire: education et développement*, vol. 2, Annex 103 (Paris: August 1973).
a. Recurrent costs of a student place relative to the recurrent cost of a place in primary school.

Recurrent costs per student appear to be increasing in real terms at all levels of education except the secondary where rapidly increasing class sizes have actually reduced them. During the 1960s, real costs of primary and secondary education per student grew at rates of approximately 3 percent a year. In short, the escalating unit costs of education are not attributable to inflation alone but to increases in the quantity and quality of inputs. Prospects for a reduction in costs in the near future do not appear good. Government estimates indicate that the rate of growth in expenditures through 1980 in constant prices will be

1. The average for the upper third of the countries was 21 percent; the middle third, 18 percent; the lower third, 14 percent. Oman, as estimated in 1972, was lowest with 3 percent. (World Bank Comparative Education Indicator, October 15, 1975.)

approximately 11.5 percent a year. This would compare with a 14 percent rate of growth in constant prices for the 1960–73 period.

With a projected real rate of growth in the economy of 6 to 7 percent a year and a revenue elasticity with respect to GDP only marginally exceeding unity, it is highly probable that the share of education and training in the government's budget will rise even further during the next plan period. Moreover, if the government begins gradually to introduce some of the innovations apparently recommended in the Report of the National Commission for Education Reforms, such as the introduction of preprimary education, this share will be higher still. Although expenditure on education is ultimately a matter of government priorities, greater economy and efficiency might be achieved with a change in policy.

Budgetary allocations

A closer examination of the total recurrent budget devoted to different levels of education does not point to any one level that has been assigned unreasonably high priority. The share allocated to the university is not excessive by international standards. A number of developing countries in Africa allocate 20 percent or more of their education budgets to higher education. Although the allocations to teacher training and technical education appear relatively low, it is problematic where reductions could be made to provide for increases in these areas. The allocations to primary and secondary education do not appear excessive by international standards.

Budgetary allocations to personnel and teaching materials reveal a similar balance. In fact, contrary to the usual tendency of countries to spend too much on personnel in relation to teaching materials, the Ivory Coast has generally maintained a good balance between the two. The UNESCO sector survey of 1973 and more recent data from the Ministry of Finance show that, for primary education, at least 10 percent of the total recurrent budget is spent on teaching materials and, for other levels of education, approximately 30 percent. The lack of a real imbalance would seem to preclude opportunities for savings in this area.

The apparent balance between levels and kinds of education, and between inputs into education, means that a reduction in the share of education and training in the total government budget could result only from reductions in the rate of growth of enrollment; the use of different educational technologies; a more intensified use of available resources; and the adoption of more appropriate educational standards. Reductions in the rates of growth in enrollments, particularly at secondary and higher levels of education, are complex and politically difficult actions to take. Prospects for attaining these reductions will be dealt with later in this appendix. The immediate discussion is devoted to the cost implications of the technology associated with educational television, and to the savings possible through a more intensified use of facilities. Consideration is also given to possible savings through the adoption of more appropriate educational standards.

Opportunities for cost reduction

There are two opportunities for cost reductions within the Ivory Coast's education sector. The first is the possibility of replacing technical assistance personnel with Ivorians. The second reduction relates to the heavy investments that have already been made in educational television.

In 1975 about 40 percent of all personnel costs and 25 percent of the total cost of all education and training were attributable to technical assistance. Since part of these costs are borne by aid donors, the government's share is only about 36 percent of the total technical assistance cost, which accounts for 13 percent of all personnel costs and 9 percent of the total recurrent cost of education and training. Because most of this aid is tied to technical assistance and probably cannot be used for other purposes, and because most technical assistance is used in secondary and higher education where there are grave shortages of teachers, it does not appear possible to make significant savings in the immediate future by replacing expatriate teachers. These teachers ought to be replaced, but, as discussed later in the section on Ivorianization, not primarily in order to cut costs.

Educational television

The Ivory Coast has made a substantial investment in educational television in order to accomplish a number of objectives. These objectives include upgrading primary school teachers, reforming the primary school curriculum, improving instruction in French, and making quality education available to a larger number of students. It was anticipated that smaller classes, better teachers, better materials, and the elimination of repeating would reduce the number of pupil years of schooling required to produce a primary school leaver. Given the high dropout rates and the fact that 26 percent of total enrollments in any year are repeaters, it has taken an average of 16 pupil years of instruction to achieve an output of one student in a six-year primary course. It has been assumed that the improved system, with automatic promotion and television, would be able to produce a pupil of former sixth-grade quality in 5.5 pupil years of instruction because of more efficient instruction, and that this would result in significant savings. In spite of rather intensive study, it is not yet clear that these objectives and these savings are being achieved. The UNESCO education survey conservatively estimates that the additional recurrent costs per student place in a television class are at least CFAF9,200 and much more when technical assistance costs are taken into account.

The capital cost of extending educational television to 695,000 students in 1980 (from 300,000 in 1976) are estimated to be CFAF24,500 per student place. Amortized over a period of ten years at 10 percent, annual capital costs per student would be about CFAF5,500. This brings the additional annual costs per student to over CFAF15,000, or about an 80 percent increase in the costs per student place in primary schools.

The initial evidence from a USAID- and UNESCO-financed study indicates that high expenditures for materials and maintenance may account for the costliness of the Ivory Coast educational television complex. The entire undertaking requires close evaluation, further experimentation, and a more intensive use of invested resources.

More intensive use of educational resources

High total and unit costs per student place in the Ivory Coast are aggravated by the high repeater rate at all levels. The total cost of repeating in 1972–73 was approximately CFAF3,250 million. With total recurrent expenditures for primary and secondary education during 1972–73 of CFAF14,426 million, repeating alone could have boosted the costs of education at these levels by as much as 30 percent. Looked at in another way, nearly 30 percent more students could have gone through the system at no additional cost with the introduction of a system of automatic promotion of students. Repeating and dropping out at the university level are even more serious matters because this is more extensive and expensive than in lower levels of education.

Academic standards

In the past the standards used to evaluate the Ivorian system of education have been essentially French. The Report of the National

Commission for Education Reform reportedly indicates that many Ivorians now regard these standards as inappropriate. The system is relatively inefficient in meeting the needs of the Ivorian economy and society; it consumes a large percentage of the public resources, and it is not thought to be preparing Ivorians for the lives they want to lead.

An educational system more consistent with Ivorian needs and resources would have lower costs per student and would not create expectations inconsistent with opportunities. Each level of education would be more closely aimed at providing people with useful knowledge and skills and less at preparing people for the next level of education. It would provide a larger number of exit points from the formal system and more opportunities for informally acquiring job-specific skills, either on the job or concurrent with a job.

The Excessive Demand for Education

The rapid increases in enrollments and costs at all levels of the educational system can be largely attributed to an excessive demand for education, a consequence of the fact that education is essentially free for private individuals and that sizable increments in income are associated with additional years of schooling. In short, the private benefits from education are far in excess of the private costs.

Moreover, there is a sharp divergence between the net private benefits and net social benefits from education. Although powerful incentives are given to individuals to continue school, the costs to society for that additional schooling may be excessive. An important objective of educational policy should be a closer correspondence between private and social benefits and costs. Until this is achieved, there will be continuing popular pressures for an expansion in enrollments at all levels. If the government is unable to resist these pressures, enrollments and costs will continue to increase.

Rising unemployment among those leaving school will result if the divergence between private and social benefits and costs is not eliminated. School leavers tend to want salaried or wage jobs in the modern urban sector because they have had access to such jobs in the past. But the opportunities for employment may fall increasingly short of expectations in the future as the number of those leaving school rises to levels far in excess of the number of jobs available in the modern sector. They will have to lower their expectations and many will have to seek jobs elsewhere—in the informal sector, for example. Or they may decide to continue in school in order to acquire the jobs that were formerly available to those with much lower levels of education. It will not be easy to find a more equitable balance between private and social benefits and costs because free public education is institutionalized and most individuals have a strong interest in retaining it. But passing on some, if not all, of the costs of education to those who benefit from it is essential if the government is to make progress in restraining future growth in enrollments, costs, and unemployment among school leavers. In addition, the current distribution of income between those employed in the modern urban sector and in other sectors of the economy makes additional years of schooling profitable for individuals. Changing the distribution of income is a slow and difficult task involving alterations in the basic structure of the economy. Thus, responsibility for controlling the costs of public education and providing employment opportunities for those leaving school will not reside entirely, or even primarily, within the ministries responsible for education and training. In the long term, progress will depend upon the action of all those ministries of government that control the instruments of income policy.

Economic structure and distribution of income

In the Ivory Coast as in many other developing and developed countries, additional years of schooling are expected to entitle one to better salaried jobs in the modern sector. But because the modern urban sector is small relative to the total economy and generally capital intensive, high growth rates do not produce many new salaried jobs. Without a consistent statistical base for salaried employment, it is difficult to estimate the precise historical relation among the growth in salaried jobs, GNP, and the number of school leavers seeking modern sector employment. The government statistical services have radically improved their coverage of establishments, but without adjusting historical information to reflect these improvements. According to official statistics, the number of salaried employees in the modern sector (excluding domestic servants) rose from 205,089 in 1971 to 227,854 in 1973–74, that is, at an annual rate of 5.4 percent. If the very substantial changes in coverage between these years are taken into account, and if allowance is made for the fact that the dates of enumeration are early in 1971 and at the end of 1973, the annual rate of growth in salaried employment in the modern sector may have been about 5 percent in the early 1970s. The real economic growth in GDP linked to this increase in salaried employment was about 6 percent a year. The growth rate in GDP in the modern sector alone (which provides a more appropriate comparison) was approximately 8 percent a year.

The 5.4 percent increase in modern sector salaried employment between 1971 and 1973–74 provided new positions for 23,000 people. If it is assumed that in the late 1970s there will be a continued substantial growth of the modern sector, a low increase in productivity (a high increase would replace labor), and an attrition from the labor force of approximately 5 percent a year owing to death and retirement (a high estimate), the modern sector would be able to absorb roughly 30,000 new entrants to the labor force a year (15,000 new jobs plus 15,000 replacements). This is the figure that must be compared with the number of school leavers looking for jobs. Table D2 provides estimates of the numbers of primary, secondary, university, technical, and craft students who entered the labor force in 1973–74. These numbers will be higher for later years. The figures are minimum estimates and are based on enrollment statistics. Table D2 is designed to give some indication of general orders of magnitude and does not include any allowance for those who leave primary school before their last year. It shows that there will not be a sufficient number of salaried openings each year to employ all those with some secondary education, to say nothing of those with only a primary school education.

According to the government's plans and projections through 1980, the prospects for modern sector salaried employment for those leaving school look bleak. By 1980 enrollments in the last year of primary school will not have increased significantly, perhaps to 130,000, because the sizable repeating rates at that level will have been significantly reduced. But the elimination of repeating, currently about 50 percent in that grade, will mean that almost the entire enrollment will either

TABLE D2. NEW JOB SEEKERS IN THE SALARIED
LABOR FORCE, 1973–74

Number of students in the last year of primary school who do not go on to secondary school, who do not repeat, or who do not go on to other formal training institutions	24,000
Number of students who completed or dropped out of secondary school	22,000
Technicians, craftsmen, and other specialists	5,000
University students	350
Total	51,350

Note: Figures are for school leavers only.
Source: World Bank estimates.

enter the labor force or go on to further education and training. According to plan projections, enrollments in the first year of secondary school will approximately double between 1974–75 and 1980–81, from 28,000 to 56,000. By 1980 planned increases in enrollments in secondary schools, at the university, and at other training institutions will add an estimated 45,000 to 50,000 new entrants to the labor force a year, an increment to the labor force of those with at least a primary education of 100,000 a year by 1980–81.

Even if salaried modern sector employment continues to grow rapidly, the number of new employees who can be absorbed by this sector in, say, 1980, will not exceed 30,000. Clearly opportunities for salaried employment in the modern sector will deteriorate during the remainder of this decade and will fall increasingly short of expectations.

Students and parents will to some extent tailor their expectations to fit this situation. If experience elsewhere is any guide, however, two factors will have an overwhelming influence on their decisions. First, the salaries for modern sector jobs are higher than those for alternative jobs, and students and parents in general are willing to assume the risks associated with the declining probability of finding a job. Second, the probability of finding a modern sector salaried job can be improved by additional schooling. Moreover, because public education is free at all levels, the private cost of additional years of schooling is probably very low. This factor alone will reduce the risks of additional years of education in the face of declining job opportunities.

The informal sector

The problem of unemployed school leavers is essentially that of excessive expectations, that is, their supply price is above that which will clear the market for their services. Over time, expectations decline, and workers will accept jobs with lower incomes and lower social status. The government is aware of the problem and is experimenting with more sophisticated types of farming, which would satisfy some of the school leavers. But an important residual employer could be found in the so-called informal or traditional sector. It will be difficult for school leavers to savor this employment prospect, however, and it will also be difficult for government officials and planners to undertake the necessary efforts required to promote the expansion of this sector without overorganizing it.

The potential for growth and the absorptive capacity of labor in the informal sector are nevertheless substantial. Small-scale enterprises in this subsector are directly responsive to the consumer needs of the less affluent in Ivorian society. The sector has other promising features: It has a low capital-output ratio, provides its own venture capital, trains much of its own labor, and requires little high-level manpower. In short, it provides both development and jobs at relatively low cost. A shift in priorities and incentives in favor of this sector is called for. More emphasis upon small-scale, labor-intensive enterprises may produce more growth, more employment, and a better distribution of income.

The issue of underemployed school leavers should be regarded in the context of rural and urban poverty in the country as a whole. The school leaver has received considerable benefits from his society and has a substantial advantage in the marketplace over those with little or no education. Although he may suffer considerable disappointment, it should be remembered that his income will generally be above average.[2]

The Geographical Maldistribution of Educational Facilities

In academic year 1973–74 about 50 percent of the population aged seven to twelve was enrolled in primary schools, but there were great differences among departments. For example, in the Touba Department only about 13 percent of the age group was enrolled while Agboville and Abengourou Departments had enrollments of 86 percent and 78 percent, respectively. Data on secondary school enrollments for each thousand inhabitants by department for 1973–74 also indicate great variability among departments. Although nationally there were 14.7 secondary school students for each thousand inhabitants, the departments of Gagnoa, Abidjan, Adzopé, Guiglo, and Agboville had between twenty and twenty-five secondary students for each thousand inhabitants, while at the other extreme Korhogo, Boundiali, Odienné, and Séguéla had only six secondary students for each thousand inhabitants and Touba had only four.

Government efforts in rural areas

The complex relation between the geographical distribution of enrollments and regional income inequalities is evident in the high correlation between the per capita income of farmers and primary and

2. World Bank, "The Ivory Coast Special Report on Employment," 3 vols., no. 297A-IVC (July 31, 1974).

secondary school enrollments by department. The government of the Ivory Coast has embarked upon a policy that encourages rural areas to establish new primary schools and seeks a wider geographic dispersion of facilities for technical and vocational education. The government has also undertaken an ambitious program of regional preinvestment studies to identify both the training needs associated with local area development and the means by which formal education can be integrated effectively with actual work experience. It should be noted that one important objective of the government's educational television program is the provision of quality education to all persons regardless of location.

Regional rural development funds.   One of the means by which the government encourages the development of primary education in poorer areas is by financing the construction of school buildings through special regional funds (Fonds Régionaux d'Aménagement Rural, FRAR). Normally, the provision of primary school buildings is a responsibility of local communities and self-help, but in poorer areas where these efforts are not sufficient, regional development funds can be used.

Teachers for rural areas.   The government is also seeking to provide teachers to self-help schools. But although preference is given to poorer areas in this program, half of all applications for teachers from local communities are turned down, and a large proportion of these are from poorer rural areas.

Technical training centers for rural areas.   With assistance from several donors, the government is currently undertaking a program to set up training facilities for craftsmen and artisans. There are twelve such centers now that are widely dispersed geographically. With forty-five students for each center, 540 students a year will be trained. Three of these centers specialize in teaching artisans skills that are in demand in rural areas.

Regional development authorities.   The development of semiautonomous regional development authorities in the more deprived rural areas is especially promising. These authorities have become involved in a wide range of activities normally undertaken by the government, including the provision and coordination of social services. They have also begun to experiment with training programs that are adapted to local needs and skills.

Regional preinvestment studies.   The experience of the regional development authorities indicates that education and training can contribute more to the welfare of individuals and regions if this education is more closely tied to specific regional economic opportunities and if it takes into account the particular social constraints of the area. The government recently undertook a sizable research program in eight different regions to modify formal education and training in ways that will better contribute to regional and national economic development.

Rural development planning.   The government's efforts to achieve greater regional equality in the distribution of educational facilities is part of a larger plan to make a minimum level of facilities available to everyone in the country by 1985. These facilities include a primary school, a market, a health center, and a government center. For administrative and planning purposes, the country has been divided into 758 rural districts, and ministries have been asked to provide FRAR with a timetable for the establishment of the minimum facilities.

Constraints

There are some major constraints—pedagogical, financial, and administrative—to the government's efforts to equalize educational and training opportunities among regions and to relate education and training to local area economic and social development. First, there is a scarcity of primary school teachers. In spite of substantial investments in the recent past, new facilities are required for 500 to 600 students in primary teaching by 1978. There is also a scarcity of teachers to train craftsmen and artisans for employment in rural areas.

In order to meet a growing financial constraint, the government must establish clear priorities within the education sector. If universal primary education and the regional equalization of educational opportunities are to be given priority, it must be at the expense of other parts of the educational and training systems. The fact that a given educational facility is likely to cost 30 percent more in a rural area than in an urban center is yet another drawback.

The Office National pour la Promotion Rurale (ONPR) has been established to mobilize farmers and to solicit their cooperation and participation in rural development efforts. FRAR is responsible for the overall planning and coordination of rural development efforts. ONPR is not adequately staffed, however, and sufficient resources are not made available to FRAR. Both organizations are consequently handicapped in meeting the government's ambitious goals.

The Supply and Demand for High-
and Middle-Level Manpower

Another aspect of the relation between education and the job market is the demand for and supply of high- and middle-level manpower—people with particular skills and educational levels. High-level manpower consists of those people with jobs requiring the equivalent in training and experience of a university education, and at the middle level are those with jobs requiring the equivalent of a secondary education. No precise data are available, but it is estimated that in 1975 a maximum of about 3,800 jobs in the Ivory Coast required university degrees and about 25,000 jobs required either a lower-secondary or upper-secondary education.

With a high GDP growth rate of 8 percent a year,[3] by 1980 the number of jobs requiring a secondary education would be approximately 40,000, and those requiring a university education about 6,000 (Table D3). If a relatively liberal rate of attrition in the labor force (through death and retirement) of approximately 5 percent a year is taken into account, the average annual requirement for high-level manpower would be 685 graduates, and for middle-level manpower, 4,625 people with at least a lower secondary school education.

TABLE D3. AVERAGE ANNUAL HIGH- AND MIDDLE-
LEVEL MANPOWER REQUIREMENTS, 1975–80

			Average annual requirements		
Manpower	1975	1980	New positions	Replacements	Total
High level	3,800	6,000	440	245	685
Middle level	25,000	40,000	3,000	1,625	4,625

Sources: 1971 and 1975 manpower surveys and World Bank estimates.

The average annual number of graduates from the University of Abidjan from 1973–74 to 1980–81 should be about 300 Ivorian graduates (excluding foreign graduates), which is not in itself excessive. But nearly 1,500 students are in universities in France, and, if as many as 200 of these return every year, there will be approximately 500 students a year entering the market for high-level manpower from universities alone. The graduates of post-secondary institutions and uni-

---

3. An 8 percent growth rate a year is optimistic. But it is difficult to forecast the rate of Ivorianization, and successful policies in this area may open up considerable additional job opportunities for Ivorians.

TABLE D4. AVERAGE ANNUAL DEMAND FOR AND SUPPLY
OF HIGH- AND MIDDLE-LEVEL MANPOWER, 1975–80

Manpower	Demand	Supply	Source
High level	685	500	Universities
		1,400	Other post-secondary institutions
Middle level	4,625	5,000	Second cycle secondary schools
		13,000	First cycle secondary schools

Source: Table D3 and World Bank estimates.

versity dropouts entering the job market should average about 1,400 a year over the next decade. Those from the second cycle of secondary schools entering the job market will number about 5,000 a year, and from the first cycle of secondary schools, over 13,000 a year (Table D4).

Although Table D4 is based upon an optimistic assessment of future demand and a rather conservative one of future supply, there still remains quite a discrepancy between demand and supply. The over-supply of high- and middle-level manpower generated by the educational system should serve as a spur to Ivorianize jobs at these levels. Although expatriates in high- and middle-level positions numbered only 9,600 in the private sector and 2,100 in the public sector, and constituted only slightly more than 5 percent of the total salaried labor force in 1973–74, they dominated employment in critical occupational groups. Expatriates, for all intents and purposes, monopolize the management of private sector enterprises. They occupy over 80 percent of all jobs in occupations requiring a university education, 60 percent of the jobs requiring an upper-secondary education, and 30 percent of those requiring a lower-secondary education. It seems likely that growing unemployment among educated people will increase popular demand for a more rapid rate of Ivorianization, especially for those jobs which require a lower- or upper-secondary education.

The quality of manpower made available

Important questions have arisen about the employability of general secondary school leavers and many of those who have had the benefit of preemployment technical and vocational training. These questions relate to attitudes as well as to the appropriateness of the training. Employers often find that those who have been educated and trained in the formal system have excessive expectations about income, amenities, and status. One reason for this may be that the excess supply of school leavers has led to an increase in minimum entry requirements for specific jobs, and actual opportunities fall increasingly short of expectations. Equally important may be the poor attitude toward work imparted by teachers and the elite.

In addition, the training provided artisans, craftsmen, and technicians is in many cases not appropriate to the job. As a consequence, one survey found that only 30 percent of industrial graduates and 35 percent of all commercial graduates could find salaried jobs in the modern sector. The inappropriateness of preemployment vocational and technical training ultimately derives from the fact that employers have had little impact upon the design of curriculum, the recruitment of trainees, and the general planning, financing, and management of training institutions. These functions have usually been performed by individuals and institutions with insufficient contact with the actual work performed on jobs or with employers.

Availability of knowledge relating to specific jobs

Student decisions to continue in school, to undertake particular courses, or to search for employment are based upon imperfect knowledge of the job market, including salary and wage prospects, minimum entry requirements for specific occupations, and available training opportunities. Better knowledge and career guidance may result in more realistic expectations, better decisions on the part of students and, as a consequence, a more efficient allocation of resources to education and training.

Ivorianization

The basic issue of Ivorianization has two aspects: the expatriates or Europeans who dominate a number of high-level manpower occupations, and the large number of non-Ivorian Africans, most of them unskilled, who occupy very nearly half of the salaried jobs in the economy.

The presence of expatriates in sizable numbers affects the educational system in many ways. The numerous expatriates who receive high incomes establish certain standards of consumption, which can be met only by those in high- and middle-level positions. Since access to these jobs is dependent upon formal schooling, the presence of expatriates stimulates an excessive demand for education. Expatriates' strong cultural influence on curricula further contributes to the creation of higher consumption standards and false expectations. Expatriate teachers and school administrators increase the cost of education because of their higher salary level, but they also make possible higher standards of education than would otherwise be possible at this stage.

Recent information indicates that the total number of Europeans in the Ivory Coast increased from 8,620 to 9,480 in the private and semi-private sectors between 1971 and 1974, and from about 2,100 to about 2,900 in the public sector over the same period. Considerable progress is being made, however, in the Ivorianization of skilled white- and blue-collar jobs and in middle-level management. Between 1971 and 1974 the proportion of Ivorians in skilled jobs rose from 70 to 75 percent and in middle management jobs from 48 to 52 percent.

In spite of these changes, non-Ivorian Africans occupied nearly half the salaried jobs in the economy between 1971 and 1974. These jobs were predominantly for unskilled, semiskilled, and blue-collar workers. Europeans, who occupied only 7 percent of all salaried jobs in the private and semiprivate sectors, either dominated or occupied large proportions of jobs in occupations requiring a secondary education or more. Ivorians dominated the middle-level manpower occupations. While similar information is not available for the public sector, it is known that 75 percent of all expatriates in that sector were employed in the formal school system. In 1974 this amounted to more than 2,100 teachers. In secondary schools 80 percent of all teachers were French expatriates.

Summary and Recommendations

The Ivory Coast has made substantial progress in expanding enrollments and in improving the quality of its educational system according to standards that are essentially French. But these achievements have not led to a system that reflects Ivorian conditions or solves important educational and training-related problems. Remaining are serious problems of costs, unemployed school leavers, geographic distribution of educational facilities, and Ivorianization. All these problems are interrelated and none is capable of simple or quick solution. Changing a country's income and incentive structure is a long-run task. All that can be hoped for is that in the short run existing problems are at least not aggravated and that some improvements can be made.

It should be underscored that the full burden of resolving the questions of education and training should not reside within the ministries directly responsible for these activities. In the long run problems can be solved only by coordinated action of the entire government, with the cooperation of the private sector. For example, it seems unlikely that increasing unemployment among school leavers in the towns during the 1976–80 period can be avoided. Actions have already been taken to increase the proportion of expenditure on education and training in the recurrent budget during the same period, but it is unlikely that significant results would appear before 1980 from the reform of secondary education. Educational and training systems, like the societies of which they are a part, have lives and momentums of their own and it is difficult to make substantial changes within a short period. Nevertheless, a start should be made to implement a number of measures that would have a positive effect on the educational system in the longer run.

Changing incentives

Ultimately, when the private costs of education are brought closer to the private benefits, pressure will be taken off the government to provide so many places in the schools. In the long run, bringing costs under control will involve a broadly conceived income policy to narrow income differences between the urban and rural populations, between skilled and unskilled workers, and between the incomes attributable to increments of education. The government is undertaking several programs that would form part of an appropriate income policy. In particular its rural and agricultural development efforts should provide for substantial improvements in the regional distribution of income.

The presence of large numbers of high-income expatriates establishes cultural and consumption standards that significantly increase the demand for education. Ivorianization policy should therefore be evaluated in terms of this influence on income distribution, the economic structure, and the social demand for access to modern sector jobs. This policy cannot be considered only in terms of the relative efficiency of Ivorians and expatriates as evaluated at current market prices and salaries.

A policy designed to change income distribution and incentives should also include promotion of the informal sector. There are a number of ways in which the government can do this:

a. By eliminating some legal constaints on training, zoning, and safety standards that affect firms in the informal sector.

b. By creating small-business extension services to identify profitable opportunities for new inputs or for the introduction of different technologies and methods.
c. By changing the content of primary school curricula to prepare children in terms of attitudes, expectations, and skills for employment in the informal sector.
d. By developing the many opportunities available for profitable training activities. Since many of the special skills required are learned in informal apprenticeship programs, the government's efforts should be directed toward training and upgrading the skills of the employer-entrepreneur himself in a variety of ways: on-the-spot training or demonstration by an extension worker; evening courses, at a site convenient to employers, in basic accounting and bookkeeping, inventory control and fundamental business principles; upgrading skills with business training for draftsmen and artisans who appear capable of operating a small-scale service enterprise; demonstration of new machinery. Because training, credit, and extension work in small businesses are perfect complements, all should be coordinated through a single agency.
e. By adopting pricing and subsidy policies that promote the use of intermediate technologies.
f. By providing roads, power, water, and sanitary facilities for areas in which small businesses are operating.

The government is working along these lines. Several international organizations have recently become involved in developing this subsector. Most assistance is channeled through OPEI (Office National de Promotion de l'Entreprise Ivoirienne). The government also decided in 1976 to seek assistance for developing *domaines industriels*, small areas equipped with public utilities where small-scale enterprises may develop under a minimum of public guidance.

Private assumption of education costs

The fact that education in the Ivory Coast is free puts tremendous pressure on demand. Passing on the social costs of education to students and families would raise revenue for the financing of education and would also reduce excessive demand. Although this policy may prove unpopular, doing little or nothing would lead not only to a rapid increase in the demand for secondary and higher education but also increasing job dissatisfaction on the part of educated people. The government should consider the following:

a. Charging students the actual costs of education at the university and the second cycle of secondary education. This action would be accompanied by a system of student loans and, in some cases where students are studying in university fields in which there are critical manpower shortages, outright grants.
b. Passing on at least some of the costs of the first cycle of secondary education to students in the form of tuition fees and boarding charges. Students who are poor and who have outstanding academic potential could be provided with grants that would defray these costs.
c. Although free primary education is probably necessary if universal primary education is to be achieved during the next decade, the government could consider initiating a series of fees for revenue purposes, provided that they could be devised in a way that poor students would not have to pay them.
d. Shifting the burden of costs from the public to the private sector would be easier in technical and vocational education. Some progress has been made in establishing a tax on employers applicable to the training of some craftsmen and artisans. This tax could be broadened to all employers and used to finance all technical and vocational training.

Reducing the quantity of educational inputs

Another way to relieve the burden of high social costs for education is by reducing the quantity and changing the kinds of inputs (for example, teachers and teaching materials). This can be accomplished by using new technologies and systems or by using more appropriate inputs for the present system. The Ivory Coast has opportunities for doing both.

The country's new capability in educational television could be extended to the first cycle of secondary education, thus spreading the fixed costs of the system over a larger number of students and realizing substantial economies of scale. Television opens up the possibilities of departing from the concept of the "school" and of making secondary education available to students who are employed either full time or part time.

Significant reductions in costs may be achieved through better management, planning, and coordination throughout the education sector. Too many ministries and agencies seem to be involved in education, and streamlining could bring about substantial improvements in efficiency. Manpower planning could also be improved. Data are not applied seriously and consistently by those responsible for determining enrollments in the university facilities or in secondary schools or for controlling costs. Strong support from the highest levels of government would be essential.

Changing educational inputs would be a subject of considerable controversy. Nevertheless, a savings of only 10 percent in the recurrent costs of financing a single student at the university for one year would finance the total costs for one year for four students in primary school. A saving of 17 percent in the recurrent costs of a single secondary school student would pay the total costs of an additional primary school student. Decisions in these fields are hard to make because changes in teaching materials, teachers, and other inputs would affect the quality of education. Clear definition of policy choices and tradeoffs would be important.

Improving geographic distribution

Three major constraints to improvement in the geographic distribution of education facilities require action. Additional facilities are needed for training primary teachers and trainers of craftsmen and artisans for employment in rural areas. More resources should be made available for educational facilities in poorer areas at the expense of other parts of the system. Both the Fonds Régionaux d'Aménagement Rural (FRAR) and the Office National pour la Promotion Rurale (ONPR) should receive more funds if the government wants to give priority to rural development.

Manpower planning

A manpower planning mechanism should be established to coordinate manpower programs and to make policy choices. These relate to specialized training and career guidance and other facets of Ivorianization. The government is already trying to achieve greater employer involvement in the planning, management, and financing of industrial and vocational training. It should take further action to expand this effort to all job-specific training, even at the university level. Where possible, employers should share the management and financial responsibility for job-specific training. A prerequisite for a professional degree, certificate, or other paper qualifications for a particular occupation should be on-the-job training under the supervision of an experienced worker whenever feasible. Employers should have an important voice in determining the curriculum of prevocational and pretechnical courses and in determining enrollments. Means should be found to link enrollments in training institutions directly to employment, and employers should assume collective responsibility for employing those who complete their courses of studies. Proposals requiring the extensive use of scarce high-level manpower skills, particularly those that are managerial and administrative, should be closely evaluated. Studies of public and parastatal organizations are required to generate proposals that will result in more efficient organization, and the formulation of a staff development program.

Career guidance

To create more realistic expectations and provide for a more efficient operation of the market for high- and middle-level manpower, students, trainees, parents, and school counselors should be provided with better information about the job market. This should include knowledge of the opportunities for training and education, the training requirements and costs for particular jobs, their salaries, the probability of finding employment in these occupations, and alternative career patterns. In view of the rapidly changing conditions in job markets in the Ivory Coast, a program for the development of a system of career guidance should be assigned a high priority.

Ivorianization

Ivorianization policy should take account of the current and undesirable structure of incentives and the potential competition of non-Ivorian Africans with Ivorians for jobs. Creation of additional teacher training capacity is required to produce enough Ivorian teachers to make progress in the Ivorianization of the teaching force during the next decade. Consideration should also be given to shortening the time teachers are required to spend in training in order to increase the numbers available at lower cost.

The government should evaluate the prospects for replacing relatively inexperienced Europeans in public service, especially in view of the increasing number of Ivorians who are university trained. Ivorianization in the private sector will not be easy, especially at the management level where there are still few Ivorians with experience. A well-defined and phased program for the replacement of expatriates is under discussion. The private sector should assume a large share of the burden of Ivorianization through on-the-job training and the financing of staff upgrading programs.

The large numbers of those leaving primary and secondary schools does not mean that skilled and semiskilled jobs currently held by expatriates can be easily Ivorianized. Schooling without vocational training will usually not satisfy minimum entry requirements for jobs. This fact will become increasingly apparent as the country is faced with more unemployed secondary school leavers and with persisting shortages of skilled people in middle-level manpower occupations. The solution can be found by shifting the burden for Ivorianization and the requisite training to the private sector. The government can promote private efforts by establishing training taxes, subsidies, training institutions, and guidelines and targets. For each vocation and profession manpower planning and Ivorianization should take account of such important subtleties as age distribution within occupations, types of training to be given priority, requirements for technical assistance, and programs for the development of trainers, teachers, and university faculties.

Curriculum reform

A number of actions have already been taken to improve the curriculum in the schools, the most noticeable of these being associated with the introduction of educational television. Studies are also being undertaken to tailor educational and training programs to the specific ethnic and development needs of communities. No action seems to be planned to bring about changes in the structure and curriculum of secondary schools consistent with the new curriculum of primary schools or with what the country can afford. It is urgent that resources be committed to such a reform. The objective should not be the achievement of excellence according to French standards, but the construction of a system that will prepare students for conditions prevailing in the Ivory Coast.

Statistical Appendix

TABLE SA1. LOCATION OF POPULATION,
SELECTED YEARS
(Thousands)

Location	1965[a]	1970	1975[b]
Cities of over 25,000 (1975)	645.5	995.2	1,534.0
Abidjan	346.0	570.0	921.0
Bouaké	85.0	122.0	173.0
Daloa	35.0	46.0	59.5
Man	30.0	38.5	48.5
Korhogo	24.0	33.0	45.0
Gagnoa	21.0	30.0	42.0
Divo	18.5	26.5	37.0
Yamoussoukro	8.0	17.0	35.0
Dimbokro	15.0	22.5	33.0
San Pédro	. . .	5.7	31.5
Abengourou	17.5	23.0	30.5
Agboville	17.5	22.0	27.0
Grand Bassam	16.5	22.0	26.0
Ferkéssédougou	11.5	17.0	25.0
Urban areas of between 4,000 and 25,000 (1975)	304.5	479.8	587.0
Rural areas	3,550.0	4,025.0	4,551.0
Total population	4,500.0	5,500.0	6,672.0

. . . Zero or negligible.

Note: Historic rates of population growth: 1920–45, 1.4 percent a year; 1945–55, 1.9 percent a year; 1955–65, 2.8 percent a year; 1965–75, 4.0 percent a year; 1973–74, 4.7 percent a year; 1974–75, 4.9 percent a year.

Source: For 1965 and 1970: "Population Rurale et Urbaine par Département et par Sous-préfecture," February 1970, Ministry of Planning. The data for these years have been adjusted by the Ministry of Planning based on the results of the 1975 population census.

a. The figures for 1965 represent mid-year estimates based on ORSTOM studies conducted between 1960 and 1967, and on counts by the Institut d'Hygiène made during its 1961–63 smallpox vaccination campaign.

b. According to the preliminary results of the first census held in April 1975.

Table SA2. Distribution of Population, 1975 (Estimated)

Department	Rural population	Urban population		Total
		Centers over 10,000	Centers between 3,000 and 10,000	
Abengourou	133,029	42,862	. . .	175,891
Abidjan	338,639	1,030,755	18,926	1,388,320
Aboisso	123,499	13,887	9,490	146,876
Adzopé	116,892	42,669	. . .	159,561
Agboville	111,846	27,210	. . .	139,056
Biankouma	69,865	. . .	4,543	74,408
Bondoukou	268,414	18,326	7,098	293,838
Bouaflé	221,211	35,323	9,341	265,875
Bouaké	546,183	242,337	16,836	805,356
Bouna	71,476	. . .	5,856	77,332
Boundiali	113,437	9,753	8,870	132,060
Dabakala	52,084	. . .	3,272	55,356
Daloa	290,087	70,346	6,933	367,366
Danané	151,176	18,413	. . .	169,589
Dimbokro	381,352	89,918	6,784	478,054
Divo	214,903	50,043	10,225	275,171
Ferkéssédougou	66,135	24,766	. . .	90,901
Gagnoa	192,250	58,505	5,251	256,006
Guiglo	108,788	21,992	4,472	135,252
Katiola	57,859	18,050	. . .	75,909
Korhogo	231,700	45,146	. . .	276,846
Man	229,127	48,521	. . .	277,648
Odienné	110,332	13,864	. . .	124,196
Sassandra	139,116	31,597	24,907	195,620
Séguéla	138,438	12,636	6,570	157,644
Touba	72,455	. . .	5,241	77,696
Total	4,550,293	1,966,919	154,615	6,671,827

. . . Zero or negligible.

Source: "Resultats Provisoires du Recensement Général de la Population," Ministry of Planning, November 1975.

TABLE SA3. NATIONAL ACCOUNTS, USES OF GROSS
DOMESTIC PRODUCT, 1960–75
(Current CFAF billion)

Item	1960	1961	1962	1963	1964	1965
GDP (market prices)	140.7	159.3	166.1	195.9	237.1	236.8
Consumption	111.5	129.6	140.5	154.1	176.6	186.1
Private	106.0	122.2	133.9	145.8	167.6	175.6
Auto consumption	29.5	28.9	32.3	34.1	35.6	38.5
Public	5.5	7.4	6.6	8.3	9.0	10.5
Gross fixed investment	19.2	24.3	25.2	28.4	39.2	43.6
Stock changes	1.3	3.1	−5.2	1.8	5.7	1.3
Exports (f.o.b.) including nonfactor services	45.5	53.1	53.8	63.4	81.4	73.5
Imports (c.i.f.) including nonfactor services	−36.8	−50.8	−48.2	−51.8	−65.8	−67.7
Gross domestic saving	29.1	29.7	25.6	41.8	60.5	50.7
Net factor income[c]	−1.8	−2.8	−4.2	−7.4	−6.7	−8.7
Net transfers[c]	−5.1	−5.6	−2.8	−5.5	−6.8	−6.7
Gross national saving	22.2	21.3	18.6	28.9	47.0	35.5

n.a. Not available.
Source: Ivory Coast national accounts and World Bank estimates.
a. Preliminary.
b. World Bank estimate.

1966	*1967*	*1968*	*1969*	*1970*	*1971*	*1972*	*1973*	*1974*[a]	*1975*[b]
257.3	274.4	325.1	364.0	414.0	439.3	471.6	564.0	742.3	826.0
198.7	217.5	243.7	263.7	299.7	330.3	351.9	418.3	526.6	618.0
186.9	205.2	229.0	242.8	274.6	298.5	319.3	377.8	479.1	n.a.
37.4	38.6	38.6	41.1	42.4	43.4	43.3	52.3	n.a.	n.a.
11.8	12.3	14.7	20.9	25.1	31.8	32.6	40.5	47.5	n.a.
44.6	45.8	54.0	61.8	83.9	92.4	94.3	121.9	148.3	198.3
5.5	1.6	1.5	7.8	7.4	3.6	3.1	7.9	17.7	8.0
81.6	87.2	115.3	133.7	149.6	151.5	167.9	212.7	322.6	341.0
−73.1	−77.7	−89.4	−103.0	−126.6	−138.5	−145.6	−196.8	−272.8	−336.0
58.6	57.0	81.4	100.3	114.3	109.0	119.6	145.7	215.7	207.0
−7.9	−8.1	−8.9	−4.6	−4.9	−6.7	−7.3	−11.1	−12.7	−15.5
−11.5	−12.5	−12.6	−18.3	−21.0	−23.7	−28.8	−26.3	−40.2	−42.3
39.2	36.4	59.9	77.4	88.4	78.6	83.5	108.3	162.8	149.2

c. The Ivorian national accounts define most foreign workers and enterprises as residents; therefore a large part of what would be called factor income (workers' remittances and profits) is included in net transfers. This definition differs in this and several other aspects from what is used in the balance of payments statistics.

TABLE SA4. NATIONAL ACCOUNTS IN ESTIMATED CONSTANT PRICES, 1960–75

(Constant 1973 CFAF billion)

Item	1960	1961	1962	1963	1964	1965
GDP (market prices)	215.5	235.6	246.1	286.4	337.7	330.3
GDY (market prices)	212.0	225.9	231.6	283.6	340.0	310.3
Consumption	164.6	181.4	192.3	221.1	253.3	240.3
Investment (including stocks)	31.4	40.5	29.6	44.3	63.9	61.8
Exports (f.o.b.) including nonfactor services	85.6	102.7	107.4	102.3	122.0	124.4
Exports (adjusted for terms of trade)	82.1	93.0	92.9	99.5	124.3	104.4
Imports (c.i.f.) including nonfactor services	−66.4	−89.0	−83.2	−81.3	−100.6	−96.2
Gross domestic saving	47.4	44.5	39.3	62.5	86.7	70.0
Net factor income	−3.2	−4.9	−7.3	−11.6	−10.2	−12.4
Net transfers	−9.2	−9.8	−4.8	−8.6	−10.4	−9.5
Gross national saving	35.0	29.8	27.9	42.3	66.1	48.1
Primary sector	n.a.	n.a.	n.a.	n.a.	n.a.	n.a.
Secondary sector	n.a.	n.a.	n.a.	n.a.	n.a.	n.a.
Tertiary sector	n.a.	n.a.	n.a.	n.a.	n.a.	n.a.
Adjustment[c]	n.a.	n.a.	n.a.	n.a.	n.a.	n.a.
GDY	n.a.	n.a.	n.a.	n.a.	n.a.	n.a.

n.a. Not available.

. . . Zero or negligible.

Note: The Ivory Coast does not publish national accounts in constant terms. These series were derived from the current series and World Bank constructed price deflators. The series are not official and should be considered only as estimates of the constant value.

Source: Ivory Coast national accounts and World Bank calculations.

1966	*1967*	*1968*	*1969*	*1970*	*1971*	*1972*	*1973*	*1974*[a]	*1975*[b]
356.4	361.5	417.9	436.4	469.4	500.9	534.1	564.0	580.9	617.1
351.0	358.0	421.4	452.4	491.7	498.3	520.2	564.0	570.1	597.0
269.0	278.4	312.2	318.1	351.3	372.7	388.0	418.3	404.4	441.3
69.8	66.0	73.1	91.7	110.8	110.1	106.9	129.8	135.3	147.9
122.5	127.9	157.3	169.7	170.7	183.4	204.5	212.7	255.6	243.8
117.1	124.4	160.8	185.7	193.0	180.8	190.6	212.7	244.8	223.7
−104.9	−110.8	−124.7	−143.1	−163.4	−165.3	−165.3	−196.8	−207.5	−215.9
82.0	79.6	109.2	134.3	140.4	125.6	132.2	145.7	172.6	155.7
−11.3	−11.6	−12.4	−6.4	−6.3	−8.0	−8.3	−11.1	−10.1	−11.1
−16.5	−17.8	−17.6	−25.4	−27.1	−28.3	−32.0	−26.3	−30.5	−30.2
54.2	50.2	79.2	102.5	107.0	89.3	91.9	108.3	132.0	114.4
n.a.	n.a.	n.a.	138.0	139.5	145.2	150.7	159.1	155.9	172.1
n.a.	n.a.	n.a.	82.9	93.1	101.5	108.6	121.6	127.1	141.0
n.a.	n.a.	n.a.	189.6	215.0	235.3	252.5	283.3	293.1	301.8
n.a.	n.a.	n.a.	42.9	44.1	16.3	8.4	...	−6.0	−18.5
n.a.	n.a.	n.a.	452.4	491.7	498.3	520.2	564.0	570.1	597.0

a. Preliminary.
b. World Bank estimate.
c. These series are derived from year-to-year volume changes by sector. By converting to a simple base year series, statistical discrepancies occur due to the changing implicit weights. This factor along with the terms of trade adjustment factor are included in this line.

TABLE SA5.   NATIONAL ACCOUNTS IN CURRENT PRICES
ON BALANCE OF PAYMENTS BASIS, 1960–75
(Current CFAF billion)

Item	1960	1961	1962	1963	1964	1965
GDP (market prices)	140.7	159.3	166.1	195.9	237.1	236.8
Consumption	116.6	132.8	144.3	160.3	182.5	188.7
Private	111.1	125.4	137.7	152.0	173.5	178.2
Auto consumption	29.5	28.9	32.3	34.1	35.6	38.5
Public	5.5	7.4	6.6	8.3	9.0	10.5
Gross fixed investment	19.2	24.3	25.2	28.4	39.2	43.6
Stock changes	1.3	3.1	−5.2	1.8	5.7	1.3
Exports (f.o.b.) including nonfactor services	52.2	61.5	62.3	72.2	88.5	81.7
Imports (c.i.f.) including nonfactor services	−48.6	−62.4	−60.5	−66.8	−78.8	−78.5
Gross domestic saving	24.1	26.5	21.8	35.6	54.6	48.1
Net factor income	−8.4	−9.3	−10.0	−10.4	−15.1	−14.8
Net transfers	0.8	1.0	1.2	1.5	2.0	2.7
Gross national saving	16.5	18.2	13.0	26.7	41.5	36.0
GNP	132.2	150.0	156.1	185.5	222.0	222.0

n.a. Not available.

Note: Trade, net factor income, and transfers are included on the basis of balance of payments definitions. These treat transfers of foreign residents and enterprises on a current basis. Thus the derived levels of saving and consumption are different from the national accounts figures in Tables SA3 and SA4.

1966	1967	1968	1969	1970	1971	1972	1973	1974[a]	1975[b]
257.3	274.4	325.1	364.0	414.0	439.3	471.6	564.0	742.3	826.0
202.7	223.8	251.3	274.7	317.9	346.2	372.4	439.3	567.1	651.4
190.9	211.5	236.6	253.8	292.8	314.4	339.8	398.8	499.5	n.a.
37.4	38.6	38.6	41.1	42.4	43.4	43.3	52.3	n.a.	n.a.
11.8	12.3	14.7	20.9	25.1	31.8	32.6	40.5	47.5	n.a.
44.6	45.8	54.0	61.8	83.9	92.4	94.3	121.9	138.5	198.3
5.5	1.6	1.5	7.8	7.4	3.6	3.1	7.9	17.7	8.2
90.4	96.5	125.2	143.9	161.0	164.9	181.1	222.9	333.4	301.2
−85.9	−93.3	−106.9	−124.2	−156.2	−167.8	−179.3	−228.0	−314.4	−333.1
54.6	50.6	73.8	89.3	96.1	93.1	99.2	124.7	185.3	192.6
−18.7	−18.8	−19.5	−20.1	−22.8	−28.0	−33.8	−43.1	−50.5	−53.6
1.9	1.4	1.4	2.6	5.1	7.2	6.1	8.5	9.8	10.4
37.3	33.2	55.7	71.8	78.4	72.3	71.5	90.1	154.6	149.4
238.6	255.6	305.6	343.9	391.2	411.3	437.8	520.9	691.8	772.2

Source: Ivorian national accounts and balance of payments data.
a. Preliminary.
b. World Bank estimate.

TABLE SA6. NATIONAL ACCOUNTS IN CONSTANT 1973 PRICES
ON BALANCE OF PAYMENTS BASIS, 1960–75
(1973 CFAF billion)

Item	1960	1961	1962	1963	1964	1965
GDP (market prices)	215.5	235.6	246.1	286.4	337.7	330.3
GDY (market prices)	211.9	224.3	229.3	283.3	340.1	308.5
Consumption	173.5	185.4	196.6	230.6	261.4	242.1
Investment (including stocks)	31.4	40.5	29.6	44.3	63.9	61.8
Exports (f.o.b.) including nonfactor services	98.3	119.0	124.4	116.4	132.7	137.9
Exports (adjusted for terms of trade)	94.7	107.7	107.6	113.3	135.1	116.1
Imports (c.i.f.) including nonfactor services	−87.7	−109.3	−104.5	−104.9	−120.3	−111.5
Gross domestic saving	38.4	38.9	32.7	52.7	78.7	66.4
Net factor income	−15.2	−16.3	−17.3	−18.7	−27.2	−25.5
Net transfers	1.4	1.8	2.1	2.8	3.6	4.7
Gross national saving	24.6	24.4	17.5	36.8	55.1	45.6
GNP	200.3	219.3	228.8	267.7	310.5	304.8
GNY	196.7	208.0	212.0	264.6	312.9	283.0

n.a. Not available.
Note: See note under Table SA5.
Source: Tables SA5 and SA10.

1966	*1967*	*1968*	*1969*	*1970*	*1971*	*1972*	*1973*	*1974*[a]	*1975*[b]
356.4	361.5	417.9	436.4	469.4	500.9	534.1	564.0	580.9	617.1
350.4	358.1	421.7	453.7	493.5	498.1	519.1	564.0	569.3	595.8
274.1	287.5	323.1	334.6	376.5	391.4	410.1	439.3	413.1	457.5
69.8	66.0	73.1	91.7	110.8	110.1	106.9	129.8	134.1	148.1
135.7	141.1	170.8	182.6	183.6	199.6	220.6	222.9	n.a.	n.a.
129.7	137.7	174.6	199.9	207.7	196.8	205.6	222.9	n.a.	n.a.
−123.2	−133.1	−149.1	−172.5	−201.5	−200.2	−203.5	−228.0	n.a.	n.a.
76.3	70.6	98.6	119.1	117.0	106.7	109.0	124.7	156.2	138.3
−30.5	−29.9	−30.0	−30.3	−35.4	−41.5	−42.1	−43.1	−40.8	−47.8
3.2	2.2	2.2	4.0	8.1	11.0	7.9	8.5	7.2	6.4
49.0	42.9	70.8	92.8	89.7	76.2	74.8	90.1	122.6	96.9
325.9	331.6	387.9	406.1	434.0	459.4	492.0	520.9	540.1	569.3
319.9	328.2	391.7	423.4	458.1	456.6	477.0	520.9	528.5	548.0

a. Preliminary.
b. World Bank estimate.

TABLE SA7. SHARES OF NATIONAL ACCOUNTS ON BALANCE
OF PAYMENTS BASIS, 1960–75
(Percent)

Item	1960	1961	1962	1963	1964	1965
GDP (market prices)	100.0	100.0	100.0	100.0	100.0	100.0
Consumption	82.9	83.4	86.9	81.5	76.7	78.8
Private	79.0	78.7	82.9	77.2	72.9	74.3
Auto consumption	21.0	18.1	19.4	17.4	15.0	16.3
Public	3.9	4.6	4.0	4.2	3.8	4.4
Gross fixed investment	13.6	15.3	15.2	14.5	16.5	18.4
Stock changes	0.9	1.9	−3.1	0.9	2.4	0.5
Exports (f.o.b.) including nonfactor services	37.1	38.6	37.5	37.0	37.8	35.1
Imports (c.i.f.) including nonfactor services	−34.5	−39.2	−36.4	−33.8	−33.4	−32.8
Gross domestic saving	17.1	16.6	13.1	18.5	23.3	21.2
Net factor income	−6.0	−5.8	−6.0	−5.2	−6.3	−6.2
Net transfers	0.6	0.6	0.7	0.8	0.8	1.1
Gross national saving	11.7	11.4	7.8	14.1	17.9	16.2

n.a. Not available.
Source: Derived from Table SA5.

1966	*1967*	*1968*	*1969*	*1970*	*1971*	*1972*	*1973*	*1974*	*1975*
100.0	100.0	100.0	100.0	100.0	100.0	100.0	100.0	100.0	100.0
78.0	81.2	77.0	75.2	76.5	78.6	79.0	77.9	76.4	78.8
73.4	76.7	72.5	69.5	70.4	71.4	72.1	70.7	69.1	n.a.
14.5	14.1	11.9	11.3	10.2	9.9	9.2	9.3	n.a.	n.a.
4.6	4.5	4.5	5.7	6.1	7.2	6.9	7.2	6.3	n.a.
17.3	16.7	16.6	17.0	20.3	21.0	20.0	21.6	18.7	24.0
2.1	0.6	0.5	2.1	1.8	0.8	0.7	1.4	2.4	1.0
36.4	35.7	38.7	38.8	38.2	36.8	37.7	39.5	45.0	36.5
−33.9	−34.2	−32.8	−33.1	−36.7	−37.2	−37.4	−40.4	−42.4	−40.3
22.0	18.8	23.0	24.8	23.5	21.4	21.0	22.1	24.5	22.6
−7.2	−6.8	−5.9	−5.4	−5.4	−6.2	−6.9	−7.6	−6.9	−7.0
0.7	0.5	0.4	0.7	1.2	1.6	1.3	1.5	1.2	1.1
15.6	12.5	17.5	20.1	19.4	16.8	15.4	16.0	18.8	16.7

TABLE SA8. NATIONAL ACCOUNTS: PRODUCTION OF GROSS
DOMESTIC PRODUCT IN CURRENT PRICES, 1960–75
(Current CFAF billion)

Sector	1960	1961	1962	1963	1964	1965
Primary sector						
Food crop and livestock	31.5	30.9	34.9	32.0	38.9	42.3
Industrial and export crops	24.8	25.5	18.5	28.4	36.3	30.0
Forestry	3.6	4.6	5.5	7.4	10.4	10.7
Fisheries	1.2	1.3	1.3	1.6	1.7	1.9
Total	61.1	62.3	60.2	74.4	87.3	84.9
Secondary						
Mining	1.0	1.8	1.5	1.0	1.2	1.7
Manufacturing	10.0	12.3	14.1	16.7	20.4	24.0
Cottage industries	6.1	7.4	7.2	7.7	8.6	10.8
Energy	2.1	2.7	2.9	3.3	3.5	2.1
Construction	6.8	8.0	9.0	9.1	11.0	12.8
Total	19.9	24.8	27.5	30.1	36.1	40.6
Tertiary						
Transports	9.9	12.2	12.9	14.3	17.9	21.0
Services[c,d]	40.6	48.8	51.4	61.1	75.9	68.4
Import duties and taxes	12.6	16.0	14.8	16.8	20.8	20.7
Administration	9.2	11.2	14.1	16.0	19.9	21.9
Total	59.7	72.2	78.4	91.4	113.7	111.3
GDP at market prices	140.7	159.3	166.1	195.9	237.1	236.8
Net indirect taxes	18.8	23.5	27.1	34.3	43.3	38.3
GDP at factor cost	121.9	135.8	139.0	161.6	193.8	198.5

n.a. Not available.
Source: National accounts and World Bank estimates.
a. Preliminary.
b. World Bank estimate.

1966	*1967*	*1968*	*1969*	*1970*	*1971*	*1972*	*1973*	*1974*[a]	*1975*[b]
41.7	43.7	44.8	46.1	46.5	49.1	47.8	60.4	n.a.	n.a.
34.1	28.6	38.5	38.5	46.9	47.0	51.4	54.9	n.a.	n.a.
10.7	13.4	15.9	21.4	16.8	18.9	22.9	40.3	n.a.	n.a.
1.9	2.0	1.9	2.2	2.4	2.6	3.0	3.5	n.a.	n.a.
88.4	87.7	101.1	108.2	112.6	117.6	125.1	159.1	195.6	233.0
1.5	1.1	1.0	1.1	0.9	1.3	1.5	1.8	1.6	n.a.
31.5	34.5	41.5	45.9	55.6	62.0	71.8	79.0	105.1	n.a.
11.9	13.4	14.0	14.9	10.7[e]	11.2[e]	12.9[e]	13.2[e]	14.4[e]	n.a.
2.5	2.8	3.4	4.1	4.6	4.8	5.7	6.3	8.1	n.a.
13.9	14.4	16.8	17.7	27.9	33.4	32.7	34.5	40.3	n.a.
49.4	52.8	62.7	68.8	89.0	101.5	111.4	121.6	155.1	179.0
22.1	23.9	26.5	30.8	31.9	37.6	42.2	53.1	72.2 ⎫	334.5
73.5	83.5	106.7	123.7	141.1	140.2	147.1	176.0	243.7 ⎭	
17.5	19.8	22.1	23.5	27.8	29.3	32.1	39.5	47.1	57.5
23.9	26.5	28.1	32.5	39.4	42.4	44.8	54.2	75.7	79.5
119.5	133.9	161.3	187.0	212.4	220.2	235.1	283.3	391.6	414.0
257.3	274.4	325.1	364.0	414.0	439.3	471.6	564.0	742.3	826.0
42.2	46.6	56.7	71.1	86.1	80.7	85.9	112.8	132.4	131.1
215.1	227.8	268.4	292.8	327.9	358.6	385.7	451.2	609.9	694.7

c. Since import duties and taxes are paid primarily by the commercial sector, importers for final distribution or agents for intermediate goods, all import duties are included in this sector, although the Ivorian data shows them separately.

d. Includes profits of the Stabilization Fund.

e. Definitions differ from 1970 to 1975 because of change in nomenclature; comparable figure for 1965 is 7.5.

TABLE SA9. NATIONAL ACCOUNTS: PERCENTAGE DISTRIBUTION
OF GROSS DOMESTIC PRODUCT AT MARKET
PRICES, 1960–75

Sector	1960	1961	1962	1963	1964	1965
Primary sector						
Food crop and livestock	22.4	19.4	21.0	16.3	16.4	17.9
Industrial and export crops	17.6	16.0	11.1	14.5	15.3	12.7
Forestry	2.6	2.9	3.3	3.8	4.4	4.5
Fisheries	0.9	0.8	0.8	0.8	0.7	0.8
Total	43.5	39.1	36.2	38.0	36.8	35.9
Secondary						
Mining	0.7	1.1	0.9	0.5	0.5	0.7
Manufacturing	7.1	7.7	8.5	8.5	8.6	10.1
Cottage industries	4.3	4.6	4.3	3.9	3.6	4.6
Energy	1.5	1.7	1.8	1.7	1.5	0.9
Construction	4.8	5.1	5.4	4.6	4.6	5.4
Total	14.1	15.6	16.6	15.3	15.2	17.1
Tertiary						
Transports	7.0	7.7	7.8	7.3	7.6	8.9
Services	28.9	30.6	30.9	31.2	32.0	28.8
Import duties and taxes	9.0	10.0	8.9	8.6	8.8	8.7
Administration	6.5	7.0	8.5	8.2	8.4	9.3
Total	42.4	45.3	47.2	46.7	48.0	47.0
GDP at market prices	100.0	100.0	100.0	100.0	100.0	100.0
Net indirect taxes	13.4	14.8	16.3	17.5	18.3	16.2

n.a. Not available.
Source: Table SA8.

1966	*1967*	*1968*	*1969*	*1970*	*1971*	*1972*	*1973*	*1974*	*1975*
16.2	15.9	13.8	12.7	11.2	11.2	10.1	10.7	n.a.	n.a.
13.3	10.4	11.8	10.6	11.3	10.7	10.9	9.7	n.a.	n.a.
4.2	4.9	4.9	5.8	4.1	4.3	4.9	7.2	n.a.	n.a.
0.7	0.8	0.6	0.6	0.6	0.6	0.6	0.6	n.a.	n.a.
34.4	32.0	31.1	29.7	27.2	26.8	26.5	28.2	26.4	28.2
0.6	0.4	0.3	0.3	0.2	0.3	0.3	0.3	0.2	n.a.
12.2	12.6	12.8	12.6	13.4	14.1	15.2	14.0	14.2	n.a.
4.6	4.9	4.3	4.1	2.6	2.5	2.7	2.6	n.a.	n.a.
1.0	1.0	1.0	1.1	1.1	1.1	1.2	1.1	1.1	n.a.
5.4	5.2	5.2	4.9	6.8	7.6	6.9	6.2	5.4	n.a.
19.2	19.2	19.3	18.9	21.5	23.1	23.6	21.6	20.9	21.7
8.6	8.7	8.2	8.5	7.7	8.6	8.9	9.4	9.7	40.5
28.5	30.4	32.8	34.0	34.1	31.9	31.2	31.2	32.8	n.a.
6.8	7.2	6.8	6.5	6.7	6.7	6.8	7.0	6.3	7.0
9.3	9.7	8.6	8.9	9.5	9.6	9.5	9.6	10.2	9.6
46.4	48.8	49.6	51.4	51.3	50.1	49.9	50.2	52.7	50.1
100.0	100.0	100.0	100.0	100.0	100.0	100.0	100.0	100.0	100.0
16.4	17.0	17.4	19.5	20.8	18.4	18.2	20.0	17.8	15.9

TABLE SA10. PRICE INDEXES, 1960–75

Category	1960	1961	1962	1963	1964	1965
Consumer price index in Abidjan for high-income families, 1960=100	100.0	n.a.[a]	108.2	109.5	113.5	118.0
Consumer price index in Abidjan for low-income families, 1960=100	100.0	102.9	112.7	112.4	113.9	117.0
Wholesale price index in Abidjan for construction goods, 1956=100	125.1	124.9	126.3	126.6	130.7	131.0
(Implicit deflators, 1973=100)[c]						
GDP	65.3	67.6	67.5	68.4	70.2	71.6
Consumption	67.7	71.4	73.1	69.6	69.7	75.5
Investment (including stocks)	65.3	67.6	67.5	68.1	70.2	72.6
Exports (including nonfactor services)	53.1	51.7	50.1	62.0	66.7	59.1
Imports (including nonfactor services)	55.4	57.1	57.9	.63.7	65.5	70.4
Terms of trade (including nonfactor services)	95.8	90.5	86.5	97.3	101.8	83.9

n.a. Not available.
Source: National accounts and World Bank calculations.
a. Price index for high-income families not computed in 1961.
b. May 1975.

1966	1967	1968	1969	1970	1971	1972	1973	1974	1975
121.0	122.2	126.7	129.7	136.2	141.8	147.0	152.9	177.8	212.9[b]
121.9	124.6	131.4	135.6	148.9	147.7	148.2	164.1	193.1	211.4[b]
133.3	133.8	136.2	136.8	148.9	184.9	186.2	n.a.	n.a.	n.a.
			(Implicit deflators, 1973=100)[c]						
72.1	75.9	77.7	83.4	88.1	87.7	88.2	100.0	127.7[d]	133.8[e]
73.9	77.7	78.7	84.1	87.1	89.2	92.3	100.0	132.3	140.3
71.7	71.9	75.9	75.8	82.4	87.1	91.0	100.0	122.5	139.3
66.6	68.4	73.3	78.8	87.7	82.6	82.1	100.0	126.2	128.3
69.7	70.1	71.7	72.0	77.5	83.8	88.1	100.0	131.8	139.8
95.6	97.6	102.2	109.4	113.2	98.6	93.2	100.0	95.8	91.8

c. Derived from Tables SA3 and 4 and subject to qualifications noted.
d. Preliminary.
e. World Bank estimate.

TABLE SA11. SAVINGS AND INVESTMENT BY AGENT, 1960–75
(CFAF billion)

Agent	1960	1961	1962	1963	1964	1965
Gross national savings						
Nonfinancial enterprises	8.1	7.2	0.4	4.0	12.9	8.2
Households	8.5	5.8	3.8	7.4	10.0	11.7
Government	5.2	7.7	13.5	16.6	22.8	14.6
Financial institutions	0.4	0.6	0.9	0.9	1.2	0.8
Total	22.2	21.3	18.6	28.9	46.9	35.3
Gross investment						
Nonfinancial enterprises	11.1	12.6	15.1	18.2	25.8	27.1
Households	1.0	1.3	1.8	2.6	3.3	4.8
Government	7.1	10.4	8.3	7.6	10.1	11.7
Financial institutions	n.a.	n.a.	n.a.	n.a.	n.a.	n.a.
Total fixed investment	19.2	24.3	25.2	28.4	39.2	43.6
Stocks	1.3	3.1	−5.2	1.8	5.7	1.3
Total	20.5	27.4	20.0	30.2	44.9	44.9
Net financing[c]	1.7	−6.1	−1.4	−1.3	2.0	−9.6

n.a. Not available.
Source: National accounts.

1966	1967	1968	1969	1970	1971	1972	1973	1974[a]	1975[b]
7.8	5.2	17.8	28.8	29.7	32.1	30.4	33.9	37.6	n.a.
13.9	13.2	17.2	15.4	21.1	21.3	22.9	25.3	41.9	n.a.
17.1	17.5	24.5	31.0	34.7	20.6	24.9	44.9	79.7	n.a.
0.4	0.5	0.4	2.2	2.9	4.7	5.4	4.2	3.7	n.a.
39.2	36.4	59.9	77.4	88.4	78.7	83.6	108.3	162.9	149.2
25.3	25.0	30.4	33.4	46.1	50.3	54.7	72.1	88.4	n.a.
6.0	5.5	8.5	5.0	8.0	8.0	10.0	11.0	12.0	n.a.
13.3	15.3	15.1	23.0	29.6	33.9	28.2	37.4	45.6	n.a.
n.a.	n.a.	n.a.	0.4	0.2	0.2	1.4	1.4	2.3	n.a.
44.6	45.8	54.0	61.8	83.9	92.4	94.3	121.9	148.3	198.3
5.5	1.6	1.5	7.8	7.4	3.6	3.1	7.9	7.6	8.0
50.1	47.4	55.5	69.6	91.3	96.0	97.4	129.8	155.9	206.3
−10.9	−11.0	4.4	7.8	−2.9	−17.3	−13.8	−21.5	7.0	−52.2

a. Preliminary.
b. World Bank estimate.
c. A minus sign represents inflow of savings.

TABLE SA12. BALANCE OF PAYMENTS, 1963–75: STANDARD INTERNATIONAL MONETARY FUND PRESENTATION (CFAF billion)

Item	1963 Credit	1963 Debit	1964 Credit	1964 Debit	1965 Credit	1965 Debit
Goods and services						
Merchandise	58.6	49.6	74.9	64.6	70.5	62.9
Freight and merchandise insurance	0.1	. . .	1.8	. . .	2.1	. . .
Other transportation	1.8	1.7	8.9	7.3	10.0	7.3
Travel	4.7	6.6	1.7	6.4	1.3	6.0
Investment income	. . .	5.1	−0.1	6.9	−0.1	6.5
On direct investment	. . .	4.7	−0.1	5.6	−0.1	5.1
Interest	. . .	0.4	. . .	1.3	. . .	1.4
Government, n.i.e.[b]	7.7	7.5	10.1	5.3	4.9	4.0
Services obtained under aid programs	. . .	2.1	. . .	2.3	. . .	2.6
Other	7.7	5.4	10.1	3.0	4.9	1.4
Other services	2.3	4.2	2.9	6.6	3.3	7.1
Total	75.2	74.7	100.2	97.1	92.0	93.8
Trade balance	9.0		10.3		7.6	
Service balance		8.5		7.2		9.4
Net goods and services	0.5		3.1			1.8
Unrequited transfers						
Private	0.9	6.3	1.5	8.8	1.5	9.0
Government	5.2	0.8	5.6	1.4	6.7	1.3
Capital grants	3.1	. . .	3.3	. . .	4.1	. . .
Other	2.1	0.8	2.3	. . .	2.6	1.3
Total	6.1	7.1	7.1	10.2	8.2	10.3
Nonmonetary capital						
Direct investment	2.6[c]	. . .	2.9[c]	. . .	4.7[b]	. . .
Other private long-term	2.1	. . .	2.2	0.4	1.9	0.6
Private short-term	. . .	. . .	0.3	. . .	. . .	1.3
Government	2.2	1.0	2.5	1.5	7.3	4.0
Total	6.9	1.0	7.9	1.9	13.9	5.9
SDR allocations	. . .	. . .	. . .	. . .	. . .	. . .
Errors and omissions	. . .	1.0	. . .	1.6	0.4	. . .
Monetary movements[d]	. . .	4.4	. . .	4.4	. . .	4.5

n.a. Not available.
. . . Zero or negligible.

1966		1967		1968		1969	
Credit	Debit	Credit	Debit	Credit	Debit	Credit	Debit
80.2	68.6	83.3	73.5	110.0	84.3	123.9	95.2
2.0	. . .	2.1	. . .	2.2	. . .	4.0	. . .
11.1	7.8	12.1	8.3	13.6	8.2	15.4	9.4
1.1	7.0	1.1	7.0	1.3	7.8	1.7	8.3
0.5	8.9	0.3	9.2	0.1	9.6	0.9	10.9
. . .	7.0	−0.2	7.1	−0.2	7.3	. . .	8.0
0.5	1.9	0.5	2.1	0.3	2.3	0.9	2.9
4.7	4.8	5.3	5.5	6.3	6.0	6.7	7.3
. . .	3.0	. . .	3.2	. . .	3.8	. . .	5.0
4.7	1.8	5.3	2.0	6.3	1.9	6.7	2.3
4.5	9.7	4.7	10.9	4.6	13.2	5.1	17.1
104.1	106.8	108.9	114.4	138.1	129.1	157.6	148.2
11.6		9.8		25.7		28.7	
	14.3		15.3		16.7		19.3
	2.7		5.5	9.0		9.4	
1.6	10.3	1.5	10.4	1.7	10.9	2.0	11.3
7.6	2.8	6.9	3.3	7.9	4.1	9.9	4.6
4.5	. . .	3.7	. . .	4.1	. . .	4.7	. . .
3.1	2.8	3.2	3.3	3.8	4.1	5.2	4.6
9.2	13.1	8.4	13.7	9.6	15.0	11.9	15.9
2.6	3.0	1.6[b]	. . .	5.1	2.1	5.9	2.9
3.2	2.5	1.5	0.1	4.6	3.6	4.3	5.5
2.7	. . .	0.1	. . .	. . .	2.1	1.0	2.5
6.2	5.6	4.5	4.5	11.0	6.3	12.5	5.8
14.7	11.1	7.7	4.6	20.7	14.1	23.7	16.7
. . .	. . .	. . .	. . .	. . .	. . .	. . .	. . .
6.1	. . .	1.4	. . .	. . .	1.5	. . .	2.9
. . .	3.1	6.3	. . .	. . .	8.7	. . .	9.5

a. Preliminary figures
b. Not included elsewhere.
c. Net.
d. Debit column indicates an increase.

(Table SA12 continues on the following page.)

TABLE SA12 *(continued)*

Item	1970 Credit	1970 Debit	1971 Credit	1971 Debit
Goods and services				
Merchandise	138.0	120.2	137.3	122.0
Freight and merchandise insurance	7.0	. . .	8.2	. . .
Other transportation	17.8	12.6	19.2	14.1
Travel	1.8	10.1	2.6	11.2
Investment income	2.4	12.7	2.1	16.7
On direct investment	. . .	8.4	. . .	11.5
Interest	2.4	4.3	2.1	5.2
Government, n.i.e.[b]	8.0	10.6	9.7	13.3
Services obtained under aid programs	. . .	6.7	. . .	8.3
Other	8.0	3.9	9.7	5.0
Other services	5.3	20.3	7.0	27.4
Total	180.3	186.5	186.1	204.7
Trade balance	17.8		15.3	
Service balance		24.0		33.9
Net goods and services		6.2		18.6
Unrequited transfers				
Private	1.7	13.5	2.2	16.5
Government	13.3	4.8	13.9	6.7
Capital grants	4.7	. . .	3.6	. . .
Other	8.6	4.8	10.3	4.7
Total	15.0	18.3	16.1	21.2
Nonmonetary capital				
Direct investment	8.5	0.4	7.3	3.2
Other private long-term	12.3	10.4	6.6	6.1
Private short-term	0.8	1.5	2.3	3.2
Government	16.6	5.9	21.3	4.5
Total	38.2	18.2	37.5	17.0
SDR allocations	0.9	. . .	1.5	. . .
Errors and omissions	. . .	2.0	. . .	1.5
Monetary movements[d]	. . .	9.4	3.2	. . .

n.a. Not available.
. . . Zero or negligible.
Source: BCEAO and World Bank estimates

1972		*1973*		*1974*		*1975*[a]	
Credit	Debit	Credit	Debit	Credit	Debit	Credit	Debit
150.2	128.0	191.9	171.6	301.4	241.4	266.3	249.3
8.2	. . .	8.3	. . .	12.5	n.a.	11.4	n.a.
19.0	14.5	2.7	7.4	6.4	17.7	6.6	20.5
2.0	12.5	3.9	16.6	5.6	20.6	6.6	23.8
1.9	16.7	1.8	25.2	3.9	27.8	4.9	35.0
. . .	10.7	. . .	17.9	n.a.	n.a.	n.a.	n.a.
1.9	6.0	1.8	7.3	n.a.	n.a.	n.a.	n.a.
12.3	17.8	7.4	7.6	9.8	10.2	10.6	11.7
. . .	12.1	. . .	. . .	n.a.	n.a.	n.a.	n.a.
12.3	5.7	7.4	7.6	n.a.	n.a.	n.a.	n.a.
8.2	28.3	8.7	24.8	10.2	24.5	11.1	27.8
201.8	217.8	224.7	253.2	349.8	342.2	317.5	368.1
22.2		20.3		60.0		17.0	
	38.2		48.8		52.4		67.6
	16.0		28.5	7.6			50.6
2.1	19.6	2.0	28.2	2.2	34.3	2.5	37.4
16.1	7.8	18.1	7.1	20.8	10.9	19.6	11.7
3.8	. . .	3.8	. . .	n.a.	n.a.	n.a.	n.a.
12.3	7.8	14.3	7.1	n.a.	n.a.	n.a.	n.a.
18.2	27.4	20.1	35.3	23.0	45.2	22.1	49.1
6.2	2.5	13.0	2.3	n.a.	n.a.	n.a.	n.a.
15.0	8.5	25.4	3.8	n.a.	n.a.	n.a.	n.a.
1.7	6.6	2.2	9.4	n.a.	n.a.	n.a.	n.a.
11.1	9.6	25.9	9.5	n.a.	n.a.	n.a.	n.a.
34.0	27.2	66.5	25.0	77.2	36.6	64.3	22.3
1.5	. . .	. . .	. . .	. . .	. . .	. . .	. . .
. . .	2.0	. . .	0.1	. . .	5.0	. . .	. . .
18.9	. . .	2.3	. . .	. . .	21.0	35.6	. . .

a. Preliminary figures
b. Not included elsewhere.
c. Net.
d. Debit column indicates an increase.

TABLE SA13. BALANCE OF PAYMENTS, 1963–75:
WORLD BANK PRESENTATION
(CFAF billion)

Item	1963	1964	1965	1966
Current account				
A. Exports (including nonfactor services)	72.2	88.5	81.7	90.4
B. Imports (including nonfactor services)	66.8	78.8	78.5	85.9
C. Resource balance (A − B)	5.4	9.7	3.2	4.5
D. Factor services (credit)	. . .	. . .	. . .	0.5
E. Factor services (debit)	11.4	16.1	16.3	20.3
Interest payments	0.4	1.3	1.4	1.9
Direct investment income	4.7	5.6	5.1	7.0
Workers' remittances	5.6	8.4	8.9	10.3
Transfers by technical assistants[b]	0.7	0.8	0.9	1.1
F. Factor services, net (D − E)	−11.4	−16.1	−16.3	−19.8
G. Goods and services (credit)	72.2	88.5	81.7	90.9
H. Goods and services (debit)	78.2	94.9	94.8	106.2
I. Goods and services, net (G − H)	−6.0	−6.4	−13.1	−15.3
J. Current transfers (credit)	3.0	3.8	4.3	4.7
K. Current transfers (debit)	1.5	1.8	1.6	2.8
L. Current transfers, net (J − K)	1.5	2.0	2.7	1.9
M. Current account balance (I + L)	−4.5	−4.4	−10.4	−13.4

n.a. Not available.
. . . Zero or negligible.

1967	*1968*	*1969*	*1970*	*1971*	*1972*	*1973*	*1974*	*1975*[a]
96.5	125.2	143.9	161.0	164.9	181.1	222.9	333.4	301.2
93.3	106.9	124.2	156.2	167.8	179.3	228.0	314.4	333.1
3.2	18.3	19.7	4.8	−2.9	1.8	−5.1	19.0	−31.9
0.5	0.3	0.9	2.4	2.1	1.9	1.8	3.8	4.0
20.7	21.8	24.0	28.1	35.5	40.0	52.7	59.9	66.9
2.1	2.3	2.9	4.3	5.2	6.0	7.3	9.2	12.0
7.1	7.3	8.0	8.4	11.5	10.7	17.9	17.2	20.0
10.4	10.9	11.3	13.1	15.9	19.1	27.5	33.5	34.9
1.1	1.3	1.8	2.3	2.9	4.2	. . .	. . .	. . .
−20.2	−21.5	−23.1	−25.7	−33.4	−38.1	−50.9	−56.1	−62.9
97.0	125.5	144.8	163.4	167.0	183.0	224.7	337.2	305.2
114.0	128.7	148.2	184.3	203.3	219.3	280.7	374.3	400.0
−17.0	−3.2	−3.4	−20.9	−36.3	−36.3	−56.0	−37.1	−94.8
4.7	5.5	7.2	10.1	12.5	14.4	16.3	n.a.	n.a.
3.3	4.1	4.6	5.2	5.3	8.3	7.8	n.a.	n.a.
1.4	1.9	2.6	4.9	7.2	6.1	8.5	7.8	9.1
−15.6	−1.3	−0.8	−16.0	−29.1	−30.2	−47.5	−29.3	−85.7

a. Preliminary figures.
b. Estimated at 35 percent of salary.

(Table SA13 continues on the following page.)

TABLE SA13 *(continued)*

Item	1963	1964	1965	1966
Capital Account				
N. Nonmonetary capital (O + P + Q)	9.0	9.3	12.1	8.1
1. Direct investment, net	2.6	2.9	4.7	−0.4
Retained earnings	1.0	1.0	1.5	1.1
2. Other long-term capital, net	1.7	1.3	1.1	−2.4
3. Short-term capital, net	. . .	0.3	−1.3	2.7
O. Private capital (1 + 2 + 3)	4.3	4.5	4.5	−0.1
4. Capital grants	3.1	3.3	4.1	4.5
5. Loans received	2.0	3.0	6.4	8.6
Central government	1.3	1.7	4.9	6.8
Public enterprises	0.7	1.3	1.5	1.8
6. Repayment	1.0	1.7	3.1	4.0
Central government	0.7	1.2	2.4	3.2
Public enterprises	0.3	0.5	0.7	0.8
7. Net (5 − 6)	1.0	1.3	3.3	4.6
8. Other capital, n.i.e.	0.6	0.2	0.2	−2.0
P. Public capital (4 + 5 + 6 + 8)	4.7	4.8	7.6	7.1
Q. Capital transactions of Air Afrique, net	n.a.	n.a.	n.a.	1.1
R. Overall balance (M + N)	4.5	4.9	1.7	−5.3
S. SDR allocations	. . .	. . .	. . .	. . .
T. Errors and omissions	−0.1	−0.5	2.8	8.4
Reserve movements[c] (R + S + T)	−4.4	−4.4	−4.5	−3.1
Reconciliation of World Bank with IMF standard presentation				
U. Goods and services, net	−6.0	−6.4	−13.1	−15.3
V. Workers' remittances	5.6	8.4	8.9	10.3
W. Air Afrique, net	0.9	1.1	2.4	2.3
X. Goods and services (standard presentation) (U + V + W)	0.5	3.1	−1.8	−2.7
Y. Current transfers (standard presentation)[d]	−1.0	−3.1	−2.1	−3.9
Capital grants	3.1	3.3	4.1	4.5
Z. Current account balance (standard presentation) (X + Y)[e]	−0.5	0.0	−3.9	−6.6

n.a. Not available.
. . . Zero or negligible.
Source: Table SA12 and BCEAO.

1967	1968	1969	1970	1971	1972	1973	1974	1975[a]
6.8	10.7	11.7	24.7	24.2	10.6	45.3	55.3	50.1
1.6	3.0	3.0	8.1	4.1	3.7	10.7	6.7	n.a.
1.4	2.0	3.0	2.9	5.4	4.3	7.8	4.3	n.a.
0.7	−0.4	−2.0	−1.7	−2.3	−1.4	−0.6	−1.0	n.a.
0.1	−2.1	−1.5	−0.7	−0.9	−4.9	−7.2	0.4	−1.3
2.4	0.5	−0.5	5.7	0.9	−2.6	2.9	6.1	3.0
3.7	4.1	4.7	4.7	3.6	3.8	3.8	3.5	4.0
5.7	12.6	14.4	19.6	29.8	20.8	46.5	52.3	72.0
4.4	8.4	7.3	10.2	18.5	5.0	22.4	26.1	n.a.
1.3	4.2	7.1	9.4	11.3	15.8	24.1	26.2	n.a.
4.9	5.6	5.8	6.6	7.6	9.3	9.2	18.4	19.0
3.6	4.0	4.0	4.5	5.3	6.6	6.1	12.2	n.a.
1.3	1.6	1.8	2.1	2.3	2.7	3.1	6.2	n.a.
0.8	7.0	8.6	13.0	22.2	11.5	37.2	33.9	53.0
−0.9	−1.2	−1.0	−1.2	−1.2	−0.4	1.4	11.8	−9.9
3.6	9.9	12.3	16.5	24.6	14.9	42.4	49.2	47.1
0.8	0.3	−0.1	2.5	−1.3	−1.7	n.a.	n.a.	n.a.
−8.8	8.9	10.9	8.7	−4.9	−19.6	−2.2	26.0	−35.6
. . .	. . .	. . .	0.9	1.5	1.5	. . .	. . .	. . .
2.5	−0.2	−1.4	−0.2	−0.2	−0.8	−0.1	−5.0	n.a.
6.3	−8.7	−9.5	−9.4	3.2	18.9	2.3	−21.0	35.6
−17.0	−3.2	−3.4	−20.9	−36.3	−36.3	−56.0	−25.9	−85.5
10.4	10.9	11.3	13.1	15.9	19.1	27.5	33.5	34.9
1.1	1.3	1.5	1.6	1.8	1.2	n.a.	n.a.	n.a.
−5.5	9.0	9.4	−6.2	−18.6	−16.0	−28.5	7.6	−50.6
−5.2	−5.5	−4.0	−3.3	−5.1	−9.2	−15.2	−22.2	−27.0
3.7	4.1	4.7	4.7	3.6	3.8	3.8	3.5	4.0
−10.7	3.5	5.4	−9.5	−23.7	−25.2	−43.7	−14.6	−77.6

a. Preliminary figures.
c. A minus sign indicates an increase.
d. Equals net unrequited transfers of Table SA12.
e. Equals net goods and services plus net unrequited transfers of Table SA12.

TABLE SA14. EXPORTS AND IMPORTS OF GOODS AND NONFACTOR SERVICES, ADJUSTED, 1963–72
(CFAF billion)

Item	1963	1964	1965	1966	1967	1968	1969	1970	1971	1972
Exports										
Exports of goods and services	63.4	81.4	73.5	81.6	87.2	115.3	133.7	149.6	151.5	167.9
Travel	1.7	1.7	1.3	1.1	1.1	1.3	1.7	1.8	2.6	2.0
Government, n.i.e.[a]	6.6	4.7	3.6	3.2	3.7	4.4	4.2	4.6	5.5	6.2
Other services[b]	0.5	0.7	3.3	4.5	4.5	4.2	4.3	5.0	5.3	5.0
Total exports (including nonfactor services)	72.2	88.5	81.7	90.4	96.5	125.2	143.9	161.0	164.9	181.1
Imports										
Imports of goods and services	51.8	65.8	67.7	73.1	77.7	89.4	103.0	130.9	138.5	145.6
Travel	6.6	6.4	6.0	7.0	7.0	7.8	8.3	10.1	11.2	12.5
Travel expenditures of technical assistants[c]	0.3	0.4	0.4	0.5	0.6	0.7	0.8	1.1	1.4	2.0
Government, n.i.e.[d]	5.4	3.0	1.4	1.8	2.0	1.9	2.3	3.9	5.0	5.7
Other services[b]	2.7	3.2	3.0	3.5	6.0	7.1	9.8	10.2	11.7	13.5
Total imports (including nonfactor services)	66.8	78.8	78.5	85.9	93.3	106.9	124.2	156.2	167.8	179.3
Resource balance	5.4	9.7	3.2	4.5	3.2	18.3	19.7	4.8	-2.9	1.8

Source: National accounts, Central Bank (BCEAO) and World Bank estimates.
a. Not included elsewhere. Excluding expenditures by technical assistants estimated at 50 percent of their salary.
b. Mainly insurance, commissions, and management fees.
c. Estimated to equal two months' salary.
d. Excluding the cost of technical assistance.

TABLE SA15. UNREQUITED TRANSFERS, 1963–75
(CFAF billion)

Item	1963	1964	1965	1966	1967	1968	1969	1970	1971	1972	1973	1974	1975ᵃ
Public transfers													
Technical assistance	2.1	2.3	2.6	3.0	3.2	3.8	5.0	6.7	8.3	12.1	14.2	14.8	16.0
Government contribution	−0.5	−1.0	−1.5	−1.8	−2.9	−3.3	−4.0	−4.2	−4.7	−6.4	−7.1	−8.9	−9.5
Other, net	−0.3	−0.4	0.2	−0.9	−0.4	−0.8	−0.4	0.4	1.5	−1.3	0.1	0.5	0.6
Total	1.3	0.9	1.3	0.3	−0.1	−0.3	0.6	2.9	5.1	4.4	7.2	6.4	7.1
Private transfers													
Pensions	0.7	1.5	1.4	1.3	1.3	1.4	1.6	1.5	1.5	1.4	1.4	1.6	1.5
Other, net	−0.5	−0.4	. . .	0.3	0.2	0.3	0.4	0.5	0.6	0.3	−0.1	−0.2	0.5
Total	0.2	1.1	1.4	1.6	1.5	1.7	2.0	2.0	2.1	1.7	1.3	1.4	2.0
Current transfers, net	1.5	2.0	2.7	1.9	1.4	1.4	2.6	4.9	7.2	6.1	8.5	7.8	9.1

. . . Zero or negligible.
Source: BCEAO and World Bank estimates.
a. Preliminary figures.

TABLE SA16. COMPOSITION OF EXPORTS, 1960–75
(CFAF billion)

Product	1960	1961	1962	1963	1964	1965
Coffee beans	18.8	20.3	18.9	24.5	31.7	25.9
Processed	. . .	. . .	0.1	0.2	0.3	0.3
Cocoa beans	8.7	9.8	10.6	11.3	14.5	10.9
Processed	. . .	. . .	. . .	. . .	0.1	1.0
Timber logs	5.8	7.6	8.4	11.2	15.9	15.0
Processed	0.7	0.9	0.9	1.2	2.0	3.3
Bananas	1.3	2.1	2.9	3.5	3.1	2.8
Pineapples, fresh	0.1	0.1	0.1	0.1	0.2	0.2
Canned	0.3	0.3	0.4	0.6	0.8	0.9
Juice	0.2	0.2	0.3	0.3	0.4	0.3
Rubber	. . .	. . .	. . .	0.1	0.2	0.3
Cotton lint	. . .	. . .	. . .	. . .	0.1	0.2
Textile	0.2	0.2	0.2	0.1	0.1	0.1
Palm oil	. . .	. . .	. . .	. . .	. . .	. . .
Palm kernels	0.6	0.4	0.3	0.3	0.3	0.5
Petroleum products	. . .	. . .	. . .	. . .	. . .	. . .
Other products	2.1	4.2	4.1	4.0	3.5	6.7
Total recorded exports	38.8	46.1	47.2	57.4	73.2	68.4
Adjustments	1.4	1.4	1.5	1.2	1.7	2.1
Total merchandise exports, (f.o.b.)	40.2	47.5	48.7	58.6	74.9	70.5

. . . Zero or negligible.

1966	1967	1968	1969	1970	1971	1972	1973	1974	1975
30.2	25.4	35.9	30.2	43.2	42.2	36.8	43.8	63.8	61.7
0.5	0.6	1.0	1.3	1.9	1.8	1.3	1.6	2.3	2.4
13.1	13.6	19.4	26.4	26.1	21.7	22.6	27.8	62.3	47.6
1.6	2.5	4.3	5.7	6.6	5.6	5.6	6.3	13.3	15.3
14.8	17.8	21.4	30.1	23.5	25.9	32.5	56.2	51.6	34.8
3.4	3.7	4.3	4.9	5.7	5.0	5.3	9.7	14.2	10.8
2.8	3.1	3.1	3.0	3.2	3.0	3.5	3.0	3.7	3.0
0.3	0.4	0.6	0.6	0.8	0.9	1.9	2.1	3.0	3.1
1.2	1.6	1.6	1.7	2.4	3.0	3.5	4.2	6.7	6.2
0.3	0.4	0.4	0.5	0.7	0.6	0.6	0.8	0.7	0.5
0.7	0.6	0.6	0.9	1.2	1.1	1.0	2.0	2.7	1.7
0.3	0.9	1.5	1.6	1.6	1.7	2.6	3.2	5.3	3.6
0.3	0.6	1.0	1.4	1.7	1.5	2.4	3.2	4.3	6.5
...	...	...	0.1	0.8	1.9	2.1	3.0	15.3	10.5
0.3	0.3	0.4	0.4	0.6	0.6	0.6	1.0	3.9	1.1
...	0.9	1.6	1.5	0.8	0.6	2.9	4.4	10.9	14.4
6.9	7.9	7.8	7.9	9.4	9.5	14.3	18.6	27.8	31.4
76.7	80.3	104.9	118.2	130.2	126.6	139.5	190.9	291.8	254.6
3.5	3.0	5.1	5.7	7.8	10.7	10.7	1.0	9.6	11.7
80.2	83.3	110.0	123.9	138.0	137.3	150.2	191.9	301.4	266.3

Source: Balance of payments and foreign trade statistics: Ministry of Economic Affairs and Finance; BCEAO, Abidjan office.

TABLE SA17. COMPOSITION OF IMPORTS, 1960–75
(CFAF billion)

	1960	1961	1962	1963	1964	1965
Constant 1973 prices						
Sugar	1.4	2.1	1.9	1.7	1.7	1.6
Wheat	0.3	0.6	0.3	0.4	1.2	1.3
Rice	2.2	2.8	2.5	1.5	3.5	4.5
Other foodstuffs	8.1	8.4	7.7	7.5	8.4	7.5
Consumer goods	20.9	25.1	22.5	23.4	31.0	29.4
Raw materials and						
semifinished products	9.4	11.6	9.7	10.5	16.2	14.9
Crude oil	. . .	. . .	. . .	. . .	. . .	1.2
Refined oil	2.9	3.4	3.4	3.4	4.2	3.6
Equipment goods	15.4	20.8	19.5	22.6	29.6	28.0
Total recorded imports	60.2	74.8	67.5	71.0	95.8	92.0
Adjustments	6.4	7.7	8.1	10.3	7.6	5.6
Total merchandise imports						
(c.i.f.)	66.6	82.5	75.6	81.3	103.4	97.6
Price indexes (1973=100)						
Sugar	66.3	57.0	58.5	60.4	81.3	86.7
Wheat	75.1	76.3	80.0	80.0	85.0	99.5
Rice	45.7	50.0	56.0	53.1	57.6	48.7
Other foodstuffs	57.0	59.5	62.2	65.0	67.0	73.5
Consumer goods	54.9	58.5	60.0	61.1	64.5	67.0
Raw materials and						
semifinished products	59.4	63.5	66.0	67.5	66.1	67.0
Crude oil	. . .	. . .	. . .	. . .	. . .	73.2
Refined oil	56.1	58.3	58.0	61.0	64.1	67.3
Equipment goods	45.4	46.1	46.6	50.5	52.0	53.5
International price index	70.8	72.3	72.4	74.5	76.3	80.0
Import price index	55.4	57.5	58.7	61.0	62.5	64.4
Current prices						
Sugar	0.9	1.2	1.1	1.0	1.4	1.4
Wheat	0.2	0.5	0.2	0.3	1.0	1.3
Rice	1.0	1.4	1.4	0.8	2.0	2.2
Other foodstuffs	4.6	5.0	4.8	4.9	5.6	5.5
Consumer goods	11.5	14.7	13.5	14.3	20.0	19.7
Raw materials and						
semifinished products	5.6	7.4	6.4	7.1	10.7	10.0
Crude oil	. . .	. . .	. . .	. . .	. . .	0.9
Refined oil	1.6	2.0	2.0	2.1	2.7	2.4
Equipment goods	7.0	9.6	9.1	11.4	15.4	·15.0
Total recorded imports	32.4	41.8	38.5	41.9	58.8	58.4
Adjustments	4.5	5.6	5.9	7.7	5.8	4.5
Total merchandise imports						
(c.i.f.)	36.9	47.4	44.4	49.6	64.6	62.9

. . . Zero or negligible.

1966	1967	1968	1969	1970	1971	1972	1973	1974	1975
2.4	2.2	2.6	2.7	3.5	3.8	3.9	4.3	3.8	4.4
2.3	1.3	1.5	1.0	1.6	0.6	1.5	2.9	2.0	2.9
4.9	1.4	2.8	3.3	4.5	5.7	4.3	8.2	3.7	0.2
7.7	7.6	9.2	10.2	13.9	13.1	13.6	17.5	19.1	19.2
30.1	33.4	35.4	39.3	41.9	41.9	41.3	44.6	48.7	47.1
17.5	19.1	20.8	21.9	29.1	29.8	26.7	30.4	35.2	31.8
3.8	4.1	4.3	5.1	4.9	3.9	6.9	5.7	10.2	9.5
1.0	0.8	3.4	1.0	1.4	1.7	0.9	1.5	0.9	0.7
27.1	26.7	28.4	33.6	37.7	36.7	33.6	42.4	49.6	46.3
96.8	96.6	108.4	118.1	138.5	137.2	132.7	157.5	173.2	162.1
6.1	10.1	8.0	10.5	14.8	12.8	13.9	14.1	10.0	6.7
102.9	106.7	116.4	128.6	153.3	150.0	146.6	171.6	183.2	168.8
53.1	60.0	62.0	62.3	68.8	76.2	90.7	100.0	165.0	145.2
99.0	100.4	103.3	117.3	93.7	116.9	113.1	100.0	108.8	91.1
63.9	62.1	67.6	57.6	44.0	38.8	49.2	100.0	189.5	100.0
75.0	77.5	75.0	73.9	75.5	85.0	89.3	100.0	123.0	135.4
66.6	67.0	70.9	69.2	73.7	77.5	82.8	100.0	115.0	127.3
68.4	72.4	73.1	76.3	81.2	83.3	89.3	100.0	120.0	141.5
70.9	73.4	76.2	72.5	80.2	96.4	92.4	100.0	304.1	330.9
70.6	74.1	77.8	81.7	85.8	90.1	94.6	100.0	237.9	328.6
57.9	60.0	68.7	76.0	81.7	85.0	87.2	100.0	125.0	145.9
81.5	82.1	83.6	84.8	84.5	87.5	98.6	100.0	110.2	122.1
66.7	68.9	72.4	74.0	78.4	81.3	87.3	100.0	132.7	142.6
1.3	1.3	1.6	1.7	2.4	2.9	3.5	4.3	6.2	6.4
2.3	1.3	1.4	1.2	1.5	0.7	1.7	2.9	2.2	2.6
3.1	0.9	1.9	1.9	2.0	2.2	2.2	8.2	7.1	0.2
5.8	5.9	6.9	7.5	10.6	11.2	12.1	17.5	23.5	26.0[a]
20.0	22.4	25.1	27.2	31.6	32.5	34.2	44.6	56.0	60.0[a]
12.0	13.8	15.2	16.8	23.7	24.8	23.8	30.4	42.2	45.0[a]
2.7	3.0	3.3	3.7	3.9	3.8	6.4	5.7	31.0	31.3
0.7	0.6	2.6	0.8	1.2	1.5	1.0	1.5	2.1	2.3
15.7	16.0	19.6	25.5	30.8	31.2	29.4	42.4	62.0	67.6[a]
63.6	65.2	77.6	86.3	107.7	110.8	114.3	157.5	232.3	241.4
5.0	8.3	6.7	8.9	12.5	11.2	13.7	14.1	9.1	8.2
68.6	73.5	84.3	95.2	120.2	122.0	128.0	171.6	241.4	249.6

Source: Balance of payments and foreign trade statistics: Ministry of Economic Affairs and Finance; BCEAO, Abidjan office.
a. World Bank estimates.

TABLE SA18. VOLUME, VALUE, AND AVERAGE PRICE
OF SELECTED EXPORTS, 1960–75
(Volume in thousands of metric tons; price in CFAF
per kilogram; value in CFAF billion)

Product	1960	1961	1962	1963	1964	1965	1966
Coffee beans							
Volume	148.4	156.0	142.6	182.1	204.3	185.7	181.5
Price per							
kilogram	126.4	130.1	132.5	134.5	155.2	139.5	166.4
Value	18.8	20.3	18.9	24.5	31.7	25.9	30.2
Cocoa beans							
Volume	62.9	88.5	101.1	99.7	124.3	126.4	124.3
Price per							
kilogram	138.3	110.7	104.8	113.3	116.7	86.2	105.4
Value	8.7	9.8	10.6	11.3	14.5	10.9	13.1
Timber (logs)							
Volume[a]	839	996	1,161	1,478	1,859	1,955	1,822
Price[b]	6,912	7,630	7,235	7,577	8,552	7,672	8,122
Value	5.8	7.6	8.4	11.2	15.9	15.0	14.8
Bananas							
Volume	72.6	92.0	125.2	133.4	125.9	128.3	131.7
Price per							
kilogram	17.9	22.8	23.2	26.2	24.6	21.8	21.3
Value	1.3	2.1	2.9	3.5	3.1	2.8	2.8
Pineapples (fresh)							
Volume	3.0	2.1	2.4	2.9	4.2	4.6	6.8
Price per							
kilogram	33.3	42.0	41.4	34.4	47.3	46.2	48.2
Value	0.1	0.1	0.1	0.1	0.2	0.2	0.3
Rubber							
Volume	...	...	...	0.4	1.6	2.8	5.5
Price per							
kilogram	...	...	...	125.0	126.0	115.0	117.2
Value	...	...	...	0.1	0.2	0.3	0.7
Cotton (lint)							
Volume	...	...	...	...	0.6	1.7	3.9
Price per							
kilogram	...	...	...	...	...	89.0	86.0
Value	...	...	...	...	0.1	0.2	0.3
Palm oil							
Volume	...	...	...	...	...	...	...
Price per							
kilogram	...	...	...	...	...	...	...
Value	...	...	...	...	...	...	...

... Zero or negligible.
Source: Balance of payments and foreign trade statistics: Ministry of Economic Affairs
and Finance; BCEAO, Abidjan office.

1967	1968	1969	1970	1971	1972	1973	1974	1975
149.0	214.4	178.3	195.3	184.8	188.5	212.6	263.6	255.0
170.5	167.4	169.4	221.0	228.2	195.2	206.0	242.0	242.0
25.4	35.9	30.2	43.2	42.2	36.8	43.8	63.8	61.7
105.2	121.5	118.9	143.2	146.9	159.4	143.0	205.3	169.7
132.1	159.7	222.0	182.3	147.7	142.1	194.4	303.3	280.5
13.9	19.4	26.4	26.1	21.7	22.6	27.8	62.3	47.6
2,172	2,620	3,327	2,511	2,933	3,168	3,497	3,017	2,372
8,195	8,168	9,047	9,359	8,831	10,259	16,071	17,300	14,671
17.8	21.4	30.1	23.5	25.9	32.5	56.2	51.6	34.8
142.6	147.3	147.3	140.5	137.1	160.1	145.0	174.7	135.9
21.7	21.0	20.4	22.8	21.9	21.9	20.9	21.2	22.1
3.1	3.1	3.0	3.2	3.0	3.5	3.0	3.7	3.0
10.0	13.7	13.3	17.4	19.7	38.0	46.5	67.0	69.7
44.2	44.1	45.2	45.2	45.8	51.0	44.9	44.4	44.5
0.4	0.6	0.6	0.8	0.9	1.9	2.1	3.0	3.1
5.8	7.0	7.1	10.9	11.8	12.7	14.9	15.2	14.9
95.0	90.0	126.0	109.0	95.0	77.0	133.0	175.5	114.1
0.6	0.6	0.9	1.2	1.1	1.0	2.0	2.7	1.7
8.6	11.3	11.7	11.7	12.9	14.7	17.0	16.2	12.2
104.0	129.0	135.0	139.0	134.0	180.0	188.5	326.5	295.1
0.9	1.5	1.6	1.6	1.7	2.6	3.2	5.3	3.6
. . .	0.5	2.0	12.4	28.0	46.6	49.8	101.6	113.8
. . .	. . .	50.0	63.5	68.2	45.7	60.2	150.6	92.3
. . .	. . .	0.1	0.8	1.9	2.1	3.0	15.3	10.5

a. In thousands of cubic meters.
b. In CFAF per cubic meter.

TABLE SA19. DIRECTION OF TRADE, 1960-75

Category	Value in CFAF billion					Percentage of total				
	1960	1965	1970	1973	1974	1960	1965	1970	1973	1974
Total exports										
France	19.6	25.8	42.5	49.2	76.2	50.5	37.7	32.6	25.8	26.1
EEC (excluding France)[a]	5.9	16.0	38.2	63.8	107.4	15.2	23.4	29.3	33.4	36.8
CEAO[b]	2.4	3.0	5.8	11.8	21.1	6.2	4.4	4.4	6.2	7.2
Other franc zone countries	1.9	3.2	3.1	8.2	13.0	4.9	4.6	2.4	4.3	4.5
United States	5.6	10.6	24.3	21.2	20.7	14.4	15.5	18.7	11.1	7.1
Other developed countries	1.4	6.4	12.2	24.9	33.5	3.6	9.4	9.4	13.0	11.5
Socialist countries	0.7	1.5	1.0	5.7	12.6	1.8	2.2	0.8	3.0	4.3
Other countries	1.3	1.9	3.1	6.1	7.3	3.4	2.8	2.4	3.2	2.5
Total	38.8	68.4	130.2	190.9	291.8	100.0	100.0	100.0	100.0	100.0
Exports of coffee beans										
France	10.2	11.3	18.6	14.4	24.1	54.3	43.6	43.1	32.9	37.8
EEC (excluding France)[a]	1.5	2.5	3.1	3.1	14.9	8.0	9.7	7.2	7.1	23.3
United States	3.3	7.0	17.5	14.4	10.7	17.5	27.0	40.5	32.9	16.8
French-speaking North Africa[c]	3.3	1.8	0.5	5.2	5.5	17.5	6.9	1.1	11.9	8.6
Japan	..	0.3	1.6	3.8	1.4	...	1.2	3.7	8.6	2.2
Other countries	0.5	3.0	1.9	2.9	7.2	2.7	11.6	4.4	6.6	11.3
Total	18.8	25.9	43.2	43.8	63.8	100.0	100.0	100.0	100.0	100.0

Exports of cocoa beans										
France	3.5	2.7	5.3	4.1	7.6	40.2	24.8	20.3	14.7	12.2
EEC (excluding France)[a]	2.3	4.8	16.1	16.7	38.3	26.5	44.0	61.7	60.1	61.5
United States	1.9	2.3	4.0	4.6	5.4	21.8	21.1	15.3	16.5	8.7
Other countries	1.0	1.1	0.7	2.4	11.0	11.5	10.1	2.7	8.7	17.6
Total	8.7	10.9	26.1	27.8	62.3	100.0	100.0	100.0	100.0	100.0
Exports of timber										
France	3.0	5.0	4.7	10.4	9.9	51.7	33.3	20.0	18.5	19.2
EEC (excluding France)[a]	2.2	6.6	12.4	29.3	24.2	37.9	44.0	52.8	52.1	46.9
United Kingdom	0.2	1.1	1.0	1.6	1.3	3.5	7.3	4.3	2.9	2.5
Spain	...	0.7	2.4	8.7	6.7	...	4.7	10.2	15.5	13.0
Other countries	0.4	1.6	3.0	6.2	9.5	6.9	10.7	12.7	11.0	18.4
Total	5.8	15.0	23.5	56.2	51.6	100.0	100.0	100.0	100.0	100.0
Total imports										
France	20.9	35.9	49.8	69.7	89.4	64.5	61.6	46.2	44.3	38.5
EEC (excluding France)[a]	3.2	7.8	24.2	27.8	40.4	9.9	13.3	22.5	17.7	17.4
CEAO	1.3	1.9	3.3	3.6	4.8	4.0	3.3	3.1	2.3	2.0
Other franc zone countries	1.7	3.4	7.1	4.3	8.6	5.2	5.8	6.6	2.7	3.7
United States	1.1	3.2	8.5	14.1	14.6	3.4	5.4	7.9	9.0	6.3
Other developed countries	1.7	2.8	8.0	13.8	19.5	5.3	4.8	7.4	8.7	8.4
Socialist countries	...	0.6	1.6	2.5	3.2	...	1.0	1.5	1.6	1.4
Other countries	2.5	2.8	5.2	21.7	51.8	7.7	4.8	4.8	13.7	22.3
Total	32.4	58.4	107.7	157.5	232.3	100.0	100.0	100.0	100.0	100.0

... Zero or negligible.

Source: Ministry of Economic Affairs and Finance; foreign trade statistics.

a. Also excluding the United Kingdom, Ireland, and Denmark, members of the EEC as of January 1, 1973.

b. Communauté Economique de L'Afrique de l'Ouest.

c. Algeria, Morocco, and Tunisia.

TABLE SA20. TRADE WITH THE CEAO, 1965–76
(CFAF million)

Category	Senegal	Mauritania	Mali	Niger	Upper Volta	Total
1965						
Exports	1,836	28	377	189	524	2,954
Imports	953	2	4	4	56	1,019
Trade balance	883	26	373	185	468	1,935
1970						
Exports	2,880	122	802	501	1,477	5,782
Imports	2,855	1	200	168	61	3,285
Trade balance	25	121	602	333	1,416	2,497
1973						
Exports	3,487	40	3,408	999	3,881	11,817
Imports	2,987	30	270	95	144	3,526
Trade balance	500	10	3,138	904	3,737	8,291
1974						
Exports	5,221	149	7,710	1,547	6,518	21,145
Imports	4,327	82	188	155	228	5,010
Trade balance	894	67	7,522	1,392	6,290	16,135
1975						
Exports	4,892	288	11,339	2,830	7,242	26,591
Imports	3,946	97	494	210	359	5,106
Trade balance	946	191	10,845	2,620	6,883	21,485
1976[a]						
Exports	4,560	89	4,759	1,572	4,704	15,684
Imports	2,582	21	689	175	123	3,590
Trade balance	1,978	68	4,070	1,397	4,581	12,094

Source: BCEAO, Abidjan office.
a. January to July 1976.

TABLE SA21. EXTERNAL PUBLIC DEBT OUTSTANDING,
INCLUDING UNDISBURSED AS OF
DECEMBER 31, 1975 (DEBT REPAYABLE
IN FOREIGN CURRENCY AND GOODS)
(Thousands of U.S. dollars)

Creditor country and type of creditor	Debt outstanding		
	Disbursed	Undisbursed	Total
Suppliers credits			
France	73,729	34,595	108,324
Germany, Federal Republic of	1,758	. . .	1,758
Israel	13,124	2,605	15,729
Italy	50,354	10,704	61,058
Lebanon	34,287	67,664	101,951
Netherlands	1,625	. . .	1,625
Norway	30,349	22,686	53,035
United States	64,690	. . .	64,690
Total	269,916	138,254	408,170
Private bank credits			
Canada	315	. . .	315
France	51,554	17,560	69,114
Germany, Federal Republic of	7,848	49	7,897
Italy	1,979	. . .	1,979
Switzerland	7,252	32,824	40,076
United States	101,937	4,111	106,048
Multiple lenders	100,415	47,178	147,593
Total	271,300	101,722	373,022
Publicly issued bonds			
France	23,213	. . .	23,213
Total	23,213	. . .	23,213

(Table SA21 continues on the following page.)

TABLE SA21 (continued)

Creditor country and type of creditor	Debt outstanding		
	Disbursed	Undisbursed	Total
Other private debt			
Germany, Federal Republic of	1,907	1,878	3,785
Italy	28,861	1,192	30,053
Total	30,768	3,070	33,838
Loans from international organizations			
African Development Bank	9,573	10,863	20,436
EEC	17,582	9,522	27,104
European Development Fund	5,915	. . .	5,915
European Investment Bank	36,246	24,015	60,261
World Bank	72,528	179,267	251,795
IDA[a]	1,333	6,167	7,500
International Coffee Organization	. . .	5,870	5,870
Total	143,177	235,704	378,881
Loans from governments			
Canada	7,912	6,797	14,709
Denmark	2,354	6	2,360
France	114,070	60,826	174,896
Germany, Federal Republic of	36,321	12,809	49,130
United Kingdom	1,083	. . .	1,083
United States	69,292	1,823	71,115
Conseil de l'Entente	4,391	1,184	5,575
Total	235,423	83,445	318,868
Total external public debt	973,797	562,195	1,535,992

. . . Zero or negligible.

Source: External Debt Division, Economic Analysis and Projections Department, World Bank.

a. International Development Association.

TABLE SA22. SERVICE PAYMENTS, COMMITMENTS, DISBURSEMENTS, AND OUTSTANDING AMOUNTS OF EXTERNAL PUBLIC DEBT (DEBT REPAYABLE IN FOREIGN CURRENCY AND GOODS), 1971–95

(Thousands of U.S. dollars)

Year	Debt outstanding at beginning of period		Transactions during period		Service payments			Other changes	
	Disbursed only	Including undisbursed	Commitments	Disbursements	Principal	Interest	Total	Cancellations	Adjustment[a]
1971	256,098	424,300	119,552	107,336	29,085	15,588	44,673	151	24,643
1972	351,722	539,259	198,435	82,719	38,556	19,339	57,895	3	3,743
1973	399,860	702,878	274,915	227,959	44,321	27,930	72,251	38,255	28,186
1974	578,645	923,403	328,752	218,815	76,644	38,433	115,077	11,333	36,131
1975	738,024	1,200,309	448,647	335,598	81,827	56,015	137,842	3,525	−27,610
					Projected				
1976	973,797	1,535,994	...	226,115	122,467	65,912	188,379	...	−826
1977	1,076,621	1,412,701	...	148,880	115,228	72,689	187,917	...	7
1978	1,110,274	1,297,480	...	93,260	140,265	75,295	215,560	...	17
1979	1,063,284	1,157,232	...	37,214	140,479	70,003	210,482	...	−2
1980	960,018	1,016,751	...	22,028	133,792	62,502	196,294	...	17
1981	848,271	882,976	...	12,423	132,633	54,202	186,835	...	−1
1982	728,062	750,342	...	6,808	118,517	45,518	164,035	...	13

. . . Zero or negligible.

Note: Projections are based on debt outstanding, including undisbursed, as of December 31, 1975.

a. This column shows the amount of arithmetic imbalance in the amount outstanding, including undisbursed, from one year to the next. The most common causes of imbalances are changes in exchange rates and transfer of debts from one category to another.

(Table SA22 continues on the following page.)

TABLE SA22 (continued)

Year	Debt outstanding at beginning of period		Transactions during period		Service payments			Other changes	
	Disbursed only	Including undisbursed	Commitments	Disbursements	Principal	Interest	Total	Cancellations	Adjustment[a]
1983	616,366	631,838	...	13,579	107,108	37,384	144,492	...	8
1984	522,845	524,738	...	1,704	87,051	30,941	117,992	...	11
1985	437,509	437,698	...	165	69,438	25,347	94,785	...	-5
1986	368,231	368,255	...	24	50,687	21,163	71,850	...	12
1987	317,580	317,580	...	...	46,374	18,027	64,401	...	-3
1988	271,203	271,203	...	...	41,676	15,210	56,886	...	3
1989	229,530	229,530	...	...	35,526	12,691	48,217	...	...
1990	194,004	194,004	...	...	27,820	10,532	38,352	...	1
1991	166,185	166,185	...	...	26,252	8,808	35,060	...	2
1992	139,935	139,935	...	...	24,575	7,146	31,721	...	2
1993	115,362	115,362	...	...	23,033	5,560	28,593	...	-3
1994	92,326	92,326	...	...	24,475	3,976	28,451	...	4
1995	67,855	67,855	...	...	11,481	2,407	13,888	...	-2

. . . Zero or negligible.

Note: Projections are based on debt outstanding, including undisbursed, as of December 31, 1975.

Source: External debt division, Economic Analysis and Projections Department, World Bank.

a. This column shows the amount of arithmetic imbalance in the amount outstanding, including undisbursed, from one year to the next. The most common causes of imbalances are changes in exchange rates and transfer of debts from one category to another.

TABLE SA23. LOAN COMMITMENTS AND DEBT SERVICE, BY DEBTOR, 1966–75
(Millions of U.S. dollars)

Item	1966	1967	1968	1969	1970	1971	1972	1973	1974	1975
External debt outstanding[a]										
Government	146.5	182.0	275.6	273.1	306.2	382.0	422.1	478.8	603.3	811.3
Public enterprises[b]	58.5	60.3	72.5	107.3	112.7	152.7	265.7	419.6	567.5	701.9
Total	205.0	242.3	348.1	380.4	418.9	534.7	687.8	898.4	1,170.8	1,513.2
New commitments										
Government	25.0	50.5	114.8	18.7	55.7	81.7	65.1	100.8	169.9	262.7
Public enterprises[b]	6.5	8.4	16.5	47.2	13.4	37.8	121.6	164.1	150.7	185.2
Total	31.5	58.9	131.3	65.9	69.1	119.5	186.7	264.9	320.6	447.9
External debt service										
Government	16.6	18.3	21.6	17.9	24.8	32.9	43.9	48.8	72.8	73.8
Interest	3.4	3.4	4.2	5.7	8.4	11.9	14.3	16.6	18.2	32.0
Principal	13.2	14.9	17.4	12.2	16.4	21.0	29.6	32.2	54.6	41.8
Public enterprises[b]	4.7	8.6	9.0	9.3	10.6	10.6	12.6	21.3	36.7	55.0
Interest	1.1	1.9	2.1	2.0	2.7	3.4	4.7	10.5	18.9	22.2
Principal	3.6	6.7	6.9	7.3	7.9	7.2	7.9	10.8	17.8	32.8
Total	21.3	26.9	30.6	27.2	35.4	43.5	56.5	70.1	109.5	128.8

Source: Data provided by the Ivorian authorities.
a. Including undisbursed; situation at end of year.
b. Including debts contracted by mixed enterprises and guaranteed by the government.

TABLE SA24. GRANT COMMITMENTS, 1960–75
(CFAF billion)

Item	1960	1961	1962	1963	1964	1965	1966	1967	1968	1969	1970	1971	1972	1973	1974	1975[a]
FAC[b]	1.7	1.1	2.3	2.3	1.1	1.7	1.4	0.5	0.6	0.9	0.7	0.8	1.1	0.9	1.1	1.2
University	...	...	0.7	0.3	0.2	0.2	0.4	0.3	0.3	0.2	0.3	...	0.1	0.1	...	...
FED[c]	1.3	4.1	0.9	1.3	1.3	8.9	0.6	0.1	0.4	0.1	1.7	0.1	4.0	1.5	2.7	0.7
Other	...	...	0.1	0.2	0.2	0.2	0.3	0.3	0.3	0.5	0.4	0.5	0.4	0.5	0.7	0.7
Total	3.0	5.2	3.3	3.8	2.6	10.8	2.3	0.9	1.3	1.5	2.8	1.4	5.5	2.9	4.5	2.6

. . . Zero or negligible.
Source: Data provided by the Ivorian authorities.
a. Preliminary figures.
b. Fonds d'Aide et de Coopération.
c. Fonds Européen de Développement.

Table SA25. French Technical Assistance, 1960–74

Item	1960–65	1966	1967	1968	1969	1970	1971	1972	1973	1974[a]
Number of technical assistants	1,346	1,579	1,715	2,102	2,252	2,476	3,034	3,115	3,250	3,390
Total cost (CFAF billion)	3.5	3.5	4.8	5.6	6.0	7.9	9.6	10.8	12.8	14.8
Contribution of France	2.2	2.1	2.1	2.1	2.1	2.1	2.4	2.6	2.8	2.8
Contribution of the Ivory Coast	1.3	1.4	2.7	3.5	3.9	5.8	7.2	8.2	10.0	12.0

Source: Mission d'Aide et de Coopération, Abidjan.
a. Preliminary figures.

TABLE SA26. PUBLIC INVESTMENT FINANCING, 1965–75
(CFAF billion)

Item	1965-67	1968	1969	1970	1971	1972	1973	1974	1975
Investments	26.2	29.7	36.4	44.2	54.3	55.0	83.3	86.8	131.2
BSIE[a]	14.5	19.9	24.9	24.8	31.1	22.3	34.2	37.7	47.1
Public enterprises	7.3	8.8	10.5	17.0	22.2	27.7	46.2	44.6	43.8
Programme du Nord	—	—	—	—	—	—	—	—	40.3
Other (grants)	4.4	1.0	1.0	2.4	1.0	5.0	2.9	4.5	
Financing	26.2	29.7	36.4	44.2	54.3	55.0	83.3	86.8	131.2
Current saving (before debt service)	11.4	13.7	18.8	18.6	22.4	24.5	29.0	32.9	35.0
Current revenue	50.1	64.3	70.2	83.2	90.4	102.2	118.7	141.5	165.0
Current expenditure	38.7	50.6	51.4	64.6	68.0	77.7	89.7	108.6	130.0
Stabilization Fund	1.4	2.2	1.8	13.8	8.3	1.1	…	…	15.0
Contribution to the BSIE	1.4	2.2	1.8	13.8	8.3	1.1	…	…	7.0
Contribution to the Programme du Nord	—	—	—	—	—	—	…	—	8.0
Resources of public enterprises[b]	5.5	4.8	6.3	7.2	7.8	9.5	18.3	24.7	29.6

Gross local resource mobilization	18.3	20.7	26.9	39.6	38.5	35.1	47.3	57.6	79.6
Public debt service	5.5	7.0	8.0	9.9	11.8	14.7	17.6	27.0	32.8
Central government	4.2	4.3	5.3	7.1	9.3	11.3	11.7	17.4	19.4
Public enterprises	1.3	2.7	2.7	2.8	2.5	3.4	5.9	9.6	13.4
Local saving (net)	12.8	13.7	18.9	29.7	26.7	20.4	29.7	30.6	46.8
Other domestic[c]	0.8	1.8	2.1	-7.6	-3.0	9.1	3.3	6.2	9.0
Total domestic resources	13.6	15.5	21.0	22.1	23.7	29.5	31.3	36.8	55.8
Foreign borrowing (gross)	8.2	13.4	14.4	19.7	29.6	20.5	47.4	45.5	71.4
Central government	5.2	8.4	7.3	10.3	18.5	5.0	22.4	26.1	33.4
Public enterprises	3.0	5.0	7.1	9.4	11.1	15.5	25.0	19.4	38.0
Grants	4.4	1.0	1.0	2.4	1.0	5.0	2.9	4.5	4.0

. . . Zero or negligible.

— Not applicable. The Programme du Nord was not established until 1975.

Source: Ministry of Economic Affairs and Finance.

a. **Budget Spécial d'Investissement et d'Equipement.** The 1970–75 data are net of transfers to public enterprises. This adjustment could not be made in the pre-1970 data, resulting in some overestimation of total investments for those years.

b. The pre-1970 data contain some transfers of the BSIE to the public enterprises that are already included in the data on current savings or foreign borrowing of the central government, so that the resources of public enterprises for those years are somewhat overstated.

c. Domestic bank borrowing and treasury financing; for 1975 this is a balancing item.

TABLE SA27. PERCENTAGE DISTRIBUTION OF PUBLIC
INVESTMENT FINANCING, 1965–75

Item	1965–67	1968	1969	1970	1971	1972	1973	1974	1975
Investment									
BSIE	55	67	68	56	57	41	41	44	36
Public enterprises	28	30	29	39	41	50	56	51	33
Programme du Nord	. . .	. . .	. . .	. . .	. . .	. . .	. . .	. . .	} 31
Other	17	3	3	5	2	9	3	5	
Financing									
Net savings	49	46	52	67	49	37	36	35	36
Other domestic[a] sources	3	6	6	−17	−6	17	4	7	7
Foreign borrowing	31	45	39	45	55	37	57	53	54
Grants	17	3	3	5	2	9	3	5	3

. . . Zero or negligible.
Source: Table SA26.
a. Domestic bank borrowing and treasury financing.

TABLE SA28. CENTRAL GOVERNMENT FINANCIAL TRANSACTIONS, 1965–75
(CFAF billion)

Item	1965	1966	1967	1968	1969	1970	1971	1972	1973	1974	1975
1. Current revenue	47.3	52.2	50.7	64.3	70.2	83.2	90.4	102.2	118.7	141.5	165.0
Ordinary budget	36.9	39.8	38.6	53.2	51.9	60.7	65.6	73.3	86.8	110.5	126.9
BSIE	7.6	7.7	7.5	10.8	10.8	12.9	14.3	17.4	18.6	16.7	17.4
CAA[a] plus FNI[b]	6.6	7.7	6.0	7.5	8.5	11.3	11.9	13.4	15.1	18.8	20.6
Adjustments[c]	-3.8	-3.0	-1.4	-7.2	-1.0	-1.7	-1.4	-1.9	-1.8	-4.5	0.1
2. Current expenditure	34.5	41.3	42.5	51.6	53.2	67.1	71.6	81.7	94.1	114.1	137.0
Ordinary budget (obligated)	34.6	38.4	40.6	49.3	50.2	61.6	65.6	75.0	87.6	109.3	126.0
Interest on public debt	0.6	0.7	0.8	1.0	1.8	2.5	3.6	4.0	4.4	5.5	7.0
Annex budgets and special accounts (net)	-0.7	2.2	1.1	1.3	1.2	3.0	2.4	2.7	2.1	-0.7	4.0
3. Current saving (1–2)	12.8	10.9	8.2	12.7	17.0	16.1	18.8	20.5	24.6	27.4	28.0
4. Investment[d]	11.5	13.7	16.5	19.9	24.9	31.0	36.6	27.4	39.0	41.8	53.4
Treasury (obligated)	n.a.	n.a.	n.a.	n.a.	15.7	20.8	21.6	18.4	16.8	17.5	n.a.
CAA (obligated)	n.a.	n.a.	n.a.	n.a.	9.2	10.2	15.0	9.0	22.2	24.3	n.a.
5. Adjustment of expenditures to cash basis	...	...	...	...	...	-1.0	2.6	-0.6	-7.8	-0.1	...
6. Surplus or deficit (3–4–5)	1.3	-2.8	-8.3	-7.2	-7.9	-13.9	-20.4	-6.3	-6.6	-14.3	-25.4

... Zero or negligible.
n.a. Not available.
a. Debt Amortization Fund.
b. National Investment Fund.
c. Changes in suspense accounts and deduction for revenues earmarked for FNI.
d. Inclusive of the transfers to public enterprises.

(Table SA28 continues on the following page.)

TABLE SA28 *(continued)*

Item	1965	1966	1967	1968	1969	1970	1971	1972	1973	1974	1975
Financing											
Foreign (net)	1.6	2.1	1.9	4.6	3.9	5.6	13.4	-1.4	15.9	14.2	21.0
Drawings	5.5	5.3	4.9	8.4	7.3	10.3	18.5	5.0	22.4	26.1	33.4
Repayments	-3.9	-3.2	-3.0	-3.8	-3.4	-4.7	-5.1	-6.4	-6.5	-11.9	-12.4
Domestic	-2.9	0.7	6.4	2.6	4.1	8.3	7.0	7.7	-9.3	0.1	4.4
Stabilization Fund	. . .	1.3	3.0	2.2	1.8	13.8	8.3	1.1	. . .	. . .	7.0
Central Bank	. . .	1.2	1.5	-2.5	-0.9	-3.4	5.9	3.0	-2.2	-10.0[e]	} -2.6
Other[f]	-2.9	-1.8	1.9	2.9	3.2	-2.1	-7.2	3.6	-7.1	10.1	

. . . Zero or negligible.
Source: Ministry of Economic Affairs and Finance.
e. Includes part of a CFAF10 billion transfer from the Stabilization Fund.
f. Includes private bank borrowing, changes in outstanding custom bills, and cash balances.

TABLE SA29. PUBLIC SECTOR REVENUE AND ITS ALLOCATION, 1965–76
(CFAF billion except as noted)

Item	1965	1966	1967	1968	1969	1970	1971	1972	1973	1974	1975	1976[a]
Ordinary budget	36.9	39.8	38.6	53.2	51.9	60.7	65.6	73.3	86.8	110.5	126.9	171.8
BSIE	7.6	7.7	7.5	10.8	10.8	12.9	14.3	17.4	18.6	16.7	17.1	21.0
CAA	4.2	4.3	4.6	5.7	6.9	9.3	9.7	11.0	12.3	14.4	16.6	18.0
Office for Support to Low Income Housing	0.0	0.0	0.0	0.0	1.3	1.4	1.6	1.7	1.9	2.3	5.5	5.8
National Office for Professional Training	0.0	0.0	0.1	0.1	0.2	0.3	0.5	0.4	0.4	0.7	0.6	0.7
National Council of Freighters	0.0	0.0	0.0	0.0	0.2	0.3	0.5	0.4	0.4	} 0.7	0.4	0.3
National Council for Export Promotion	0.0	0.0	0.0	0.0	0.0	0.0	0.2	0.2	0.4		0.4	0.3
Total for central government	48.7	51.8	50.8	69.8	71.1	84.6	92.1	104.2	120.8	145.3	167.5	217.9
FNI	2.2	1.4	1.4	1.8	2.6	2.0	2.2	2.4	2.8	4.4	4.0	4.5
Central government plus FNI	50.9	53.2	52.2	71.6	73.7	86.0	94.3	106.6	123.6	149.7	171.5	222.4
Stabilization Fund[b]	−2.3	−1.1	4.4	6.1	8.9	17.3	9.3	−1.8	4.9	43.2	18.1	30.0[c]
Social Security	2.5	2.6	2.7	2.5	2.5	4.0	4.4	5.0	6.2	7.5	9.4	10.0[c]
Price Equalization Fund	n.a.	n.a.	n.a.	n.a.	n.a.	n.a.	n.a.	n.a.	n.a.	2.6	2.6	2.6[c]
Municipalities	n.a.	n.a.	n.a.	n.a.	1.8	2.4	2.1	2.4	2.8	3.3	3.5	3.5[c]
Total public revenue	n.a.	n.a.	n.a.	n.a.	86.9	109.7	110.1	112.2	137.5	206.3	205.1	268.5
Central government revenue as percentage of GDP	20.6	20.1	18.5	21.5	19.5	20.4	21.0	22.1	21.4	19.6	20.3	n.a.
Total revenue as percentage of GDP	n.a.	n.a.	n.a.	n.a.	23.8	26.5	25.1	23.8	24.4	27.8	24.8	n.a.

n.a. Not available.
Source: Ministry of Economic Affairs and Finance.
a. Estimated by the Ministry of Economic Affairs and Finance.
b. The fiscal year of the Stabilization Fund covers parts of two calendar years. The revenue is here allocated to the latter of the two calendar years. Revenue is taken before subsidy payments and before contributions to BSIE. It also excludes "other revenue," which compensates for contributions to international organizations.
c. World Bank estimates.

TABLE SA30. CENTRAL GOVERNMENT REVENUE, 1965–76
(CFAF billion)

Item	1965	1966	1967	1968	1969	1970	1971	1972	1973	1974	1975	1976[a]
Current revenues	47.3	52.2	50.7	64.3	70.2	83.2	90.4	102.2	118.7	141.5	165.0	213.6
Total tax revenue	47.3	48.6	47.7	69.3	69.4	82.8	89.9	102.2	117.7	141.6	160.6	210.8
Taxes on income and profits	5.0	6.5	8.4	10.7	10.9	12.5	14.2	17.4	22.1	28.3	31.6	45.8
Taxes on profits	0.0	0.0	0.0	0.0	5.4	6.0	6.8	8.2	10.3	14.0	15.6	17.9
Income taxes	0.0	0.0	0.0	0.0	3.3	4.0	4.7	5.8	7.8	9.4	10.6 }	27.9
Other	0.0	0.0	0.0	0.0	2.2	2.5	2.7	3.4	4.0	4.9	5.4 }	
Taxes on property	1.2	1.3	0.9	1.5	1.3	1.9	1.5	1.6	1.3	2.3	2.4	2.5
Real estate	0.7	0.7	0.6	1.1	0.9	1.5	1.1	1.1	0.9	1.9	1.9	1.9
Motor vehicles	0.5	0.6	0.3	0.4	0.4	0.4	0.4	0.5	0.4	0.4	0.5	0.6
Taxes on production, consumption, and transactions[b]	16.7	16.4	16.8	25.2	14.9	18.3	21.1	24.5	26.7	30.6	35.6	43.0
Tax on intermediate transactions	11.7	11.4	11.6	18.0	7.7	8.8	10.8	12.2	14.4	17.4	19.5	31.1
Excise taxes	4.3	4.5	4.4	5.8	6.1	8.2	8.9	10.2	11.3	12.2	15.7	11.2
Tobacco	1.6	1.7	1.7	2.1	2.1	2.4	2.6	3.0	3.1	3.8	4.0	n.a.
Alcoholic beverages	1.2	1.2	1.1	1.5	1.7	1.8	2.0	2.4	2.5	2.9	3.0	n.a.
Gasoline	1.5	1.6	1.6	2.2	2.3	4.0	4.3	4.8	5.7	5.5	8.7	n.a.
Timber tax	0.7	0.5	0.8	1.4	1.1	1.3	1.4	2.1	1.0	1.0	0.7	0.7

Taxes on international trade[b]	21.7	22.3	19.8	28.9	39.5	47.0	49.7	53.5	64.0	74.5	86.3	122.1
Import duties	11.7	12.0	11.9	16.1	27.2	30.4	32.5	35.1	41.3	49.1	59.5	84.9
Export duties	10.0	10.3	7.9	12.8	12.3	16.6	17.2	18.4	22.7	25.4	26.8	37.2
Other taxes	2.7	2.1	1.8	3.0	2.8	3.1	3.4	5.2	3.6	4.3	4.5	5.0
Business tax and licenses	0.7	0.7	0.6	0.9	0.8	0.6	0.7	0.7	1.3	1.5	1.3	1.6
Registration fees and stamps	0.9	1.0	0.8	1.0	1.1	1.3	1.9	2.3	2.3	2.8	3.2	3.4
Other	1.1	0.4	0.4	1.1	0.9	1.2	1.2	2.2	0.0	0.0	0.0	0.0
Nontax revenues	1.6	2.0	1.9	2.2	1.8	2.1	1.9	1.9	2.8	4.7	3.4	4.0
Service charges	1.2	1.6	0.8	1.4	1.1	1.0	1.3	1.2	1.1	1.7	1.8	1.8
Revenue from property	0.4	0.4	0.4	0.6	0.5	0.5	0.5	0.5	0.6	0.5	0.7	0.7
Other	0.0	0.0	0.7	0.2	0.2	0.6	0.1	0.2	1.1	2.5	0.9	1.5
Total (final accounts)	48.9	50.6	49.6	71.5	71.2	84.9	91.8	104.1	120.5	144.7	164.1	222.4
Adjustments[c]	-1.6	1.6	1.1	-7.2	-1.0	-1.7	-1.4	-1.9	1.8	-3.2	0.9	-11.6

n.a. Not available.

Source: Ministry of Economic Affairs and Finance.

a. Estimated by the Ministry of Economic Affairs and Finance.

b. Up to 1968 the value added tax on imports was classified under the taxes on production, consumption, and transactions; thereafter it was added to import duties.

c. Changes in suspense accounts and deductions of revenue earmarked for FNI.

TABLE SA31. PERCENTAGE DISTRIBUTION OF CENTRAL GOVERNMENT REVENUE, 1965–76

Item	1965	1966	1967	1968	1969	1970	1971	1972	1973	1974	1975[a]	1976[a]
Current revenues	100.00	100.00	100.00	100.00	100.00	100.00	100.00	100.00	100.00	100.00	100.00	100.00
Total tax revenue	100.00	93.10	94.08	107.78	98.86	99.52	99.45	100.00	99.16	100.07	97.30	98.70
Taxes on income and profits	10.57	12.45	16.57	16.64	15.53	15.02	15.71	17.03	18.62	20.00	19.20	21.40
Taxes on profits	0.00	0.00	0.00	0.00	7.69	7.21	7.52	8.02	8.68	9.89	n.a.	n.a.
Income taxes	0.00	0.00	0.00	0.00	4.70	4.81	5.20	5.68	6.57	6.64	n.a.	n.a.
Other	0.00	0.00	0.00	0.00	3.13	3.00	2.99	3.33	3.37	3.46	n.a.	n.a.
Taxes on property	2.54	2.49	1.78	2.33	1.85	2.28	1.66	1.57	1.10	1.63	1.50	1.20
Real estate	1.48	1.34	1.18	1.71	1.28	1.80	1.22	1.08	0.76	1.34	n.a.	n.a.
Motor vehicles	1.06	1.15	0.59	0.62	0.57	0.48	0.44	0.49	0.34	0.28	n.a.	n.a.
Taxes on production, consumption, and transactions[b]	35.31	31.42	33.14	39.19	21.23	22.00	23.34	23.97	22.49	21.63	21.20	20.10
Tax on intermediate transactions	24.74	21.84	22.88	27.99	10.97	10.58	11.95	11.94	12.13	12.30	n.a.	n.a.
Excise taxes	9.09	8.62	8.68	9.02	8.69	9.86	9.85	9.98	9.52	8.62	n.a.	n.a.
Tobacco	3.38	3.26	3.35	3.27	2.99	2.88	2.88	2.94	2.61	2.69	n.a.	n.a.
Alcoholic beverages	2.54	2.30	2.17	2.33	2.42	2.16	2.21	2.35	2.11	2.05	n.a.	n.a.
Gasoline	3.17	3.07	3.16	3.42	3.28	4.81	4.76	4.70	4.80	3.89	n.a.	n.a.
Timber tax	1.48	0.96	1.58	2.18	1.57	1.56	1.55	2.05	0.84	0.71	n.a.	n.a.

Taxes on international trade[b]	45.88	42.72	39.05	44.95	56.27	56.49	54.98	52.35	53.92	52.65	52.30	57.20
Import duties	24.74	22.99	23.47	25.04	38.75	36.54	35.95	34.34	34.79	34.70	n.a.	n.a.
Export duties	21.14	19.73	15.58	19.91	17.52	19.95	19.03	18.00	19.12	17.95	n.a.	n.a.
Other taxes	5.71	4.02	3.55	4.67	3.99	3.73	3.76	5.09	3.03	3.04	2.70	2.30
Business tax and licenses	1.48	1.34	1.18	1.40	1.14	0.72	0.77	0.68	1.10	1.06	n.a.	n.a.
Registration fees and stamps	1.90	1.92	1.58	1.56	1.57	1.56	1.66	2.25	1.94	1.98	n.a.	n.a.
Other	2.33	0.77	0.79	1.71	1.28	1.44	1.33	2.15	0.00	0.00	0.00	0.00
Nontax revenues	3.38	3.83	3.75	3.42	2.56	2.52	2.10	1.86	2.34	3.32	2.10	1.90
Service charges	2.54	3.07	1.58	2.18	1.57	1.20	1.44	1.17	0.93	1.20	n.a.	n.a.
Revenue from property	0.85	0.77	0.79	0.93	0.71	0.60	0.55	0.49	0.51	0.35	n.a.	n.a.
Other	0.00	0.00	1.38	0.31	0.28	0.72	0.11	0.20	0.93	1.98	n.a.	n.a.
Total (final accounts)	103.38	96.93	97.83	111.20	101.42	102.04	101.55	101.86	101.52	102.26	99.00	104.10
Adjustments[c]	-3.38	3.07	2.17	-11.20	-1.42	-2.04	-1.55	-1.86	-1.52	-2.26	1.00	-4.10

n.a. Not available.
Source: Ministry of Economic Affairs and Finance. The 1976 figures are estimates.
a. Breakdowns were not available.
b. Up to 1968, the value added tax on imports was classified under the taxes on production, consumption, and transactions; thereafter it was added to import duties.
c. Changes in suspense accounts and deductions of revenue earmarked for FNI.

TABLE SA32. EXPENDITURE IN ANNEX BUDGETS, 1970–75
(CFAF billion)

Item	1970	1971	1972	1973	1974	1975
Postal services	3.7	4.1	4.7	5.1	6.1	6.9
Public works	0.7	1.0	1.0	1.1	1.2	1.8
Radio and television	0.7	0.7	0.7	0.8	1.1	1.3
University Hospital Center	0.2	0.4	0.4	0.5	0.5	0.6
Press agency	0.1	0.2	0.2	0.2	0.2	0.4
Sassandra wharf	0.1	0.1	0.1	. . .	. . .	. . .
Port of Abidjan[a]	1.8	. . .	. . .	. . .	. . .	. . .
National printing press	. . .	. . .	. . .	0.2	0.3	0.3
Total	7.3	6.5	7.1	7.9	9.4	11.3

. . . Zero or negligible.
Source: Ministry of Economic Affairs and Finance.
a. Transformed into public enterprise in 1971.

TABLE SA33. CENTRAL GOVERNMENT EXPENDITURE: FUNCTIONAL CLASSIFICATION, 1965–76
(CFAF billion)

Item	1965	1966	1967	1968	1969	1970	1971	1972	1973	1974	1975	1976[a]
Total current expenditure	34.5	41.3	42.5	51.6	53.2	66.6	71.6	81.7	94.1	114.1	136.7	167.0[b]
General services	12.8	13.5	13.4	14.3	15.8	17.6	17.5	17.6	19.0	23.8	26.9	30.2
Defense	2.8	3.3	3.6	4.0	4.2	4.9	5.3	5.7	6.1	8.0	10.0	n.a.
Social services	9.8	11.6	12.8	15.3	16.6	20.1	24.3	30.5	30.9	39.1	45.7	58.9
Education	6.2	7.2	8.0	9.5	10.1	13.1	14.9	18.5	22.0	28.6	32.0	n.a.
Public health	3.3	4.0	4.4	5.3	5.3	6.2	6.8	7.0	7.8	9.1	11.1	n.a.
Economic services	7.3	8.0	9.2	10.6	11.1	13.9	13.4	13.9	17.4	23.8	24.5	31.2
Agriculture	1.6	2.0	2.2	2.5	2.6	3.2	2.7	2.7	3.3	4.0	4.6	n.a.
Public works	4.5	4.6	5.4	6.2	5.7	6.3	4.4	4.2	6.0	8.9	8.3	n.a.
Other expenditure	4.7	5.3	5.2	9.1	6.7	9.5	10.4	13.0	20.3	22.6	28.6	33.4
Total on cash basis	34.6	38.4	40.6	49.3	50.2	61.1	65.6	75.0	87.6	109.3	125.7	153.7
CAA interest payments	0.6	0.7	0.8	1.0	1.8	2.5	3.6	4.0	4.4	5.5	7.0	9.8
Annex budgets and special accounts	−0.7	2.2	1.1	1.3	1.2	3.0	2.4	2.7	2.1	−0.7	4.0	n.a.

n.a. Not available.
Source: Ministry of Economic Affairs and Finance.
a. Estimated by the Ministry of Economic Affairs and Finance.
b. World Bank estimate.

TABLE SA34. PERCENTAGE DISTRIBUTION OF CENTRAL EXPENDITURE:
FUNCTIONAL CLASSIFICATION, 1965–76
(Percent of total)

Item	1965	1966	1967	1968	1969	1970	1971	1972	1973	1974	1975	1976[a]
Total current expenditure	100.00	100.00	100.00	100.00	100.00	100.00	100.00	100.00	100.00	100.00	100.00	100.00
General services	37.10	32.69	31.53	27.71	29.70	26.43	24.44	21.54	20.19	20.86	19.68	18.10
Defense	8.12	7.99	8.47	7.75	7.89	7.36	7.40	6.98	6.48	7.01	7.31	n.a.
Social services	28.41	28.09	30.12	29.65	31.20	30.18	33.94	37.33	32.84	34.27	33.43	35.30
Education	17.97	17.43	18.82	18.41	18.98	19.67	20.81	22.64	23.38	25.07	23.41	n.a.
Public health	9.57	9.69	10.35	10.27	9.96	9.31	9.50	8.57	8.29	7.97	8.12	n.a.
Economic services	21.16	19.37	21.65	20.54	20.86	20.87	18.72	17.01	18.49	20.86	17.92	18.70
Agriculture	4.64	4.84	5.18	4.84	4.89	4.80	3.77	3.30	3.51	3.51	3.36	n.a.
Public works	13.04	11.14	12.71	12.02	10.71	9.46	6.15	5.14	6.38	7.80	6.07	n.a.
Other expenditure	13.62	12.83	12.24	17.64	12.60	14.26	14.53	15.91	21.57	19.80	20.92	20.00
Total on cash basis	100.29	92.98	95.53	95.54	94.36	91.74	91.62	91.80	93.09	95.79	91.95	92.10
CAA interest payments	1.74	1.69	1.88	1.94	3.38	3.75	5.03	4.90	4.68	4.82	5.12	5.90
Annex budgets and special accounts	−2.03	5.33	2.59	2.52	2.26	4.50	3.35	3.30	2.23	−0.61	2.93	2.00

n.a. Not available.
Source: Ministry of Economic Affairs and Finance.
a. Estimated by the Ministry of Economic Affairs and Finance.

TABLE SA35. ORDINARY BUDGET EXPENDITURE: ECONOMIC CLASSIFICATION, 1966–76

Item	1966	1967	1968	1969	1970	1971	1972	1973	1974	1975	1976[a]
Expenditure in CFAF billion											
Wages and salaries	16.7	18.1	22.3	22.6	28.8	32.1	38.3	43.5	56.2	64.0	80.2
Materials and maintenance	13.6	14.1	17.2	16.5	19.0	18.7	18.5	25.8	30.7	35.3	40.1
Subsidies and transfers	8.1	8.4	9.8 {	10.1	11.8	13.0	15.3	15.7	21.4	25.2	31.6
Contracted debt payments				1.0	0.5	0.5	0.5	0.7	1.0	1.3	1.8
Other	. . .	. . .	. . .	. . .	1.0	1.3	2.4	1.9	0.5	. . .	. . .
Total	38.4	40.6	49.3	50.2	61.1	65.6	75.0	87.6	109.8	125.8	153.7
Expenditure in percent of total											
Wages and salaries	43.5	44.6	45.3	45.0	47.2	48.9	51.1	49.7	51.2	50.9	52.1
Materials and maintenance	35.5	34.7	34.8	32.9	31.1	28.5	24.7	29.4	28.0	28.1	26.1
Subsidies and transfers	21.0	20.7	19.9 {	20.1	19.3	19.8	20.4	17.9	19.5	20.0	20.6
Contracted debt payments				2.0	0.8	0.8	0.7	0.8	0.9	1.0	1.2
Other	. . .	. . .	. . .	. . .	1.6	2.0	3.1	2.2	0.4	. . .	. . .
Total	100.0	100.0	100.0	100.0	100.0	100.0	100.0	100.0	100.0	100.0	100.0

. . . Zero or negligible.
Source: Ministry of Economic Affairs and Finance.
a. Estimated by the Ministry of Economic Affairs and Finance.

TABLE SA36. PERSONNEL PROVISIONS OF THE ORDINARY BUDGET, 1965–76

Item	1965	1966	1967	1968	1969	1970	1971	1972	1973	1974	1975	1976[a]
Ministers and assimilated ranks	36	38	41	42	45	52	50	58	70	n.a.	122	n.a.
Civil servants	13,077	16,340	18,372	20,384	22,055	24,332	27,919	28,604	30,400	39,601[b]	42,357[b]	45,100
Technical assistants	1,556	1,615	1,801	1,988	2,185	1,729	2,151	2,725	2,635	3,336	3,160	3,700
Contractual workers	550	537	568	657	708	701	7,793[d]	1,003	1,089	1,069	612[c]	n.a.
Temporary workers	6,241	6,125	6,315	6,806	6,866	6,681		7,194	7,080	—[b]	—[b]	n.a.
Total	21,460	24,655	27,097	29,877	31,859	33,495	37,913	39,584	41,274	43,844	46,315	n.a.
Total less technical assistants	19,904	23,040	25,296	27,889	29,674	31,766	35,762	36,859	38,639	40,670	42,969	n.a.

n.a. Not available.
Source: Ivory Coast current budget, various years.
a. Estimated by the Ministry of Economic Affairs and Finance.
b. In 1974 and 1975 temporary workers are grouped together with civil servants.
c. In 1971 contractual and temporary workers are grouped together.
d. Not fully comparable with earlier years.

TABLE SA37. INDICATORS IN THE COCOA, COFFEE, AND
COTTON SECTORS PER CROP YEAR

Indicator	1955–56	1960–61	1965–66
Cocoa			
Production area (thousands of hectares)	n.a.	243	366
Production (thousands of tons)	n.a.	94	113
Exports (thousands of tons)	76	94	124
Average export cost, f.o.b. (CFAF per kilogram)[a]	67	136	93
Average export price, f.o.b. (CFAF per kilogram)	n.a.	n.a.	68
Export taxes (CFAF per kilogram)	n.a.	28.0	22.4
Producer price (CFAF per kilogram)	60	95	55
Tax reference price (CFAF per kilogram)	110	125	100
Coffee			
Production (thousands of hectares)	n.a.	534	558
Production (thousands of tons)	n.a.	178	272
Exports (thousands of tons)	119	158	177
Average export cost, f.o.b. (CFAF per kilogram)[a]	n.a.	128	116
Average export price, f.o.b. (CFAF per kilogram)	n.a.	n.a.	148
Export taxes (CFAF per kilogram)	n.a.	24.6	22.4
Producer price (CFAF per kilogram)	n.a.	90	75
Tax reference price (CFAF per kilogram)	n.a.	$\left\{ \begin{array}{c} 110^b \\ 115^b \end{array} \right\}$	100
Cotton			
Production area (thousands of hectares)	n.a.	n.a.	n.a.
Production (thousands of tons)	n.a.	n.a.	n.a.
Exports (thousands of tons)	n.a.	n.a.	n.a.
Average export cost, f.o.b. (CFAF per kilogram)[a]	n.a.	n.a.	n.a.
Average export price, f.o.b. (CFAF per kilogram)	n.a.	n.a.	n.a.
Export taxes (CFAF per kilogram)	n.a.	n.a.	n.a.
Producer price (CFAF per kilogram)	n.a.	n.a.	n.a.

n.a. Not available.

a. Excludes transport cost within the Ivory Coast, packing, insurance, and miscellaneous other items. For coffee the figures also exclude the cost of financing stocks. The result, therefore, of Stabilization Fund activities computed on the basis of the above figures do not correspond to those given in Table SA38.

b. Figure changed during the crop year.

(Table SA37 continues on the following page.)

TABLE SA37 *(continued)*

Indicator	1966–1967	1967–68	1968–69
Cocoa			
Production area (thousands of hectares)	340	332	347
Production (thousands of tons)	150	147	144
Exports (thousands of tons)	148	145	140
Average export cost, f.o.b. (CFAF per kilogram)[a]	112	112	112
Average export price, f.o.b. (CFAF per kilogram)	117	146	188
Export taxes (CFAF per kilogram)	22.4	25.7	25.7
Producer price (CFAF per kilogram)	70	70	70
Tax reference price (CFAF per kilogram)	115	115	115
Coffee			
Production (thousands of hectares)	473	647	652
Production (thousands of tons)	131	288	210
Exports (thousands of tons)	165	198	174
Average export cost, f.o.b. (CFAF per kilogram)[a]	135	134	134
Average export price, f.o.b. (CFAF per kilogram)	159	153	149
Export taxes (CFAF per kilogram)	25.7	25.7	31.3
Producer price (CFAF per kilogram)	90	90	90
Tax reference price (CFAF per kilogram)	115	115	115
Cotton			
Production area (thousands of hectares)	23	38	48
Production (thousands of tons)	8	12	16
Exports (thousands of tons)	6	10	12
Average export cost, f.o.b. (CFAF per kilogram)[a]	132	132	132
Average export price, f.o.b. (CFAF per kilogram)	124	141	135
Export taxes (CFAF per kilogram)	3.5	3.5	3.5
Producer price (CFAF per kilogram)	33.5	33.5	33.5

n.a. Not available.
Source: Ministry of Agriculture; Stabilization Fund.

1969–70	*1970–71*	*1971–72*	*1972–73*	*1973–74*	*1974–75*	*1975–76*	*1976–77*[c]
353	373	404	430	441	480	531	550
181	179	226	185	214	242	227	210
178	177	222	181	199	237	217	200
140	146	147	148	176	246	245	261
211	161	125	159	283	346	319	400
42.5	42.5	42.5	43.7	43.7	43.7	50.6	50.6
80	85	85	85	110	175	175	180
190	190	190	190	190	190	{ 190[b] 220[b] }	220
653	658	674	689	741	760	890	820
280	240	268	302	196	270	308	300
184	194	215	212	261	227	332	250
147	158	159	160	178	213	224	272
193	212	203	205	256	245	385.5	550
31.3	31.3	31.3	32.2	32.2	43.7	57.5	57.5
95	105	105	105	120	150	150	180
140	140	140	140	140	{ 140[b] 190[b] }	{ 190[b] 250[b] }	250
33	35	51	56	58	58	65	64
13	11	19	21	23	23	26	24
10	6	16	17	16	14	15	10
130	141	148	150	178	256	261	299
146	167	178	196	313	241	344	408
3.6	3.6	3.6	3.6	4.0	3.9	3.9	4.0
34.5	39.5	39.6	39.7	44.8	69.8	69.9	79.9

a. Excludes transport cost within the Ivory Coast, packing, insurance, and miscellaneous other items. For coffee the figures also exclude the cost of financing stocks. The results, therefore, of Stabilization Fund activities computed on the basis of the above figures do not correspond to those given in Table SA38.

b. Figures changed during the crop year.

c. Estimated by the Stabilization Fund.

TABLE SA38. FINANCIAL RESULTS OF THE STABILIZATION FUND
(CSSPPA) for Crop Years 1963–64 to 1976–77
(CFAF billion)

Item	1963–64	1964–65	1965–66	1966–67	1967–68
Net results of stabilization					
Coffee	6.8	−1.1	2.6	4.3	1.6
Cocoa ⎫	1.5	−1.0	−3.5	0.5	4.9
Cotton ⎬					
Oil seeds	. . .	. . .	−1.0	. . .	. . .
Total	8.3	−2.2	−1.0	4.8	6.5
Other revenues	. . .	. . .	. . .	. . .	. . .
Net administrative cost	−0.4	−0.1	−0.1	−0.4	−0.4
Contributions to international organizations (membership dues) ⎫ Direct subsidy payments[b] ⎭	−0.6	−0.3	−1.3	−1.3	−1.1
Contribution to investment budget	. . .	. . .	−1.3	−3.0	−2.0
Net financial results	7.3	−2.6	−3.7	0.1	3.0
Reserve account					
Cumulative net financial results	12.6[c]	10.0	6.4	6.5	9.5

. . . Zero or negligible.
n.a. Not available.
Source: Ministry of Economics and Finance and Stabilization Fund.

1968–69	1969–70	1970–71	1971–72	1972–73	1973–74	1974–75	1975–76	1976–77[a]
−0.4	5.9	7.7	4.0	4.4	19.0	−0.5	46.0	45.7
9.9	11.9	2.1	−5.4	1.2	20.6	19.3	7.0	16.5
0.1	0.2	0.3	0.4 {	0.5	1.4	0.7	−0.6	−2.3
				−0.2	3.3	0.1	−0.3	−0.5
9.6	18.0	10.1	−1.0	5.9	44.3	19.6	52.1	59.4
0.8	1.3	1.0	0.6	0.6	1.8	1.6	2.1	2.2
−0.7	−0.7	−0.8	−0.8	−1.0	−1.1	−1.5	−1.7	−2.1
−1.7	−3.9	−2.9	−2.7	−3.8 {	−1.6	−1.7	−2.0	−1.5
					−4.0	−6.9 }	−37.5	n.a.
−1.6	−13.5	−8.0	. . .	. . .	. . .	−7.0 }		
6.4	1.2	−0.6	−3.9	1.7	39.4	4.1	13.2	58.0
					39.4	4.1	13.2	
15.8	17.0	16.4	12.6	14.3	14.3	14.3	14.3	n.a.

a Estimated by Stabilization Fund.
b. Including diversification funds (SATMACI, MOTORAGRI, and others).
c. Including a carryover of CFAF 5.4 billion from the period prior to September 30, 1963.

TABLE SA39. FOREIGN RESERVES, 1969–76
(CFAF billion)

Item	1969	1970	1971	1972	1973	1974	1975	1976 (August)
Central Bank								
Foreign assets	19.8	29.1	22.9	22.3	20.4	14.6	23.1	13.2
Foreign liabilities	0.2	1.8	0.1	0.3	1.7	4.0	5.5	7.8
Net	19.6	27.3	22.8	22.0	18.7	10.6	17.6	5.4
Deposit money banks								
Foreign assets	21.5	25.3	25.9	8.1	11.0	36.8	8.3	12.1
Foreign liabilities	13.0	14.1	14.0	16.2	19.6	25.8	33.6	42.3
Net	8.5	11.2	11.9	−8.1	−8.6	11.0	−25.3	−30.2
Net foreign assets	28.1	38.5	34.7	13.9	10.1	21.6	−7.7	−24.8

Source: International Monetary Fund, *International Financial Statistics.*

TABLE SA40. INTEREST STRUCTURE
           (Percent)

Item	To January 1973	January 1973–June 1975	From July 1, 1975
Basic discount rate	3.50	5.50	priority: 5.50 normal: 8.00
Interest rate charged by commercial banks			
Short-term			
Discountable	4.50–6.00	6.50– 9.50	6.50–7.50[a]
Nondiscountable	6.00–9.00	8.00–11.00	13.00 maximum[b]
Medium-term			
Discountable	5.50–7.75	7.25–10.50	6.50–8.50[c]
Nondiscountable	8.00–8.50	11.00	13.00 maximum[b]
Interest paid on deposits			
Demand deposits	0.00–2.50	0.00–3.75	0.00–3.00 minimum
Time deposits	0.00–4.50	2.50–6.50	3.25–6.50 minimum
Savings accounts	3.25	4.75	5.50

Note: In the new system there is no distinction between rediscountable and nonrediscountable credits.

Source: BCEAO.

a. For crop financing and advances on stocks.

b. All other credits.

c. For small- and medium-scale enterprises run by nationals and mortgage loans of less than CFAF10 million to nationals.

TABLE SA41. MONETARY AND BANKING STATISTICS, 1965–75
(CFAF billion)

Item	1965	1966	1967	1968	1969	1970	1971	1972	1973	1974	1975
					Monetary survey						
Foreign assets (net)	15.7	19.1	14.5	22.4	28.1	38.6	34.9	20.1	17.5	30.3	4.3
Claims on government	−9.3	−10.0	−6.8	−10.3	−8.8	−16.2	−16.3	−10.2	−25.2	−38.1	−25.2
Claims on private sector	44.7	48.2	54.8	65.5	79.1	92.7	111.4	132.9	175.4	243.7	292.5
Money	42.3	46.4	48.5	59.1	69.8	83.6	92.1	103.2	117.9	162.8	179.8
Currency	22.9	26.4	27.6	30.6	34.0	39.8	47.0	51.5	57.0	77.5	89.6
Demand deposits	19.5	20.1	20.9	28.5	35.8	43.7	45.1	51.7	60.9	84.3	89.2
Quasi-money	6.6	7.5	9.7	13.4	22.2	23.2	25.5	19.7	30.0	60.4	64.7
					Assets and liabilities of the Central Bank						
Foreign assets	14.9	15.0	17.1	19.3	19.8	29.1	22.9	22.3	20.4	14.7	23.0
Claims on government	...	1.2	1.8	0.3	...	...	1.5	4.8	0.1	3.0	1.8
Claims on banks	12.0	13.3	12.7	15.7	19.6	22.9	29.2	35.0	51.5	91.1	90.4
Total	26.9	29.5	31.6	35.3	39.4	52.0	53.6	62.1	72.0	108.8	115.2
Currency	25.4	28.8	30.9	33.3	37.4	45.0	50.2	56.7	62.5	87.5	99.2
Foreign liabilities	0.3	0.1	0.1	1.1	0.2	0.9	0.1	0.3	1.3	4.0	5.5

Government deposits	1.2	0.6	0.6	0.9	1.8	5.2	0.8	1.1	3.8	13.4	6.7
Other liabilities (net)	...	...	...	...	...	0.9	2.5	4.0	4.4	3.9	3.8
Total	26.9	29.5	31.6	35.3	39.4	52.0	53.6	62.1	72.0	108.8	115.2
Assets and liabilities of the deposit money banks[a]											
Foreign assets	8.5	11.4	5.9	14.6	21.5	25.3	25.9	8.1	11.0	36.8	8.3
Claims on private sector	41.6	45.8	52.2	62.4	76.1	89.3	107.5	128.8	167.4	238.5	286.4
Other assets	2.4	2.2	2.8	2.6	3.2	4.7	3.1	4.9	5.4	9.4	8.4
Total	52.5	59.4	60.9	79.6	100.8	119.3	136.5	141.8	183.8	284.7	303.1
Demand deposits	18.1	19.0	19.6	27.2	34.2	42.0	43.2	50.0	59.5	82.8	87.9
Time deposits	6.6	7.5	9.7	13.4	22.2	23.2	25.4	19.6	30.0	60.4	64.7
Foreign liabilities	7.5	7.2	8.4	10.4	13.0	14.1	14.0	16.2	19.6	25.8	33.4
Government deposits	8.4	11.3	9.0	9.6	7.4	9.5	15.3	11.5	15.1	25.2	16.8
Credit from Central Bank	12.0	13.3	12.7	15.6	19.7	22.9	29.2	35.0	51.5	91.1	90.4
Other liabilities	...	1.1	1.5	3.4	4.3	7.5	9.4	9.5	8.1	-0.6	9.9
Total	52.5	59.4	60.9	79.6	100.8	119.3	136.5	141.8	183.8	284.7	303.1

. . . Zero or negligible.
Note: Figures are as of end of year.
Source: International Monetary Fund, *International Financial Statistics.*
a. Including CAA.

TABLE SA42. LABOR DEMAND AND SUPPLY AND UNEMPLOYMENT, 1973

Category	Total population	Active population aged 15–59[a]	Participation rates assumed		Employment		Unemployment	
			Number	Percent	1970	1973[b]	Number	As percentage of labor force
Rural								
Male	n.a.	1,087,000	1,087,000	100	n.a.	1,087,000	...	...
Female	n.a.	1,006,000	1,006,000	100	n.a.	1,006,000	...	...
Total	4,056,000	2,093,000	2,093,000	100	n.a.	2,093,000	...	...
Urban								
Male	n.a.	532,000	392,100	73.7[c]	n.a.	n.a.	n.a.	n.a.
Female	n.a.	484,000	122,100	25.3[c]	n.a.	n.a.	n.a.	n.a.
Total	1,830,800	1,016,000	514,200	50.6[c]	{ 370,400[d] / 384,100[e]	435,100[d] / 448,800[e]	79,100[d] / 65,400[e]	15.4[d] / 12.7[e]
Rural and urban								
Male	n.a.	1,619,000	1,479,100	91.4	n.a.	n.a.	n.a.	n.a.
Female	n.a.	1,490,000	1,128,100	75.7	n.a.	n.a.	n.a.	n.a.
Total	5,886,800	3,109,000	2,607,200	83.9	n.a.	{ 2,528,100[d] / 2,541,800[e]	79,100[d] / 65,400[e]	3.0[d] / 2.5[e]

. . . Zero or negligible.

n.a. Not available.

Source: Ministry of Planning and SETEF, *L'Image base, 1970* (Paris, 1973).

a. Rural males, 51.3 percent; rural females, 51.9 percent; urban males, 56.5 percent; urban females, 54.5 percent.

b. Ministry of Planning, estimated job creation, 1971–73: industry, 8,000; construction, 3,000; transport and communications, 3,600; trade, 3,900; housing and other services, 2,400; financing institutions, 300; domestic servants, 3,000; government, 6,300; cottage industries, 34,200; total, 64,700.

c. Rates found for Adjame in 1971 as quoted by the Ministry of Planning, *Dossier de situation emploi,* April 1974, p. 5. For 1974–75 a BCEOM study for Abidjan found even lower participation rates (around 58 percent), which seem unrealistic.

d. Reestimates of original SETEF figures, *L'Image base, 1970,* were orally communicated by the Ministry of Planning.

e. Original SETEF figures.

TABLE SA43. PROJECTIONS OF EMPLOYMENT, EXCLUSIVE OF THE PRIMARY SECTOR

Sector	Source[a]	1965	Average annual growth	1970	Percent annual growth	1975	Percent annual growth	1980
Modern sector								
Industry (05–22) {	SETEF	29,000	6.6	40,800 }	5.8	57,000	7.5	82,000
{	MOP	30,000	12.6	43,000 }				
Construction and public works {	SETEF	25,000	10.9	42,000 }	4.9	33,000	6.0	44,000
{	MOP	22,000		26,000 }				
Tertiary sector	SETEF	36,600	5.9	48,830	6.0	65,000	6.0	87,000
Civil servants, private sector managers	SETEF	36,200	5.7	47,860	6.0	64,000	6.0	85,500
Financial institutions	SETEF	1,500	5.4	1,950	5.5	2,500	5.5	3,000
Household help	SETEF	14,400	5.4	18,720	5.5	24,500	5.5	32,000
Total {	SETEF	142,700	7.0	200,160	5.75	246,000	6.3	333,800
{	MOP	140,700	5.8	186,360				
Informal sector								
Industry	SETEF	89,380	7.9	130,520	6.4	178,000	6.1	239,000
Tertiary sector	SETEF	37,820	7.8	53,460	7.0	75,000	7.0	105,000
Total	SETEF	127,200	7.7	183,980	6.6	253,000	6.3	344,000
Grand total {	MOP	267,900	—	370,340	—	499,000	—	678,000
{	SETEF	269,900	—	384,140	—	n.a.	—	n.a.

—Not applicable.
n.a. Not available.
a. Ministry of Planning (MOP) and SETEF, *L'Image base, 1970.*

TABLE SA44. INCOME DISTRIBUTION, 1973–74

Department	Non-agricultural population (thousands)	Distribution (Percent)	Individual entrepreneurs, nonagricultural (CFAF million)	Public and para-public (CFAF million)	Private modern (CFAF million)	Civil service (CFAF million)
Abengourou	31.1	1.7	2,114.9	142	2,532	1,219
Abidjan	909.0	49.3	61,302.6	17,373	34,357	23,042
Aboisso	23.3	1.3	1,616.5	321	982	993
Adzopé	30.4	1.6	1,989.5	45	982	1,038
Agboville	22.3	1.2	1,492.2	114	1,188	1,228
Biankouma	4.6	0.2	248.7	2	. . .	45
Bondoukou	57.3	3.1	3,854.7	38	103	1,580
Bouaflé	30.2	1.6	1,989.5	35	207	1,309
Bouaké	195.5	10.6	13,180.7	646	2,945	5,398
Boundiali	11.7	0.6	746.1	52	52	451
Daloa	69.4	3.8	4,725.1	208	1,447	1,896
Danané	27.0	1.5	1,865.2	24	52	451
Dimbokro	68.6	3.7	4,600.8	95	827	1,828
Divo	43.8	2.4	2,984.3	208	465	1,038
Ferkéssédougou	18.3	1.0	1,243.5	30	517	474
Gagnoa	44.1	2.4	2,984.3	142	1,808	1,535
Guiglo	17.1	0.9	1,119.1	28	982	858
Katiola	15.4	0.8	994.8	23	155	812
Korhogo	74.9	4.1	5,098.2	189	207	1,354
Man	52.7	2.9	3,606.0	65	258	1,377
Odienné	14.5	0.8	994.8	31	52	767
Sassandra	44.1	2.4	2,984.3	653	1,498	1,286
Séguéla	27.5	1.5	1,865.2	44	52	654
Touba	10.7	0.6	746.1	10	. . .	271
Total	1,843.5	100.0	124,346.0	20,518	51,668	50,904

. . . Zero or negligible.
Source: Ministries of Planning and Agriculture, and World Bank estimates.

Informal sector salaries (CFAF million)	Agricultural money and subsistence income (CFAF million)	Subtotal[a] (CFAF million)	Total population (thousands)	Per capita income subtotal (CFAF)	Population (Percent)	Income (Percent)
1,130	3,789.8	10,927.7	148.0	73,836	2.5	2.7
32,700	7,900.9	176,675.5	1,236.4	142,895	21.0	44.5
860	4,093.7	8,866.2	123.1	72,024	2.1	2.2
1,060	3,014.6	7,175.1	143.5	50,001	2.4	1.8
800	2,030.6	6,852.8	116.0	59,076	2.0	1.7
130	703.7	1,129.4	62.2	18,158	1.1	0.3
2,060	5,607.5	13,243.2	303.5	43,635	5.2	3.3
1,060	4,054.0	8,654.5	224.7	38,516	3.8	2.2
7,030	11,539.6	40,739.3	740.4	55,023	12.6	10.2
400	1,668.1	3,369.2	118.3	28,480	2.0	0.8
2,520	4,938.8	15,734.9	346.0	45,477	5.9	3.9
990	2,293.9	5,676.1	164.0	34,610	2.8	1.4
2,450	10,157.2	19,958.0	386.3	51,665	6.6	5.0
1,590	5,210.9	11,496.2	231.0	49,767	3.9	2.9
660	722.7	3,647.2	73.6	49,554	1.3	0.9
1,590	4,473.6	12,532.9	203.5	61,587	3.5	3.1
600	1,175.7	4,762.8	123.7	38,503	2.1	1.2
530	1,631.4	4,146.2	116.0	35,743	2.0	1.0
2,720	2,750.6	12,318.8	273.5	45,041	4.6	3.1
1,920	3,051.0	10,277.0	253.0	40,621	4.3	2.6
530	1,181.9	3,556.7	122.5	29,034	2.1	0.9
1,590	1,607.3	9,618.6	156.1	61,618	2.7	2.4
990	1,666.4	5,271.6	149.1	35,356	2.5	1.3
400	943.8	2,370.9	72.5	32,702	1.2	0.6
66,310	86,207.7	399,002.0	5,886.9	67,679	100.2	99.0

a. Does not include profits and dividends.

TABLE SA45. INCOME DISTRIBUTION EXCLUDING
AND INCLUDING PROFITS, 1973–74

Department	Income distribution, excluding profits		Income distribution, including profits	
	Percentage of population	Percentage of income	Percentage of population	Percentage of income
Biankouma	1.1	0.3	1.1	0.2
Boundiali	2.0	0.8	2.0	0.7
Odienné	2.1	0.9	2.1	0.8
Touba	1.2	0.6	1.2	0.5
Danané	2.8	1.4	2.8	1.2
Subtotal	9.2	4.0	9.2	3.4
Séguéla	2.5	1.3	2.5	1.1
Katiola	2.0	1.0	2.0	0.9
Guiglo	2.1	1.2	2.1	1.0
Bouaflé	3.8	2.2	3.8	1.9
Subtotal	10.4	5.7	10.4	4.9
Man	4.3	2.6	4.3	2.2
Bondoukou	5.2	3.3	5.2	2.8
Subtotal	9.5	5.9	9.5	5.0
Korhogo	4.3	3.1	4.3	1.6
Daloa	5.9	3.9	5.9	3.4
Subtotal	10.2	7.0	10.2	5.0
Ferkéssédougou	1.3	0.9	1.3	0.8
Divo	3.9	2.9	3.9	2.5
Adzopé	2.4	1.8	2.4	1.5
Dimbokro	6.6	5.0	6.6	4.3
Subtotal	14.2	10.6	14.2	9.1
Bouaké	12.6	10.2	12.6	8.8
Agboville	2.0	1.7	2.0	1.5
Gagnoa	3.5	3.1	3.5	2.7
Sassandra	2.7	2.4	2.7	2.1
Aboisso	2.1	2.2	2.1	1.9
Abengourou	2.5	2.7	2.5	2.3
Subtotal	12.8	12.1	12.8	10.5
Abidjan	21.0	44.5	21.0	52.2
Total	99.9	100.0	99.9	98.9

Source: World Bank estimates. See Table SA42.

TABLE SA46. HISTORICAL PERFORMANCE OF VARIOUS INDICATORS
COMPARED WITH VARIOUS RUNS

Indicator	Historical performance		Base run with saving unconstrained		Base run with saving constrained	
	1965–70	*1970–75*	*1976–80*	*1981–85*	*1976–80*	*1981–85*
Annual growth in gross domestic income (percent)	9.9	3.9	8.6	7.0	8.6	7.1
Investment/gross domestic income	19.9	22.9	29.1	28.1	29.0	28.0
Domestic saving/gross domestic income	23.0	23.2	29.2	27.8	20.8	18.5
National saving/gross domestic income	16.4	17.0	22.8	21.2	12.9	7.3
Investment minus national saving/gross domestic income	3.5	5.9	6.3	6.9	16.1	20.7
Net public saving/public investment	55.0	40.0	43.7	26.4	32.8	−45.0
Debt service ratio (percent)	6.9[b]	8.9	10.8	12.3	16.1	45.9
Import elasticity	1.1	1.1	1.2	0.8	2.10	0.55
Incremental capital-output ratio	2.7	4.1	3.8	4.3	3.8	4.3

Source: World Bank.   *(Table SA46 continues on the following page.)*

TABLE SA46 (*continued*)

More rapid growth with saving unconstrained		Base run with policy package and saving constrained		No special projects with saving unconstrained		No special projects with policy package and saving constrained		Paper pulp project with policy package[a] and saving constrained	
1976–80	*1981–85*	*1976–80*	*1981–85*	*1976–80*	*1981–85*	*1976–80*	*1981–85*	*1976–80*	*1981–85*
9.3	8.0	8.9	7.8	7.6	6.7	7.2	6.5	7.5	6.9
28.6	27.0	27.3	25.5	25.4	26.0	24.0	24.3	26.0	24.1
28.6	25.9	25.5	24.9	27.4	25.7	25.3	24.7	24.5	24.6
22.3	19.5	18.8	17.8	20.8	19.4	18.4	18.1	17.4	17.3
6.3	7.5	8.5	7.7	4.6	6.6	5.6	6.2	8.6	6.8
45.7	30.4	63.2	51.1	44.1	22.8	61.9	50.3	53.4	33.6
10.7	13.1	11.1	18.2	10.5	13.4	11.0	15.5	12.1	20.1
1.12	0.78	1.46	0.42	0.99	0.93	1.18	0.81	1.43	0.52
3.4	3.7	3.5	3.6	3.9	3.7	4.1	3.6	4.1	3.6

a. Excluding tax increase.
b. For 1967–70 only.

TABLE SA47. BASE RUN WITH SAVING UNCONSTRAINED: BALANCE OF PAYMENTS, 1976–85
(1973 CFAF billion and basic ratios)

Item	1976	1977	1978	1979	1980	1981	1982	1983	1984	1985
Exports	398.683	467.267	541.092	608.162	679.885	759.150	859.414	996.631	1137.965	1318.483
Imports	390.356	446.389	538.590	625.270	701.437	809.020	905.733	963.678	1104.958	1303.616
Trade balance	51.075	75.947	64.430	44.148	39.301	14.192	24.925	111.590	122.293	112.331
Resource balance	8.327	20.878	2.503	-17.108	-21.552	-49.870	-46.319	32.954	33.007	14.867
Current balance	-56.440	-53.400	-81.904	-113.949	-133.318	-175.591	-192.468	-134.014	-151.137	-187.765
Net direct foreign investment	14.999	16.799	27.345	39.412	53.046	47.437	52.079	33.158	50.002	82.891
Capital grants	4.509	4.509	4.509	4.509	4.509	4.509	4.509	4.509	4.509	4.509
Net transfers, traditional lenders	25.605	24.437	46.147	90.703	120.193	108.641	107.459	33.521	36.719	36.397
Net transfers, additional lenders	20.404	17.013	19.301	-6.200	-31.710	32.970	44.571	72.503	83.501	97.144
Change in reserves	-9.077	-9.358	-15.398	-14.476	-12.720	-17.966	-16.151	-9.677	-23.594	-33.176
Disbursed public capital	68.331	66.496	99.160	121.692	132.641	189.848	199.737	157.977	180.865	210.838
Amortized public capital	-22.321	-25.047	-33.712	-37.189	-44.158	-48.236	-47.706	-51.953	-60.645	-77.297
Net transfers, public capital	46.010	41.449	65.448	84.503	88.483	141.611	152.031	106.024	120.220	133.541
Price index, export goods	138.965	157.492	173.915	185.041	194.302	205.102	219.095	233.873	248.065	264.951
Price index, import goods	154.423	163.344	173.442	185.513	197.987	212.284	227.847	245.092	263.041	282.065
Terms of trade (1973=100)[a]	91.820	97.254	100.430	99.887	98.448	97.122	96.740	96.142	95.157	94.809
Import elasticity	1.250	1.306	1.641	0.933	0.611	1.270	0.670	0.162	0.849	1.178
Growth, exports of goods (percentage)	4.838	3.968	5.326	5.548	6.432	5.697	6.115	9.072	8.121	8.780
Debt service ratio (percentage)	9.901	9.894	10.853	11.095	12.044	12.252	12.179	12.221	12.240	12.591

Source: World Bank.
a. Goods and nonfactor services.

TABLE SA48. BASE RUN WITH SAVING UNCONSTRAINED: NATIONAL ACCOUNTS, 1976–85
(1973 CFAF billion and basic ratios)

Item	1976	1977	1978	1979	1980	1981	1982	1983	1984	1985
Gross domestic product	649.596	687.206	742.582	809.241	875.895	928.350	988.968	1047.754	1132.867	1229.472
Gross national income	576.434	627.220	690.050	752.254	810.219	854.777	908.522	959.652	1037.233	1128.345
Gross domestic income	626.301	679.068	743.922	808.870	870.471	917.732	976.222	1031.371	1110.747	1203.757
Consumption	460.775	497.711	531.565	554.626	584.823	648.027	698.452	754.351	809.995	879.065
Investment	160.065	168.477	210.909	263.489	296.554	293.248	298.155	263.520	288.146	319.395
Imports	256.014	275.376	311.794	337.919	354.931	381.923	398.623	394.788	422.001	464.383
Terms of trade adjustments	−261.475	−288.256	−313.242	−328.673	−344.025	−358.380	−378.237	−408.288	−434.607	−469.679
Gross domestic saving	165.526	181.357	212.357	254.244	285.648	269.705	277.770	277.020	300.752	324.691
Gross national saving	121.437	134.553	162.881	201.144	228.712	209.849	212.741	207.587	229.187	251.093
Basic ratios										
Public borrowing/public investment	46.664	52.618	57.130	60.279	64.633	68.413	70.073	73.736	76.611	79.004
Investment/gross domestic income	25.557	24.810	28.351	32.575	34.068	31.954	30.542	25.550	25.942	26.533
Domestic saving/gross domestic income	26.429	26.707	28.546	31.432	32.815	29.388	28.454	26.859	27.077	26.973
Public saving/gross domestic saving	36.282	33.612	31.829	28.142	25.598	26.242	25.421	24.745	22.793	22.017
Incremental capital-output ratio	4.564	4.256	3.042	3.164	3.953	5.653	4.838	5.072	3.096	2.983

Source: World Bank.

TABLE SA49. BASE RUN WITH SAVING UNCONSTRAINED: GOVERNMENT SAVING AND INVESTMENT, 1976–85
(1973 CFAF billion)

Indicator	1976	1977	1978	1979	1980	1981	1982	1983	1984	1985
Government current revenue[a]	162.492	171.589	187.073	200.590	212.484	221.287	233.164	244.105	258.153	276.257
Government current expenditure	102.436	110.631	119.481	129.040	139.363	150.512	162.553	175.557	189.602	204.770
Government gross national saving	69.384	69.561	76.135	79.363	79.607	76.341	73.312	68.801	68.597	71.335
Total gross domestic saving	137.031	142.281	154.674	166.030	175.244	179.262	186.129	191.048	200.882	214.607
Total public investment	101.600	113.500	131.500	148.750	161.480	168.978	174.037	179.700	192.516	206.037
Total private investment	58.464	54.976	59.407	64.739	70.072	74.268	79.117	83.820	90.629	98.358
Total special projects investment	0.000	0.000	20.000	50.000	65.000	50.000	45.000	0.000	5.000	15.000
Total public investment, current prices	145.337	175.281	219.000	264.912	305.453	341.208	376.512	416.539	476.898	546.553

Source: World Bank.
a. Includes Stabilization Fund.

TABLE SA50. BASE RUN WITH SAVING CONSTRAINED: BALANCE OF PAYMENTS, 1976–85
(1973 CFAF billion and basic ratios)

Item	1976	1977	1978	1979	1980	1981	1982	1983	1984	1985
Exports	398.683	467.267	541.092	608.162	679.885	759.150	859.414	996.631	1137.965	1318.483
Imports	433.545	509.446	637.511	786.864	917.260	998.595	1111.782	1171.952	1364.148	1609.558
Trade balance	7.886	12.889	-34.491	-117.447	-176.522	-175.382	-181.125	-96.685	-136.897	-193.611
Resource balance	-34.862	-42.180	-96.419	-178.702	-237.375	-239.445	-252.369	-175.321	-226.183	-291.075
Current balance	-99.629	-121.414	-192.678	-298.698	-391.148	-432.792	-490.036	-462.446	-561.570	-684.785
Net direct foreign investment	14.999	16.799	27.345	39.412	53.046	47.437	52.079	33.158	50.002	82.891
Capital grants	4.509	4.509	4.509	4.509	4.509	4.509	4.509	4.509	4.509	4.509
Net transfers, traditional lenders	25.605	24.437	46.147	90.703	120.193	108.641	107.459	33.521	36.719	36.397
Net transfers, additional lenders	70.806	88.345	136.064	189.016	235.176	285.788	344.891	401.306	502.437	601.972
Change in reserves	-16.290	-12.675	-21.387	-24.942	-21.776	-13.583	-18.902	-10.048	-32.097	-40.984
Disbursed public capital	118.733	137.829	224.137	337.591	442.700	525.451	641.862	684.438	870.841	1067.112
Amortized public capital	-22.321	-25.047	-41.927	-57.872	-87.330	-131.022	-189.512	-249.611	-331.685	-428.743
Net transfers, public capital	96.411	112.782	182.211	279.719	355.369	394.429	452.351	434.828	539.156	638.369
Price index, export goods	138.965	157.492	173.915	185.041	194.302	205.102	219.095	233.873	248.065	264.951
Price index, import goods	152.725	161.678	171.694	183.370	195.566	210.081	225.375	242.223	259.592	278.261
Terms of trade (1973 = 100)[a]	92.485	97.929	101.175	100.791	99.425	97.933	97.575	97.010	96.122	95.809
Import elasticity	3.655	1.812	2.171	1.716	1.122	0.235	0.586	-0.310	1.063	1.184
Growth, exports of goods (percentage)	4.838	3.968	5.326	5.548	6.432	5.697	6.115	9.072	8.121	8.780
Debt service ratio (percentage)	9.901	11.074	14.912	18.951	25.659	33.691	41.395	46.330	51.750	56.188

Source: World Bank.
a. Goods and nonfactor services.

TABLE SA51. Base Run with Saving Constrained: National Accounts, 1976–85
(1973 CFAF billion and basic ratios)

Item	1976	1977	1978	1979	1980	1981	1982	1983	1984	1985
Gross domestic product	649.596	687.217	742.582	809.266	875.895	928.365	988.985	1047.744	1132.867	1229.481
Gross national income	578.330	626.107	685.426	742.628	792.233	825.588	871.082	913.361	982.863	1063.905
Gross domestic income	628.197	681.079	746.246	811.870	873.885	920.739	979.504	1035.046	1115.156	1208.718
Consumption	491.162	538.802	591.569	645.828	698.636	741.472	793.378	843.997	914.270	994.104
Investment	160.065	168.478	210.909	263.494	296.554	293.248	298.155	263.520	288.146	319.397
Imports	286.401	316.456	371.798	429.100	468.744	475.354	493.530	484.444	526.276	579.414
Terms of trade adjustments	−263.371	−290.255	−315.566	−331.648	−347.439	−361.373	−381.502	−411.973	−439.017	−474.632
Gross domestic saving	137.035	142.277	154.677	166.043	175.249	179.267	186.126	191.048	200.887	214.615
Gross national saving	92.946	92.349	98.253	100.614	96.913	87.215	80.376	71.650	70.543	71.614
Basic ratios										
Public borrowing/public investment	46.664	55.415	66.128	76.413	91.602	110.907	129.817	147.374	161.939	174.730
Investment/gross domestic income	25.480	24.737	28.263	32.455	33.935	31.849	30.439	25.460	25.839	26.424
Domestic saving/gross domestic income	21.814	20.890	20.727	20.452	20.054	19.470	19.002	18.458	18.014	17.756
Public saving/gross domestic saving	43.825	42.846	43.699	43.095	41.724	39.482	37.939	35.878	34.124	33.310
Incremental capital-output ratio	4.564	4.255	3.043	3.163	3.955	5.652	4.838	5.074	3.096	2.982

Source: World Bank.

TABLE SA52. BASE RUN WITH SAVING CONSTRAINED: GOVERNMENT SAVING AND INVESTMENT, 1976–85
(1973 CFAF billion)

Indicator	1976	1977	1978	1979	1980	1981	1982	1983	1984	1985
Government current revenue[a]	162.492	171.591	187.073	200.596	212.484	221.289	233.167	244.102	258.153	276.259
Government current expenditure	102.436	110.631	119.481	129.040	139.363	150.512	162.553	175.557	189.602	204.770
Government gross national saving	69.384	66.386	69.117	66.640	58.049	43.949	32.431	18.667	9.662	1.754
Total gross domestic saving	137.031	142.283	154.674	166.038	175.244	179.266	186.133	191.044	200.882	214.609
Total public investment	101.600	113.500	131.500	148.750	161.480	168.978	174.037	179.700	192.516	206.037
Total private investment	58.464	54.977	59.407	64.741	70.072	74.269	79.119	83.820	90.629	98.358
Total special projects investment	0.000	0.000	20.000	50.000	65.000	50.000	45.000	0.000	5.000	15.000
Total public investment, current prices	145.337	175.283	219.000	264.907	305.453	341.208	376.517	416.545	476.898	546.553

Source: World Bank.
a. Includes Stabilization Fund.

TABLE SA53. MORE RAPID GROWTH WITH SAVING UNCONSTRAINED: BALANCE OF PAYMENTS, 1976–85
(1973 CFAF billion and basic ratios)

Item	1976	1977	1978	1979	1980	1981	1982	1983	1984	1985
Exports	401.383	471.533	547.422	617.186	692.400	776.157	882.170	1026.708	1177.325	1369.573
Imports	392.624	451.247	546.900	638.193	720.273	835.620	942.374	1013.186	1170.855	1390.265
Trade balance	51.507	75.355	62.450	40.249	32.980	4.599	11.040	92.158	95.756	76.771
Resource balance	8.759	20.286	0.522	-21.007	-27.873	-59.463	-60.204	13.522	6.470	-20.693
Current balance	-56.008	-53.982	-83.971	-118.189	-140.460	-186.786	-209.150	-157.996	-184.719	-233.838
Net direct foreign investment	14.999	16.799	27.345	39.412	53.046	47.437	52.079	33.158	50.002	82.891
Capital grants	4.509	4.509	4.509	4.509	4.509	4.509	4.509	4.509	4.509	4.509
Net transfers, traditional lenders	25.605	24.437	46.147	90.703	120.193	108.641	107.459	33.521	36.719	36.397
Net transfers, additional lenders	20.351	18.027	21.945	-1.190	-23.580	45.461	62.931	98.634	119.820	146.682
Change in reserves	-9.456	-9.790	-15.974	-15.246	-13.707	-19.263	-17.828	-11.826	-26.331	-36.641
Disbursed public capital	68.277	67.511	101.795	126.859	141.372	203.844	221.178	189.801	226.687	275.340
Amortized public capital	-22.321	-25.047	-33.703	-37.345	-44.759	-49.741	-50.788	-57.646	-70.147	-92.260
Net transfers, public capital	45.956	42.464	68.092	89.513	96.613	154.103	170.390	132.155	156.539	183.079
Price index, export goods	139.023	157.504	173.870	185.013	194.343	205.223	219.257	234.088	248.404	265.372
Price index, import goods	154.380	163.283	173.372	185.417	197.843	212.119	227.648	244.811	262.729	281.758
Terms of trade (1973 = 100)[a]	91.861	97.279	100.435	99.911	98.516	97.220	96.852	96.279	95.324	94.983
Import elasticity	1.201	1.261	1.574	0.925	0.634	1.207	0.694	0.013	0.855	1.136
Growth, exports of goods (percentage)	5.617	4.280	5.664	5.914	6.823	6.134	6.580	9.488	8.582	9.238
Debt service ratio (percentage)	9.828	9.795	10.734	11.009	12.034	12.399	12.563	12.911	13.306	14.069

Source: World Bank.
a. Goods and nonfactor services.

TABLE SA54. MORE RAPID GROWTH WITH SAVING UNCONSTRAINED: NATIONAL ACCOUNTS, 1976–85
(1973 CFAF billion and basic ratios)

Item	1976	1977	1978	1979	1980	1981	1982	1983	1984	1985
Gross domestic product	654.176	696.269	757.064	830.276	904.749	966.487	1038.077	1109.786	1210.095	1324.501
Gross national income	580.981	636.289	704.512	773.176	838.797	892.286	956.507	1019.906	1111.770	1219.486
Gross domestic income	630.848	688.131	758.436	829.978	899.468	956.003	1025.452	1093.517	1188.023	1298.716
Consumption	464.625	506.411	546.068	576.163	614.717	687.792	749.880	819.490	891.226	979.094
Investment	160.478	169.202	212.065	265.172	298.862	296.299	302.084	268.483	294.324	326.997
Imports	257.535	278.427	316.682	345.024	364.656	394.699	414.995	415.366	447.479	495.541
Terms of trade adjustments	−263.281	−290.944	−316.984	−333.667	−350.544	−366.612	−388.483	−420.910	−449.952	−488.165
Gross domestic saving	166.223	181.719	212.367	253.815	284.751	268.212	275.572	274.027	296.796	319.622
Gross national saving	122.134	134.922	162.840	200.826	227.396	207.594	209.298	202.702	222.493	242.205
Basic ratios										
Public borrowing/public investment	45.813	51.106	55.083	57.791	61.718	65.040	66.259	69.596	72.383	74.787
Investment/gross domestic income	25.438	24.589	27.961	31.949	33.227	30.993	29.459	24.552	24.774	25.179
Domestic saving/gross domestic income	26.349	26.408	28.001	30.581	31.658	28.056	26.873	25.059	24.982	24.611
Public saving/gross domestic saving	36.650	34.488	33.119	29.758	27.591	29.071	28.990	29.295	28.019	27.994
Incremental capital-output ratio	4.000	3.812	2.783	2.897	3.561	4.841	4.139	4.213	2.677	2.573

Source: World Bank.

TABLE SA55. MORE RAPID GROWTH WITH SAVING UNCONSTRAINED: GOVERNMENT SAVING AND INVESTMENT, 1976–85

(1973 CFAF billion)

Indicator	1976	1977	1978	1979	1980	1981	1982	1983	1984	1985
Government current revenue[a]	163.357	173.302	189.816	204.569	217.928	228.483	242.440	255.833	272.760	294.244
Government current expenditure	102.436	110.631	119.481	129.040	139.363	150.512	162.553	175.557	189.602	204.770
Government gross national saving	70.249	71.278	78.822	83.148	84.620	82.757	81.320	78.607	80.429	85.457
Total gross domestic saving	138.341	144.876	158.825	172.056	183.498	190.171	200.185	208.813	223.004	241.839
Total public investment	101.600	113.500	131.500	148.750	161.480	168.978	174.037	179.700	192.516	206.037
Total private investment	58.876	55.702	60.565	66.422	72.380	77.319	83.046	88.783	96.808	105.960
Total special projects investment	0.000	0.000	20.000	50.000	65.000	50.000	45.000	0.000	5.000	15.000
Total public investment, current prices	145.353	175.311	219.034	264.994	305.653	341.513	376.876	416.967	477.475	547.241

Source: World Bank.
a. Includes Stabilization Fund.

TABLE SA56. BASE RUN WITH POLICY PACKAGE AND SAVING CONSTRAINED: BALANCE OF PAYMENTS, 1976–85
(1973 CFAF billion and basic ratios)

Item	1976	1977	1978	1979	1980	1981	1982	1983	1984	1985
Exports	401.383	471.533	547.422	617.186	692.400	776.157	882.170	1026.708	1177.325	1369.573
Imports	393.968	453.227	560.270	687.160	793.919	848.220	928.512	991.222	1144.862	1360.573
Trade balance	50.163	73.375	49.080	-8.718	-40.666	-8.001	24.902	114.122	121.750	106.463
Resource balance	7.415	18.306	-12.848	-69.974	-101.519	-72.063	-46.342	35.487	32.464	9.000
Current balance	-57.353	-56.116	-97.713	-169.059	-221.558	-215.076	-212.521	-153.025	-174.915	-219.169
Net direct foreign investment	14.999	16.799	27.345	39.412	53.046	47.437	52.079	33.158	50.002	82.891
Capital grants	4.509	4.509	4.509	4.509	4.509	4.509	4.509	4.509	4.509	4.509
Net transfers, traditional lenders	25.605	24.437	46.147	90.703	120.193	108.641	107.459	33.521	36.719	36.397
Net transfers, additional lenders	21.920	20.268	37.589	55.626	61.639	63.557	61.882	92.309	109.343	131.395
Change in reserves	-9.681	-9.896	-17.876	-21.191	-17.829	-9.068	-13.409	-10.473	-25.658	-36.024
Disbursed public capital	69.846	69.752	117.694	184.321	229.896	234.948	248.900	219.849	260.234	309.265
Amortized public capital	-22.321	-25.047	-33.959	-37.992	-48.064	-62.750	-79.559	-94.019	-114.171	-141.473
Net transfers, public capital	47.525	44.705	83.736	146.329	181.832	172.198	169.341	125.831	146.062	167.792
Price index, export goods	139.023	157.504	173.870	185.013	194.343	205.223	219.257	234.088	248.404	265.372
Price index, import goods	154.239	163.065	172.892	184.443	196.631	211.630	227.456	244.667	262.556	281.551
Terms of trade (1973 = 100)[a]	91.920	97.372	100.638	100.313	98.993	97.399	96.922	96.331	95.383	95.048
Import elasticity	1.398	1.395	1.962	1.578	0.948	-0.094	0.271	-0.095	0.869	1.164
Growth, exports of goods (percentage)	5.617	4.280	5.664	5.914	6.823	6.134	6.580	9.488	8.582	9.238
Debt service ratio (percentage)	9.828	9.831	10.859	11.462	13.729	16.402	18.159	18.450	18.731	19.019

Source: World Bank.
a. Goods and nonfactor services.

TABLE SA57. BASE RUN WITH POLICY PACKAGE AND SAVING CONSTRAINED: NATIONAL ACCOUNTS, 1976–85

(1973 CFAF billion and basic ratios)

Item	1976	1977	1978	1979	1980	1981	1982	1983	1984	1985
Gross domestic product	650.868	689.348	746.045	815.714	886.978	945.399	1013.237	1080.923	1176.503	1286.094
Gross national income	577.840	629.548	693.916	758.919	818.929	864.402	924.276	984.207	1072.164	1175.957
Gross domestic income	627.708	681.487	748.057	816.759	883.396	935.589	1000.889	1064.885	1154.709	1260.644
Consumption	466.762	510.032	557.827	607.232	655.581	694.057	741.474	805.375	873.636	957.347
Investment	156.080	160.149	197.685	247.509	279.460	275.633	279.838	244.953	268.658	300.088
Imports	258.583	279.915	325.080	372.991	403.888	401.387	409.183	406.584	437.815	485.291
Terms of trade adjustments	–263.449	–291.221	–317.625	–335.009	–352.242	–367.286	–388.761	–421.140	–450.230	–488.501
Gross domestic saving	160.946	171.454	190.230	209.527	227.815	241.532	259.416	259.509	281.073	303.298
Gross national saving	116.857	124.560	140.485	155.500	166.664	173.444	185.474	181.118	200.477	220.424
Basic ratios										
Public borrowing/public investment	34.043	35.088	35.987	37.191	41.822	47.640	49.182	49.656	49.558	48.509
Investment/gross domestic income	24.865	23.500	26.426	30.304	31.635	29.461	27.959	23.003	23.266	23.804
Domestic saving/gross domestic income	25.640	25.159	25.430	25.653	25.789	25.816	25.919	24.370	243.341	24.059
Public saving/gross domestic saving	43.272	43.339	44.879	45.177	44.929	44.223	44.092	46.633	46.606	47.909
Incremental capital-output ratio	4.392	4.056	2.825	2.837	3.473	4.784	4.063	4.134	2.563	2.451

Source: World Bank.

TABLE SA58. BASE RUN WITH POLICY PACKAGE AND SAVING CONSTRAINED: GOVERNMENT SAVING AND INVESTMENT, 1976–85
(1973 CFAF billion)

Indicator	1976	1977	1978	1979	1980	1981	1982	1983	1984	1985
Government current revenue[a]	169.236	178.876	195.172	209.946	223.407	233.918	247.843	261.150	278.137	299.804
Government current expenditure	99.590	104.570	109.798	115.288	121.053	127.105	133.461	140.134	147.140	154.497
Government gross national saving	79.502	83.940	95.441	103.781	107.970	108.415	113.547	118.881	129.889	145.201
Total gross domestic saving	160.941	171.452	190.225	209.522	227.809	241.528	259.423	276.633	301.014	331.334
Total public investment	97.500	105.000	118.000	132.250	143.500	150.000	153.780	158.478	169.537	182.200
Total private investment	58.578	55.148	59.684	65.257	70.958	75.632	81.059	86.474	94.120	102.888
Total special projects investment	0.000	0.000	20.000	50.000	65.000	50.000	45.000	0.000	5.000	15.000
Total public investment, current prices	139.490	162.198	196.588	235.657	271.690	303.219	333.071	367.779	420.525	483.959

Source: World Bank.
a. Includes Stabilization Fund.

TABLE SA59. NO SPECIAL PROJECTS WITH SAVING UNCONSTRAINED: BALANCE OF PAYMENTS, 1976–85
(1973 CFAF billion and basic ratios)

Item	1976	1977	1978	1979	1980	1981	1982	1983	1984	1985
Exports	398.683	467.267	541.092	608.162	679.885	751.650	844.414	949.984	1047.934	1182.526
Imports	390.356	446.389	508.701	571.941	640.993	727.911	830.415	948.215	1083.943	1240.294
Trade balance	51.075	75.947	94.320	97.476	99.745	87.802	85.243	80.405	53.277	39.695
Resource balance	8.327	20.878	32.392	36.221	38.892	23.739	13.999	1.769	-36.009	-57.769
Current balance	-56.440	-53.400	-52.015	-58.298	-67.210	-93.747	-118.459	-148.547	-207.640	-256.610
Net direct foreign investment	14.999	16.799	18.815	21.072	23.601	26.433	29.605	33.158	37.137	41.593
Capital grants	4.509	4.509	4.509	4.509	4.509	4.509	4.509	4.509	4.509	4.509
Net transfers, traditional lenders	25.605	24.437	20.557	17.343	22.043	24.625	28.799	35.121	42.904	48.716
Net transfers, additional lenders	20.404	17.013	18.541	25.935	28.589	52.695	72.664	95.433	145.758	187.903
Change in reserves	-9.077	-9.358	-10.406	-10.561	-11.532	-14.515	-17.118	-19.673	-22.667	-26.111
Disbursed public capital	68.331	66.496	72.809	80.468	94.666	130.657	164.600	201.966	273.434	342.387
Amortized public capital	-22.321	-25.047	-33.712	-37.189	-44.034	-53.337	-63.138	-71.413	-84.772	-105.768
Net transfers, public capital	46.010	41.449	39.097	43.278	50.632	77.320	101.463	130.554	188.661	236.619
Price index, export goods	138.965	157.492	173.915	185.041	194.302	205.296	219.410	234.113	247.657	263.675
Price index, import goods	154.423	163.344	173.732	185.940	198.379	212.822	228.382	245.111	263.022	282.355
Terms of trade (1973 = 100)[a]	91.820	97.254	100.330	99.738	98.316	97.038	96.715	96.245	95.070	94.406
Import elasticity	1.250	1.306	1.030	0.693	0.660	0.897	0.937	0.926	0.980	0.908
Growth, exports of goods (percentage)	4.838	3.968	5.326	5.548	6.432	4.397	5.131	5.388	4.222	5.887
Debt service ratio (percentage)	9.901	9.894	10.853	10.671	11.106	11.868	12.526	12.927	14.133	15.805

Source: World Bank.
a. Goods and nonfactor services.

TABLE SA60. NO SPECIAL PROJECTS WITH SAVING UNCONSTRAINED: NATIONAL ACCOUNTS, 1976–85
(1973 CFAF billion and basic ratios)

Item	1976	1977	1978	1979	1980	1981	1982	1983	1984	1985
Gross domestic product	649.596	687.206	732.801	784.722	843.521	899.069	960.172	1027.124	1096.174	1176.514
Gross national income	576.434	627.220	679.957	728.510	780.268	829.224	885.959	947.145	1006.766	1077.535
Gross domestic income	626.301	679.068	733.829	783.861	837.635	888.258	947.568	1011.939	1075.418	1151.569
Consumption	460.775	497.711	528.971	563.036	603.519	647.165	696.065	749.344	808.961	871.977
Investment	160.065	168.477	186.126	201.279	214.463	229.905	245.352	261.870	280.211	300.159
Imports	256.014	275.376	294.198	308.637	323.911	343.042	364.900	388.455	414.036	441.575
Terms of trade adjustments	−261.475	−288.256	−312.931	−328.183	−343.564	−354.230	−371.051	−389.179	−400.281	−421.008
Gross domestic saving	165.526	181.337	204.859	220.825	234.117	241.093	251.503	262.595	266.456	279.592
Gross national saving	121.437	134.553	155.382	169.288	180.065	185.158	192.566	200.087	199.754	207.370
Basic ratios										
Public borrowing/public investment	46.664	52.618	57.259	59.803	63.332	68.681	72.601	76.043	81.729	87.112
Investment/gross domestic income	25.557	24.810	25.364	25.678	25.603	25.883	25.893	25.878	26.056	26.065
Domestic saving/gross domestic income	26.429	26.707	27.916	28.171	27.950	27.142	26.542	25.950	24.777	24.279
Public saving/gross domestic saving	36.282	33.612	32.077	30.268	28.577	27.029	25.885	24.613	23.128	22.002
Incremental capital-output ratio	4.564	4.265	3.695	3.585	3.423	3.861	3.763	3.665	3.792	3.488

Source: World Bank.

TABLE SA61. No Special Projects with Saving Unconstrained: Government Saving and Investment, 1976–85

(1973 CFAF billion)

Indicator	1976	1977	1978	1979	1980	1981	1982	1983	1984	1985
Government current revenue[a]	162.492	171.589	185.194	195.880	206.267	215.677	227.655	240.189	251.227	266.287
Government current expenditure	102.436	110.631	119.481	129.040	139.363	150.512	162.553	175.557	189.602	204.770
Government gross national saving	69.384	69.561	74.255	75.951	76.326	74.871	74.271	72.748	68.120	64.971
Total gross domestic saving	137.031	142.281	151.846	158.943	165.888	170.811	177.825	185.126	190.384	199.478
Total public investment	101.600	113.500	127.500	138.500	146.980	157.978	168.537	179.700	192.516	206.037
Total private investment	58.464	54.976	58.624	62.778	67.482	71.925	76.814	82.170	87.694	94.121
Total special projects investment	0.000	0.000	0.000	0.000	0.000	0.000	0.000	0.000	0.000	0.000
Total public investment, current prices	145.337	175.281	212.419	246.879	278.345	319.259	364.860	416.513	476.502	545.641

Source: World Bank.
a. Includes Stabilization Fund.

TABLE SA62. NO SPECIAL PROJECTS WITH POLICY PACKAGE AND SAVING CONSTRAINED: BALANCE OF PAYMENTS, 1976–85

(1973 CFAF billion and basic ratios)

Item	1976	1977	1978	1979	1980	1981	1982	1983	1984	1985
Exports	398.683	467.267	541.092	608.162	679.885	751.650	844.414	949.984	1047.934	1182.526
Imports	392.867	452.476	522.616	587.260	655.734	728.935	818.515	926.308	1058.008	1210.661
Trade balance	48.564	69.860	80.404	82.157	85.003	86.777	97.143	102.312	79.212	69.328
Resource balance	5.816	14.791	18.477	20.901	24.150	22.715	25.899	23.676	-10.074	-28.135
Current balance	-58.952	-59.775	-66.897	-76.160	-86.231	-100.853	-113.035	-132.318	-185.597	-228.681
Net direct foreign investment	14.999	16.799	18.815	21.072	23.601	26.433	29.605	33.158	37.137	41.593
Capital grants	4.509	4.509	4.509	4.509	4.509	4.509	4.509	4.509	4.509	4.509
Net transfers, traditional lenders	25.605	24.437	20.557	17.343	22.043	24.625	28.799	35.121	42.904	48.716
Net transfers, additional lenders	23.335	23.985	34.730	44.031	47.513	57.511	65.082	77.532	123.042	159.356
Change in reserves	-9.497	-9.955	-11.713	-10.796	-11.435	-12.225	-14.960	-18.001	-21.994	-25.493
Disbursed public capital	71.262	73.469	89.476	100.226	118.140	143.710	169.925	199.644	266.910	326.890
Amortized public capital	-22.321	-25.047	-34.189	-38.852	-48.584	-61.574	-76.044	-86.992	-100.965	-118.817
Net transfers, public capital	48.941	48.422	55.287	61.374	69.556	82.136	93.881	112.653	165.945	208.072
Price index, export goods	138.965	157.492	173.915	185.041	194.302	205.296	219.410	234.113	247.657	263.675
Price index, import goods	154.227	162.997	173.179	185.367	197.814	212.420	228.134	244.961	262.838	282.131
Terms of trade (1973 = 100)[a]	91.899	97.397	100.556	99.964	98.527	97.180	96.801	96.300	95.133	94.477
Import elasticity	1.556	1.597	1.372	0.724	0.625	0.574	0.710	0.814	1.010	0.938
Growth, exports of goods (percentage)	4.838	3.968	5.326	5.548	6.432	4.397	5.131	5.388	4.222	5.887
Debt service ratio (percentage)	9.901	9.963	11.146	11.426	12.516	13.929	14.996	15.323	16.179	17.130

Source: World Bank.

a. Goods and nonfactor services.

TABLE SA63. No Special Projects with Policy Package and Saving Constrained:
National Accounts, 1976–85
(1973 CFAF billion and basic ratios)

Item	1976	1977	1978	1979	1980	1981	1982	1983	1984	1985
Gross domestic product	646.288	680.285	721.779	770.157	826.179	877.982	935.332	998.268	1062.576	1138.105
Gross national income	573.349	620.539	669.074	713.302	761.483	805.758	858.569	916.152	971.920	1038.823
Gross domestic income	623.217	672.569	723.513	770.038	821.031	867.688	923.059	983.307	1042.083	1113.477
Consumption	463.733	504.008	541.060	575.119	612.706	647.728	688.563	735.261	791.390	850.252
Investment	155.667	159.423	171.744	183.614	196.095	209.240	223.106	238.341	254.544	273.249
Imports	257.883	279.540	302.926	317.620	332.071	344.026	359.992	379.698	404.396	431.348
Terms of trade adjustments	−261.700	−288.678	−313.636	−328.924	−344.301	−354.747	−371.383	−389.403	−400.546	−421.324
Gross domestic saving	159.485	168.561	182.453	194.919	208.325	219.960	234.496	248.046	250.693	263.225
Gross national saving	115.395	121.576	132.410	141.995	152.094	161.130	172.678	183.177	182.478	190.384
Basic ratios										
Public borrowing/public investment	34.977	36.891	38.389	38.858	41.501	45.923	48.289	49.063	51.645	53.394
Investment/gross domestic income	24.978	23.704	23.737	23.845	23.884	24.115	24.170	24.239	24.426	24.540
Domestic saving/gross domestic income	25.591	25.062	25.218	25.313	25.374	25.350	25.404	25.226	24.057	23.640
Public saving/gross domestic saving	43.098	43.012	44.125	43.870	43.281	42.431	42.140	42.148	43.209	44.019
Incremental capital-output ratio	5.082	4.579	3.842	3.550	3.278	3.785	3.648	3.545	3.706	3.370

Source: World Bank.

TABLE SA64. No Special Projects with Policy Package and Saving Constrained: Government Saving and Investment, 1976–85
(1973 CFAF billion)

Indicator	1976	1977	1978	1979	1980	1981	1982	1983	1984	1985
Government current revenue[a]	168.325	177.072	190.305	200.799	211.218	220.438	232.277	244.681	255.463	270.367
Government current expenditure	99.590	104.570	109.798	115.288	121.053	127.105	133.461	140.134	147.140	154.497
Government gross national saving	78.592	82.047	90.277	95.778	100.799	104.482	110.513	116.899	121.218	128.072
Total gross domestic saving	159.480	168.559	182.449	194.914	208.329	219.956	234.507	250.235	264.652	284.114
Total public investment	97.500	105.000	114.000	122.000	130.000	139.000	148.280	158.478	169.537	182.200
Total private investment	58.166	54.423	57.742	61.613	66.094	70.239	74.827	79.861	85.006	91.048
Total special projects investment	0.000	0.000	0.000	0.000	0.000	0.000	0.000	0.000	0.000	0.000
Total public investment, current prices	139.475	162.171	189.969	217.525	246.255	280.969	321.071	367.380	419.667	482.533

Source: World Bank.
a. Includes Stabilization Fund.

TABLE SA65. PAPER PULP PROJECT WITH POLICY PACKAGE[a] AND SAVING CONSTRAINED: BALANCE OF PAYMENTS, 1976–85

(1973 CFAF billion and basic ratios)

Item	1976	1977	1978	1979	1980	1981	1982	1983	1984	1985
Exports	398.683	467.267	541.092	608.162	679.885	759.150	859.414	979.984	1092.934	1240.526
Imports	401.233	461.844	565.947	659.433	716.863	751.022	847.238	963.044	1077.292	1230.581
Trade balance	40.198	60.491	37.073	9.984	23.875	72.191	83.420	95.575	104.928	107.409
Resource balance	-2.550	5.422	-24.855	-51.271	-36.978	8.128	12.176	16.940	15.642	9.945
Current balance	-67.317	-70.104	-112.197	-154.179	-159.060	-132.435	-145.848	-160.675	-183.527	-213.007
Net direct foreign investment	14.999	16.799	27.345	39.412	33.416	26.433	29.605	33.158	37.137	41.593
Capital grants	4.509	4.509	4.509	4.509	4.509	4.509	4.509	4.509	4.509	4.509
Net transfers, traditional lenders	25.605	24.437	46.147	63.193	61.303	24.625	28.799	33.521	38.439	41.797
Net transfers, additional lenders	33.098	34.481	51.582	62.677	69.422	82.573	99.003	108.827	122.522	150.707
Change in reserves	-10.894	-10.122	-17.385	-15.612	-9.591	-5.704	-16.068	-19.340	-19.079	-25.599
Disbursed public capital	81.024	83.965	133.510	168.187	186.136	179.901	220.800	252.937	296.149	354.839
Amortized public capital	-22.321	-25.047	-35.781	-42.317	-55.410	-72.703	-92.998	-110.589	-135.188	-162.334
Net transfers, public capital	58.703	58.918	97.729	125.870	130.726	107.198	127.802	142.348	160.961	192.505
Price index, export goods	138.965	157.492	173.915	185.041	194.302	205.102	219.095	233.630	247.225	263.359
Price index, import goods	153.867	162.724	172.650	184.496	197.088	212.120	227.716	244.483	262.723	282.065
Terms of trade (1973 = 100)[b]	92.036	97.504	100.762	100.306	98.799	97.197	96.802	96.248	94.992	94.362
Import elasticity	2.075	1.577	2.050	1.189	0.259	-0.464	0.747	0.802	0.605	0.880
Growth, exports of goods (percentage)	4.838	3.968	5.326	5.548	6.432	5.697	6.115	7.099	5.508	6.544
Debt service ratio (percentage)	9.901	1.0191	11.865	13.102	15.489	17.844	19.312	19.913	21.324	22.157

Source: World Bank.
a. Excluding tax increase.
b. Goods and nonfactor services.

TABLE SA66. PAPER PULP PROJECT WITH POLICY PACKAGE[a] AND SAVING CONSTRAINED: NATIONAL ACCOUNTS, 1976–85

(1973 CFAF billion and basic ratios)

Item	1976	1977	1978	1979	1980	1981	1982	1983	1984	1985
Gross domestic product	646.288	680.280	730.320	784.807	836.941	882.618	943.534	1013.493	1083.754	1163.365
Gross national income	573.742	620.248	677.103	725.890	767.237	802.254	858.047	921.668	982.374	1054.163
Gross domestic income	623.609	672.883	732.696	785.814	832.745	872.275	931.031	997.814	1061.727	1136.956
Consumption	469.618	510.107	553.707	592.854	628.067	658.325	701.905	751.302	799.512	858.143
Investment	155.667	159.423	193.426	220.785	223.455	210.110	223.763	239.559	256.235	275.269
Imports	263.768	285.644	328.715	357.877	364.031	354.815	373.118	395.300	411.875	438.489
Terms of trade adjustments	−262.092	−288.997	−314.279	−330.052	−345.253	−358.656	−378.480	−402.254	−417.855	−442.033
Gross domestic saving	153.991	162.776	178.989	192.960	204.677	213.951	229.126	246.512	262.215	278.813
Gross national saving	109.902	115.186	127.792	136.849	142.486	147.029	158.813	172.652	184.811	197.834
Basic ratios										
Public borrowing/public investment	41.606	43.957	45.599	47.492	54.109	61.529	64.572	65.766	69.287	70.681
Investment/gross domestic income	24.962	23.693	26.399	28.096	26.834	24.088	24.034	24.008	24.134	24.211
Domestic saving/gross domestic income	24.694	24.191	24.429	24.555	24.579	24.528	24.610	24.705	24.697	24.523
Public saving/gross domestic saving	40.439	40.361	41.862	41.783	41.026	39.936	39.732	39.542	38.799	39.201
Incremental capital-output ratio	5.082	4.580	3.186	3.550	4.235	4.892	3.449	3.198	3.410	3.219

Source: World Bank.
a. Excluding tax increase.

TABLE SA67. PAPER PULP PROJECT WITH POLICY PACKAGE[a] AND SAVING CONSTRAINED: GOVERNMENT SAVING AND INVESTMENT, 1976–85
(1973 CFAF billion)

Indicator	1976	1977	1978	1979	1980	1981	1982	1983	1984	1985
Government current revenue[b]	161.862	170.268	184.728	195.912	205.024	212.548	224.497	237.610	248.876	263.796
Government current expenditure	99.590	104.570	109.798	115.288	121.053	127.105	133.461	140.134	147.140	154.497
Government gross national saving	72.129	74.628	83.535	87.658	88.573	88.281	93.913	100.242	104.610	112.380
Total gross domestic saving	153.987	162.775	178.989	192.957	204.677	213.946	229.124	246.509	262.230	282.317
Total public investment	97.500	105.000	115.000	123.000	131.500	139.500	148.280	158.478	169.537	182.200
Total private investment	58.166	54.422	58.426	62.785	66.955	70.609	75.483	81.079	86.700	93.069
Total special projects investment	0.000	0.000	20.000	35.000	25.000	0.000	0.000	0.000	0.000	0.000
Total public investment, current prices	139.475	162.172	191.575	219.188	248.999	281.932	320.988	367.252	419.551	482.448

Source: World Bank.
a. Excluding tax increase.
b. Includes Stabilization Fund.

TABLE SA68. VOLUME OF AGRICULTURAL PRODUCTION, 1965–85
(Thousand tons)

Crop	1965	1970	1975[a]	Plan targets 1980	Plan targets 1985	World Bank forecasts[b] 1980	World Bank forecasts[b] 1985
Coffee	213	240	270	336	361	350	400
Cocoa	134	182	240	350	483	320	375
Oil palm, total fresh fruit bunches	329	480	980	1,262	1,700	1,260	1,700
Industrial fresh fruit bunches	74	223	750	1,012	1,480	1,030	1,480
Industrial palm oil	10	43	162	233	340	237	340
Copra	3.5	10	15	61	155	55	130
Rubber	2.0	11	17	21	47	n.a.	n.a.
Bananas, for export	107	134	170	200	220	n.a.	n.a.
Pineapples, for canning	33	87	170	215	270	n.a.	n.a.
Fresh	4.6	16.5	80	150	230	n.a.	n.a.
Cotton	10.4	33	65	105	195	95	120
Sugar	. . .	. . .	5	230	550	110	200
Paddy	250	316	400	740	1,030	700	850
Maize	200	231	280	360	560	n.a.	n.a.
Sorghum–millet	45	43	50	n.a.	n.a.	n.a.	n.a.
Yam	1,300	1,551	1,750	2,170	2,550	n.a.	n.a.
Cassava	500	540	650	750	890	n.a.	n.a.
Plantain	600	650	780	900	1,060	n.a.	n.a.
Taro	160	182 }	240	275	325	n.a.	n.a.
Sweet potato	20	21				n.a.	n.a.
Groundnuts	28	42.5	45	60	80	n.a.	n.a.
Citrus, for essential oil	4.5	19	50	60	80	n.a.	n.a.
Avocado, for export	. . .	. . .	0.5	4	10	n.a.	n.a.
Soya	. . .	. . .	. . .	10	75	n.a.	n.a.
Vegetables	n.a.	n.a.	26	69	159	n.a.	n.a.

. . . Zero or negligible.
n.a. Not available.
Source: Ministry of Planning.
a. Preliminary.
b. Forecasts were made for major products only and are listed only when different from plan targets.

TABLE SA69. PAST AND EXPECTED GROWTH OF AGRICULTURAL
CROP PRODUCTION, 1965–85
(CFAF billion)

Crop	(CFAF per kilo- grams)	1965	1970	1975	1980	1985
Main industrial crops						
Coffee	109	23.2	26.2	28.3	38.2	43.6
Cocoa	105	14.1	19.1	24.2	33.6	39.4
Oil palm (fresh fruit bunches)	3.9	1.3	1.9	3.8	4.9	6.6
Copra	35	0.1	0.4	0.5	1.9	5.3
Rubber (latex)	109	0.2	1.2	1.9	2.3	5.1
Bananas	18.8	2.0	2.5	3.2	3.8	4.1
Pineapple	13.3	0.6	1.5	3.3	4.9	6.7
Cotton	39.6	0.4	1.3	2.6	3.8	4.8
Sugar	65[a]	. . .	. . .	0.3	7.1	13.0
Subtotal		41.9	54.1	68.1	100.5	128.6
Index		100.0	129.1	162.5	239.9	306.9
Annual rate of growth (percent)			5.3	4.7	8.1	5.0
Main food crops						
Paddy	25	6.3	7.9	10.0	17.5	21.3
Maize	12.9	2.6	3.0	3.6	4.6	7.2
Sorghum and millet	25	1.1	1.1	1.2	1.3	1.4
Yam	10	13.0	15.5	18.8	21.7	25.5
Cassava	10	5.0	5.4	6.5	7.5	8.9
Plantain	6.2	3.7	4.0	4.8	5.6	6.6
Taro–sweet potato	7.1	1.3	1.4	1.7	1.9	2.3
Groundnuts	18.3	0.5	0.8	0.8	0.9	1.0
Subtotal		33.5	39.1	47.4	61.0	73.3
Index		100.0	116.7	141.5	182.1	218.8
Annual rate of growth (percent)			3.1	4.0	5.2	3.8
Total crops		75.4	93.2	115.5	161.5	201.9
Index		100.0	123.6	153.2	214.2	267.8
Annual rate of growth (percent)			4.3	4.4	6.9	4.6

. . . Zero or negligible.
Note: Production is valued at constant 1973 producer prices.
Sources: Ministries of Agriculture and Planning, and World Bank estimates.
a. Using World Bank production forecasts (SA68).

TABLE SA70. RETAIL FOOD PRICES, ABIDJAN MARKETS, 1955 AND 1960–75
(CFAF per kilogram)

Year	Rice (imported)	Rice (hulled)	Yam	Cassava (fresh)	Attiéké	Banana/plantain	Maize (grain)	Bread[a]	Millet
1955	39	n.a.	20	n.a.	n.a.	n.a.	n.a.	35	n.a.
1960	37.5	45	19	14	37	14	38	40	46
1961	37.5	54	25	16	39	19	29	40	33
1962	37.5	51	23	20	40	18	26	40	27
1963	37.5	54	20	18	40	15	25	40	30
1964	41	46	22	18	41	17	25	41	30
1965	45[b]	51	26	21	44	16	25	44	30
1966	45	56	30	23	46	19	27	44	32
1967	53	61	26	17	39	14	30	44	35
1968	50	58	25	18	45	15	30	54	35
1969	50	61	30	27	60	15	30	54	35
1970	50	74	36	34	88	22	42	54	49
1971	50	40	35	33	73	23	49	54	50
1972	50	50	33	27	60	20	50	54	50
1973[c] (first quarter)	70[d]	50	37	34	61	23	50	54	50
1973 (second quarter)	70	60	35	34	61	24	51	61	50
1974 (second quarter)	125	120	52	54	92	35	68[e]	77	68
1975 (first quarter)	125	120	52	55	117	33	70[e]	91	70
1975 (April)	100	100	51	53	117	33	73[e]	118	66

n.a. Not available.
Note: Prices are yearly or quarterly averages.
Sources: Figures for 1960–73 (first quarter): *Bulletins Mensuels de Statistique.* Figures for 1973–75 (second quarter): Ministry of Economy and Finance, Department of Statistics.
 a. Until 1967, for one kilogram loaf; from 1968 based on price of "baguette" of 555 grams.
 b. From September 1964.
 c. January and February only.
 d. From May 11, 1973.
 e. Price for maize meal.

TABLE SA71. PLAN PROJECTIONS OF PER CAPITA NET
CONSUMPTION OF MAIN FOOD STAPLES,
1975 AND 1985
(Kilograms per capita)

Food staple	1975			1985		
	Rural	Urban	Average	Rural	Urban	Average
Cereal						
Rice	34	72	47	35	77	55
Maize	40	14	31	41	13	28
Wheat flour	4	30	13	7	30	18
Millet, and other	8	4	7	8	3	5
Subtotal	86	120	97	91	123	106
Roots						
Yam	200	102	168	199	103	153
Cassava	122	59	101	122	61	93
Plantain	130	68	109	128	68	99
Taro, and other	34	14	27	34	14	24
Subtotal	488	243	405	483	246	369
Total	574	363	502	574	369	475

Source: Ministry of Planning.

TABLE SA72. PLAN PROJECTIONS
OF REQUIREMENTS FOR
MAIN FOOD STAPLES,
1975 AND 1985
(Thousand tons)

	1975		1985		Percent increase
Food staple	Gross	Net	Gross	Net	
Cereal					
Rice-paddy	598	302	1,030	530	72
Maize	253	200	335	265	32
Wheat flour	84	84	175	175	108
Millet and other	49	42	59	50	20
Subtotal	984	628	1,599	1,020	62
Roots					
Yam	1,880	1,080	2,550	1,470	36
Cassava	650	650	890	890	37
Plantain	780	700	1,060	955	36
Taro and other	240	175	325	235	35
Subtotal	3,550	2,605	4,825	3,550	36
Total	4,534	3,233	6,424	4,570	41

Note: Conversion factors used by plan (gross to net): paddy to rice, 50.5 percent (only 55 percent milling yield assumed); maize, 79 percent; wheat, already in terms of flour; millet and sorghum, 85 percent; yam, 58 percent; cassava, 100 percent; plantain, 90 percent; taro and other, 72.5
Source: Ministry of Planning.

TABLE SA73. BASIC FOOD REQUIREMENTS, TOTAL
AND PER RURAL INHABITANT, 1970–85

Item	Average 1970–75	1975	1980	1985	Percentage increase, 1975–85
Population		*Thousands*			
Urban	1,780	2,200	3,300	4,620	110
Rural	4,010	4,245	4,650	5,000	18
Total	5,790	6,445	7,950	9,620	49
Food consumption[a]		*Kilograms per capita in thousands of tons*			
Cereals					
Urban	71	156	234	328	n.a.
Rural	91	386	423	455	n.a.
Total	85	542	657	783	44
Roots					
Urban	244	537	805	1,127	n.a.
Rural	440	1,868	2,046	2,200	n.a.
Total	380	2,405	2,851	3,327	38
Food production required[b]		*Kilograms per capita of rural population*			
Total					
Cereals	—	127	141	157	24
Roots	—	567	613	665	17
Calories per day	—	2,720	2,980	3,270	20
Surplus					
Cereals	—	36	50	66	83
Roots	—	127	173	225	77
Calories per day	—	680	940	1,230	80

n.a. Not available.
—Not applicable.
Source: World Bank estimates.
a. Includes only locally produced staples (for example, the category cereals excludes wheat). Cereal and root elements of ration kept constant.
b. Net quantities before allowing for seed, feed, and losses, or for industrial use (for example, substitution of local cereals for wheat flour).

TABLE SA74. PRODUCER PRICES
FOR SELECTED
CROPS, 1970–75
(CFAF per kilogram;
index, 1972=100)

Year	Cocoa	Coffee	Seedcotton	Paddy
1970	80	95	34.5	20
1971	85	105	39.5	20
1972	85	105	39.5	25
1973	85	105	39.5	28
1974	110	120	44.5	70
1975	175	150	69.5	70
1970	94	90	87	80
1971	100	100	100	80
1972	100	100	100	100
1973	100	100	100	112
1974	129	114	113	280
1975	206	143	176	280

Source: Ministry of Agriculture.

TABLE SA75. OFFICIAL FACTORY PRICES FOR FERTILIZER, 1970–75
(Prices in CFAF per kilogram; index, 1972 = 100)

Year	12–15–18[a] (cocoa) Price	Index	14–14–14[a] (cotton) Price	Index	Ammonium sulphate (cotton, rice) Price	Index	10–18–18[a] (rice) Price	Index
1970	20.9	91	n.a.	—	11.0	104	n.a.	—
1971	23.0	100	n.a.	—	10.6	100	n.a.	—
1972	23.0	100	25.0	100	10.6	100	25.0	100
1973	27.9	121	28.1	112	16.0	151	28.6	114
1974	47.5	206	48.5	173	46.3	289	47.3	189
1975	47.5	206	48.5	173	46.3	289	47.3	189
1975 production cost	67.5	—	67.5	—	59.5	—	70.4	—
Subsidy	20.0	—	19.0	—	13.2	—	23.1	—
Subsidy/cost (percent)	30	—	28	—	22	—	33	—

n.a. Not available.
— Not applicable.
a. Type of fertilizer is denoted by its NPK (nitrogen-phosphorous-potassium) concentration—that is, the fertilizer for cocoa has a 12–15–18 NPK concentration; cotton, a 14–14–14 NPK, and rice, a 10–18–18 NPK.

Source: Ministry of Agriculture.

TABLE SA76. NET RETURNS PER HECTARE AND PER MAN-DAY FOR MAIN CROPS, 1974

Crop	Yield (kilograms per hectare)	Price (CFAF per kilogram)	Gross value (CFAF per hectare)	Cash costs (CFAF per hectare)	Net value (CFAF per hectare)	Labor (man-days)	Return per man-day (CFAF)
Upland rice[a]							
Traditional	750	70	52,500	4,000	48,400	90	539
Improved (manual)	1,800	70	126,000	14,000	112,000	110	1,018
Improved (ox cultivation)	2,000	70	140,000	21,000	119,000	80	1,488
Irrigated rice							
Manual	5,700[b]	70	399,000	87,500[c]	311,500	300	1,038
Mechanized	8,300[d]	70	581,000	152,700[c]	428,300	288	1,487
Cocoa							
Traditional	300	175	52,500	700[e]	51,800	35	1,480 {2,055[f]
Improved	1,000	175	175,000	4,470	170,530	83	{710[g]
Coffee							
Traditional	350	150	52,500	4,750[h]	47,750	70	682
Improved	1,100	150	165,000	28,070	136,930	140	978[f] {537[g]
Cotton[a]							
Manual	1,000	69.5	69,500	12,000	57,500	143	402
Ox cultivation	1,300	69.5	90,350	19,700	70,650	116	609
Yams[a]	6,000	15	90,000	27,000	63,000	210	300
Maize[a]	750	20	15,000	900	14,100	70	201

Source: World Bank estimates.

a. For detailed calculation see "Appraisal of Cotton Areas Rural Development Project," World Bank Report No. 606-IVC.

b. At 150 percent cropping intensity.

c. Including development charge of CFAF13,000 a year (200 kilogram paddy).

d. At 200 percent cropping intensity.

e. Tools at CFAF700 a year.

f. On existing established mature plantations, with no allowance for costs of establishment.

g. Value of prospective future cash flow on new plantings, discounted at 10 percent; yields and inputs as in note f; cocoa as in Appraisal of Second Cocoa Project, but with maintenance of price of CFAF175 a kilogram.

h. Tools at CFAF500, insecticides and sprayer at 2,500, milling at CFAF5 a kilogram.

TABLE SA77. PADDY PRODUCTION, RICE IMPORTS, AND RETAIL
AND PRODUCER PRICES, 1960 AND 1965–74

Year	Paddy production	Rice imports	Price c.i.f. Abidjan	Official retail price white rice	Market price bulled rice	Official producer price paddy
	(thousand tons)			(CFAF per kilogram)		
1960	160	35	26.0	37.5	45	n.a.
1965	250	78	28.2	40	51	n.a.
1966	275	83	37.3	40	56	18
1967	345	24	37.3	50	61	20
1968	365	47	40.2	50	58	20
1969	363	56	36.0	50	61	20
1970	315	79	25.8	50	74	20
1971	385	97	22.6	50	40	20
1972	320	77	28.5	50	50	25[a]
1973	335	148	58.2	70	60	28[b]
1974	406	73	112.9	125[a]	120	65,70[c],75[d]

n.a. Not available.
Sources: Ministries of Agriculture, Economy, and Finance.
a. From October 17, 1972 (Grade I).
b. From May 11, 1973 (Grade I).
c. The price was lowered to CFAF100 per kilogram in mid-1975.
d. From March 7, 1974 (65 at farmgate, 70 at store, 75 at mill).

TABLE SA78. ESTIMATED RICE PRODUCTION
AND CONSUMPTION, 1970–75
(Thousand tons)

Item	1970	1971	1972	1973	1974	1975 forecast
Paddy production	316	385	320	335	406	470
Less seed and losses (10 percent)	32	39	32	34	41	47
Net production	284	346	288	301	365	423
Rice equivalent (60 percent)	170	208	173	181	219	254
Share of SODERIZ	n.a.	7	11	9	33	72
Rice Imports[a]	79	97	77	148	73	. . .
Stocks[b]						
Opening	n.a.	n.a.	25+2	6+7	15+39	33+73
Closing	n.a.	(25+2)	(6+7)	(15+39)	(33+73)	(55+50)[c]
Total rice consumption						
Abidjan Chamber of Commerce sales	249	278[d]	264	288	240	255
Imports	79	95	72	116	39	23
Local	. . .	. . .	30[e]	. . .	15	50
Total	79	95	102	116	54	73
Consumption[f]						
Urban	84	100	107	121	59	73
Rural	165	178	157	167	181	182
Population (thousands)						
Urban	1,424	1,547	1,682	1,831	2,000	2,200
Rural	3,779	3,870	3,963	4,049	4,150	4,245
Total	5,203	5,417	5,645	5,880	6,150	6,445
Consumption per capita (kilograms)						
Urban	60	65	64	66	30	33
Rural	44	46	40	41	44	43
Average	48	51	47	49	39	40

n.a. Not available.
. . . Zero or negligible.
Source: World Bank estimates based on official government figures.
a. Ministry of Agriculture figures from customs statistics; for each year except 1973 these are about 10,000 tons a year lower than figures provided by SODERIZ based on Ministry of Commerce information.
b. The first figure refers to SODERIZ (local) rice; the second to imported rice.
c. Closing stock forecasts for 1975 assume July–December sales of SODERIZ rice at 5,000 tons a month, imported rice at 2,000 tons a month, and SODERIZ production of 42,000 tons of rice.
d. It is estimated that stock figures for local rice (including small traders) would show a carryover from the heavy 1971 crop of perhaps 25,000 tons, which would even out urban per capita consumption over 1970–73 at around 65 kilograms.
e. Estimate.
f. Abidjan Chamber of Commerce sales plus 5,000 tons from small traders (SODERIZ estimate).

TABLE SA79. PUBLIC SECTOR INVESTMENT IN AGRICULTURE
UNDER THE 1971–75 PLAN
(CFAF million)

Crop	1971–72	1973	1974	1975	1971–75
Oil palm	6,250	4,200	3,750	4,600	18,800
Coconut	1,000	1,100	1,350	1,650	5,100
Rubber	1,050	1,300	1,750	2,550	6,650
Coffee	1,300	2,350	1,600	2,250	7,500
Cocoa	1,550	2,150	1,300	2,950	7,950
Cotton	950	800	200	n.a.[a]	1,950
Kenaf	300	750	650	. . .	1,700
Fruits	550	150	450	300	1,450
Sugar	2,750	9,450	4,900	9,500	26,600
Vegetables	100	50	50	450	650
Rice	2,650	2,450	2,850	2,250	10,200
Other crops	50	50	. . .	. . .	100
Regional projects	200	1,100	2,150	5,750	9,200[b]
Miscellaneous	200	200	200	100	700
Subtotal	18,900	26,100	21,200	32,350	98,550
Livestock	600	400	900	3,400	5,300
Fisheries	300	200	400	500	1,400
National parks	300	200	250	200	950
Forestry	1,500	900	1,050	1,100	4,550
Subtotal	2,700	1,700	2,600	5,200	12,200
Total agriculture	21,600	27,800	23,800	37,550	110,750
Total public investment	121,000	73,000	95,000	135,000	425,000
Agriculture as percentage of total investment	17.9	38.1	25.0	27.8	26.1
Index of international prices (1970=100) (average)	111	137	166	184	n.a.
Agricultural investment at 1970 prices	19,500	20,300	14,300	20,400	74,500

n.a. Not available.
. . . Zero or negligible.
Source: Ministry of Planning.
a. From 1975 included under regional projects.
b. ARSO, 900; AVB, 2,200; Savannah, 6,100; total, 9,200.

TABLE SA80. PLAN TARGETS AND ACTUAL RESULTS RELATING TO AREA AND COST OF ESTABLISHMENT OF PLANTATION CROPS, 1971–75

| | Plan | | | Actual | | | |
| | (1) | (2) | (3) | (4) | (5) | (6) | (7) |
Crop	Area to be planted (hectares)	Total cost[a] (CFAF million)	Average cost per hectare (CFAF thousand)	Area planted (hectares)	Total cost[b] (CFAF million)	Average cost per hectare (CFAF thousand)	(6) ÷ (3)
Coffee	68,000	2,150	31.6	37,000	7,500	202.7	6.4
Cocoa	86,500	6,300	72.8	58,500	7,950	135.9	1.9
Rubber	9,150	2,750	300.5	4,700	6,650	1,414.9	4.7
Oil palm	28,000	11,700	417.9	15,000	18,800	1,253.3	3.0
Coconut	15,000	4,200	280.0	8,500	5,100	600.0	2.1
Sugar	5,000	8,900	1,780.0	5,000	26,600	5,320.0	3.0
Total	211,650	36,000	—	128,700	72,600	—	—
Average	—	—	170.1	—	—	564.1	3.3

— Not applicable.

Source: World Bank estimates based on official government figures.

a. Total costs include all costs recorded in the Loi Programmes for respective crop programmes, including some industrial and infrastructural investments; therefore average costs a hectare planted are not indicative of direct costs of plantation establishment.

b. Planned costs (before revisions of 1971) were in terms of 1970 constant CFAF; application of the World Bank's index of international inflation (without allowing for exchange rate variations) would give a ratio of about 1.5.

TABLE SA81. DRAFT AGRICULTURAL
            INVESTMENT
            PLAN, 1976–80
            (CFAF billion, at 1975 prices)

Program	Preliminary plan estimates	World Bank estimates
Agriculture		
Sugar	120.6	40.0
Cotton	28.0[a]	28.0
Rice	21.0	14.6
Cocoa	19.2	15.0
Coffee	11.4	6.0
Rubber	13.8	13.8
Oil palm	11.2	11.2
Coconut	9.9	6.1
Horticulture	8.0	6.0
AVB	22.0	15.0
ARSO[b]	1.8	1.8
Motorization[c]	15.5	5.0
Other rural development projects	. . .	10.0
Subtotal	282.4	172.5
Livestock	29.2	15.0
Forestry[d]	24.0	20.0
Fisheries	7.0	5.0
Subtotal	60.2	40.0
Total	342.6	212.5

. . . Zero or negligible.
Source: Ministry of Planning and World Bank estimates.
   a. Includes CFAF19.2 billion for insect control, which should be largely offset by Stabilization Fund profits on cotton sales.
   b. Middle Sassandra settlement project.
   c. This program, covering 20,000 hectares in the north, is still in the early study stage.
   d. Excluding pulpwood.

TABLE SA82. VALUE ADDED AT CURRENT MARKET PRICES IN
MANUFACTURING, 1970–74
(CFAF million)

Industry and handicrafts	1970	1971	1972	1973	1974
Grain and flour processing	4,020	4,642	5,498	6,838	7,906
Canned and processed foods	3,557	4,565	5,956	4,844	9,357
Beverages, ice	2,066	2,651	3,034	3,414	3,872
Edible oils and fats	2,341	2,417	2,307	3,645	13,187
Other food industries, tobacco	2,687	3,625	3,931	4,373	4,777
Subtotal	14,671	17,900	20,726	23,114	39,099
Textile industry	8,905	9,698	11,610	11,013	13,580
Leather, footwear	1,042	999	1,029	1,149	1,306
Wood products	4,187	3,848	4,290	6,138	8,196
Petroleum products	10,775	11,658	14,556	15,524	15,743
Chemical products	2,570	3,270	3,684	3,642	3,860
Rubber products	481	490	356	456	530
Building materials, glass	1,349	1,507	1,502	1,513	2,219
Basic metal products	511	587	497	524	1,132
Transport equipment	5,971	6,148	6,571	8,085	10,093
Mechanical and electrical industries	2,782	3,181	4,053	4,540	5,407
Other	2,367	2,693	2,959	3,202	3,967
Total	55,611	61,979	71,833	78,900	105,132

Source: National accounts.

TABLE SA83. VALUE ADDED AT CURRENT FACTOR COST IN
MANUFACTURING, 1970–74
(CFAF million)

Industry and handicrafts	1970	1971	1972	1973	1974
Grain and flour processing	3,950	4,535	5,391	6,672	7,588
Canned and processed foods	2,830	3,572	5,103	3,848	7,260
Beverages, ice	1,268	1,666	1,797	2,214	2,315
Edible oils and fats	2,440	2,066	2,375	3,335	11,297
Other food industries, tobacco	498	836	956	1,169	896
Subtotal	10,986	12,675	15,622	17,238	29,356
Textile industry	8,064	8,557	10,253	9,423	11,627
Leather, footwear	813	784	796	938	1,041
Wood products	3,653	3,231	3,722	4,888	6,578
Petroleum products	1,225	960	1,773	1,599	1,886
Chemical products	1,731	2,389	2,859	2,916	2,869
Rubber products	430	412	283	352	408
Building materials, glass	889	982	979	867	1,417
Basic metal products	504	459	339	466	953
Transport equipment	5,019	5,167	5,377	6,949	8,561
Mechanical and electrical industries	2,207	2,399	3,249	3,543	4,163
Other	2,218	2,536	2,733	2,971	3,695
Total	37,739	40,551	47,985	52,150	72,554

Source: National accounts.

TABLE SA84. VALUE ADDED AT CURRENT MARKET PRICES BY SMALL
INDUSTRY AND HANDICRAFTS, 1970–74
(CFAF million)

Industry and crafts	1970	1971	1972	1973	1974
Grain and flour processing	2,157	2,512	2,471	3,373	2,596
Canned and processed foods	680	795	1,261	771	928
Beverages, ice	. . .	. . .	. . .	. . .	. . .
Edible oils and fats	315	302	168	164	754
Other food industries, tobacco	. . .	. . .	. . .	. . .	. . .
Subtotal	3,152	3,609	3,900	4,308	4,278
Textile industry	3,134	3,013	3,222	3,222	3,153
Leather, footwear	235	234	148	248	269
Wood products	755	841	946	1,218	1,308
Petroleum products	. . .	. . .	. . .	. . .	. . .
Chemical products	. . .	. . .	. . .	. . .	. . .
Rubber products	. . .	. . .	. . .	. . .	. . .
Building materials, glass	. . .	. . .	. . .	. . .	. . .
Basic metal products	. . .	. . .	. . .	. . .	. . .
Transport equipment	1,218	1,204	1,288	1,781	2,252
Mechanical and electrical industries	797	825	891	891	1,011
Other	1,445	1,444	1,595	1,550	1,770
Total	10,736	11,170	11,190	13,218	14,041

. . . Zero or negligible.
Source: National accounts.

TABLE SA85. VALUE ADDED AT CURRENT FACTOR COST BY SMALL
INDUSTRY AND HANDICRAFTS, 1965 AND 1970–74
(CFAF million)

Industry and crafts	1965	1970	1971	1972	1973	1974
Grain and flour processing	1,649	2,148	2,503	2,461	3,361	2,576
Canned and processed foods	498	680	791	1,261	770	928
Beverages, ice	. . .	. . .	. . .	. . .	. . .	. . .
Edible oils and fats	238	315	302	168	164	754
Other food industries, tobacco	. . .	. . .	. . .	. . .	. . .	. . .
Subtotal	2,385	3,143	3,596	3,890	4,295	4,258
Textile industry	2,440	3,086	2,968	3,174	3,174	3,097
Leather, footwear	207	228	228	227	241	262
Wood products	674	745	830	935	1,206	1,295
Petroleum products	. . .	. . .	. . .	. . .	. . .	. . .
Chemical products	. . .	. . .	. . .	. . .	. . .	. . .
Rubber products	. . .	. . .	. . .	. . .	. . .	. . .
Building materials, glass	. . .	. . .	. . .	. . .	. . .	. . .
Basic metal products	. . .	. . .	. . .	. . .	. . .	. . .
Transport equipment	421	1,202	1,188	1,271	1,764	2,202
Mechanical and electrical industries	372	771	798	863	861	973
Other	972	1,430	1,429	1,580	1,535	1,756
Total	2,891	10,605	11,037	11,940	13,076	13,843

. . . Zero or negligible.
Source: National accounts.

TABLE SA86. VALUE ADDED AND PRODUCTION VALUE IN MANUFACTURING, 1973
(CFAF million)

Industry and crafts	Material inputs and services	Labor cost	Percent labor cost in value added	Other components of value added	Total value added at factor cost	Indirect taxes	Total value added at market prices	Production value (value of output at factor cost)	Percent value added at factor cost in production value
Grain and flour processing	11,883	1,654	24.8	5,018	6,672	156	6,828	18,555	36.0
Canned and processed foods	24,806	1,406	36.5	2,442	3,848	996	4,844	28,654	13.4
Beverages, ice	2,165	820	37.0	1,394	2,214	1,200	3,414	4,379	50.6
Edible oils and fats	8,109	1,474	44.2	1,861	3,335	310	3,645	11,444	29.1
Other food industries, tobacco	2,204	302	25.8	867	1,169	3,204	4,373	3,373	34.7
Subtotal	49,167	5,656	32.8	11,582	17,238	5,866	23,104	66,405	26.0
Textile industry	15,412	3,547	37.6	5,876	9,423	1,590	11,013	24,835	37.9
Leather, footwear	1,470	519	55.3	419	938	211	1,149	2,408	39.0
Wood products	13,445	3,612	73.9	1,276	4,888	1,250	6,138	18,333	26.7
Petroleum products	9,091	572	35.8	1,027	1,599	13,925	15,524	10,690	15.0
Chemical products	9,409	1,820	62.4	1,096	2,916	726	3,642	12,325	23.7
Rubber products	2,331	158	44.9	194	352	104	456	2,683	13.1
Building materials, glass	4,385	417	48.1	450	867	646	1,513	5,252	16.5
Basic metal products	888	107	23.0	359	466	58	524	1,354	34.4
Transport equipment Mechanical and electrical industries	14,917	3,371	48.5	3,578	6,949	1,136	8,085	21,866	31.8
Other	7,457	1,716	48.4	1,827	3,543	997	4,540	11,000	32.2
Other	3,499	972	32.7	1,999	2,971	231	3,202	6,470	45.9
Total	131,471	22,467	43.1	29,683	52,150	26,740	78,890	183,621	28.4

Note: Crafts and small industry are included.
Source: National accounts.

TABLE SA87. PRODUCTION OF SELECTED INDUSTRIAL PRODUCTS, 1965 AND 1969–75

Product	Unit	1965	1969	1970	1971	1972	1973	1974	Plan 1975
Grain and flour processing									
Rice (hulled)[a]	1,000 tons	n.a.	12	6.7	4.6	10.5	9.2	18.9	85.7
Wheat flour	1,000 tons	32	41	45	60	73	90	83	81
Canned and processed foods									
Canned pineapple	1,000 tons of input	32	71	87	110	130	152	147	175
Canned tuna fish	tons of input	1,300	1,900	3,600	4,170	4,500	5,000	8,000	10,000
Instant coffee	tons of input	2,100	4,300	5,300	4,500	5,550	7,650	8,900	10,000
Cocoa products	1,000 tons of input	16.6	32.1	35.8	33.0	33.0	36.0	38.0	50.0
Beverages and ice									
Beer	1,000 hectoliters	109	185	248	330	470	569	635	270
Soft drinks	1,000 hectoliters	192	300	399	380	400	484	495	430
Ice	1,000 tons	63	91	99	95	106	109	95	130
Edible oils and fats									
Crude palm oil	1,000 tons	18	30	50	66	96	93	139	166
Refined oil	1,000 tons	10	14	15	19	23	24	28	22
Soap	1,000 tons	12	16	16	20	21	22	17	19
Detergents	1,000 tons	500	1,200	1,200	1,570	1,895	2,300	2,900	2,500
Textiles and footwear									
Ginned cotton	1,000 tons	4	17	13	12	21	23	23	38.5
Cotton yarn	tons	2,880	4,100	4,100	4,100	4,300	4,000	5,000	20,400[b]
Cotton cloth	tons	1,400	2,100	2,200	3,000	3,300	3,000	3,000	18,100[b]
Printed cotton cloth	million meters	4	14	16	40	53	47	51	n.a.
String (rope)	tons	600	700	800	800	n.a.	900	1,000	1,200
Jute bags	million bags	n.a.	7.2	7.5	4.3	n.a.	4.4	5.6	n.a.
Shoes, sandals	million pairs	2.7	5.4	5.7	5.3	n.a.	7.0	7.5	8.0

(Table SA87 continues on the following page.)

TABLE SA87 (continued)

Product	Unit	1965	1969	1970	1971	1972	1973	1974	Plan 1975
Wood products									
Logs	1,000 cubic meters	2,550	4,277	3,464	3,887	4,118	5,189	4,626	3,000
Sawn lumber	1,000 cubic meters	250	290	308	298	345	453	564	465
Veneer	1,000 cubic meters	23	58	60	64	74	53	57	96
Plywood	1,000 cubic meters	9	17	20	24	29	32	40	50
Chemical products									
Oxygen, acetylene	1,000 cubic meters	444	456	461	650	n.a.	780	790	800
Paint	1,000 tons	1.9	3.0	3.4	6.0	n.a.	7.0	7.0	6.4
Matches	million boxes	98	89	95	100	n.a.	133	122	155
Cement	1,000 tons	n.a.	388	433	508	592	665	630	535
Metal products									
Steel bars and shapes	1,000 tons	n.a.	n.a.	4	6.2	11.9	13.4	15.0	37.0
Galvanized sheets	1,000 tons	n.a.	n.a.	3	12	12.5	13	11	14
Aluminum sheets	1,000 tons	n.a.	n.a.	2.5	4.0	3.7	4.8	5.3	3.8
Nails	1,000 tons	n.a.	n.a.	4.4	4.0	4.8	4.6	4.5	6.3
Metal cans	million boxes	n.a.	n.a.	n.a.	100	n.a.	142	143	n.a.
Vehicle assembly									
Cars and trucks	1,000 units	1.9	3.2	3.8	5.5	5.4	5.7	5.3	6.4
Bicycles	1,000 units	30	28	28	35	33	36	36	30
Motorcycles	1,000 units	2.8	4.1	4.2	6.0	3.6	5.0	4.0	8.0
Radio assembly	1,000 units	n.a.	n.a.	n.a.	32	113	120	85	n.a.

n.a.: Not available.
Sources: Ministry of Planning and Chamber of Industry.
a. SODERIZ rice mills.
b. Revised target for 1977.

TABLE SA88. ACTUAL AND PLANNED INDUSTRIAL EMPLOYMENT

Industry and crafts	1970 (mid-year)	1974 (mid-year)	Increase 1970–74	Planned increase 1971–75	Percent achievement
	4,182	5,500	688	800	86
Grain and flour processing	1,667	2,112	445	440	101
Canned and processed foods	1,180	2,054	874	190	460
Beverages, ice	926	1,475	549	1,170	
Edible oils and fats					47
Other food industries, tobacco	257	665	408	500	82
Subtotal	8,842	11,806	2,964	4,100	72
Textile industry	6,179	8,010	1,831	7,520	24
Leather, footwear	797	714	(83)	440	—
Wood products	9,320	11,820	2,500	2,880	87
Petroleum products	229	308	79	40	198
Chemical products	2,684	3,339	645	760	85
Rubber products	563	560	(3)	260[a]	—
Building materials	865	845	(20)	640	—
Basic metal products	38	133	95	220	43
Transport equipment	1,092	1,624	532	3,630	15
Mechanical and electrical industries	1,741	2,597	846	1,440	59
Other	1,002	1,487	485	570[b]	85
Total	33,352	43,233	9,881	22,500	44

— Not applicable.
Note: Figures in parentheses indicate decreases.
Source: Chamber of Industry and 1971–75 Plan.
a. Tire plant project excluded.
b. Paper pulp project excluded.

TABLE SA89. WAGE COST IN MANUFACTURING, SELECTED YEARS
(Index: January 1, 1961 = 100)

Worker category	1961 (January 1)	1963 (November 1)	1968 (July 1)	1970 (January 1)	1973 (August 1)	1974 (August 1)
Unskilled workers						
Category 1	100	106	117	146	183	230
Category 2	100	106	116	140	169	209
Category 3	100	106	115	138	165	201
Category 4	100	106	114	133	155	187
Skilled workers						
Category 1	100	105	112	126	143	166
Category 2	100	105	111	122	135	153
Category 3	100	103	109	117	125	139
Foremen and supervising personnel						
Shift supervisors						
Category 1	100	100	100	107	118	133
Category 2	100	100	100	107	114	127
Foremen	100	100	100	107	114	127
Workshop supervisors	100	100	100	107	114	127
Category 1	100	100	100	111	119	132
Category 2	100	100	100	107	114	127
Engineers and executives						
Category 1	100	100	100	105	110	122
Category 2	100	100	100	105	110	122
Category 3A	100	100	100	105	110	122
Category 3B	100	100	100	105	110	122
Cost of living index (1960 = 100)						
African-type family	100	n.a.	131	149	164	193
European-type family	100	n.a.	127	136	153	178

n.a. Not available.
Note: In addition to wages, social charges amounted to about 45 percent of wages for African labor in 1975.
Source: Chamber of Industry.

TABLE SA90. IVORIAN OWNERSHIP IN MANUFACTURING
ON JANUARY 1, 1975
(CFAF million)

Industry and crafts	Total share capital in branch	Ivorian ownership			Percent Ivorian ownership
		Government	Private	Total	
Grain and flour processing	3,320	372	90	462	13.9
Canned and processed foods	3,843	790	577	1,367	35.6
Beverages, ice	2,384	80	62	142	6.0
Edible oils and fats	7,271	2,475	309	2,784	38.3
Other food industries, tobacco	1,402	641	210	851	60.7
Subtotal	18,220	4,358	1,248	5,606	30.8
Textile industry	11,421	2,899	1,059	3,958	34.7
Leather, footwear	445	. . .	1	1	. . .
Petroleum products	1,115	100	. . .	100	9.0
Chemical products	3,414	529	363	892	26.1
Rubber products	4,220	2,123	169	2,292	54.3
Building materials, glass	1,190	334	78	412	34.6
Basic metal products	200	80	112	192	96.0
Transport equipment	1,565	245	28	273	17.4
Mechanical and electrical industries	3,290	25	645	670	20.4
Other	883	306	192	498	56.4
Total	45,963	10,999	3,895	14,894	32.4

. . . Zero or negligible.
Note: Data on the wood products industry are not available.
Source: Chamber of Industry.

TABLE SA91. GROSS INVESTMENT IN MANUFACTURING, 1971–75
(CFAF billion)

	Actual, at current prices					1971–75 (planned, at 1968 prices)
Industry	1971	1972	1973	1974	Total	
Grain and flour processing	0.6	. . .	1.7	0.7	3.0	0.8
Canned and processed foods	0.7	0.4	2.1	0.8	4.0	2.3
Beverages, ice	0.6	1.7	0.5	0.4	3.2	0.6
Edible oils and fats	2.1	3.5	. . .	0.3	5.9	4.9
Other food industries, tobacco	0.1	0.2	0.5	11.1	11.9	4.4
Subtotal	4.1	5.8	4.8	13.3	28.0	13.0
Textile industry	1.1	0.7	1.4	6.0	9.2	15.3
Leather, footwear	0.5	0.2	0.1	. . .	0.8	0.6
Wood products	. . .	0.9	0.8	9.1	10.8	4.6
Petroleum products	0.7	0.4	2.8	0.1	4.0	2.1
Chemical products	(0.5)	1.7	0.9	0.8	2.9	1.2
Rubber products	0.1	0.1	0.1	. . .	0.3	0.3[a]
Building materials, glass	0.1	0.1	0.2	0.9	1.3	2.6
Basic metal products	. . .	. . .	0.5	0.1	0.6	0.4
Transport equipment	0.3	0.2	0.4	0.7	1.6	1.7
Mechanical and electrical industries	0.4	0.6	. . .	0.4	1.4	1.9
Other	0.2	0.4	0.3	0.3	1.2	0.7[b]
Total	8.0	11.1	12.3	31.7	62.1	44.4[c]
Total (estimated at 1968 prices)	5.8	9.2	8.9	18.6	42.5	44.3

. . . Zero or negligible.
Note: Figures in parentheses indicate decreases.
Source: Chamber of Industry.
a. Excluding rubber tire plant project.
b. Excluding paper pulp project.
c. Excluding CFAF32.2 billion for replacement.

TABLE SA92. PROFITABILITY OF IVORIAN MANUFACTURING
INDUSTRY, 1961 AND 1966–73
(Percent)

Indicator	1961	1966	1967	1968	1969	1970	1971	1973
Net profits/sales[a]	8.8	4.5	4.0	4.0	4.7	3.9	3.2	6.2
Cash flow/sales[a]	14.7	10.2	10.1	9.7	10.2	8.9	8.3	10.9

Sources: 1961–71: ORSTOM, "Income Distribution by Ivorian Industries" (March 1975).
        1973: Central Bank, "Centrale des Bilans" (1973).
   a. Taxes included.

TABLE SA93. VALUE OF SELECTED INDUSTRIAL EXPORTS,
1965 AND 1970–74
(CFAF million)

Exports	1965	1970	1971	1972	1973	1974
Instant coffee	340	1,877	1,790	1,246	1,635	2,285
Cocoa products	1,000	6,600	5,600	5,600	6,270	13,329
Canned fish	. . .	1,200	1,300	1,300	1,253	2,232
Pineapple products	1,280	3,027	3,632	4,110	5,052	7,414
Canned pineapple	910	2,379	2,990	3,530	4,241	6,679
Pineapple juice	370	648	642	580	811	735
Palm oil	. . .	790	1,910	2,130	3,045	15,300
Ginned cotton	150	1,620	1,720	2,640	3,204	5,290
Wood products	3,479	5,714	4,999	5,256	9,304	13,251
Sawn lumber	3,177	4,414	3,543	3,573	7,442	10,780
Veneer, plywood	302	1,300	1,456	1,683	1,862	2,471
Rubber (latex)	320	1,190	1,120	980	1,982	2,668
Subtotal (A)	6,569	22,018	22,071	23,262	31,745	61,769
Total industrial exports (B)[a]	12,000	30,500	30,380	40,811	51,675	97,200[b]
A/B	54.7	72.2	72.6	57.0	61.4	63.5
Total exports (C)	73,500	149,600	151,500	166,700	213,000	324,000
A/C	8.9	14.7	14.6	14.0	14.9	19.1
B/C	16.3	20.4	20.1	24.5	24.3	30.0

. . . Zero or negligible.

Note: Other main industrial exports include petroleum products, textiles, cement, tobacco products, motor vehicles, insecticides, fertilizers, essential oils, and plastic articles. In 1974 these items represented CFAF20.4 billion (of which 9.9 billion was for petroleum products), that is, about 21 percent of industrial exports.

Source: Trade statistics and national accounts.

a. See Table SA94.

b. Estimated.

TABLE SA94. DEVELOPMENT OF INDUSTRIAL EXPORTS,
1965 AND 1970–74
(CFAF billion)

Exports	1965	1970	1971	1972	1973	1974
Grain and flour processing	0.1	0.1	0.3	0.3	1.0	0.7
Canned and processed						
foods	3.2	11.7	12.3	13.0	15.1	24.9
Beverages, ice	0.1	0.1	0.2	0.2	0.2	0.1
Edible oils and fats	0.8	1.8	2.8	3.2	4.5	16.7
Other food industries,						
tobacco	0.3	0.3	0.4	0.5	0.5	0.8
Subtotal	2.5	14.0	16.0	17.2	21.3	43.2
Textile industry	0.7	3.6	3.1	6.3	6.1	11.2
Leather, footwear	0.1	0.2	0.3	0.5	0.4	0.3
Wood products	3.5	5.8	5.3	5.4	10.0	14.5
Petroleum products	0.4	2.1	0.8	3.3	4.3	9.8
Chemical products	0.9	0.9	1.2	1.9	2.2	5.0
Rubber products	n.a.	1.2	1.2	1.1	2.0	2.7
Building materials, glass	0.1	0.2	0.3	0.2	0.4	0.8
Basic metal products	0.2	0.8	0.6	0.7	0.8	n.a.
Transport equipment	0.4	0.9	0.8	1.7	1.5	3.0
Mechanical and						
electrical industries	1.1	0.7	0.8	2.1	2.0	3.7
Other	0.1	0.1	0.1	0.4	0.7	3.0
Total	12.0	30.5	30.5	40.8	51.7	97.2

n.a. Not available.
Source: National accounts and Chamber of Industry for 1974.

TABLE SA95. PROJECTS ASSISTED BY OPEI WHICH RECEIVED CAPITAL FROM A BANK, 1968–73

Sector	Number of enterprises	Number of projects	Total investment cost (CFAF million)	Loan financing (CFAF million)	Employment generated	Bank concerned			
						CCI	SGBCI	BICISI	Other
Agriculture	5	7	76.7	53.8	52	...	1	...	6
Forestry	3	3	82.6	44.4	103	...	1	2	...
Fishing	1	1	2.8	0.4	10	...	1	...	...
Quarries	5	5	114.5	75.6	140	2	1	1	1
Bakeries	27	27	321.3	230.2	359	6	10	5	6
Agrobusiness	1	1	46.0	34.1	62	...	...	...	1
Textile	8	9	28.2	25.7	50	2	1	3	3
Woodworking	14	14	63.2	50.7	132	6	2	4	2
Chemicals	1	1	39.0	25.0	12	...	...	1	...
Construction materials	2	2	10.1	9.6	19	...	2	...	...
Mechanical repairs	3	3	47.5	31.6	58	1	1	1	...
Other mechanicals	3	3	25.9	19.7	42	1	...	2	...
Printing, paper	6	6	137.6	50.8	74	1	...	2	3
Construction	11	11	65.2	63.5	112	7	2	2	...
Transport	5	5	18.8	15.1	22	...	2	2	1
Real estate	3	3	23.4	18.2	27	1	2	2	2
Other services	22	22	191.8	136.8	128	5	7	5	5
Commerce	32	32	271.6	201.4	124	2	13	11	6
Schools	7	7	112.9	89.0	115	...	3	2	2
Total	159	162	1,679.1	1,175.6	1,641	34	47	43	38
Manufacturing share	65	67	718.8	477.4	920	17	16	18	15
Percent of total	40.9	41.4	42.8	40.6	56.0	50.0	34.0	41.9	39.5

... Zero or negligible.
Source: OPEI.

Index

Abidjan, 13; development project for, 206; growing importance of, 272; housing in, 145, 206; industry in, 50, 51, 233–35, 256; investment program for, 147, 149; population movement to, 6, 124, 205; port of, 14, 270; revenues of, 84; tourism and, 50; unemployment in, 123, 192, 195

Abidjan-Niger railway, 14, 270, 274

Africa: income distribution in, 130, 135; regional cooperation in, 122; wages in, 139

Afrique Occidentale Française (AOF), 11–12, 16, 17

Agriculture: capital expenditures in, 175; diversification of, 5, 17, 18, 22, 26, 32, 33, 37, 44, 140, 188, 200; employment in, 195, 197–98; expansion into forest areas of, 14, 45, 199, 210, 211, 224; foreign labor for, 43, 125; growth rate of, 182; incentives for, 5, 36, 38–39; investment in, 196–201, 210, 212–13, 214; mechanization of, 38, 123, 158, 159, 200, 224; opening new areas for, 126; organization of, 40–43; plantation, 33–34, 122, 196, 198; price policies of, 24, 42, 66, 122, 123, 136, 140; production in, 32–33, 35–36, 43–44, 199; profits from, 195; public expenditures for, 74, 192; regional development program for, 223–25;

research in, 41; SODE for, 41–43, 192, 211; subsidization of industry by, 8, 36, 51, 126; under *1971–75* plan, 32–34, 210–211; under *1976–80* plan, 212–25; value added in, 182; wages in, 40, 139. *See also* Farm income.

AGRIPAC, 223

Air Afrique, 119, 120

Angola, 109

AOF. *See* Afrique Occidentale Française

Arabusta, 146

Arbitration, 28, 31, 94

ARSO. *See* Autorité pour l'Aménagement de la Région du Sud-Ouest

Assets, foreign, 103–04

Assimilation policy, 12

Autorité pour l'Aménagement de la Région du Sud-Ouest (ARSO), 41, 223, 224

Autorité pour l'Aménagement de la Vallée du Bandama (AVB), 41, 223

Avocados, 33, 222–23

Baas, Hessel, 69n

Balance of payments, 5, 104, 111; accounting system for, 117–20; foreign exchange earnings and, 110; projection model for, 162; testing hypotheses relating to, 161, 162

82156